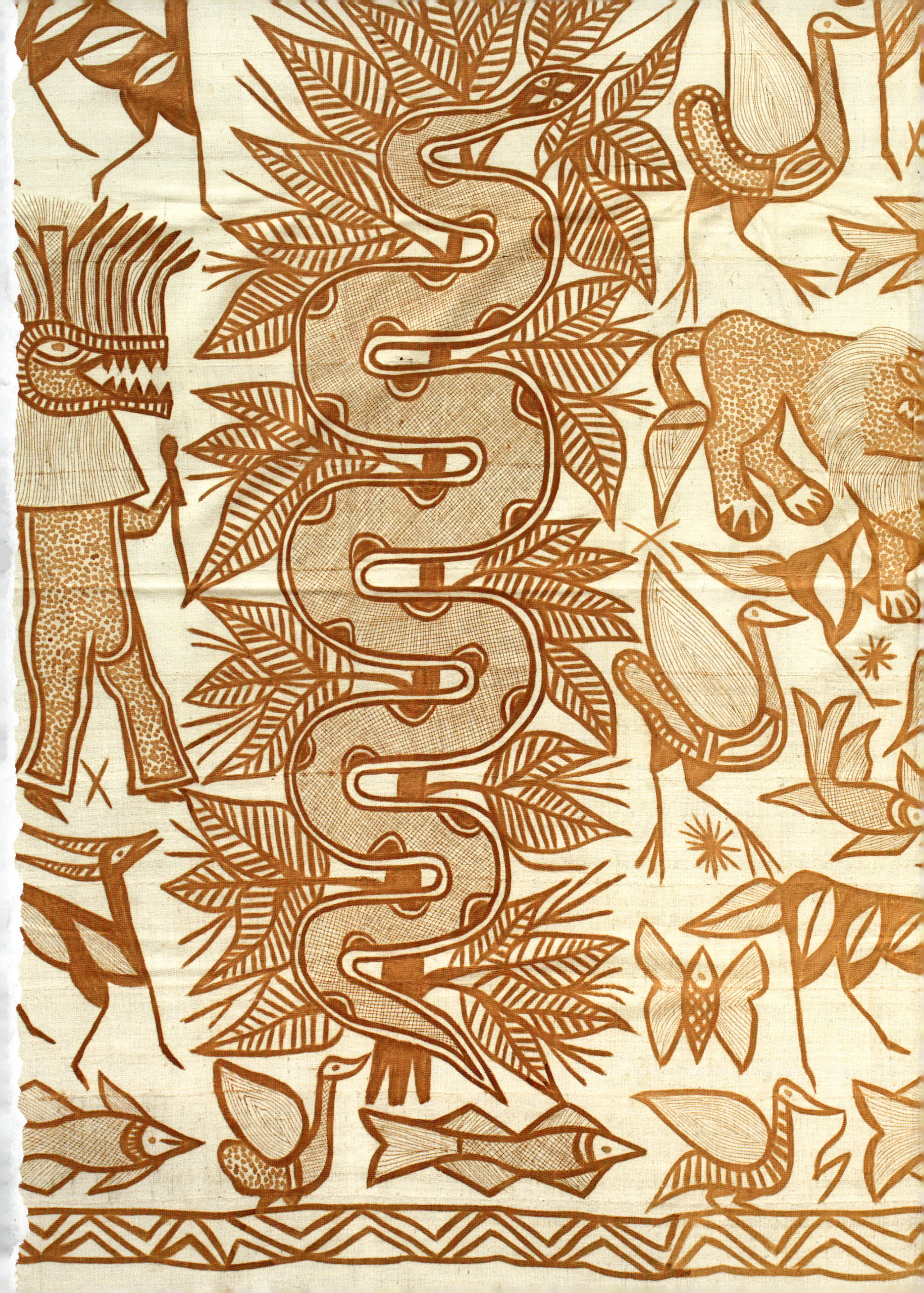

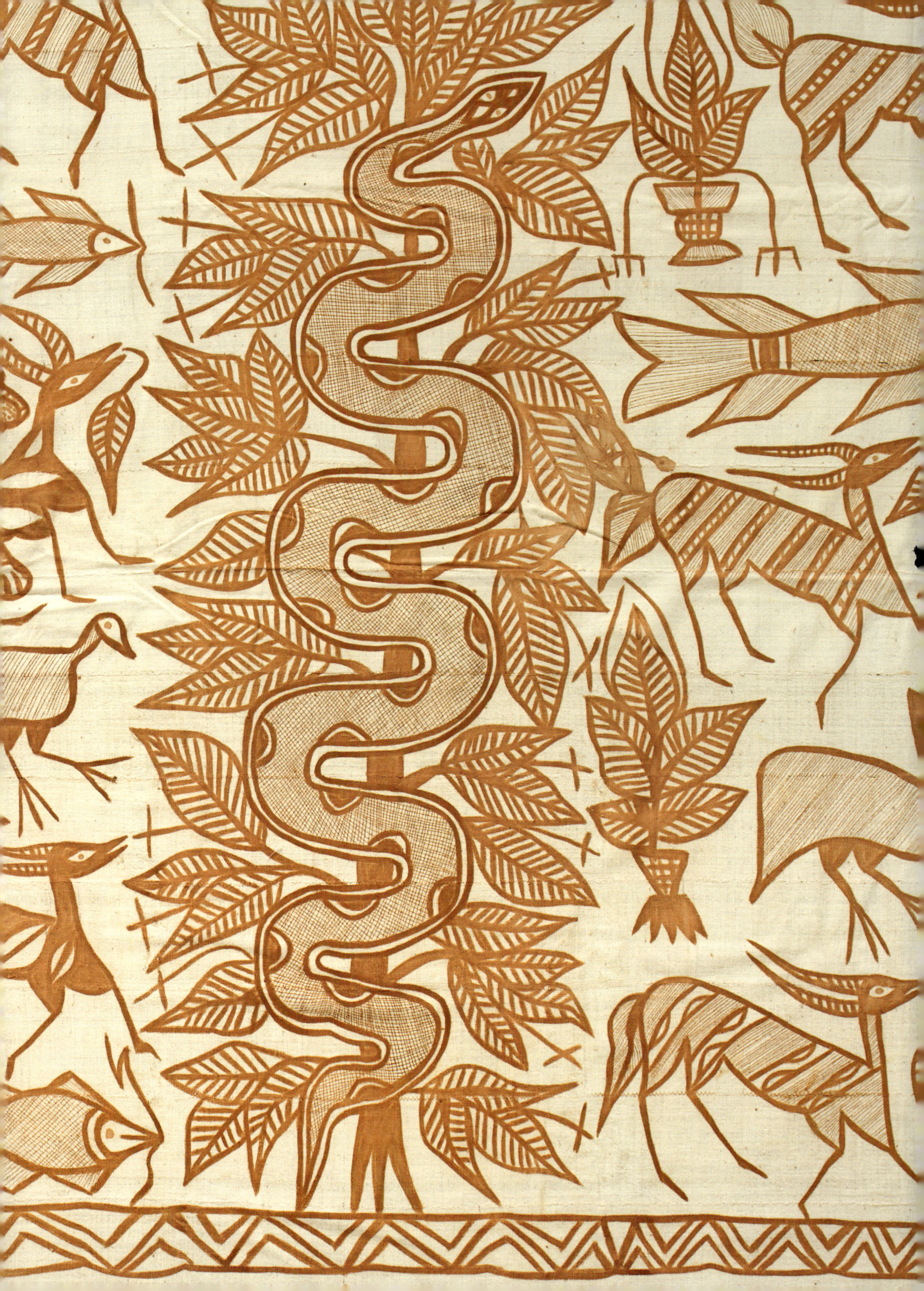

AFRICA *in the* MARKET

AFRICA *in the* MARKET

TWENTIETH-CENTURY ART

FROM THE AMRAD AFRICAN ART COLLECTION

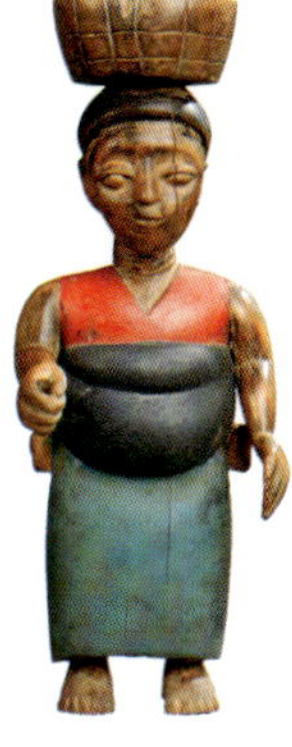

Edited by

SILVIA FORNI
CHRISTOPHER B. STEINER

R•M

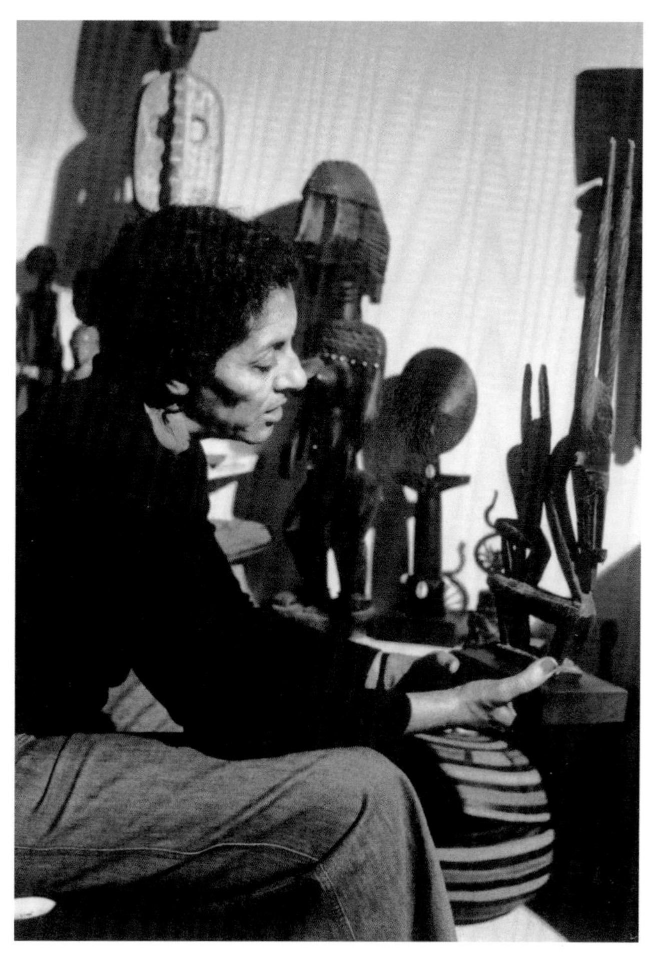

Esther Dagan dedicated her donation of the Amrad African Art Collection in memory of her daughter Halit and in homage to the unknown African artists

Published by the Royal Ontario Museum with the generous support of the Louise Hawley Stone Charitable Trust. The Stone Trust generates significant annual funding for the Museum, providing a steady stream of support that is used to purchase new acquisitions and to produce publications related to the ROM's collection. The Louise Hawley Stone Charitable Trust was established in 1998 when the ROM received a charitable trust of nearly $50 million—the largest cash bequest ever received by the Museum—by its long-time friend and supporter, the late Louise Hawley Stone (1904–1997).

Library and Archives Canada Cataloguing in Publication
Africa in the Market: Twentieth-Century Art from the Amrad African Art Collection / edited by Silvia Forni, Christopher B. Steiner.

Includes bibliographical references.
ISBN 978-0-88854-506-0 (paperback)

1. Galerie Amrad art africain. 2. Art, African--20th century. 3. Art, African--Collectors and collecting. I. Forni, Silvia, editor, author II. Steiner, Christopher B., editor, author III. Galerie Amrad art africain IV. Royal Ontario Museum, issuing body

N7391.65.A37 2016 709.67 C2015-907998-5

Managing Editor: Sheeza Sarfraz
Senior Designer: Rose Pereira
Editor: Dimitra Chronopoulos
Production Designer: Alexandra Tanner

Printed and bound in Canada.

The Royal Ontario Museum is an agency of the Government of Ontario.

CONTENTS

9 Foreword

11 Acknowledgements

13 The Dislocation of Culture: The Amrad African Art Collection at the Royal Ontario Museum
SILVIA FORNI AND CHRISTOPHER B. STEINER

37 A Community of Art Lovers: Collecting and Dealing African Art in Canada between the 1960s and the 1990s
CATHERINE M. HALE AND SILVIA FORNI

59 The Art Market in Burkina Faso: A Personal Recollection
CHRISTOPHER D. ROY

75 New Markets, New Patrons: Work-Trade Relationships in a West African Art Market
TILL FÖRSTER

101 Markets and Matrilineages: Asante Stools in the Twentieth Century
CATHERINE M. HALE

119 Canonical Inventions and Market Knowledge in the Grassfields of Cameroon
SILVIA FORNI

147 The Secret of the Masks: On the Social Construction of Power and Desire in the African Art Market
CHRISTOPHER B. STEINER

165 Map of Africa

167 Amrad African Art Collection Catalogue

191 List of Plates

193 List of Galerie Amrad African Arts Publications

195 Contributors

FOREWORD

For many in the art world and beyond, authenticity is a key component of the value and appreciation of a piece. Yet, when looking at the production and market of African art, it appears evident that the attribution of authenticity is not as straightforward as one may imagine. Authenticity is not just the result of the act of creation of a piece, the hard work of the artist, and his or her inspiration. The greater context, the art market and the process of the piece's journey from the artist's hands to the display case of a patron also come into play in determining whether or not a piece may be considered authentic or not. For many who love African art, authenticity is based on the cultural significance of a piece and ultimately on the fact that they were made for local consumption rather than for the market. Yet, in many cases, it is exactly because of the existence of an art market that these pieces were made or produced in the first place. The double standard by which an African art object is considered authentic or "real" (a Western object can be authentic if created for a larger market and broad appeal) continues to be a polarizing intellectual debate. There are less than subtle power imbalances at work in these distinctions. Focusing on the trade of African art, its markets, and the impact of economic and political forces on the pieces themselves, this book seeks to place African art, its production, and its trade in a cultural context.

Esther Amrad Dagan's collection of African art in the Royal Ontario Museum (ROM) offers a great vantage point to look at some stories of the production and circulation of African art in the second half of the twentieth century. Do the works' provenance, materials and purpose prove sufficient when examining their history? Or does the background merit a deeper study into the circumstances surrounding the creation and sale of the artworks—not merely their birth but also their development? *Africa in the Market* is an exploration of the environment surrounding the creation and exchange of art in and from Africa, with pieces from the ROM's Amrad African Art Collection providing the framework of that study.

The Amrad African Art Collection arrived at the ROM in 2009. It comprises more than four hundred objects collected by Dagan, an extensive library and document archive. The artworks were mostly purchased by the collection between 1959 and 2001, during her trips in Africa from the east to the west of the continent. As the ROM enters the second year of its *Of Africa* initiative—a three-year, multi-platform project featuring exhibitions, talks, and programming aimed at rethinking historical and contemporary representations of Africa—this book brings to the fore a fresh perspective on the African market.

The ROM is extremely grateful to Esther Dagan for her substantial donation to the Museum's collection. This book was both inspired by, and documented with, her collection. Our appreciation also goes to Silvia Forni and Christopher B. Steiner for spearheading this anthology and to all the authors for their contributions within this authoritative collection of essays. Special thanks are due to the Louise Hawley Stone Charitable Trust, for the production and printing of this book would not have been possible without their generous support.

MARK ENGSTROM
INTERIM DIRECTOR & CEO, ROYAL ONTARIO MUSEUM

ACKNOWLEDGEMENTS

This book was inspired by the life and travels of Esther Dagan. Her vision, passion and love for the experiences and encounters gained in over 50 years of travel and collecting art throughout the African continent were the main driving force for the completion of this project. Mrs. Dagan's activity as a dealer and promoter of African creativity beyond the strictures of the canon highlight her interest in the continuous transformations in society and her emphasis on the makers and brokers that enable the circulation of objects from Africa to the rest of the world.

We are grateful to the authors that have accepted to contribute their own reflections on the complicated historical narratives of the art market and on the contemporary intersections between creators and dealers in different parts of Africa. While all these accounts are localized, they also reflect broader trends that are still often unacknowledged in scholarship and institutional collecting. Beyond those who have contributed to this volume, we are indebted to many colleagues who have shared their thoughts, reflections and critical remarks at various stages of this project. In particular, we wish to acknowledge Yaëlle Biro, Jonathan Fine, Susan Gagliardi, Christraud Geary, Paula Girshick, Elizabeth Harney, Bennetta Jules-Rosette, Kinsey Katchka, John Monroe, Trudy Nicks, Sylvester Ogbechie, Constantine Petridis, Ruth Phillips, Ciraj Rassool, Doran Ross, and Raymond Silverman.

We also wish to express our gratitude to those people at the Royal Ontario Museum who have championed the acquisition of the Amrad African Art Collection and the publication of this book project despite its unconventional approach. Janet Carding, Mark Engstrom, and Dan Rahimi have been great supporters of this project. ROM collection, conservation and curatorial staff moved the project along since its inception in 2012. Special thanks go to Stephanie Allen, Brian Boyle, Charlotte Chaffey, Julia Fenn, Tracey Forster, Molly Minnick, James Nixon, Rose Pereira, Judith Pudden, Angela Raljic, Sheeza Sarfraz, Heidi Sobol, Arthur Smith, and Tara Winterhalt.

SILVIA FORNI & CHRISTOPHER B. STEINER

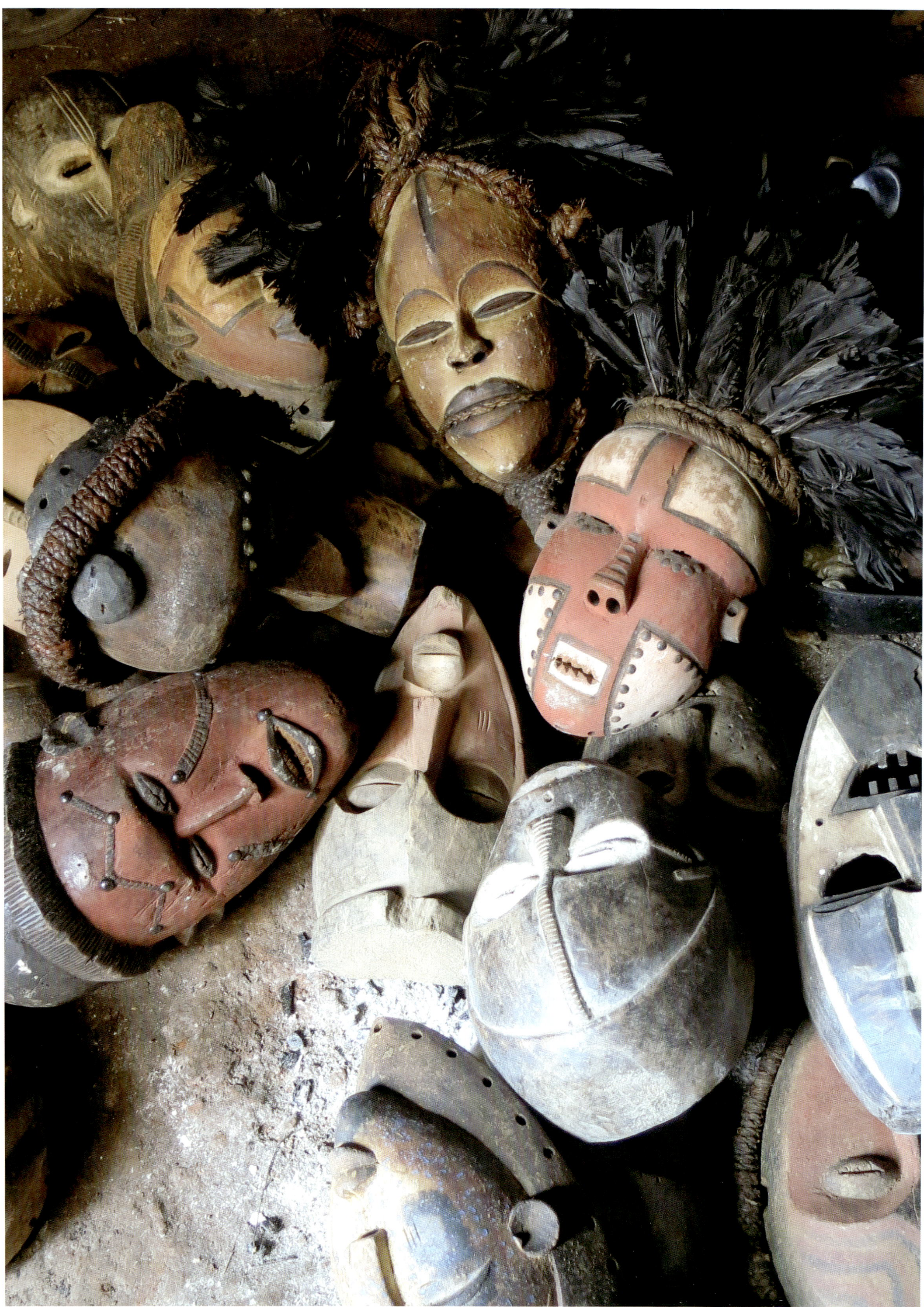

CHAPTER 1

THE DISLOCATION OF CULTURE: THE AMRAD AFRICAN ART COLLECTION AT THE ROYAL ONTARIO MUSEUM

SILVIA FORNI AND CHRISTOPHER B. STEINER

In his review of the 2007 exhibition *African Vision: The Walt Disney-Tishman African Art Collection* at the Smithsonian's National Museum of African Art, art critic Holland Cotter noted the absence of any representation of African participants in the equation of transatlantic exchange. In this exhibition, he says, collectors are represented as "benign heroes," and art "magically appears in their hands from nowhere, or rather from a vague somewhere called Africa, for our entertainment."[1] He goes on to note that in survey exhibitions from a private collection such as this one, "the only thematic thread [is] the taste and money of a single owner" and exhibits like this "are at least as much about the Western market as about African art." In this perceptive exhibition review, Cotter alludes to a more general phenomenon in the field of African art collecting—namely, the privileging of an object's history within the Western context of discovery and exhibition over an object's history within the African context of creation and exchange.

Even a cursory glance at auction records and market prices for the sale of African art over the past several decades reveals a predominant emphasis on an object's provenance in the Western sphere of art collecting, with little or often no mention of the object's circulation prior to its "extraction" from Africa. One of the underlying motivations for hiding the physical trajectory of an object from its indigenous context of creation and origin to its new context of exhibition and collection outside of Africa, is to de-emphasize its entanglement in the ignoble world of commodities and markets. Authenticity in African art is often predicated on negating the concept of the economic value of art production and art marketing. Objects that were created for consumption or export are summarily dismissed as inauthentic because any affiliation with a market economy is seen as a threat to the collector's fragile notion of an art created purely for ritual or religious purposes.[2] In explaining why he chose never to visit Africa, for example, American collector Brian Leyden sheds light on the connoisseur's insistence that authenticity is undermined by any association with modernity or the fruits of a capitalist economy: "If Adidas sneakers, payphones and Sony Walkmen were absent from the Côte d'Ivoire, I might reconsider my position, but, at present, my romantic vision of pre-colonial Côte d'Ivoire is too fragile to tamper with."[3]

One of the aims of this book is to demystify some of the "magic" in this system of cultural exchange by exploring the social networks and economic structures that both produce and circulate works of African art in global markets today. Holland Cotter's critique of the Walt Disney-Tishman exhibition may be explained in part by acknowledging that many African objects end up in museum or private collections with little or no documentation regarding their trajectory from Africa to the West. Certainly, until recently, the emphasis in museum records was more on documenting

detail
Masks piled in dealer's storage room. Foumban, Cameroon. July 2013. Photo by Silvia Forni

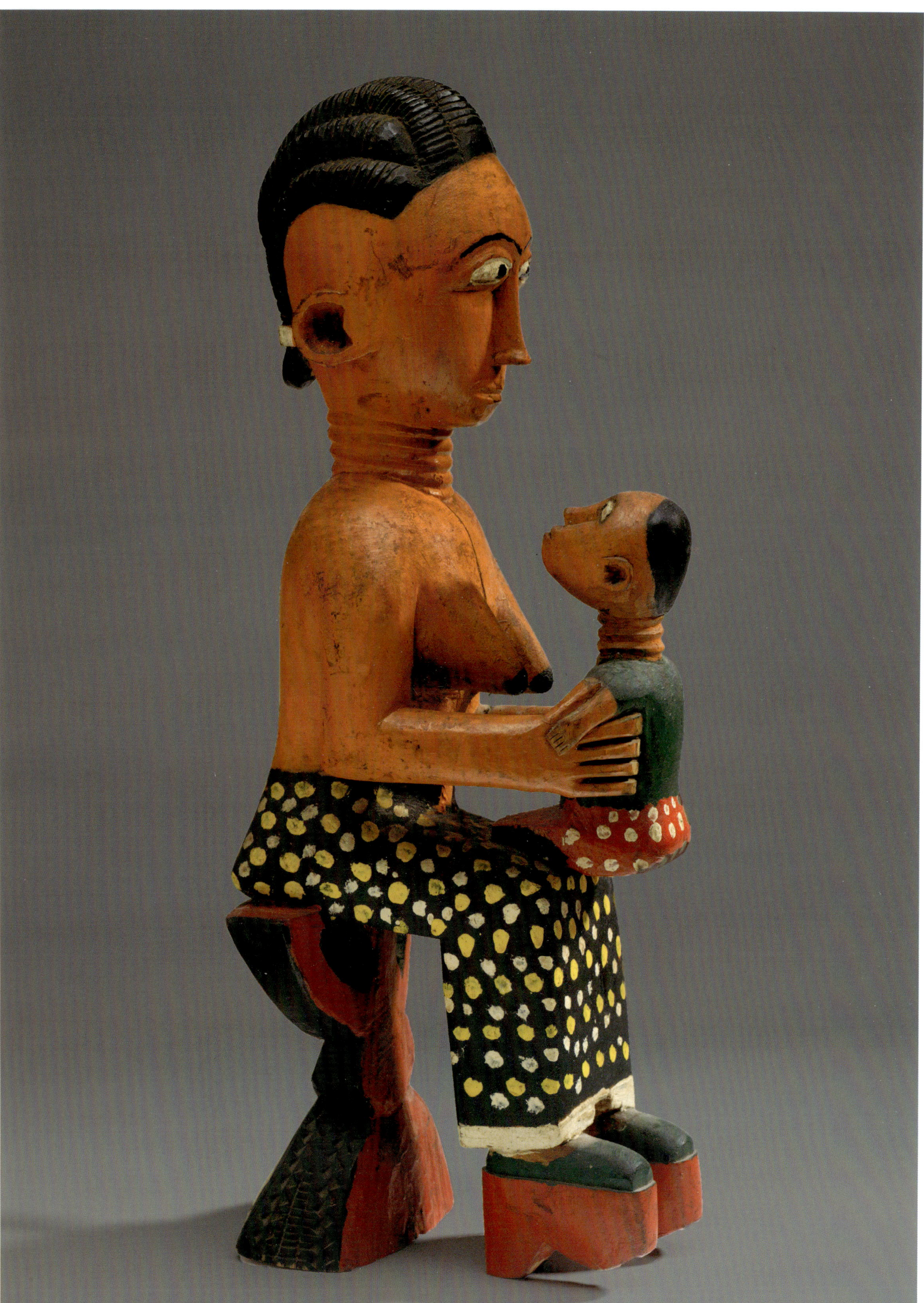

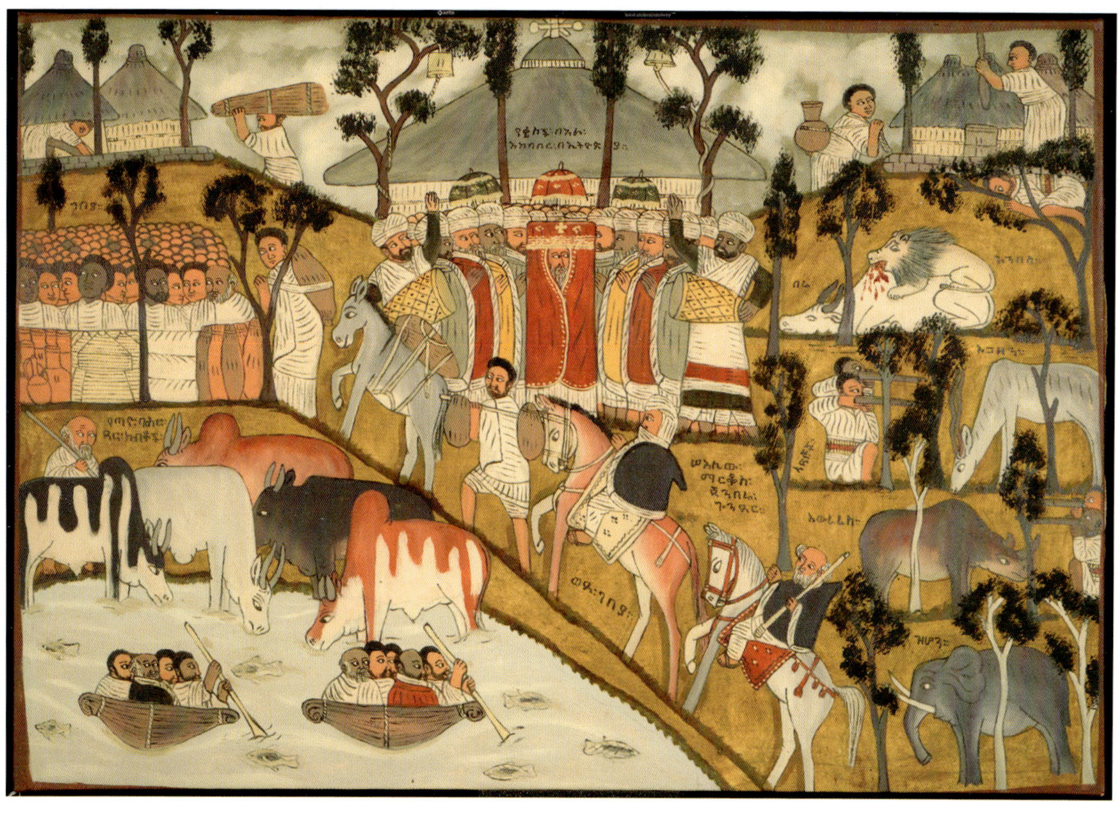

figure 1 (opposite)
Mother and child figure
Unidentified artist or workshop
Baule style
Wood, pigment
Purchased in 1986 from a dealer in Bouaké, Côte d'Ivoire
Height: 47.5 cm, Width: 16 cm, Depth: 20 cm
ROM 2009.126.51

figure 2
Painting
Marqos Jembere (b. 1958)
Ethiopia
Oil on canvas
Gift received in Ethiopia
Date unrecorded
Height: 81.9 cm, Width: 118.7 cm
ROM 2009.126.306

the indigenous function and meaning of an object than recording the details of purchase and acquisition.

In fact, in one of the earliest articles dedicated to a full description and analysis of the West African art market, Daniel Crowley concludes his discussion, quite surprisingly, by stressing the immediate need for scholarship not on the market but on "traditional" artistic forms and practices in Africa.

> If work is not begun immediately to record the cultural context in which traditional art is used, most of the forms we so admire will remain enigmas. Africans still living could tell us most of what we want to know about the divinities represented, the associated songs and dances, and their ritual significance, but scholars ... must seek them out, and quickly.[4]

The knowledge Crowley gained from studying the art market is not, in the end, the critical point of his article. Rather, it is the speed with which he sees the market growing and overtaking the production of "traditional" art in Africa and the way this could be a catalyst for urging scholars to train their attention on "vanishing" traditions before they are lost in the expansive sprawl of the commodity world. Writing at a time when the study of African art in both art history and anthropology was just emerging as a "legitimate" field of scholarship, it is not surprising that Crowley and his cohort of pioneers in the discipline should have attended to the indigenous context of object creation, aesthetics, and use. But today, we would argue, the "cultural context" of the art market—a space that so many Africanist scholars overlooked as they as they raced to record what was considered to be the "real thing"—is itself irrecoverable in the history and ethnography of Africa and its arts. It is to these cultural narratives of commerce, collecting and the economy of taste that we must with urgency turn our attention before they too are lost.

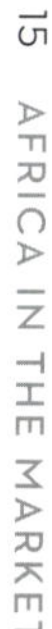

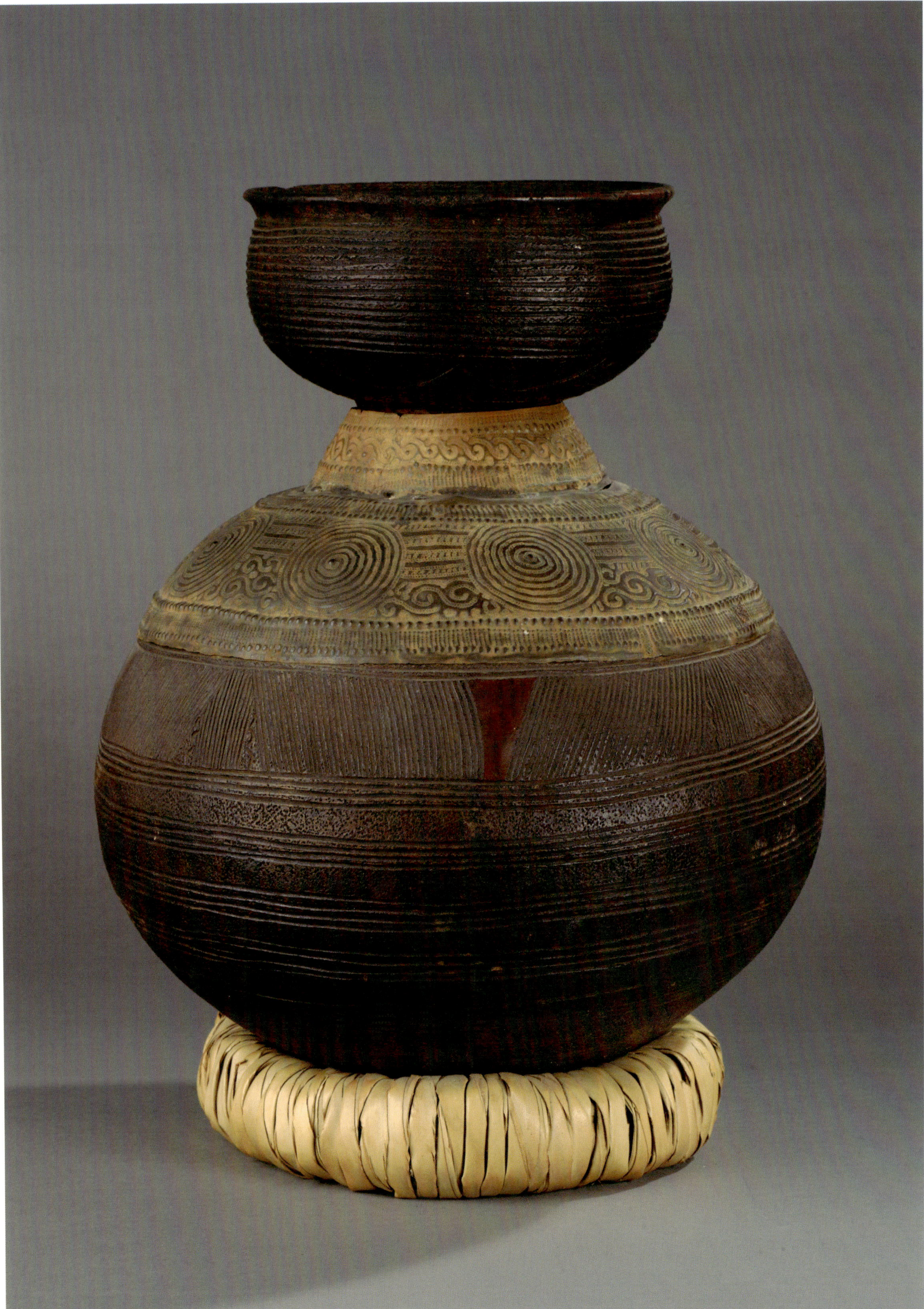

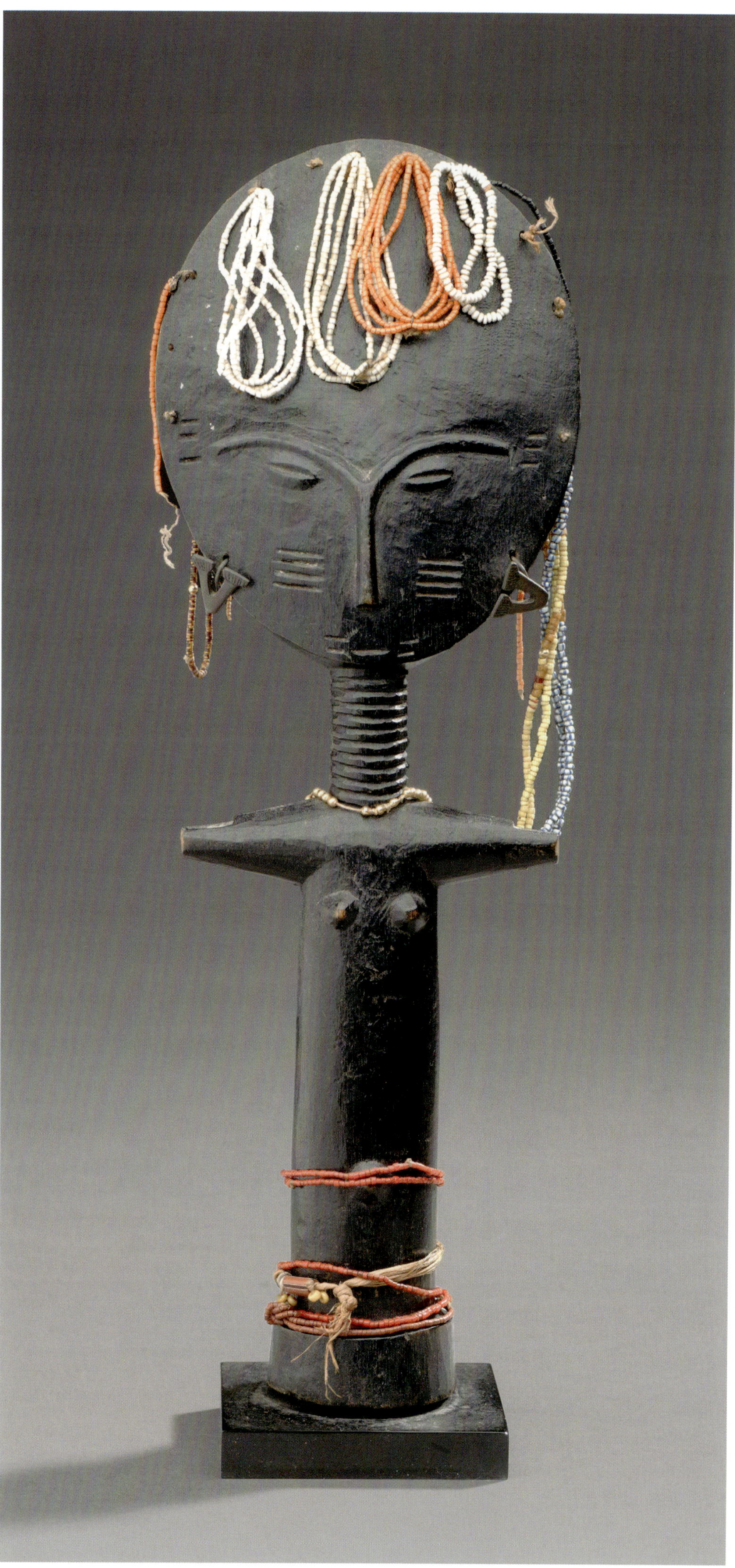

figure 3 (opposite)
Water or palm wine container
Unidentified artist
Nupe style
Terracotta
Purchased from a dealer in Dakar, Senegal, in 1988
Height: 41.5 cm, Diameter: 30 cm
ROM 2009.126.238

figure 4
Akua-ba doll
Unidentified artist or workshop
Asante style
Wood, fibre, glass beads
Purchased from the Kahan Gallery, New York, in 1985
Height: 25 cm, Width: 8.9 cm, Depth: 5 cm
ROM 2009.126.97

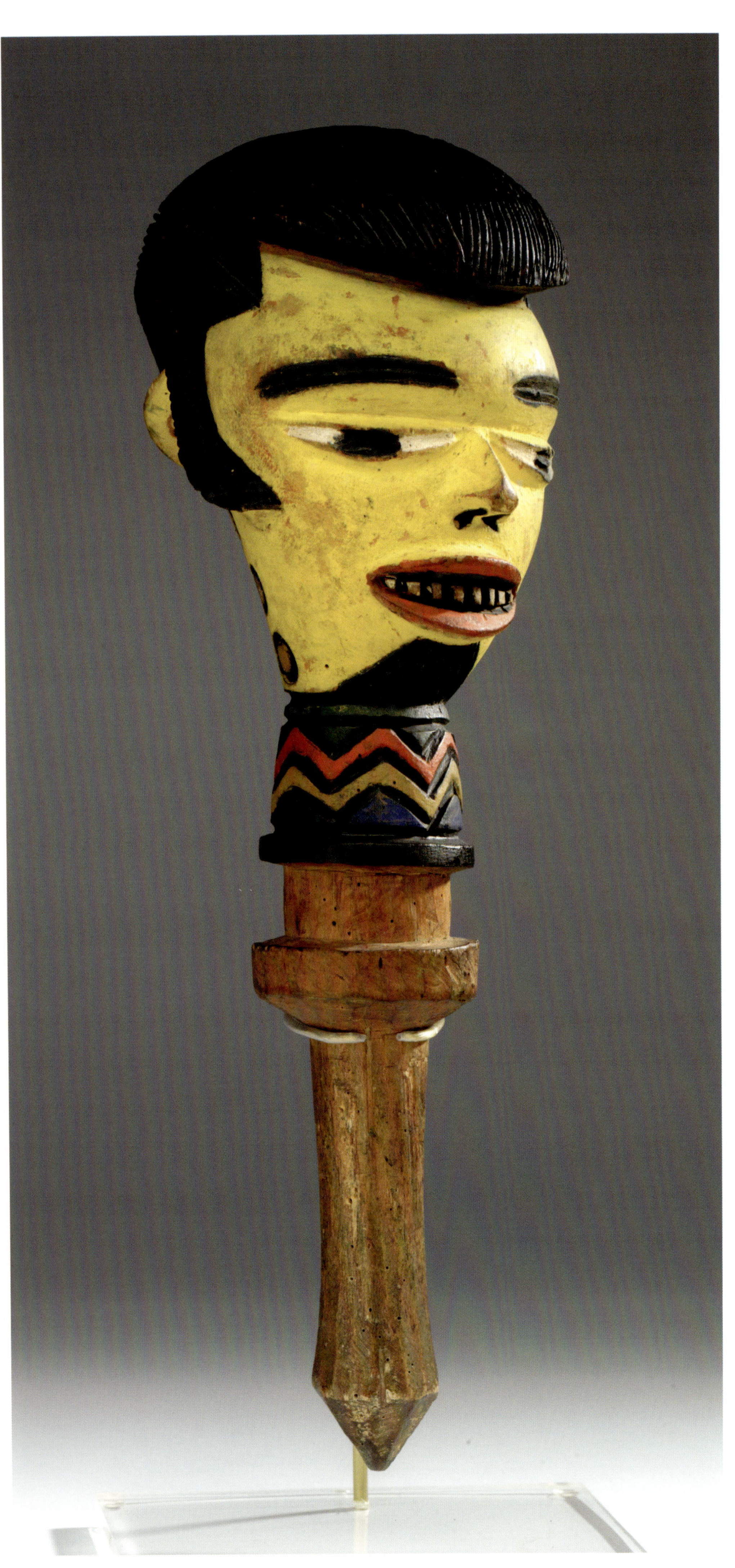

figure 5
Kebe-kebe puppet head
Unidentified artist or workshop
Kuyu style
Wood, pigment
Acquired in 1966 in the village of Mokambi, Gabon, from itinerant theatre troupe
Height: 39.8 cm, Width: 14.4 cm, Depth: 13.7 cm
ROM 2009.126.2

figure 6 (opposite)
Mother and child figure
Unidentified artist or workshop
Ewe style
Wood
Purchased in 1983 from Arouna, a dealer in Lomé, Togo
Height: 50 cm, Width: 28 cm, Depth: 28 cm
ROM 2009.126.58

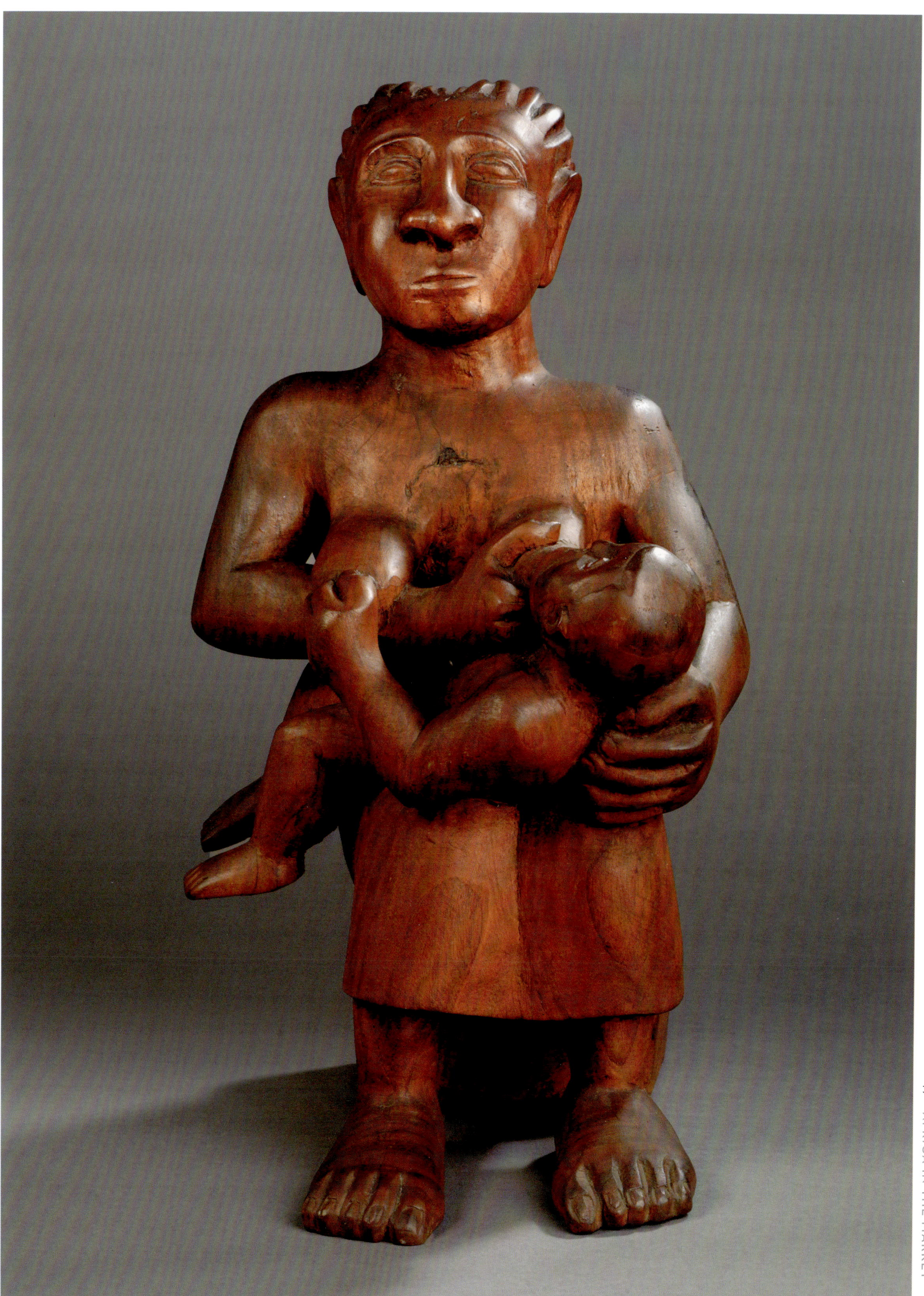

The Amrad African Art Collection

The impetus for this book stems from the acquisition by the Royal Ontario Museum of the Amrad African Art Collection, donated by Esther Amrad Dagan in 2009. Born in Jerusalem in 1931, Esther Dagan was a dancer, dance ethnographer, African art teacher, author and gallerist. The objects donated to the ROM were collected by her in Africa, or purchased from European and North American galleries, between 1959 and 2001.

A prolific author and the publisher of more than thirteen books on African art,[5] Dagan dedicated her career to sharing with the public (first in Israel; after 1978 in Canada) her passion for African cultures, arts and aesthetics. Through exhibitions at her gallery in Montreal and through her many publications, Dagan focused on particular themes—such as mother and child, bodily movement, theatre, puppets, masks, dolls, stools, and calabashes—that could be illustrated through artworks from different regions of Africa. These themes were also the driving inspiration for her explorations of the African continent, which she visited for extended periods as a young dance researcher in the 1960s and 1970s and then almost yearly for purchasing trips during her time as an active gallerist, between 1980 and 1992.

The objects collected by Dagan are representative of a large body of African works produced and sold into Western collections since the middle of the last century. Though art made for sale can certainly be traced in Africa back to the advent of European contact itself,[6] large-scale production for export began in earnest during the 1950s and 1960s, in response to the growth of expatriate communities and mass tourism. The Amrad African Art Collection exhibits a typical mix of object types collected during this period—from utilitarian objects made for indigenous use, to ritual objects intended for local consumption but eventually introduced into the international market (Fig. 1), to works that replicate traditional forms associated with particular ethnic styles. With the exception of a few objects that she acquired as gifts (Fig. 2), barters, or field purchases, most of the pieces in the Amrad Collection were bought in some of the large African art markets in West Africa in the 1980s (Fig. 3) or from other Canadian or US galleries mostly supplied by itinerant African dealers (Fig. 4).

Dagan shared with collectors of her generation a fascination with the bold "modernist" aesthetic of many African forms. Her first formative encounter with African art as a child was with a Songye *kifwebe* mask in an antique store. This deep impression was reawakened in the late 1950s when, as a dancer and choreographer-in-training, she was exposed to African dance performed in Paris, and later on, by an inspiring visit to Picasso's atelier in southern France.[7] Yet her inquisitive mind and desire to go beyond a superficial fascination pushed her to travel to Africa and investigate firsthand the context of production and use of these art forms. Unlike many collectors of her generation, Dagan travelled extensively in Africa, mostly in the western part of the continent from Senegal to Gabon, but also in Kenya, Uganda, Tanzania and Ethiopia. Though interested in seeking out "authentic" objects that she considered to be the most meaningful expressions of African creativity, Dagan was also fascinated by the innovations and variations stimulated by global trends and the market. While in Gabon in 1966, she acquired from an itinerant Gabonese theatre troupe six brightly painted Kuyu puppet heads, with the main character modelled as a portrait of Elvis Presley (Fig. 5). In her purchasing expeditions of the 1980s and early 1990s, Dagan sought different pieces based on the theme that she had selected for her exhibitions. For this purpose she would acquire traditionally inspired commercial pieces that she believed represented interesting contemporary transformations of traditional ideas rather than aesthetic degenerations (Fig. 6). Though in many of her publications and interviews she adopted a rather strict definition of authenticity,[8] her own experience travelling and communicating with artists and dealers inspired a much broader appreciation of African creativity as well as recognition of her African partners' active role in her journey of discovery.

Locating African "Tourist" Art

Over several decades it has become increasingly clear that to understand the full context of African art one must understand the frameworks within which that art has been produced and sold in Africa and internationally. Some of the earliest research on this topic was initiated by scholars in the fields of anthropology and sociology under the rubric of tourist art studies. In his now-classic 1976 edited volume, *Ethnic and Tourist Arts: Cultural Expressions from the Fourth World*, Nelson Graburn established the foundation for the field of tourist art studies by bringing together over twenty scholars whose work examined the production of arts and crafts by indigenous populations from across the world intended for sale to outsiders.[9]

Evaluators of African tourist arts have always been divided between those who view such work as having a negative impact on the artistic traditions of Africa and those who consider it vital to the survival of both traditional styles and the spirit of creativity. The former, who regard tourist art as a threat to the cultural survival of "traditional" arts, argue that commercialization encourages shoddy workmanship through the limitations imposed by mass production and the ever-lower expectations of tourist patrons with putatively undeveloped taste. Critics of commercialism argue that tourist art leads inevitably to the cultural demise of true artistic genius.[10] Frank McEwen, the first director of the National Gallery of Zimbabwe, coined the term "airport art" in 1960 to reflect his disapproval of all aspects of commercialism in African art, which he described as one of "the saddest forms of art prostitution that ignorant tourists support."[11]

Admirers and defenders of African tourist art, on the other hand, value commercial developments for at least four reasons.

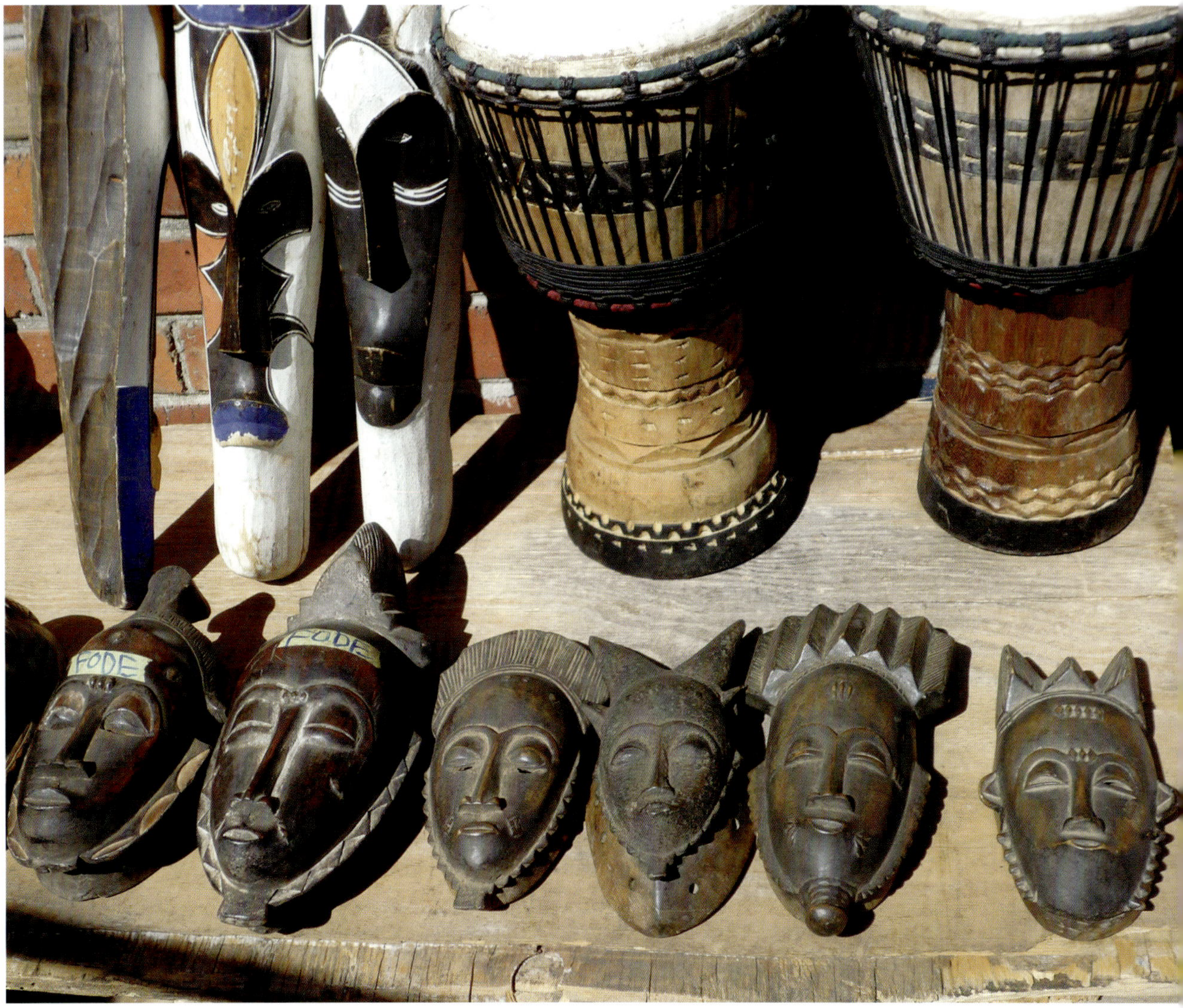

figure 7
Guro-style masks and Fang masks made in Foumban at a market stall in Cape Town, South Africa
Photo by Till Förster, 2011

First, they argue that the rise of a tourist art trade often leads to the continuation or even revival of earlier art forms that might otherwise have vanished. In certain areas, for example, where missionary conversion may have suppressed the religious practices that once relied on using masks and statues, banished art forms persist only as a result of secular, commercial production for outsiders. Second, they suggest that commercial production for export encourages young artists to develop their skills and aptitude as workshop apprentices and "line" carvers. Such abilities may then be transferred back into more traditional artistic practices for indigenous consumption.

Third, from an economic perspective, tourist arts are championed as a financial survival strategy in areas where other forms of income may be hard to come by. Tourist art networks employ not only artists but also a vast array of related personnel, including itinerant street-hawkers, marketplace traders, wholesale and international middlemen, gallery employees and owners, and government bureaucrats. Finally, some argue that African tourist art should not be viewed as a degraded or inferior version of "traditional" art, but rather analyzed as a category of artistic production with its own aesthetic sensibilities, merits and values. Turning to a linguistic parallel to underscore this last point, Paula Ben-Amos suggested that tourist art might even be compared to a pidgin language, because both are created as means of communication in transcultural exchange.[12] Just as linguists confirm that pidgin languages are not "simplified foreign talk" but complex language systems, so too one could argue that tourist art represents a sophisticated form of cultural expression that can be accorded equal intellectual and aesthetic value and study at the same level of analysis as "traditional" arts.

Taking a lead from the linguistic model in Ben-Amos's 1977 article, Bennetta Jules-Rosette published in 1984 *The Messages of Tourist Art*, a book that examined the production of art for market consumption across the African continent. By imagining the tourist art market as a kind of semiotic system of exchange, Jules-Rosette opened up the possibility of interpreting tourist art as an authentic mode of communication between producers and consumers.[13] One reviewer noted that in *The Messages of Tourist Art*, Jules-Rosette "broadens our minds and decolonizes our perception of a mode of African expression."[14] Following in her footsteps, Christopher Steiner's book *African Art in Transit* (1994) focused specifically on art traders in Côte d'Ivoire. He describes these traders as "culture brokers" who mediate both knowledge and value in a complex system of transnational exchange. Focusing on an area of African art that had previously been largely neglected, Steiner shed light on the economic and cultural interactions that occur in the "contact zone" between

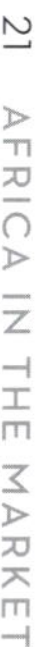

the worlds of production/use and consumption/collecting. And though mostly focused on European and North American protagonists, Raymond Corbey's more recent *Tribal Art Traffic* (2000), an overview of the history and negotiations that shaped museum collections and the art market, provides a rare profile of an African art dealer.

Much of the literature on African tourist art and the commercial dimensions of the African art market has reprimanded scholars, collectors and museums that fail to acknowledge the legitimacy of art made for trade. Sidney Kasfir, for example, in her 1992 article "African Art and Authenticity," says,

> In the biological model of stylistic development [tourist art] exemplifies "decay" or even "death"; in discussions of quality it is dismissed as crude, mass produced and crassly commercial; in the metaphors of symbolic anthropology it is impure, polluted; in the salvage anthropology paradigm it is already lost. The Center for African Art in New York decided to omit it from its supposedly definitive contemporary art exhibition "Africa Explores," because presumably for some or all of the above reasons.[15]

We believe the moment has come to move beyond criticism and to build a legitimate framework within which to collect and interpret African art of recent production intended for an external market. Our goal is not to disparage museums for exhibiting works that are perceived to be "traditional" (and not intended for external audiences), nor are we seeking to persuade the cultures of Western art collecting to embrace one type of African material production over another. Markets are complex, self-regulating economic structures, determined through the forces of supply and demand. Instead, our aim here is to provide an ethnographic and historical context within which to understand and interpret a collection of African art objects assembled during the latter part of the twentieth century by a collector whose passion for African art was strongly connected with her love for travel and for the human interactions of the large African markets.

There is a tendency, we think, among some art museum curators and private collectors to confound the assessment of African art objects made for trade with a canonical paradigm constructed out of a set of near-mythological objects that are held in extraordinary esteem by the high-end market. The categories "fine" art and "commercial" or "trade" art emerge out of highly subjective criteria that are often based less on objective differences and more on perceived values and skewed concepts of authenticity. We are not suggesting here that trade pieces be elevated to the category of fine art, we are simply suggesting that such works ought to be taken seriously and situated within their appropriate ethnohistorical context. Scholarship on commercial art in Africa sheds light not only on a neglected area of the aesthetic production and circulation of material culture, but also brings into sharp focus the categorical distinction between "high" art and "low" art—thereby encouraging a critical re-examination of a system of classification whose boundaries have sometimes been treated as more real than they are imagined (Fig. 7).

In the nearly forty years that have passed since the publication of Graburn's edited volume on tourist art, the fields of anthropology and art history have, for the most part, embraced a new reading of commercial art and seen value in the analysis and understanding of artworks created in the nexus of cross-cultural exchange. With few exceptions, mainly amongst museums with an ethnographic or historical focus, the museum world has lagged a bit in its acceptance of non-traditional pieces or art made for commercial export. This discrepancy might be explained in part by the fact that while it costs nothing for scholars to *write* about a huge range of objects that exemplify commercial and economic production, it is quite another thing to acquire such objects within the limited and costly space of physical museum storage. The acceptance of Esther Dagan's collection by the Royal Ontario Museum is meant to explicitly stake a museological claim on a body of materials that might, in the past, have been rejected.

Museum Context: The Indeterminacy of Authenticity

The motivation to acquire the Amrad African Art Collection for the Royal Ontario Museum is, at least in part, to redress some of the bias against African objects that fall outside the strict canonical definition of African art—a bias which usually finds its final endorsement through museum acquisitions and exhibitions. "Museum quality" is often used as a shorthand phrase for those pieces that have passed the most rigorous assessment or are endorsed by a collector or curator whose expertise is recognized by the market. These expert-vetted pieces are deemed to be outstanding examples of the art of specific peoples or periods. By and large, these pieces are attributed to a time that preceded the art market or to domains that are not influenced by commercial motives.

According to the strict definition of value recognized in the high-end art market, the authenticity of an African art object is predicated on the artist's intention to produce for local use, and on the original functional, spiritual or symbolic purpose of the piece. "Traditional" African "museum quality" pieces are thus all hypothetically produced with no regard for the demands and pressures of the international art market. Paradoxically, very few collections—usually only those acquired under scientific rather than aesthetic premises—have followed a direct trajectory from the field to the museum. In most other cases, it is precisely through their market circulation that objects are assigned aesthetic and monetary value. Commodification, however, is only acceptable according to the logic of the high-end market once the pieces have been positioned entirely within the Western world.

This approach *de facto* creates somewhat fictional representations of artistic production and object circulation that completely overlook the powerful impulse of the market in African art well before mass tourism of the 1960s.[16] The value attributed to artworks is thus determined less by the intrinsic aesthetic quality of the object itself, and more by its known or supposed context of production. Recent scholarship in museum studies and the sociology of art demonstrates quite clearly that museums commonly function as sites of inclusion and exclusion based on the social class and economic status of the visitor.[17] It is equally true, however, that museums commonly function as sites of inclusion and exclusion of the very objects they collect and exhibit. Like the visitors, objects that are perceived as crass in character and wanting in style are excluded in favour of those that demonstrate elitist values and good taste.[18]

The reproduction of these tropes—tropes that continue to dictate price and value on the marketplace—have created a rather complicated impasse, which basically denies any sort of cultural and aesthetic legitimacy to those artworks produced for the greatest part of the twentieth century in the many artistic workshops throughout the African continent. Usually defined as fakes, or in some cases "firewood" or "junk," these works and their production settings are routinely ignored in art museum contexts, or amongst art collectors and galleries which continue to reproduce a rather Manichean narrative of a traditional and untouched spiritual past—a past unspoiled by the same conditions that in the West have warranted the recognition of African aesthetics as art. While, as mentioned earlier, several scholars have challenged these premises through in-depth studies of the African contexts of production and circulation of pieces made for the market, these insights are rarely embraced in museum collections. Only rather recently have curators started to address the issues of acquisition and market circulation of the objects that eventually find their way to museums. One seminal example in this direction is Christraud Geary and Stephanie Xatart's catalogue for the 2007 exhibition *Material Journeys* at the Museum of Fine Arts, Boston, which provides a fascinating account of Geneviève McMillan's travels and the situation of the art market in the places she visited in her collecting explorations during the second half of the twentieth century. Quite meaningfully, in the same review mentioned at the beginning of this chapter, *Material Journeys* was presented as a counter-example to the Walt Disney–Tishman exhibition. This exhibition, according to Cotter, presents

> a view that challenges and redefines all kinds of orthodoxies: purity, beauty, authenticity, value, and art among them. If as a result, Material Journeys is shorter on convention-vetted masterpieces than the Tishman show, it offers a far truer, newer, more various and surprising vision of Africa.[19]

Exhibitions and catalogues such as this are inspiring in that they take into serious historical consideration not only unquestionably old and "authentic" pieces but also some twentieth-century objects that fall outside the strict limitations of the art canon—objects for which the provenance is unknown or muddy, objects whose ceremonial or ritual life may have been short or objects fabricated quite explicitly for the export market. As many of the authors in this book note, in relation to productive and commercial contexts in different parts of Africa, the market was a strong driving force for innovation and creativity and a fundamental component of the system well before the advent of mass tourism. While the second half of the twentieth century has undoubtedly seen an expansion of commercial opportunities for African artists working with traditional forms, changes and adaptations in response to the demands of new customers have always been an element of the creative process.

In any field of art connoisseurship, the public assumes that "experts" can tell the difference between "real" art and "fake" art, between masterpieces and forgeries. But what the public is not told is that the categories themselves are constructed by the very experts charged with making these imprecise and highly contentious distinctions. The public's perception of "the museum" as an emblem of authority underscores, validates and even "naturalizes" the arbitrary and imprecise systems of classification generated by the gatekeepers of authenticity. "Once it is in the museum," writes Duncan Cameron, "we make our judgment in the knowledge, if not awe, of the fact that experts have already said 'This is good', or 'This is important', or 'This is real.'"[20] By routinely denying contemporary artistic expressions generated under conditions of commerce and market exposure access to in museum collections and exhibitions, the "system" effectively encourages the production in Africa of copies and fakes that replicate the canonical works that are perceived to gain entry into the museum. Through this rigid framework of inclusion/exclusion we are left, in the end, with a highly contradictory and problematic situation where artists in Africa reproduce the canon (as imagined by outsiders) in order to sell their work and survive economically.

Out of the Shadows: African Traders as (Invisible) Creative Partners

In the world of African art collecting, "provenance" is another complicated and potentially fraught word. Whereas often concealed while an object is in Africa, the commercial and collecting biography of the object is very carefully documented once it becomes part of the Western art–culture system.[21] There are countless examples from recent auctions that could be cited here, but an excellent case in point would be the sale in Paris in June 2014 of a Guro mask from Côte d'Ivoire. First collected by Paul Guillaume, then sold to André Breton and then to Charles Ratton, the mask was photographed in 1927 by Man Ray, and an image of the mask was included in Nancy

Cunard's influential book *Negro Anthology* (1934). The mask then disappeared from public view until it was accidentally rediscovered eighty years later. This narrative of discovery, loss, and rediscovery, coupled with a stellar pedigree of celebrity provenance, was so compelling that Tajan held an entire auction at Hôtel Drouot for this single object, which was estimated to fetch between €100,000 and €150,000 but sold for €1,375,000. Although there are some speculations on the identity of the artist, known only by attribution as the Master of Bouaflé, the trajectory of the object from Côte d'Ivoire to Paris remains a complete mystery.

Well-known dealers and collectors, such as Guillaume, Breton and Ratton, are important contributors to the creation of the price and value of an object. Dealers and collectors are often recognized for their role in shaping or influencing institutional holdings and trends in the field, but not if they are African. The biography of an artwork and its history of exchange, once it has been severed from its context of production and use, are important elements in determining its importance and desirability. However, if the dealer is African, he or she is rarely mentioned—they are relegated to anonymous "middlemen" or "runners."

It is rare to see a catalogue, whether for a museum exhibition or a private collection, that acknowledges partnership with African dealers or attributes any agency to African counterparts in the equation of collecting practices. The introductory text in the catalogue of the Smithsonian's Walt Disney–Tishman collection, for instance, makes no mention of the role of Africans in the formation of the collection, noting only this:

> Although the Tishmans made several trips to remote regions of Africa during the late 1960s to see the origins of the works they owned, the bulk of their extensive collection was acquired over a period of 20 years from reputable galleries around the world.[22]

With few exceptions, African dealers have been erased from the pedigree of an object or artwork and from the scholarship associated with it—and with them is erased quite relevant information about the life history of the object. Many African dealers are, in fact, also field collectors, and they acquire objects thanks to their knowledge and understanding of social and political shifts in the communities where the objects are produced and used. African dealers carry a rather diversified inventory, ranging from well-documented pieces that they collected in the field, to objects acquired by some of their collaborators, and objects produced by local workshops and finished with antique-looking patinas.

The uncharacteristically candid text in the catalogue accompanying Yale University Art Gallery's recent exhibition of the Charles B. Benenson Collection of African Art offers a rare glimpse into the role played by African dealers and traders in supplying a Western collector with objects brought

figure 8
Mask
Unidentified artist or workshop
We style
Wood, pigment, cloth, cowrie shells
Purchased from a dealer in Abidjan, Côte d'Ivoire, in 1985
Height: 150 cm, Width: 21 cm, Depth: 47.2 cm
ROM 2009.126.174

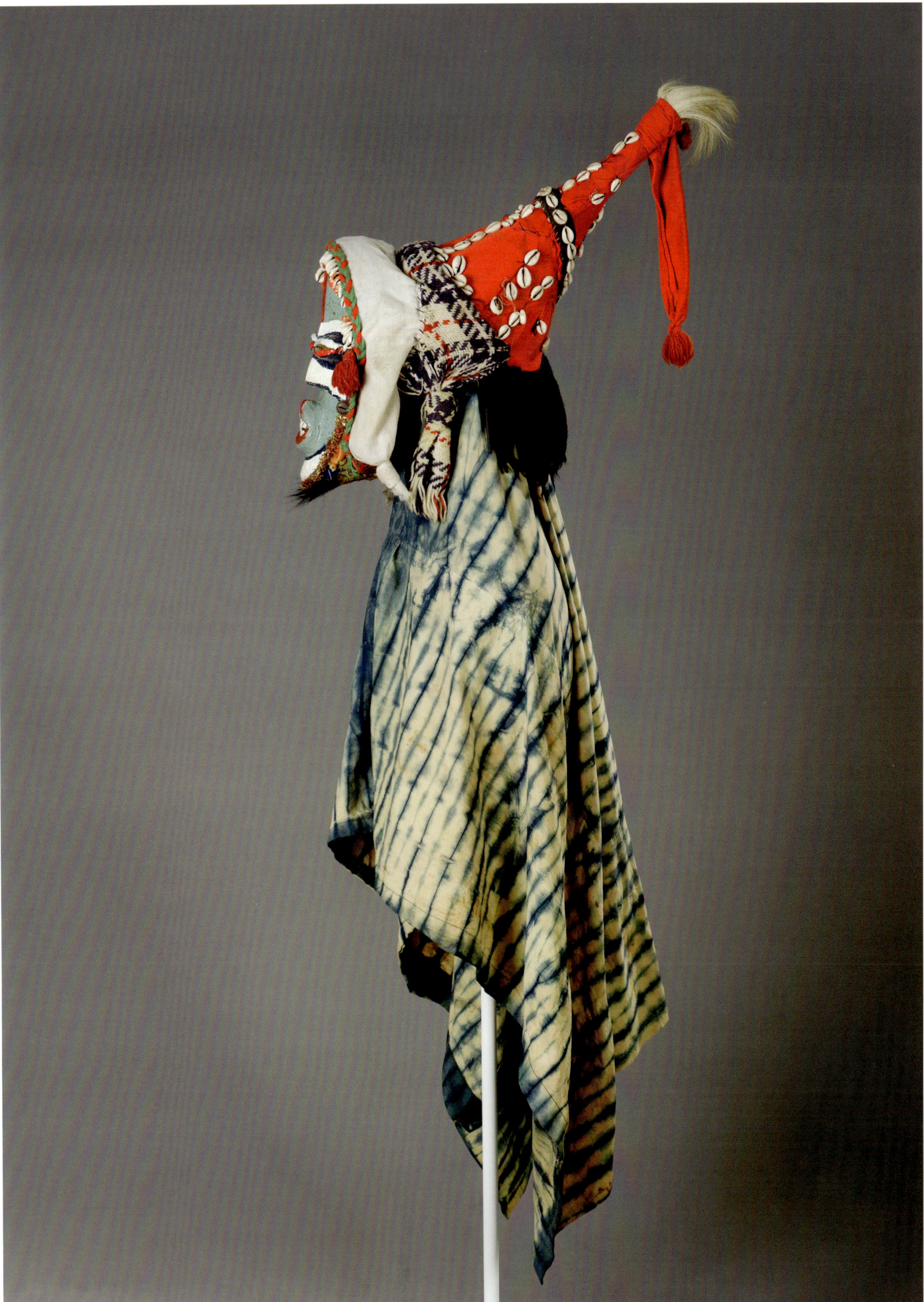

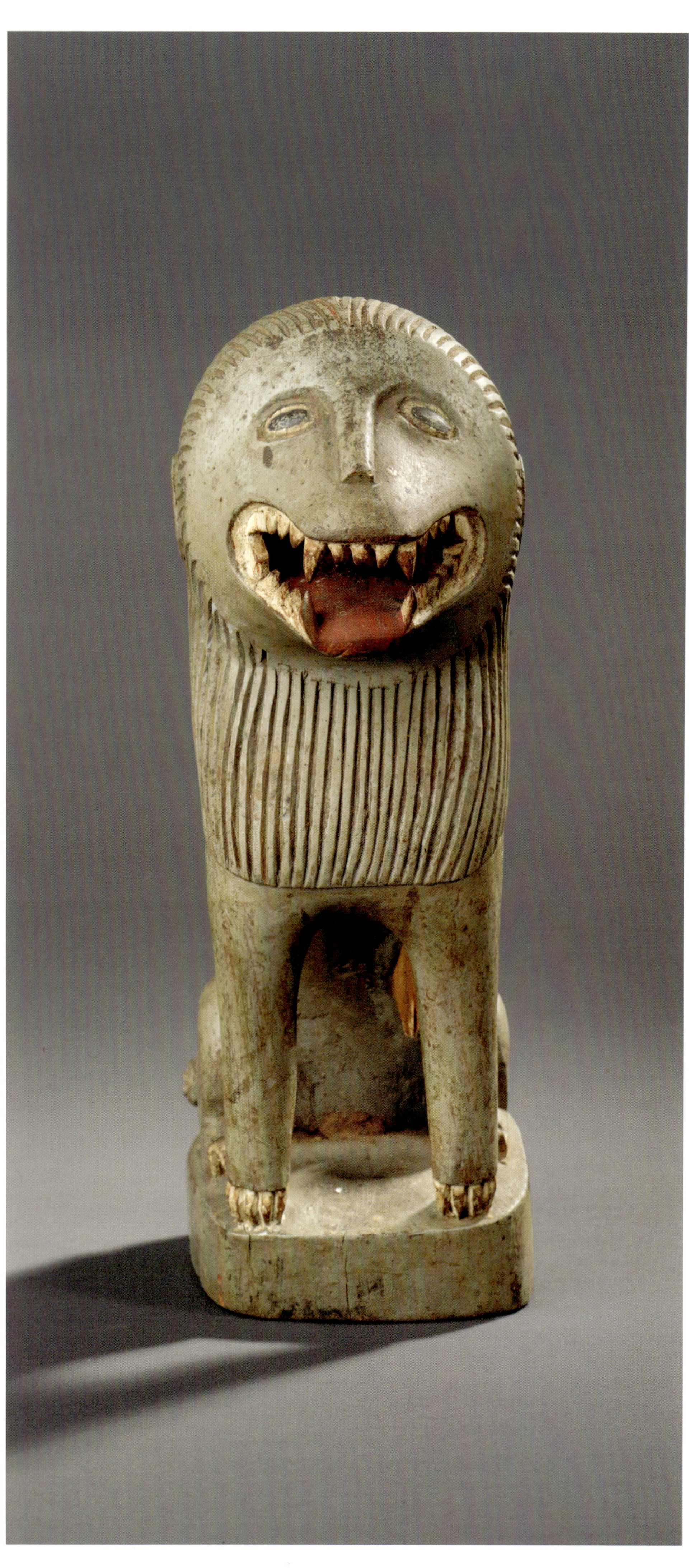

figure 9
Lion figurine
Unidentified artist or workshop
Fon style
Wood, pigment
Purchased from a private collector in Cotonou, Benin in 1988
Height: 30.3 cm, Width: 11 cm, Depth: 19.5 cm
ROM 2009.126.29

figure 10 (opposite)
Hunting decoy in the shape of a bird
Unidentified artist
Hausa style
Wood, leather, bird beak
Purchased in Ouagadougou, Burkina Faso, in 1981
Height: 38 cm, Width: 10.7 cm, Depth: 26 cm
2009.126.241

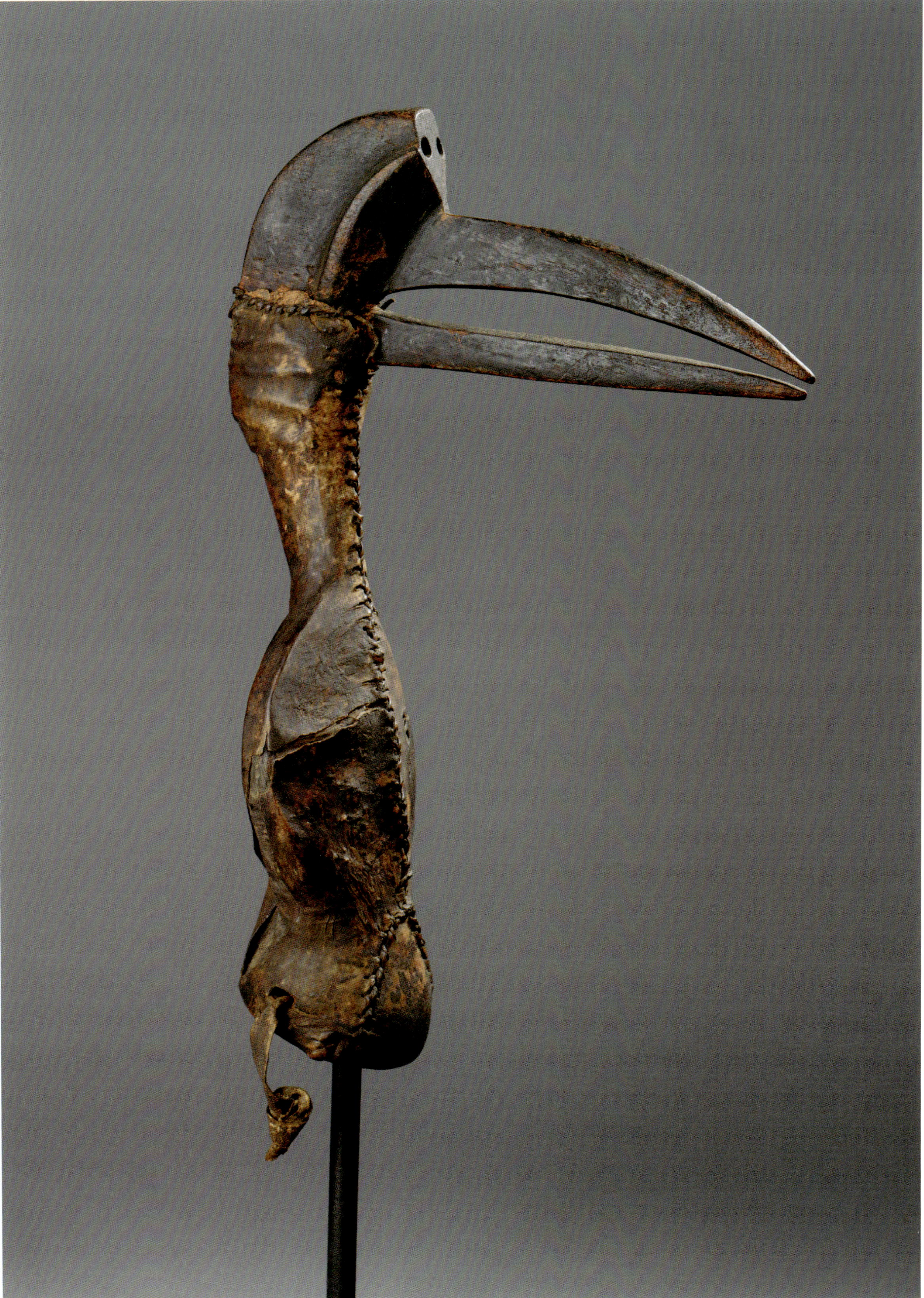

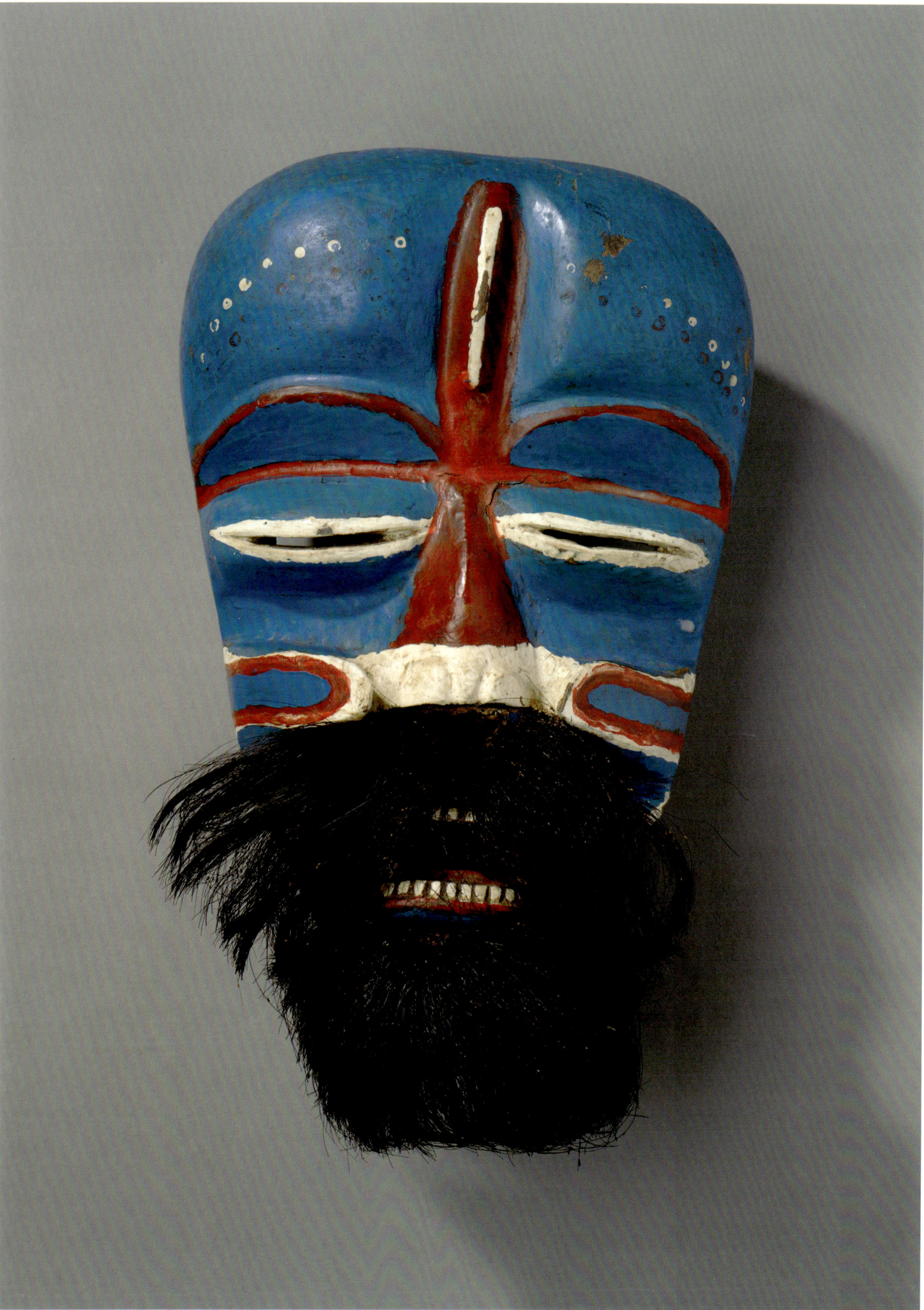

from Africa: "Dealers would land at JFK airport," writes one of Charles's sons, Lawrence, "get in taxis, and bring duffel bags filled with sculptures and tattered wrapping paper straight to his workplace."[23] Another one of Charles's sons, William, goes on to say,

> He would have dealers, African art-dealers, sitting in the lobby with duffle bags and things, knapsacks stuffed with pieces.... In general, he would only buy after he would have one of his experts look at it. So, it was, on the one hand, impulsive, and on the other, cautious, with needing to have the provenance and antiquity of it researched or confirmed by people he liked or trusted as professional advisors.[24]

Unlike most catalogues of African art, here the role of African traders is revealed and presented with respectful acknowledgement. Yet the text in the catalogue also makes clear that the power to validate "authenticity" still rested in the hands of Charles Benenson's "experts," who were not African. (These included Michael Kan, while he served as curator of African art at the Brooklyn Museum of Art in the 1960s and 1970s; and Susan Vogel, beginning in the 1970s while she was curator of African collections at the Metropolitan Museum of Art.)

Some complicated mental gymnastics are exercised by various voices of "authority" quoted in the exhibition catalogue to validate the Benenson pieces acquired from African sources. Not only are we told that everything he bought was vetted by non-African authorities, but it is also suggested that Benenson benefited from collecting at a time when "real" pieces could still be had from African sources. Because Benenson collected from "runners" in the late 1960s and 1970s, Michael Kan believes that "the Benenson Collection has particular value because it contains the last wave of 'authentic' art from the continent."[25] "While dealing with African traders may have been acceptable in the 1960s and 1970s," write the authors of the Benenson catalogue, "more recent transactions with them, according to American and European dealers, have been more likely to be inauthentic."[26]

Although Benenson is represented in the catalogue as a man of integrity with the utmost respect for the African traders that supplied him with many of the core objects in his collection, it is also noted that he kept few if any records of those transactions.

> The top collectors in New York generally disdained the itinerant African dealers, at least publicly, although many profited from the few good pieces that were to be found, but this provenance often went unmentioned and unrecorded. This is the case with the Benenson records: even though Charlie kept his receipts with the names of African dealers, the same African dealers' names are rarely mentioned in the copious notebooks he kept, to the point that absence of a record implies a probable African provenance.[27]

figure 11
Mask
Unidentified artist or workshop
Wè style
Wood, pigment, hair
Purchased from a dealer in Abidjan, Côte d'Ivoire, in 1985
Height: 32.5 cm, Width: 19.9 cm, Depth: 11.2 cm
ROM 2009.126.190

Significantly, the only recent collection publication that records the names of the African dealers from which pieces were acquired and gives ample recognition to their critical role as intermediaries and brokers is Sylvester Okwunodu Ogbechie's *Making History*,[28] which, incidentally, is also the first scholarly publication to document a collection of African art owned by an African collector based in Africa. In documenting the Akinsanya Collection, Ogbechie stresses, once more, the almost paradoxical foundations of the canonical understanding of African art, whereby objects become more valuable and "authentic" the further they are removed geographically, historically and conceptually from the human interactions in Africa that determined their creation, appreciationand circulation.

While these human interactions are an important and acknowledged factor in the building of the Nigerian collection studied by Ogbechie, silence and absence are more typical in the records and narratives associated with Western-based collections of African art. Interestingly, we find similar silences in the records kept by Esther Dagan. Although, in conversation, Dagan consciously recognized the role of dealers as creative partners in the building of her collections and exhibitions—and often relied heavily on the information that she gathered through her exchanges with them—she did not always document dealers' names and roles. While the dealers would provide her with objects and stories, Dagan did not consider their identity an important part of the narrative of indigenous meanings and context of use that define and document African artworks (Fig. 8).

Contributions to this Book

While gaps in documentation can often not be filled, the relatively recent history of the Amrad African Art Collection makes it possible to research and investigate some aspects of the human interactions and exchanges that informed the background of Dagan's collecting. Each chapter in this book offers a perspective on one of the particular regions of Africa from which the objects in the Amrad's collection originate. All the authors analyze in detail the changes and transformations in the art markets where Dagan purchased many pieces throughout the years.

Many, if not all, scholars doing fieldwork on art in Africa have encountered the market in one way or another, but few have provided written accounts of their discoveries and exchanges in this realm. Dagan herself, despite recalling fondly the hours spent interacting, negotiating and speaking with dealers in Ouagadougou, Lomé, Accra, Abidjan, Korhogo and Foumban29 did not include stories of and from those exchanges amongst the many that she chose to recount about the arts of Africa. The commercial exchanges that enable objects to circulate within and beyond their original context of production continue to be concealed or ignored as incidental, distracting or irrelevant components of the biography of these objects (Fig. 9).

The contributors to this book, while focusing on specific market contexts, provide insight on more general continental trends and issues. Indeed, while cultural premises, historical precedents, stylistic tradition, and market and patronage systems influence in unique ways the development of local artistic scenes, all contributors highlight the meaningful role of the market—whether local or international—in determining the viability and ultimately the continuity of specific artistic productions. All contributors also reveal that the dichotomy between a past, spiritually imbued and uncommodified authentic art and a modern, commercially driven production is often more a fiction of Western imagination than a reflection of the creative settings found in Africa. Most importantly, the authors emphasize the *longue durée* of the fruitful intersection between "traditional" artistic production and the international tourist and art market, whereby the changes in artistic production reflect quite "authentically" social and cultural transformation informed by local and international events and trends.

In Chapter 2, Catherine M. Hale and Silvia Forni focus on the historical and cultural premises that have influenced the building of the Amrad African Art Collection. If, on the one hand, collecting art from Africa is predicated on what is available on the market at any specific time, on the other, collectors' personal choices play a fundamental role in determining the character of the collection as a whole. This essay looks at the community of African art lovers, collectors and dealers active in Montreal, Toronto and Ottawa in the second half of the twentieth century. While each individual or couple had a personal approach to collecting, the Montreal group also formed a tight-knit community whose members followed similar paths in their discovery of an African aesthetic and shared a fascination with contemporary art. In addition, the key figures in this circle all aspired to educate the Canadian public about what they perceived to be rather neglected yet powerful art forms. Dagan in particular took this mission beyond the curation of gallery displays by editing and publishing several books on African art. In her publications, as in her displays, Dagan promoted a broad range of artworks, challenging with her passion and enthusiasm the strictures of canonical definitions of authenticity and museum quality.

Christopher D. Roy's chapter, "The Art Market in Burkina Faso," offers a history of the Burkina Faso art market during the second half of the twentieth century. Told in the voice of a personal narrative, this chapter explores the range of objects that were sold in the capital, Ouagadougou, from the 1970s onward. Although Roy's own field research and publications have focused on the traditional role of arts (and especially masks and masking) in communities throughout Burkina Faso, these previously unpublished observations of the art market go a long way to filling the gaps and silences in the ethnographic record of the African art trade. We suspect that many art historians and anthropologists made comparable observations of the art market while studying the "traditional" arts, then considered a more distinguished research destination. But as Roy's chapter here demonstrates, important knowledge can be gleaned from even informal observations of the market. His essay helps us to better frame the context of the Dagan collection, as it was assembled in West Africa during the same time period discussed by Roy (Fig. 10).

In the fourth chapter, Till Förster investigates the changes brought about to the art market in Korhogo, Côte d'Ivoire, over the last hundred years. As an art-rich area with a longstanding tradition of specialized carving, northern Côte d'Ivoire lends itself well to a long-term analysis of variations in production modes and aesthetic choices dictated by shifting forms of patronage. Förster recounts the interactions between carvers and customers since pre-colonial times, when ritual and ceremonial objects were commissioned from carvers' colonies through the intermediation of the elder members of *poro* lodges. The arrival of European officials in the early 1900s shifted compensation to currency and expanded the range of small entertainment masks known as *kpelie*, an instant favourite of the new customers. The years from the 1950s to the 1990s saw a rather dramatic increase in artistic production, both of traditionally inspired carvings and new two-dimensional artworks such as the *toiles de Fakaha* developed by artistic co-operatives as a novel representation of traditional motifs for the external market. This wave of creativity and international success for artists was brought to a halt by the *coup d'état* of 1999 and the subsequent military crisis. At the same time different forms of patronage, namely that of rebel commanders looking for visual statements of their newly acquired status, started to emerge. This new patronage was able to sustain many of the artist workshops until 2011 when the fall of the rebels' regime caused an even deeper crisis for the artist colonies of the north. Förster's analysis highlights the complexity of the history of artistic production in northern Côte d'Ivoire, whereby the ideas of tradition and authenticity need to be understood within a system of diversified patronage that has promoted meaningful and culturally relevant stylistic changes and innovation for over a century.

Catherine Hale's essay focuses on the transformations in the iconography and use of Asante stools in history and particularly in the second half of the twentieth century. Stools amongst the Asante are an essential material and visual element of the display of political and spiritual leadership. Hale demonstrates how, during the twentieth century, important political and social transformations, combined with an increase in market demand, stimulated a diversified production of stools that resemble only very superficially the seats of office of the Asante chiefs and queen mothers. These stools, smaller in size and often featuring *Adinkra* symbols at their base, are produced in a number of contemporary workshops and purchased by tourists or members of the urban middle class as decorative elements for their households. While royals would never use these stools publicly as insignia of status, this new production has come to represent, on many levels, a simplified symbol of nationhood for both internal and external consumption. In Hale's lively account, the different nuances and variations in seat forms, uses and meanings contrast sharply with the rather simplified and often misguided representation of these artworks in Western museums and collections, where meaning was assigned based on preconceived assumptions of the function of a "royal stool" rather than on the understanding of local context.

In Chapter 6, Silvia Forni analyzes the Cameroonian market of African art, with a particular focus on the kingdom of Foumban. This art-rich centre, already active in pre-colonial times, and one of the main art-collecting centres for officers, administrators, missionaries, scholars and traders during the colonial era, has maintained till today its reputation as the main centre for art production and commerce in the Republic of Cameroon. Looking at the trajectory of Foumban workshops and dealers over the course of the twentieth century, it becomes quite difficult to draw a neat line between "authentic" traditional art made for local use and artistic productions influenced by market demands. Forni argues that exchange networks, diplomacy and market consciousness on the part of local producers and dealers have been important influences in the shaping of regional aesthetics and creativity for well over a century. Indeed, the Grassfields region of Cameroon had been characterized by extensive circulation and reinterpretation of forms, iconography, objects and ideas long before the growth of the international tourist art market in the last decades of the twentieth century. Forni highlights the agency of many of the producers and traders that have participated in the expansion and transformation of local production, and, in more recent times, in the creative appropriation of commercial artworks of different styles to introduce into local material culture.

In conclusion, Christopher Steiner presents a more theoretical discussion of the role of secrecy and obfuscation in the African art trade. Grounded in his field research among African art traders in Côte d'Ivoire during the late 1980s and early 1990s, Steiner attempts to draw an interpretive connection between the function of secrecy in traditional African ritual and religious practices (such as the "cult" of the masks) and the function of secrecy in establishing the economic value and artistic authenticity of an African object in the art market. Central to his thesis is the parallel he draws between secrecy and power in both an object's indigenous milieu and the context of collection and consumption. Steiner's chapter also addresses some key issues regarding the role of publications in validating for the market certain objects and objects types.

As we have suggested throughout this introductory chapter, the field of study surrounding African art made for trade and export is young, amorphous and still rough around the edges. Even the key terms of our project—"tourist art," "commercial art," "art made for the market"—are imprecise, unstable and problematic. If the chapters in this book appear to offer fragmented perspectives, it is because our field of inquiry is by nature disjointed. Some chapters approach the topic from the viewpoint of personal narrative; some take a more diachronic approach, looking at the ethnohistory of particular regions or workshops; and some seek to extend theoretical models of interpretation from indigenous context to transnational trade. In the end, however, all these different approaches suggest a common conclusion: that objects of African art that are now located outside of Africa (whether in museums, galleries or private collections) cannot be understood without tracking them back to their sites of creation and, most importantly, exchange. Without understanding the transactions, both cultural and economic, that propelled their journey from one continent to another, we are left with an imperfect and largely incomplete history of Africa and its arts.

---

1 Cotter, "Out of Africa, Eclectic Visions," *The New York Times*, June 1, 2007.

2 Christopher B. Steiner, *African Art in Transit* (Cambridge University Press, 1994), 157–64.

3 Quoted in Susan Vogel, *The Art of Collecting African Art* (New York: The Center for African Art, 1988), 58.

4 Crowley, "The West African Art Market Revisited," *African Arts* 7, no. 4 (1974): 59.

5 A list of the books of the Galerie Amrad African Art publishing house is provided in the appendix of this volume.

6 William Fagg, *Afro-Portuguese Ivories* (London: Batchworth Press, 1959).

7 Esther Dagan, personal communication to Silvia Forni, July 1, 2009. See also Dorota Kozinska, "A Passion for Africa," *Montreal Gazette*, February 14, 1998, J1–J2.

8 See for example Esther A. Dagan, *Man at Rest: Stools and Seats from 14 African Countries*, (Montreal: Galerie Amrad African Art, 1985), 4. And also Sarah Scott, "Search for African Art Took Many Strange Turns," *Montreal Gazette*, July 25, 1981, 47.

9 See also Graburn, "Epilogue: Ethnic and Tourist Arts Revisited," in *Unpacking Culture: Art and Commodity in Colonial and Postcolonial Worlds*, eds. Ruth B. Phillips and Christopher B. Steiner (Berkeley: University of California Press, 1999).

10 These different positions are illustrated in the heated and inconclusive dialogue that was published in the journal *African Arts* following the publication of Sidney Kasfir's "African Art and Authenticity: A Text with a Shadow," *African Arts* 25, no. 4 (1992): 41–53, 96.

11 McEwen, "Art Promotes Racial Understanding," *Museum News* (1960): 39.

12 Ben-Amos, "Pidgin Languages and Tourist Arts," *Studies in the Anthropology of Visual Communications* 4, no. 2 (1977).

13 See also Jules-Rosette, "Aesthetics and Market Demand: The Structure of the Tourist Art Market in Three African Settings," *African Studies Review* 29 , no. 1 (1986) and Harry R. Silver, "Beauty and the 'I' of the Beholder: Identity, Aesthetics, and Social Change among the Ashanti," *Journal of Anthropological Research* (1979).

14 Simon Battestini, review of *The Messages of Tourist Art: An African Semiotic System in Comparative Perspective*, by Bennetta Jules-Rosette, *African Studies Review* 30, no. 2 (1987).

15 Kasfir, "African Art and Authenticity," 39.

16 See Alice Horner, "Tourist Arts in Africa Before Tourism," *Annals of Tourism Research* 20, no. 1 (1993).

17 Pierre Bourdieu and Alain Darbel, *The Love of Art: European Art Museums and Their Public* (Cambridge: Polity Press, 1997).

18 See Shelly Errington, *The Death of Authentic Primitive Art and Other Tales of Progress* (Berkeley: University of California Press, 1998), 57–63, and Ruth B. Phillips, "Why Not Tourist Art?" in *After Colonialism: Imperial Histories and Postcolonial Displacements*, ed. Gyan Prakash (Princeton, NJ: Princeton University Press, 1994).

19 Cotter, "Out of Africa, Eclectic Visions," *The New York Times*, 2007.

20 Duncan F. Cameron, "The Museum, a Temple or the Forum," reprinted in *Reinventing the Museum: Historical and Contemporary Perspectives on the Paradigm Shift*, ed. Gail Anderson (Lanham, MD: Alta Mira Press, 2004), 70.

21 See James Clifford, *The Predicament of Culture: Twentieth-Century Ethnography, Literature, and Art* (Cambridge, MA: Harvard University Press, 1998), 189–214, and Sally Price, *Primitive Art in Civilized Places* (Chicago: University of Chicago Press, 1989), 100–7.

22 Martin A. Sklar, "Guardians of an International Treasure: The Walt Disney-Tishman African Art Collection," in *African Vision: The Walt Disney-Tishman African Art Collection*, ed. Christine Mullen Kreamer (Washington, DC: National Museum of African Art, Smithsonian Institution, 2007), 2.

23 Frederick John Lamp, Amanda M. Maples and Laura M. Smalligan, *Accumulating Histories: African Art from the Charles B. Benenson Collection at the Yale University Art Gallery*. (New Haven, CT: Yale University Press, 2012), 9.

24 Ibid., 26.

25 Ibid., 27.

26 Ibid.

27 Ibid.

28 Sylvester Okwunodu Ogbechie, *Making History: African Collectors and the Canon of African Art: The Femi Akinsanya African Art Collection* (Milan: 5 Continents Editions, 2011), 99–102.

29 Esther Dagan, personal communication to Silvia Forni, October 13, 2010.

Bibliography

Battestini, Simon. Review of *The Messages of Tourist Art: An African Semiotic System in Comparative Perspective*, by Bennetta Jules-Rosette. *African Studies Review* 30, no. 2 (1987): 104–105.

Ben Amos, Paula. "Pidgin Languages and Tourist Arts." *Studies in the Anthropology of Visual Communications* 4, no. 2 (1977): 128–39.

Bourdieu, Pierre and Alain Darbel. *The Love of Art: European Art Museums and Their Public*. Cambridge: Polity Press, 1997.

Cameron, Duncan F. "The Museum, a Temple or the Forum." Reprinted in *Reinventing the Museum: Historical and Contemporary Perspectives on the Paradigm Shift*, edited by Gail Anderson, 61–73. Lanham, MD: Alta Mira Press, 2004.

Clifford, James. *The Predicament of Culture: Twentieth-Century Ethnography, Literature, and Art*. Cambridge, MA: Harvard University Press, 1988.

Corby, Raymond. *Tribal Art Traffic. A Chronicle of Taste, Trade and Desire in Colonial and Postcolonial Times*. Amsterdam: Royal Tropical Institute, 2000.

Cotter, Holland. "Out of Africa, Eclectic Visions," *The New York Times*, June 1, 2007.

Crowley, Daniel J. "The West African Art Market Revisited," *African Arts* 7, no. 4 (1974): 54–59.

Dagan, Esther A. *Man at Rest: Stools and Seats from 14 African Countries*. Montreal: Galerie Amrad African Art, 1985.

Dutton, Denis. "Tribal Art and Artifact." *Journal of Aesthetics and Art Criticism* (1993): 13–21.

Errington, Shelly. *The Death of Authentic Primitive Art and Other Tales of Progress*. Berkeley: University of California Press, 1998.

Fagg, William. *Afro-Portuguese Ivories*. London: Batchworth Press, 1959.

Geary, Christraud M. and Stephanie Xatart. *Material Journeys: Collecting African and Oceanic Art, 1945–2000*. Boston: Museum of Fine Arts, 2007.

Geismar, Haidy. "What's in a Price? An Ethnography of Tribal Art at Auction." *Journal of Material Culture* 6, no. 1 (2001): 25–47.

Graburn, Nelson H. H. "Epilogue: Ethnic and Tourist Arts Revisited." In *Unpacking Culture: Art and Commodity in Colonial and Postcolonial Worlds*, edited by Ruth B. Phillips and Christopher B. Steiner, 335–354. Berkeley: University of California Press, 1999.

———, ed. *Ethnic and Tourist Arts: Cultural Expressions from the Fourth World*. Berkeley: University of California Press, 1976.

Horner, Alice. "Tourist Arts in Africa Before Tourism," *Annals of Tourism Research* 20, no. 1 (1993): 52–63.

Jules-Rosette, Bennetta. "Aesthetics and Market Demand: The Structure of the Tourist Art Market in Three African Settings." *African Studies Review* 29.01 (1986): 41–59.

———. *The Messages of Tourist Art: An African Semiotic System in Comparative Perspective*. New York: Plenum Press, 1984.

Kasfir, Sidney Littlefield. "African Art and Authenticity: A Text with a Shadow." *African Arts* 25, no. 4 (1992): 41–97.

Lamp, Frederick John, Amanda M. Maples and Laura M. Smalligan. *Accumulating Histories: African Art from the Charles B. Benenson Collection at the Yale University Art Gallery*. New Haven: Yale University Press, 2012.

MacClancy, Jeremy. *Contesting Art: Art, Politics and Identity in the Modern World*. Berg Publisher Ltd, 1997.

McEwen, Frank. "Art Promotes Racial Understanding," *Museum News* (1960): 36–39.

Ogbechie, Sylvester Okwunodu. *Making History: African Collectors and the Canon of African Art: The Femi Akinsanya African Art Collection*. Milan: 5 Continents Editions, 2011.

Phillips, Ruth B. "Why Not Tourist Art? Significant Silences in Native American Museum Representations." In *After Colonialism: Imperial Histories and Postcolonial Displacements*, edited by Gyan Prakash, 98–125. Princeton, NJ: Princeton University Press, 1995.

Price, Sally. *Primitive Art in Civilized Places*. Chicago: University of Chicago Press, 1989.

Shiner, Larry. "'Primitive Fakes,' 'Tourist Art,' and the Ideology of Authenticity." *Journal of Aesthetics and Art Criticism* (1994): 225–34.

Silver, Harry R. "Beauty and the 'I' of the Beholder: Identity, Aesthetics, and Social Change among the Ashanti." *Journal of Anthropological Research* (1979): 191–207.

Sklar, Martin A. "Guardians of an International Treasure: The Walt Disney-Tishman African Art Collection." In *African Vision: The Walt Disney-Tishman African Art Collection*, edited by Christine Mullen Kreamer, 1–5. Washington, DC: National Museum of African Art, Smithsonian Institution, 2007.

Steiner, Christopher B. *African Art in Transit*. Cambridge University Press, 1994.

Stoller, Paul. "Circuits of African Art/Paths of Wood: Exploring an Anthropological Trail." *Anthropological Quarterly* 76, no. 2 (2003): 207–34.

Vogel, Susan. *The Art of Collecting African Art*. New York: The Center for African Art, 1988.

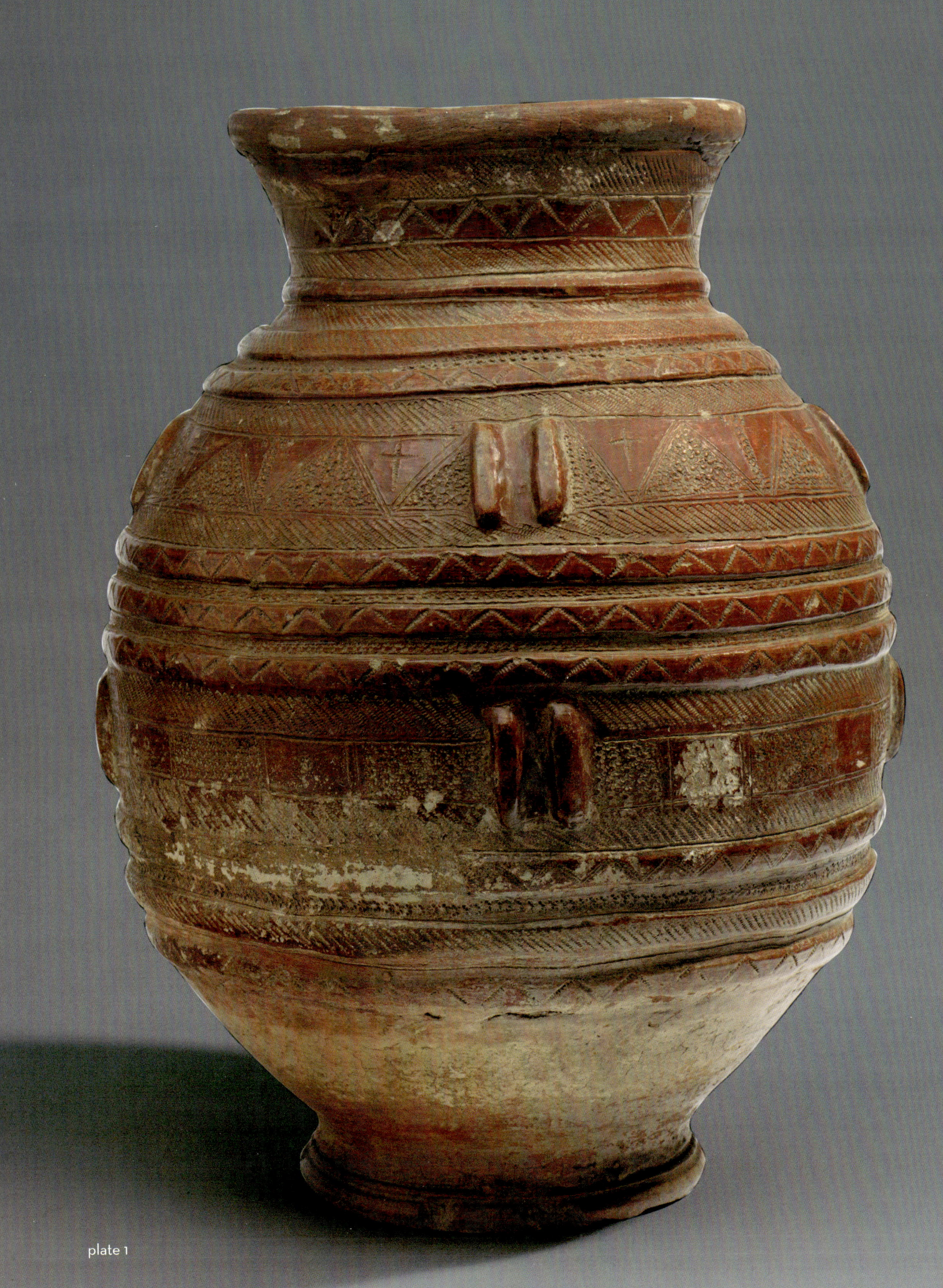

plate 1

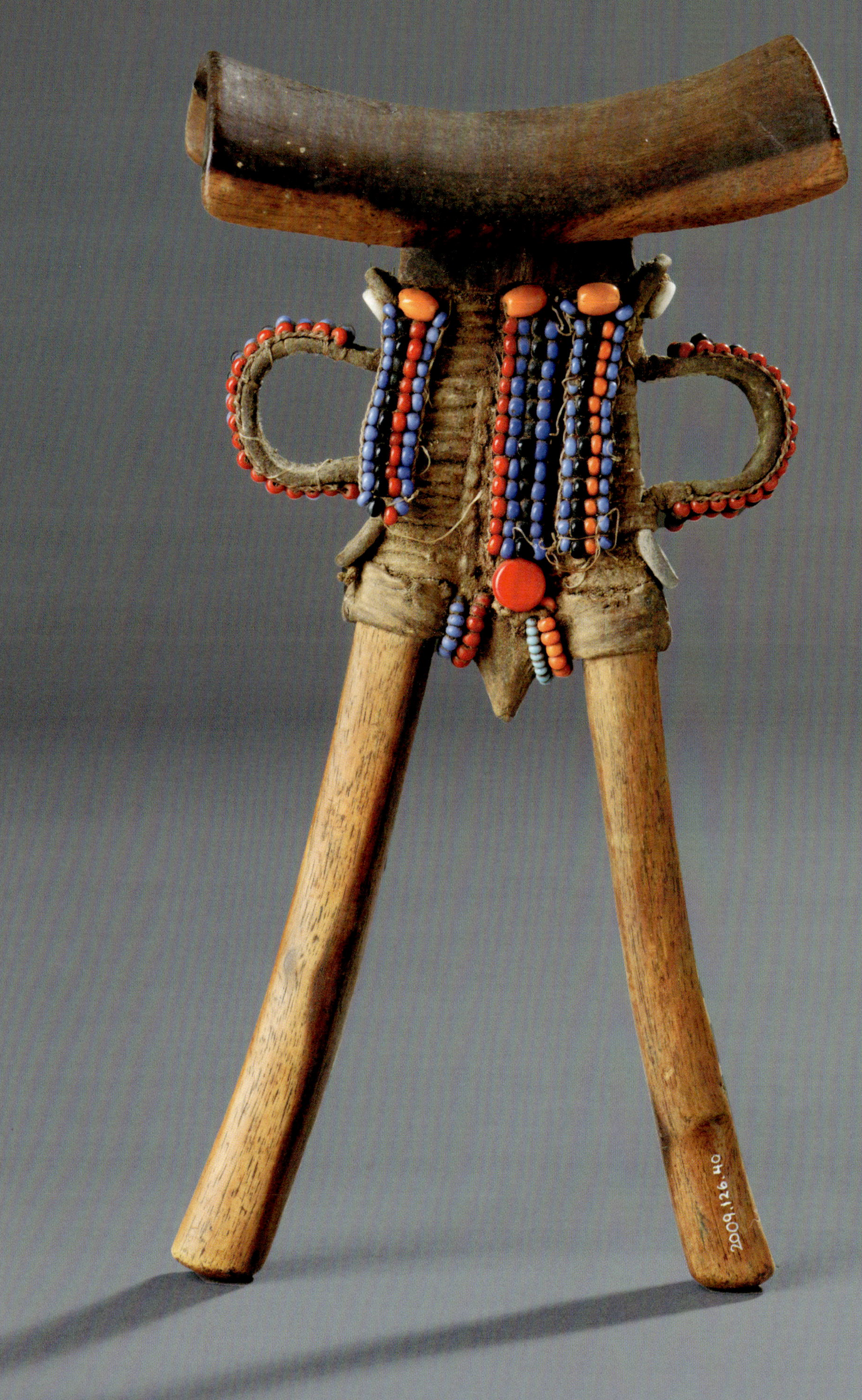

plate 2

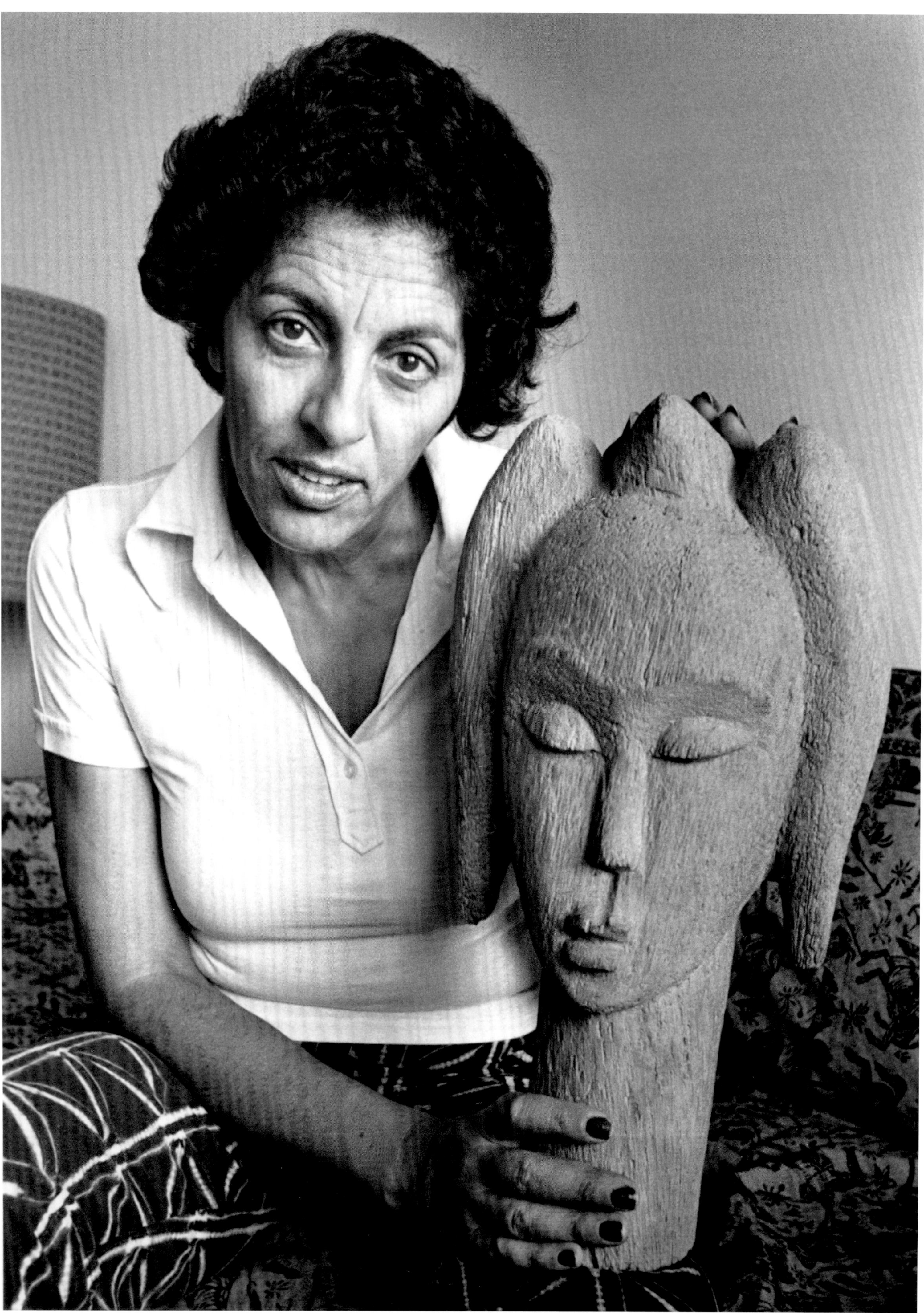

CHAPTER 2

A COMMUNITY OF ART LOVERS: COLLECTING AND DEALING AFRICAN ART IN CANADA BETWEEN THE 1960S AND THE 1990S

CATHERINE M. HALE AND SILVIA FORNI

The act of collecting is at once a very personal endeavour and the result of broader social, political and economic circumstances. Almost three decades ago, in a classic essay, James Clifford pointed out how Western collections of African artworks are predicated on the ability of specific individuals and groups to identify and select the "pure products of others" to be celebrated as art objects. These objects, absorbed within the Western art-culture system, are then attributed cultural relevance and economic value.[1] Collectors, dealers, curators and scholars all participate, in various ways, in the creation and affirmation of the value in the Western art system, which is based on the biography of the objects, the relationships that originated their displacement, and the broader national and local cultural scene in which they are reinterpreted and resignified. While collections each reflect the idiosyncratic tastes and passions of the individuals assembling them, it is possible to trace commonalities and shared perspectives among collectors.

This is particularly true of the small Montreal art scene that Esther Dagan joined in 1978. She was a relative latecomer into a community with a shared admiration of contemporary and African art. At that time, appreciation for the aesthetic dimension of African objects was not widely established in Canada. In the few Canadian institutions that held historically and sometimes numerically significant African collections, the focus was mostly ethnographic and historical.

In general terms, the presence of African objects in Canadian museums is attributable to two significant phases of collecting. The first phase was brought about by Canada's involvement in colonial activities in Africa during the nineteenth and early twentieth centuries and accounts for the largest number of objects in Canadian institutions. Wide ranges of object types, and narrow geographic and cultural representation, characterize these collections.[2] For the most part, missionaries and military personnel collected such objects as souvenirs, trophies or curios, or as a way to finance and support their activities. The second phase of Canadian collecting of African objects, detailed in this chapter, is traceable to an intertwined group of intellectuals and art dealers in Montreal, Ottawa and Toronto, many of whom were European immigrants. This phase began around the time of World War II and flourished for several decades before waning in the late twentieth century. It was characterized by a catholic appreciation of African, Oceanic and Native American (or, the so-called Primitive[3]) arts in association with an interest in the arts of modern movements like Abstract Expressionism and Surrealism. In many cases, collectors did not obtain objects directly from their original contexts in Africa. Instead, dealers, auction houses and "runners" were their main sources for purchase. Yet, unlike early field collectors who did not value aesthetically the pieces that they were purchasing, the urban intellectuals of the second half of the twentieth century more explicitly expressed in their collecting the fascination for the bold aesthetic of what was by then quite broadly understood as "African Art."

detail
Esther Dagan with one of the pieces in her collection. Circa 1980. From the Amrad African Art Collection Archive.

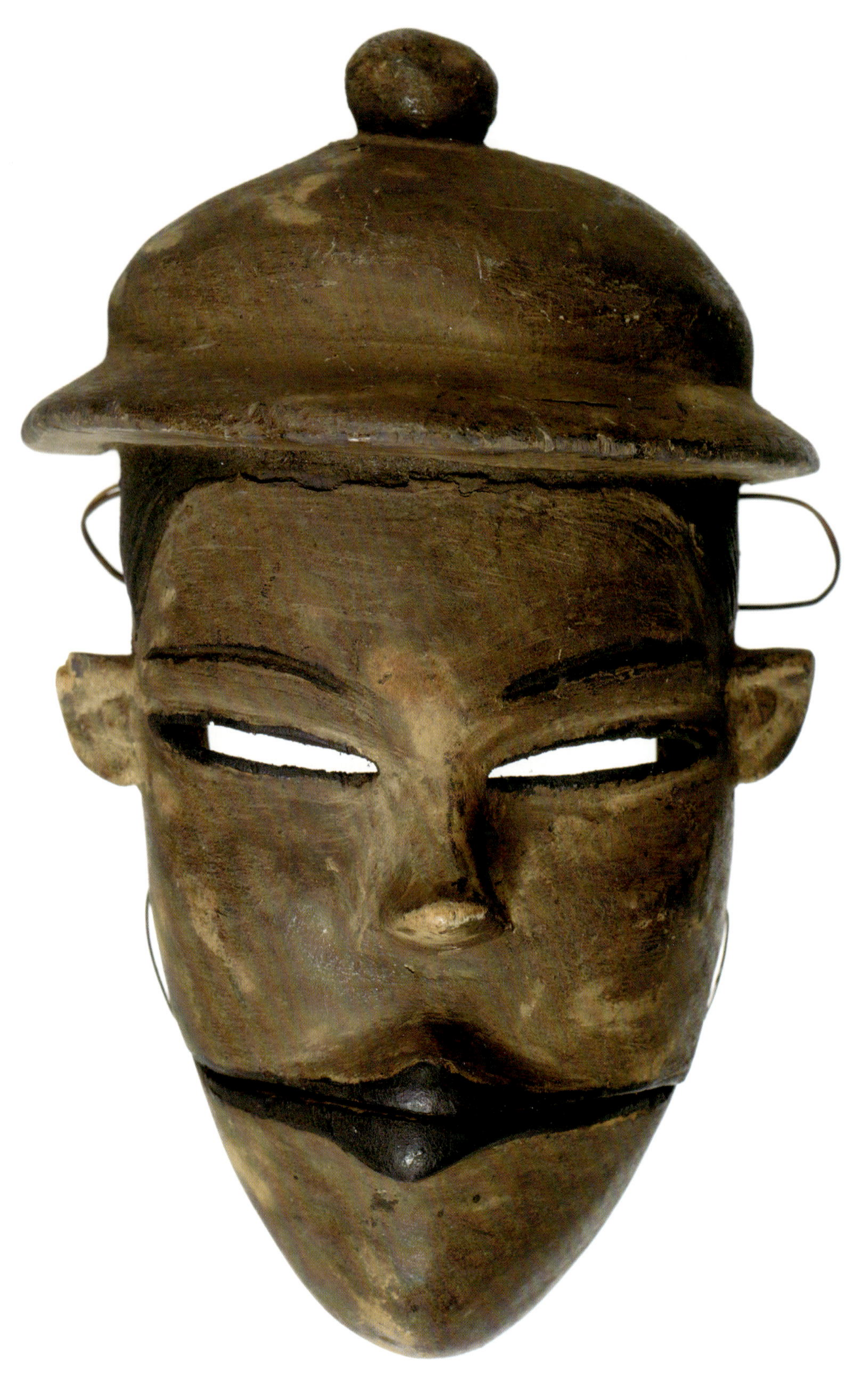

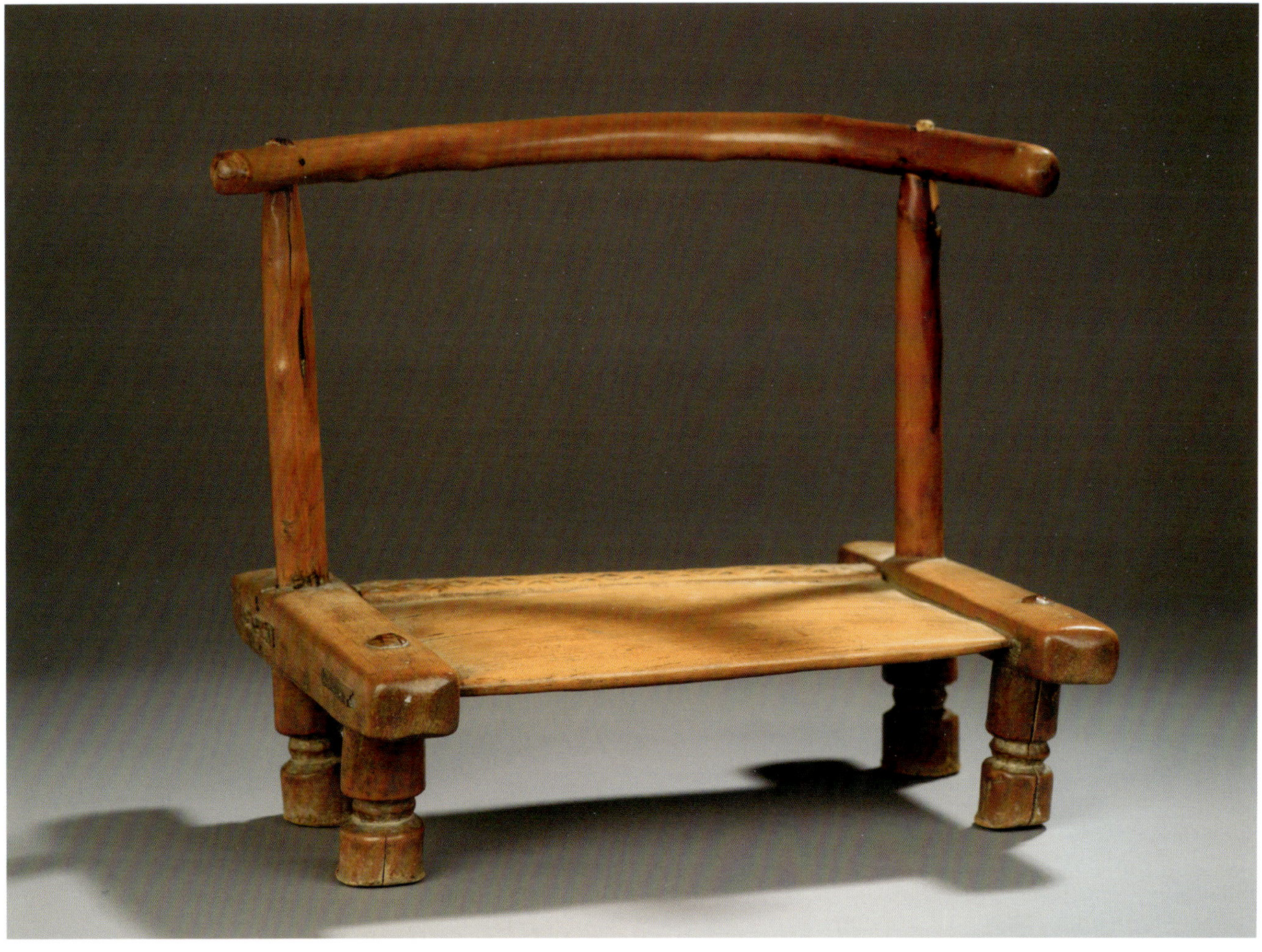

figure 2
Chair
Unidentified artist or workshop
Wood
Dan or Bété style
Purchased from an African dealer in Montreal in 1982
Height: 32 cm, Width: 37 cm, Depth: 27 cm
ROM 2009.126.17

figure 1 (opposite)
Mask
Unidentified artist or workshop
Ogoni style
Wood, fibre, pigment
Purchased from Lippel Gallery, Montreal, in 1988
Height: 22 cm, Width: 13.3 cm, Depth: 10.5 cm
ROM 2009.126.207

Modernist Primitivism at Home and Abroad

Canadian collectors developed an interest in African aesthetics at a time when this appreciation was well established in Europe and the United States. Scholars have credited several European artists working during the early twentieth century—especially those of the Montparnasse group in Paris—with instigating the development of a serious artistic interest in the primitive arts.[4] When they encountered African and other indigenous sculptures in museums, flea markets or elsewhere, the artists expressed admiration for the formal innovation and emotional expression they felt they embodied. Motifs and formal elements inspired by such sculptures soon found their way into the work of artists like Pablo Picasso, which was most famously exemplified in his 1907 work *Les Demoiselles d'Avignon*. In some cases, it was not the specific formal qualities that inspired Western artists, but rather, the belief that primitive arts were a direct product of the artist's subconscious, which they thought was free from modern concerns. Anti-modern sentiments played an important role in Western artists' emulation of indigenous material culture.[5] At the same time, there was a prevailing confidence in the universality of modern European aesthetics. Many individuals claimed that objects made by supposedly primitive peoples appealed to Western artists because they were aesthetic masterpieces whose power could transcend cultural and temporal boundaries.

This Western artistic phenomenon, labelled "Modernist Primitivism" retrospectively, has since been normalized within the canon of Art History. In recent years, scholars have researched the impact of this movement in the United States, Britain, and elsewhere. However, the Canadian involvement with Modernist Primitivism, especially in terms of African art collecting, has received less attention. Prior to World War II, individuals who embraced Modernist Primitivist values in Canada focused primarily on the material culture of First Peoples. The 1927 exhibition *Canadian West Coast Art, Native and Modern*, presented at the National Gallery, exemplified this early manifestation. It was the first time in the gallery's history that it exhibited indigenous objects as "Art." The show, which focused exclusively on British Columbia, brought together a range of Northwest Coast ceremonial objects and paintings by artists such as Paul Kane, Anne Savage, members of the Group of Seven, and Emily Carr.[6] The presentation encouraged viewers to evaluate the Northwest Coast arts for their aesthetic beauty while recognizing their formal "affinities" with the modern paintings. For much of the twentieth century, indigenous Canadian material culture remained central to the local Modernist Primitive discourse.

During and after the Second World War, the taste for Primitive arts in Canada began to expand to include African and Oceanic objects. Galleries that sold African arts appeared in cities such as Montreal, Ottawa and Toronto, and there was an intimate circle of African art collectors, scholars and gallery owners who associated with one another. The context for African art in Canada is particularly interesting because of a number of social and historical circumstances. World War II brought an increase in immigration from Western European countries; most notably, a number of Jewish refugees who had been forced to flee the Nazi regime and who brought with them a Western fine arts tradition that privileged aesthetic contemplation, and exposure to the Modernist partiality to Primitive arts. There also seems to have been an extensive commitment among new immigrants to support and foster the growth of specifically Canadian art and artists. In this way, collectors and scholars who came to Canada with an existing interest in the arts of Africa often transitioned into collecting or studying the arts of the indigenous North American cultures as well. Similarly, the work of Québécois artists like Les Automatistes, which was based on Surrealist principles, found an eager audience among collectors who were familiar with its European models.

A Community of Art Lovers

When Esther Amrad Dagan moved to Montreal from Israel, she quickly inserted herself into a rather tight community of like-minded intellectuals sharing a common passion for Primitive art. By the late 1970s the Montreal circle of African art enthusiasts revolved around a few key collectors-turned-dealers, whose intellectual and professional paths prefigured in many ways Dagan's own commercial approach and choices.

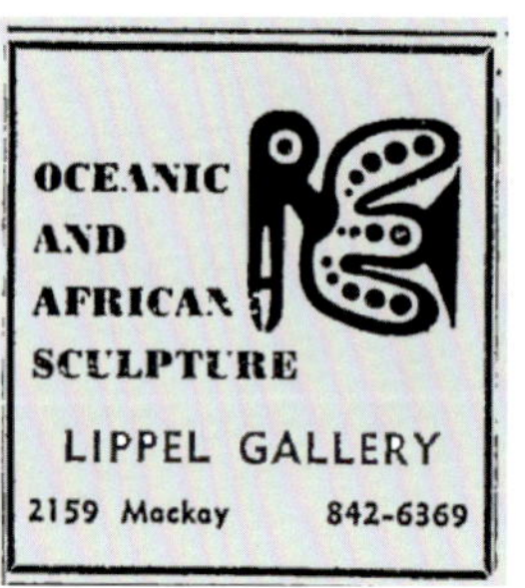

figure 3
Advertisement for the Lippel Gallery Appeared in the *Montreal Gazette*, April 8, 1972 p. 48

Leon and Louise Lippel ran the Lippel Gallery that dealt in a range of non-Western arts but specialized primarily in African art, which was Leon Lippel's first love. Lippel initially encountered African art during his days as an art student in London, England. He later recalled that when he saw the African works at the British Museum, their "power, originality and honesty" filled him with awe.[7] Lippel felt that African sculpture presented a stark contrast to Western arts, stating that "the freedom with which Africans regarded sculpture was a denial...the very opposite of Western concepts."[8] Lippel started collecting African art, and, when his home began to fill with the objects, he and his wife rented a small gallery space on Crescent Street in Montreal. They had so much success exhibiting their African works that in 1961 they decided to open a permanent gallery in a basement on Mackay Street (Fig. 3).

Lippel later abandoned his day job as an importer and exporter so he could devote himself to the gallery full time. At that point, the Lippels moved to an even larger gallery space on Sherbrooke Street.[9] The Lippel Gallery was a social gathering place. Leon Lippel did not pressure visitors to buy and spent a great deal of his time sipping tea in a large armchair in the gallery. He also had a solid client base of people from Canada and the United States who bought from him on a regular basis. Lippel claimed to have sold Toronto collector Murray Frum his first piece of African sculpture.[10] In addition to collecting, exhibiting, and selling African works, Lippel reportedly had a fine personal collection of Inuit and Northwest Coast objects that was admired by many.[11]

Other important figures in Montreal were Justin and Elisabeth Lang. The couple met when they were living in Amsterdam, Justin having fled his native Germany and Elisabeth her native Austria to escape the Nazi regime. When Hitler threatened to invade Holland, each was able to leave the country separately, after which they reunited in Montreal in 1941 and married soon after. Elisabeth Lang was deeply interested in African art, which she had

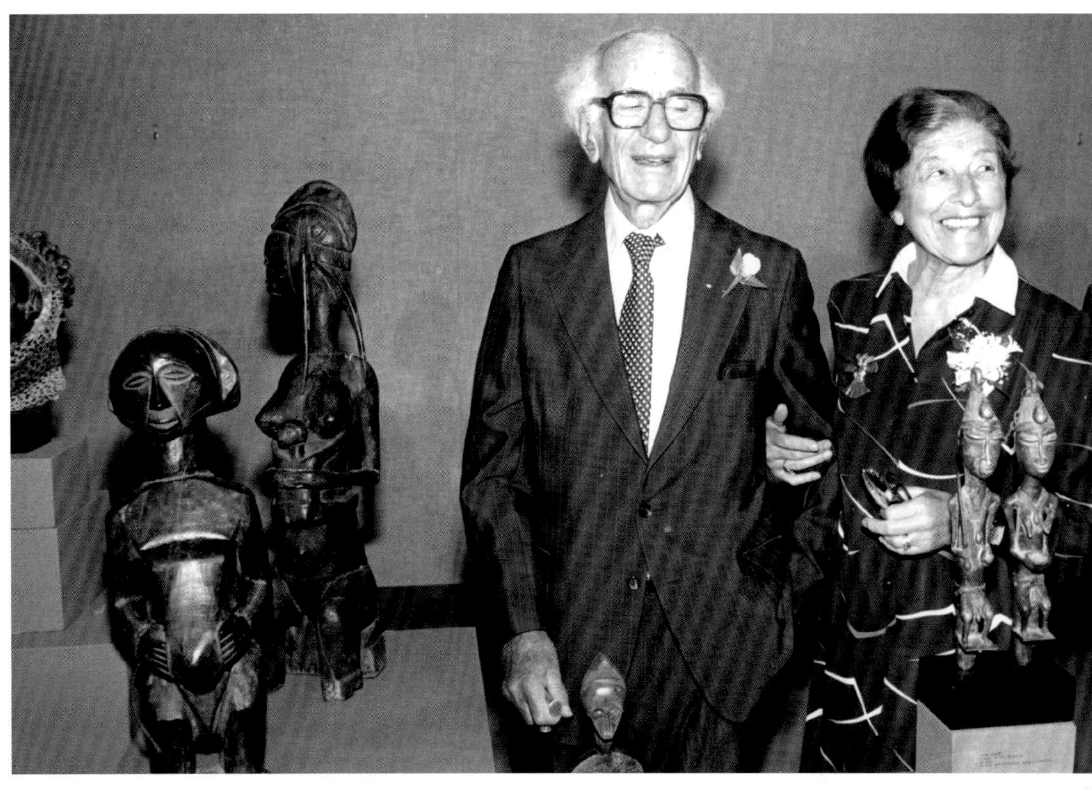

figure 4
Justin and Elisabeth Lang with their collection in the Agnes Etherington Art Centre, 1984
Courtesy of the Agnes Etherington Art Centre, Queen's University, Kingston

originally encountered in Amsterdam. She also had a strong commitment to supporting Canadian, and specifically Québécois, artists.[12] Although African art comprised the main body of the Langs' art collection, and Canadian modern artists were well represented, they also collected First Peoples art in comparatively smaller numbers.[13]

Like Lippel, in addition to being a collector, Elisabeth Lang took on the role of art dealer. In 1978, she opened the Galerie des 5 Continents on Greene Avenue in Montreal. The gallery, which specialized in African, First Peoples, and Canadian folk arts, quickly became a social gathering place for people who were interested in talking about, collecting, or learning more about these lesser-known art forms. Coffee and tea were always available and Elisabeth Lang did not expect anyone to buy.[14] Robert Swain, former director of the Agnes Etherington Art Centre at Queen's University, compared the gallery to a "European coffee house" because of the constant stream of people strolling in and out and chatting.[15] The ideas Elisabeth Lang shared with her clientele and their resonance with the universalist values inherent in Modernist Primitivism are evidenced in her introduction to the catalogue for her gallery's tenth anniversary in 1988 (Fig. 4). She wrote that,

> the arts of Africa not only enlarge our understanding of the indigenous people of that rich continent—of their fears, longings and mythical beliefs—but may also reveal to us the deepest longings of mankind. I believe that the African sculptor who carves objects of authentic value feels basic human emotions and passes them on to us in great depth and intensity.[16]

Two other gallerists connected to the Montreal circle were Max Klein, who ran the gallery Petit Musée on Sherbrooke Street, and Max Stern, owner of the Dominion Gallery of Fine Art. Originally housed in a basement, Petit Musée displayed and sold works from all over the world. Members of the Montreal circle visited the gallery on a regular basis and frequently purchased African objects from Klein.[17] Max Stern had known Justin and Elisabeth Lang in Europe. Stern studied art history in Berlin, Cologne and Vienna before receiving his doctorate from the University of Bonn. After completing his studies, he returned to Düsseldorf to manage his family's gallery, Galerie Julius Stern.[18] The rise of the Nazis forced Stern to close the gallery, and in 1937 he fled to London, England. He was interned as an enemy alien after the war began, first in England, then in New Brunswick and Quebec.[19] Stern was able to get an exemption from the limitations imposed by his refugee status in Montreal by having William Birks, the head of the Canadian Refugee Organization, vouch for him based on a letter of recommendation from Tancred Borenius, dean of art history at the University of London and editor of *Burlington Magazine*.[20] By 1944 Stern was a partner in the Dominion Gallery, and in 1947 he and his wife became the sole proprietors.[21]

In addition to the range of Old Masters and Primitive arts that Stern exhibited and sold, he undertook the ambitious task of marketing contemporary Canadian artists.[22] He held exhibitions of the work of artists such as Goodridge Roberts, Paul-Émile Borduas, Eric Goldberg, Stanley Cosgrove, Philip Surrey, Emily Carr and the Bouchard sisters.[23] Although these artists have become standard members of the canon of modern Canadian art, when Stern began to exhibit them, their modernism would

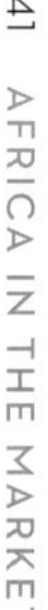

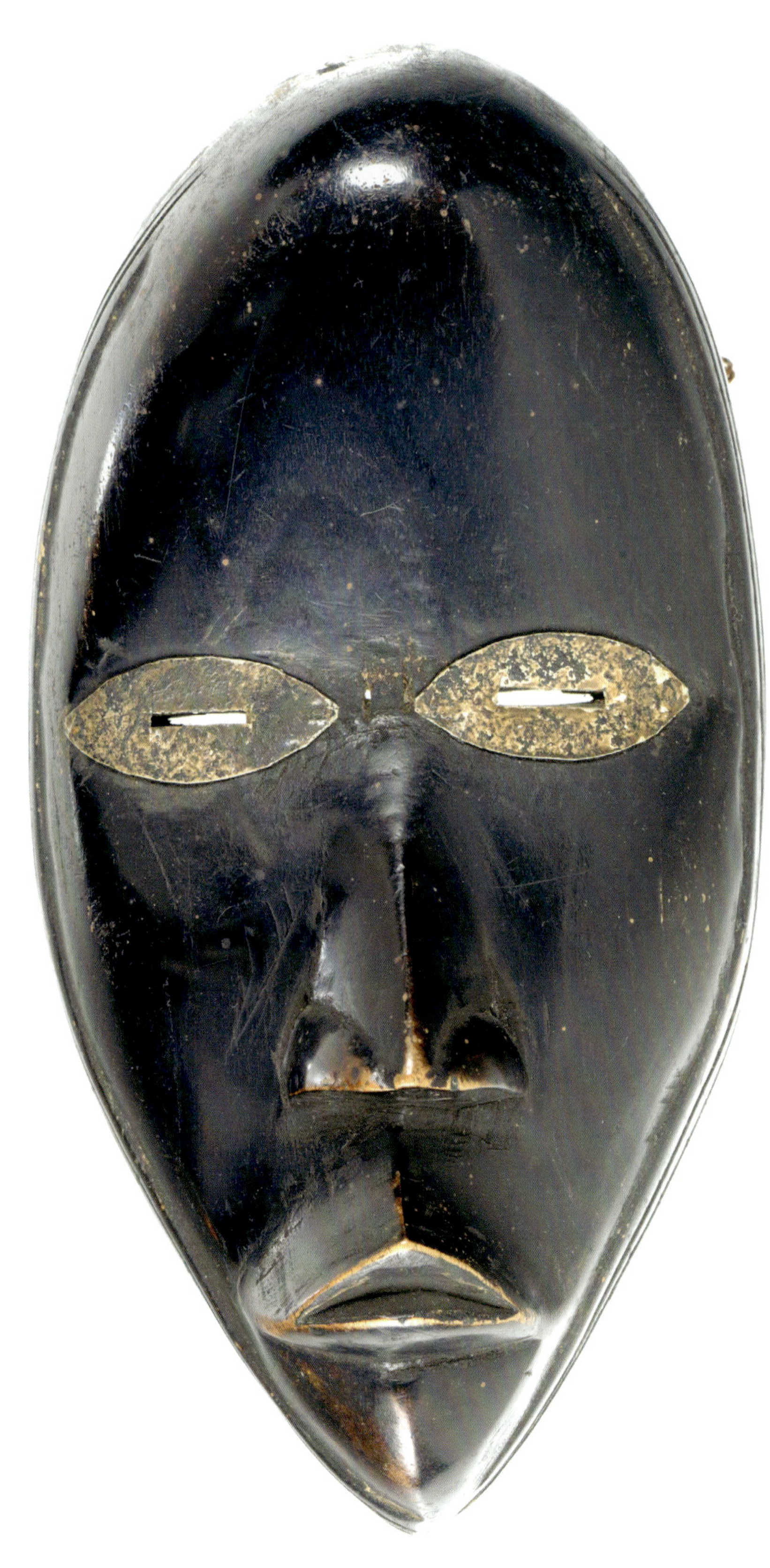

figure 5 (opposite)
Deangle mask
Unidentified artist or workshop
Dan style
Wood, metal strips
Acquired in 1959 from
a gallery in Paris
Height: 21.7cm, Width: 11.2cm,
Depth: 7cm
ROM 2009.126.169

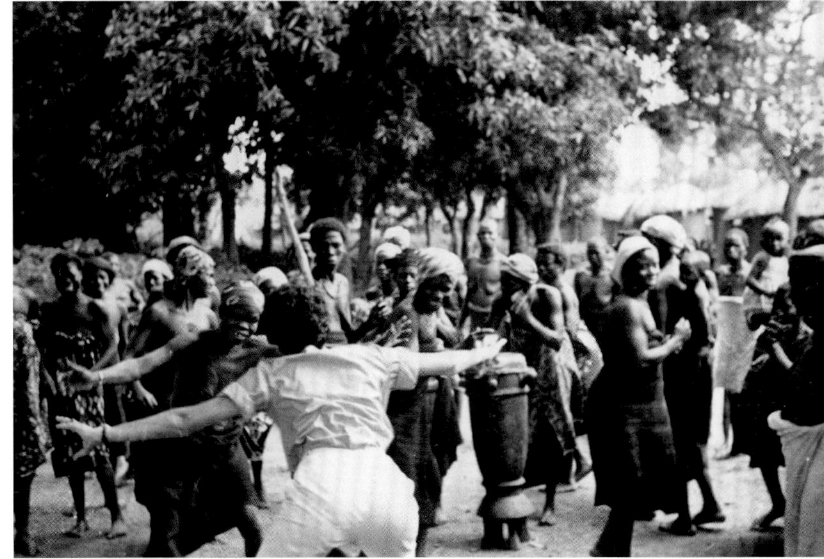

figure 6
Esther Dagan performing
with a group of women
in Côte d'Ivoire.
From the Amrad African
Art Collection Archive

have been considered daring. In the 1940s, most Canadians were interested in art that expressed ideas of nationalism through Post-Impressionist styles of landscape painting that were conservative and formal.[24] Stern's own personal collection of modern Canadian art included works by artists like Borduas, indicating that his commitment to promoting Canadian artists was more than mere business strategy.[25]

Bruno and Ruby Cormier were also important members of the Montreal circle. Their personal collection included Inuit art in addition to works by Jean-Paul Riopelle, Paul-Émile Borduas and Fernand Leduc, among others. Bruno Cormier was a pioneer in the field of forensic psychiatry in Canada who taught at the Université de Montréal and McGill University.[26] He has been described as "a rebel and iconoclast, an art connoisseur, and, in its second acceptation, a dilettante of all things cultural."[27] Cormier's rebellious nature became evident in 1948 when he, along with fifteen others, signed *Le Refus Global* (Total Refusal). Paul-Émile Borduas authored the document, which was considered "one of the most influential artistic and social documents in modern Quebec society," and "called for a total rejection of conventional thinking and advocated a freedom of ideas."[28] The artists who signed the manifesto were called Les Automatistes because of their interest in Surrealism and its theory of automatism. *Le Refus Global* was inspired by André Breton's 1924 Surrealist manifesto that celebrated the power and creativity of the subconscious.[29] The signatories and their close associates belonged to an avant-garde in the context of mid-twentieth-century Montreal.

In 1978, Esther Amrad Dagan arrived in Montreal from Tel Aviv with her Canadian husband and two children. Somewhat of a latecomer to the scene, she fit easily within this community of intellectuals/collectors/dealers who shared a common interest in modern avant-garde and Primitive arts. Dagan had become passionate about African art from the time of her training as a dancer and choreographer in Paris in the late 1950s. In 1959, she had acquired her first piece of African art, a Dan mask (Fig. 5), which she had paid for by saving each month a portion of her small student income.[30] For Dagan, the plastic dimension of African art could not be understood separately from the movement and the life that animated other forms of aesthetic expression, and in particular theatre and dance (Fig. 6).

To fully grasp this powerful lived aesthetic, Dagan set off to Africa by herself in 1961 to learn African dances. After her first six-week trip in Côte d'Ivoire and Upper Volta (now Burkina Faso), Dagan travelled to Africa more than fifteen times, visiting several countries, exploring, learning, collecting and, on a few occasions, working with ministry officials on large-scale dance surveys for the newly formed independent national governments. Her two main official professional engagements of this kind, on the basis of her dance scholarship, were in Gabon in 1966 and Togo in 1973.[31] Though mostly focused on performance and dance, Dagan was always interested in plastic art, and she often acquired masks, musical instruments and sculptures on her travels. Many of the pieces in her collection are connected to very compelling and personal stories. She purchased brightly painted Kuyu *kebe-kebe* puppet heads from an itinerant Gabonese theatre troupe (Fig. 9); she exchanged her car for a drum in a village outside Libreville (Fig. 10); she sacrificed a goat for a *kpelie* mask that was hanging in a seemingly abandoned shrine on the outskirts of a northern Côte d'Ivoire village (Fig. 7).[32]

Just like the Lippels and Langs, Dagan began her commercial activity several years after becoming a collector and developing a passion for African art. Unlike the other Montreal collectors, though, her approach to acquisition and trade always implied a very strong experiential and relational aspect which was often more important than the quest for unique or indisputably "authentic" pieces. When, in 1981, she opened the Galerie Amrad African Arts on Sherbrooke Street in Montreal, she saw it as a way to promote the broader cultural understanding of African cultures for which she became a very vocal advocate.[33]

Dagan also distinguished herself from the other Montreal collectors and gallerists in that she specialized exclusively in African art and acquired most of the pieces directly in Africa, where she would travel periodically and collect extensively based on the themes that she intended to explore in her

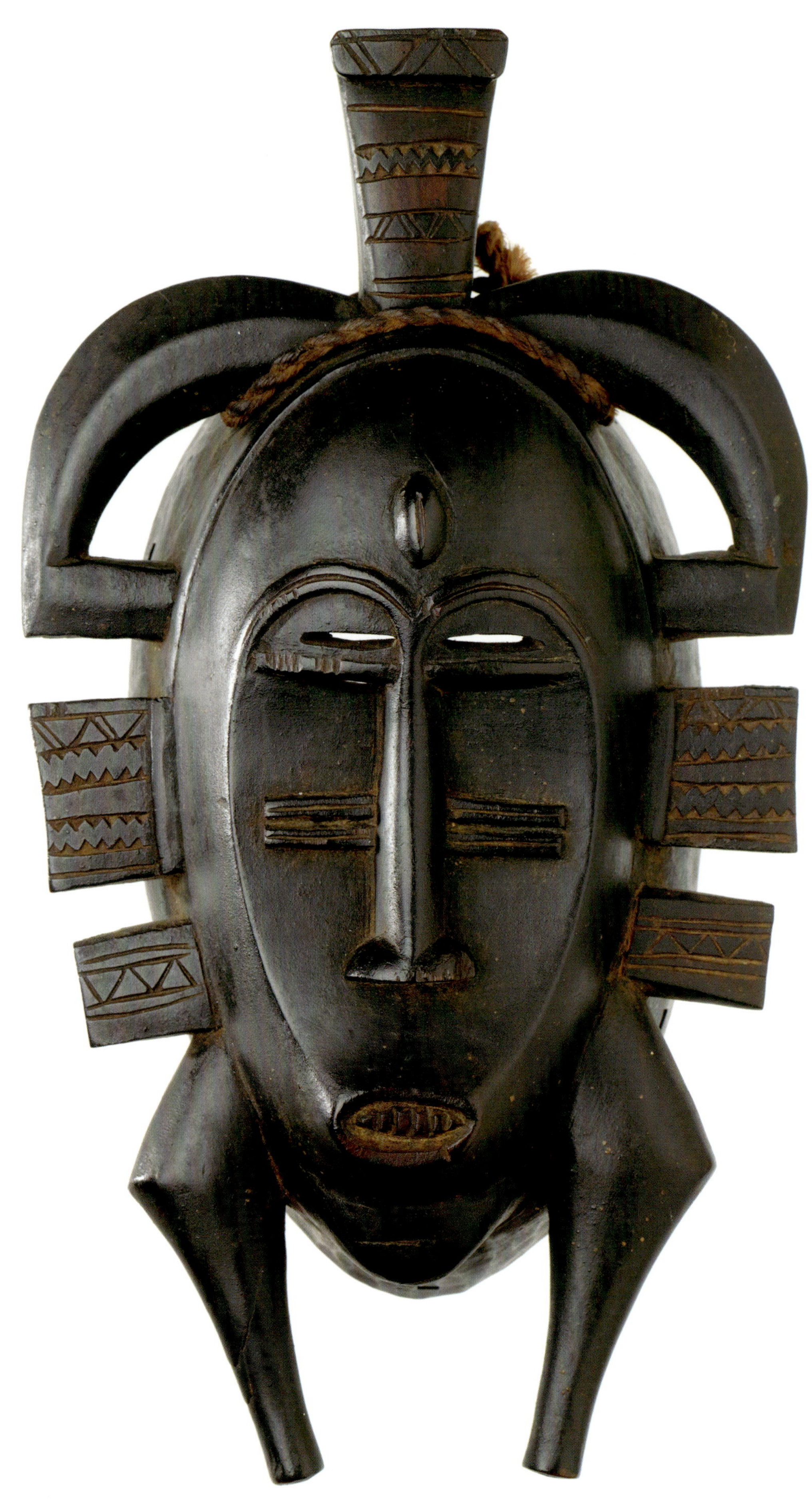

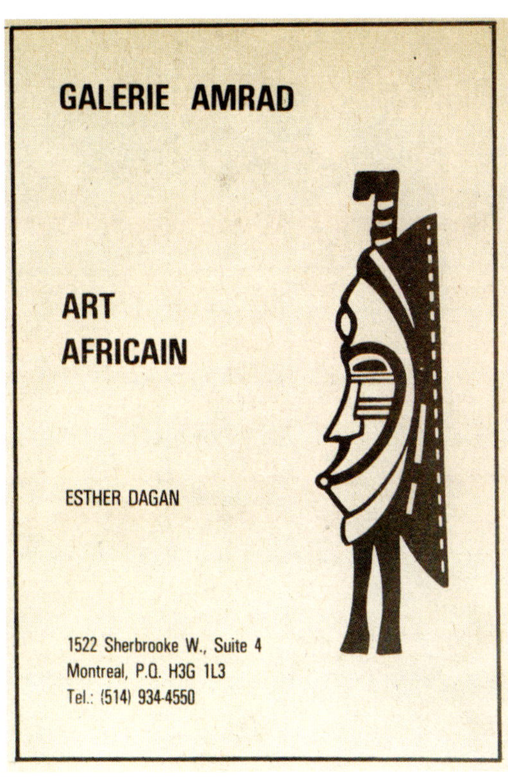

figure 8
Advertisement for the Galerie Amrad Art Africain.
From the Amrad African Art Collection Archive

figure 7 (opposite)
Kodali ye'e mask
Unidentified artist or workshop
Senufo style
Wood, fibre
Received in 1961 as a gift while in the village
of Djigo-dougou, Côte d'Ivoire
Height: 28 cm, Width: 15.5 cm, Depth: 9 cm
ROM 2009.126.183

exhibitions (Fig. 8). During the eleven years of her activity as a gallerist, Dagan worked quite closely with a number of African dealers in Senegal, Ghana, Côte d'Ivoire, Burkina Faso, Cameroon and Gabon, whom she would visit repeatedly and often alert several months before her arrival of the themes and focus of her collecting.[34] This strong connection to Africa and her long-term relationships with specific individual dealers set Esther Dagan somewhat apart from the other collector/gallerists of the Montreal circle. Indeed, while often affirming the common canonical understanding of authenticity in African art (i.e., "made in Africa, for Africans, for African purposes"),[35] she applied this criteria very broadly to include a number of recent and contemporary creations based on well-known "traditional" styles. She also incorporated the work of contemporary urban and studio artists, whom she started promoting more systematically through her publishing house after closing her gallery in 1992.[36]

African Art Connections in Ottawa and Toronto

The Montreal community was connected to a broader circle of African art collectors and dealers in Ottawa and Toronto, some of whom took an even more openly commercial approach to their interest. In Ottawa, two galleries were dealing with African arts during the seventies. Victoria Henry opened Ufundi Gallery on St. Patrick Street in 1975. She sold primarily East African work from Tanzania and Zambia but had a few West African objects as well. Unlike many in the Montreal group who were more concerned with conventional or historical pieces, Victoria Henry was very much interested in contemporary African arts. Prior to opening her gallery, Henry had worked in Africa as a volunteer with Canadian University Service Overseas (CUSO) and, after her CUSO work ended, she continued to travel to Africa every year for at least fourteen years.[37] The types of objects Henry sold at her gallery reflected her commitment to the contemporary arts of Africa. She saw women wearing textiles, commemorative cloths, and beadwork in Africa and wanted to bring home part of that living history to share with members of the Canadian public.[38] Where Elisabeth Lang and the Lippels exhibited primarily sculptural works, Henry displayed numerous pieces of beadwork, textiles, jewellery and basketry in addition to sculptural works.[39]

The other gallery dealing in African arts during the seventies in Ottawa was Giraffe Gallery on Sparks Street. Run by Betty Kieran, Giraffe specialized in African art and wearables.[40] Jewellery was a major source of income for the gallery, and Kieran, who was born and raised in Uganda, designed much of it. As at Ufundi Gallery, the majority of the arts for sale at Giraffe were products of contemporary African cultures.[41] It was common at both Ufundi and Giraffe to purchase beads and other materials in Africa and then put together their own designs, a practice gallery owners like the Langs and the Lippels likely would have found "inauthentic."[42]

In Toronto, one of the better-known galleries working with African art was Susan and George Barkley and Robert and Barbara Barde's The Best of Africa, which opened in 1976 and closed in 1983.[43] The Best of Africa specialized, like Ufundi and Giraffe, in contemporary African art. The gallery included some more figural and sculptural pieces, but the focus was on a variety of crafts.[44] Victoria Henry often collaborated with this Toronto gallery, showing contemporary artists and work. The owners of The Best of Africa had also been CUSO volunteers and had worked as photographers in Africa.[45]

The cluster of dealers and collectors of African art in Canada during this period formed a small and interconnected group. Gallery owners often purchased works from each other for their personal collections and discussed their respective activities (Fig. 12). They also shared a notable trait: the conviction that one of their main missions was to educate the public about African art by creating a welcoming environment where people could come to learn and talk and not just to buy. While there

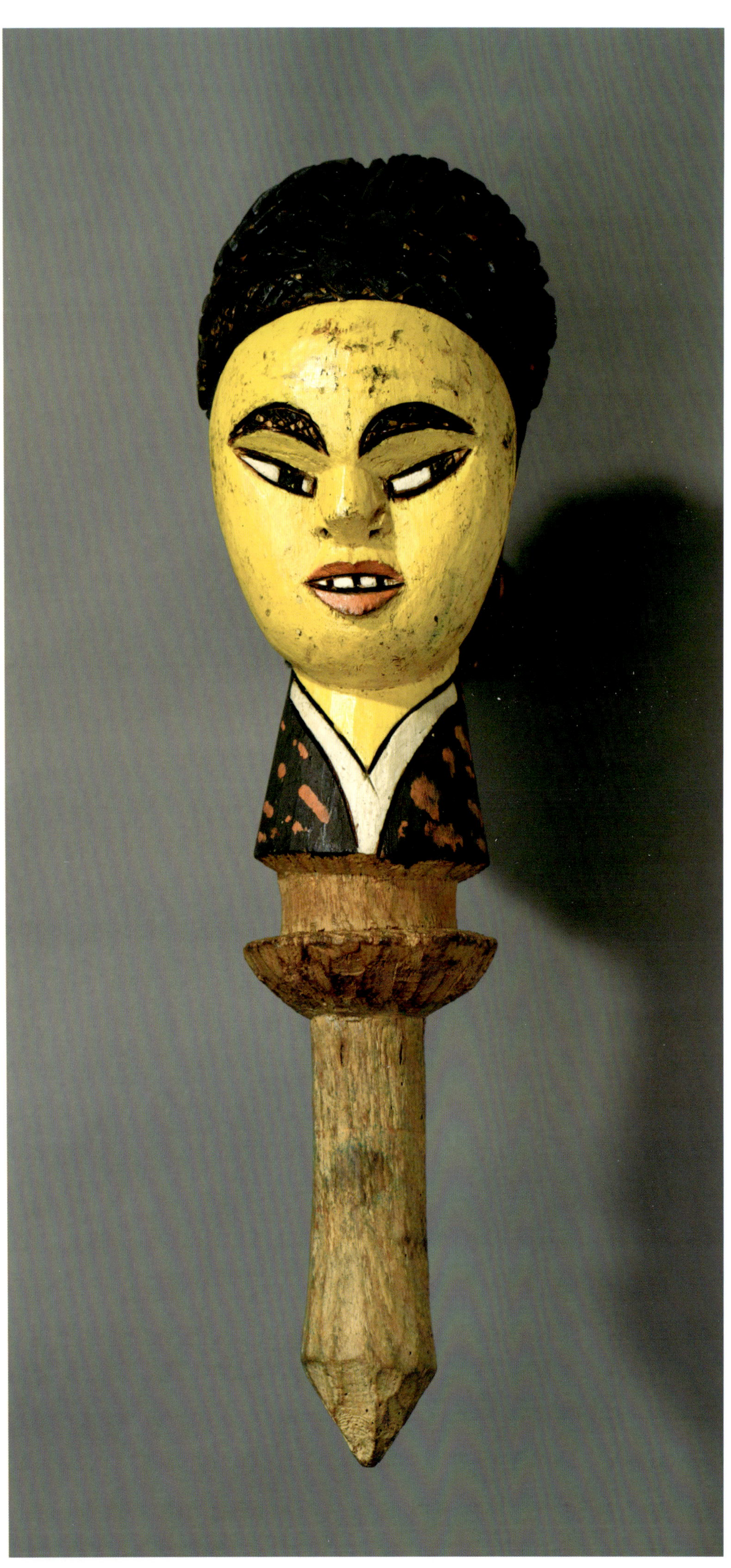

figure 9
Kebe-kebe puppet head
Unidentified artist or workshop
Kuyu style
Wood, pigment
Acquired in 1966 in the village of Mokambi, Gabon, from itinerant theatre troupe
Height: 40.1 cm, Width: 10 cm, Depth: 14 cm
ROM 2009.126.6

figure 10 (opposite)
Drum
Unidentified artist or workshop
Fang style
Wood, hide, fibre, pigment
Acquired from owner in 1964, in village outside Libreville, Gabon
Exchanged for collector's car
Height: 71 cm,
Outside diameter: 29 cm
ROM 2009.126.222

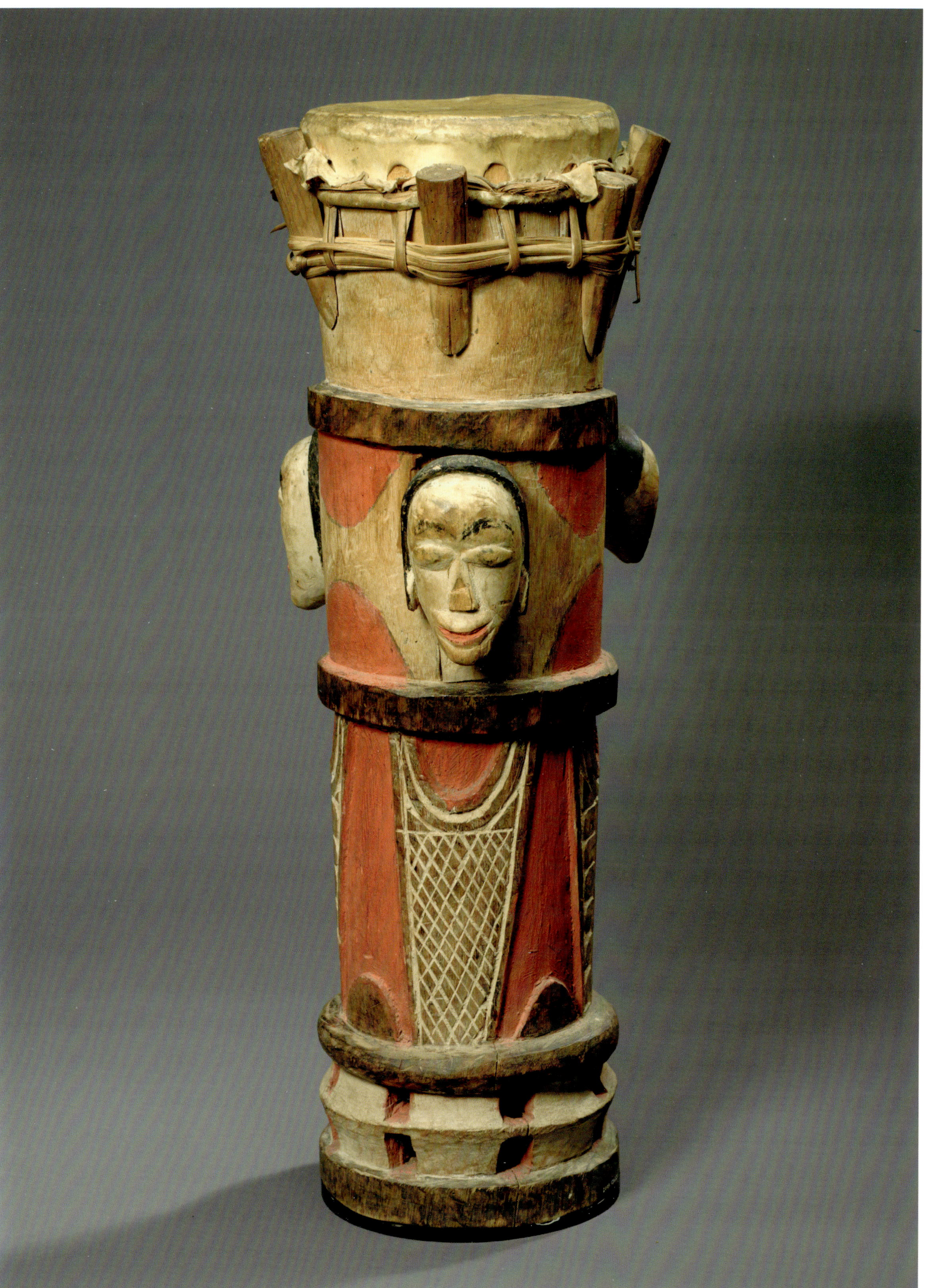

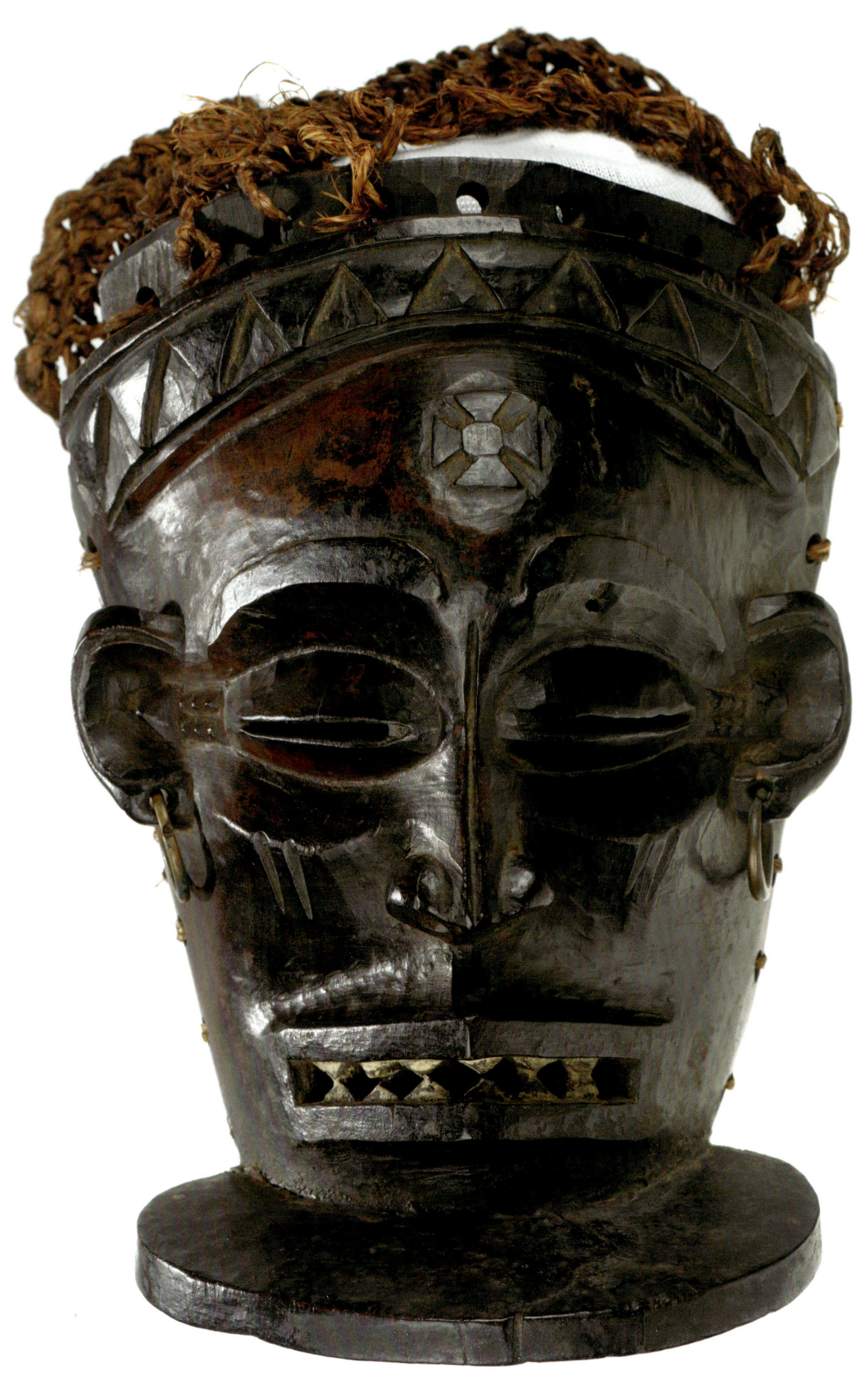

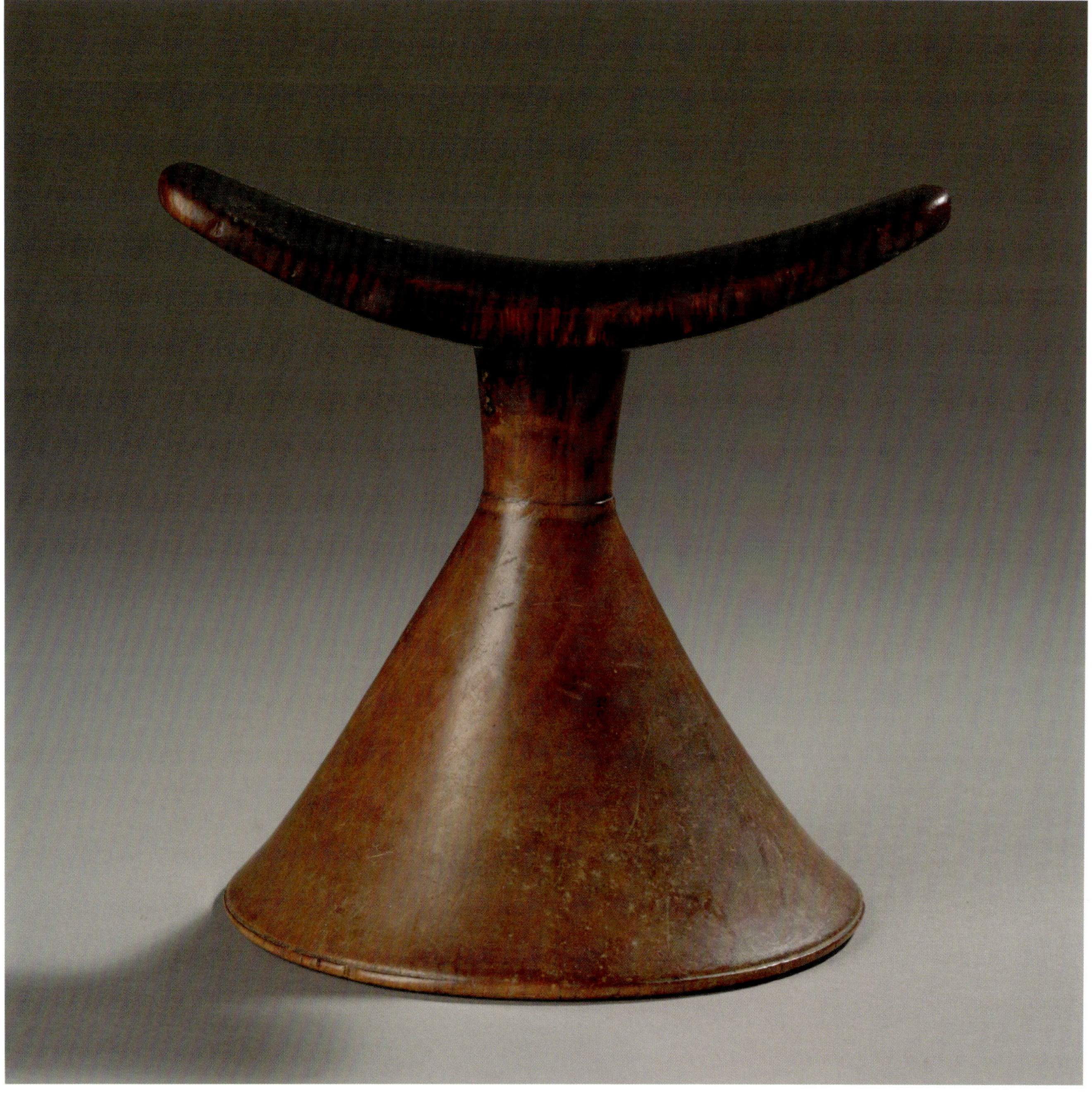

figure 11 (opposite)
Mask
Unidentified artist or workshop
Chokwe style
Wood, fibre, metal
Purchased from Galerie des 5 Continents, Montreal, in the late 1980s
Height: 30.5 cm, Width: 17 cm, Depth: 17 cm
ROM 2009.126.219

figure 12
Headrest
Unidentified artist or workshop
Kaffa style
Wood
Purchased from Giraffe Gallery, Montreal, in 2001
Height: 15.3 cm, Width: 16 cm, Depth: 13.5 cm
ROM 2009.126.34

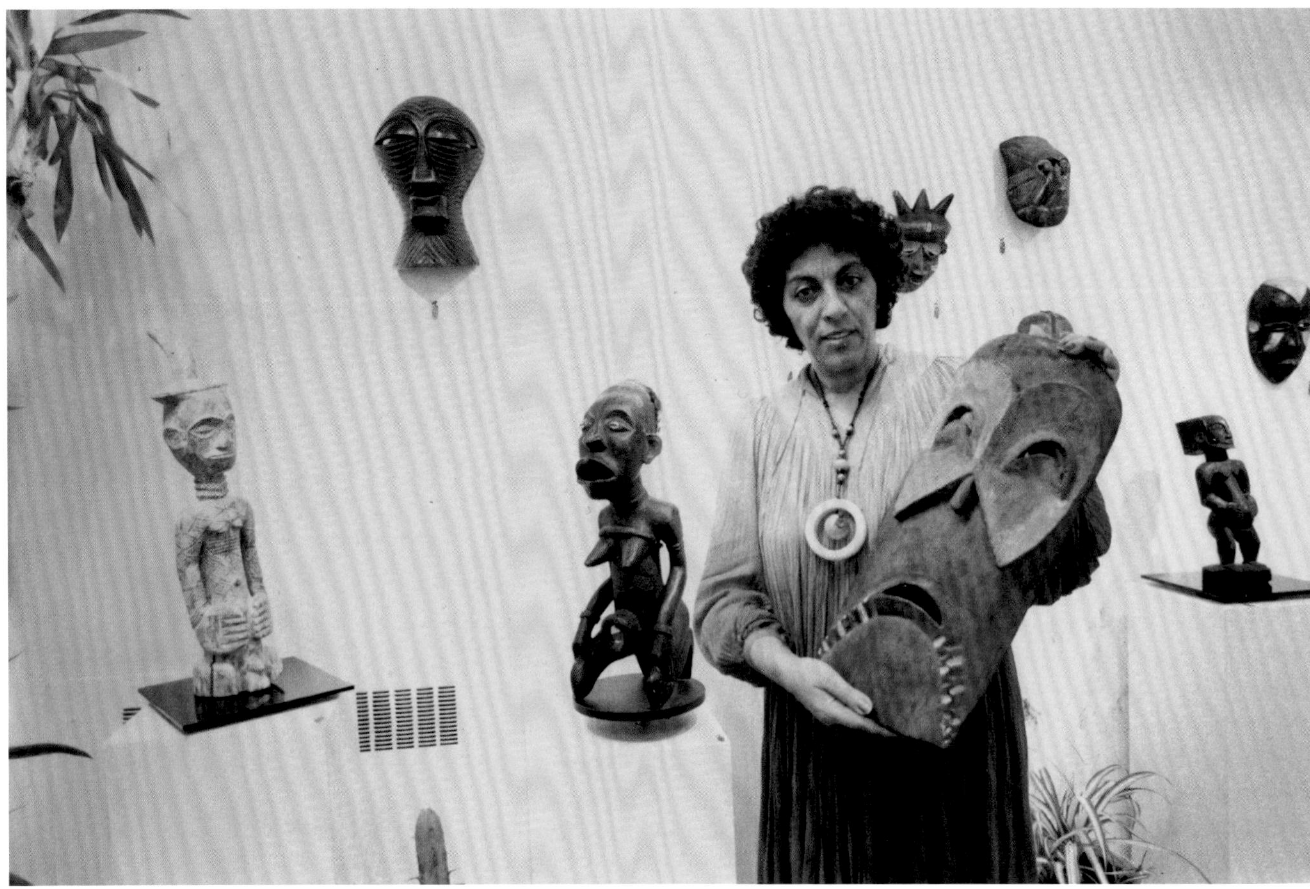

figure 13
Esther Dagan in her Gallery
Circa 1980
From the Amrad African Art Collection Archive

seems to have been a genuine sense of camaraderie among the individual galleries, they displayed two distinct collecting attitudes. Collectors like the Langs and the Lippels, who came from a strong European tradition and spent less time in Africa, focused on collecting older, more traditional African works that were primarily sculptural (Fig. 11). The gallery owners who had spent lengthy amounts of time in Africa—exploring and collecting (like Esther Dagan), through work with CUSO, or because they had grown up there (like Betty Kieran)—seem to have been more interested in fostering a broader appreciation of contemporary African arts and crafts in Canada.

As previously mentioned, members of the Montreal group also had connections to Barbara and Murray Frum, the Toronto couple responsible for amassing the highly regarded African collection that is now at the Art Gallery of Ontario. They began collecting African art in the late 1960s, when Murray Frum bought his first piece. The couple was committed to developing a collection of sculptural masterpieces and made the majority of their acquisitions through dealers and auction houses.[46] According to Philip Fry, they meticulously researched and rigorously evaluated every piece before they acquired it, seeking the input of scholars such as William Fagg and Jacqueline Fry.[47] William J. Withrow emphasized this approach in his foreword to the 1981 exhibition catalogue for *African Majesty: From Grassland and Forest, The Barbara and Murray Frum Collection*:

> The Frums have made no attempt to assemble a comprehensive ethnographic group of objects to represent each of the dozens of African tribes and geographic regions. Rather, the emphasis has been on individual aesthetic and sculptural qualities. Each carving has been chosen on its merits from the very best examples available. The fact that almost every major publication on African art in the last few years has included works in this collection attests to the Frums' standard of taste and judgement.[48]

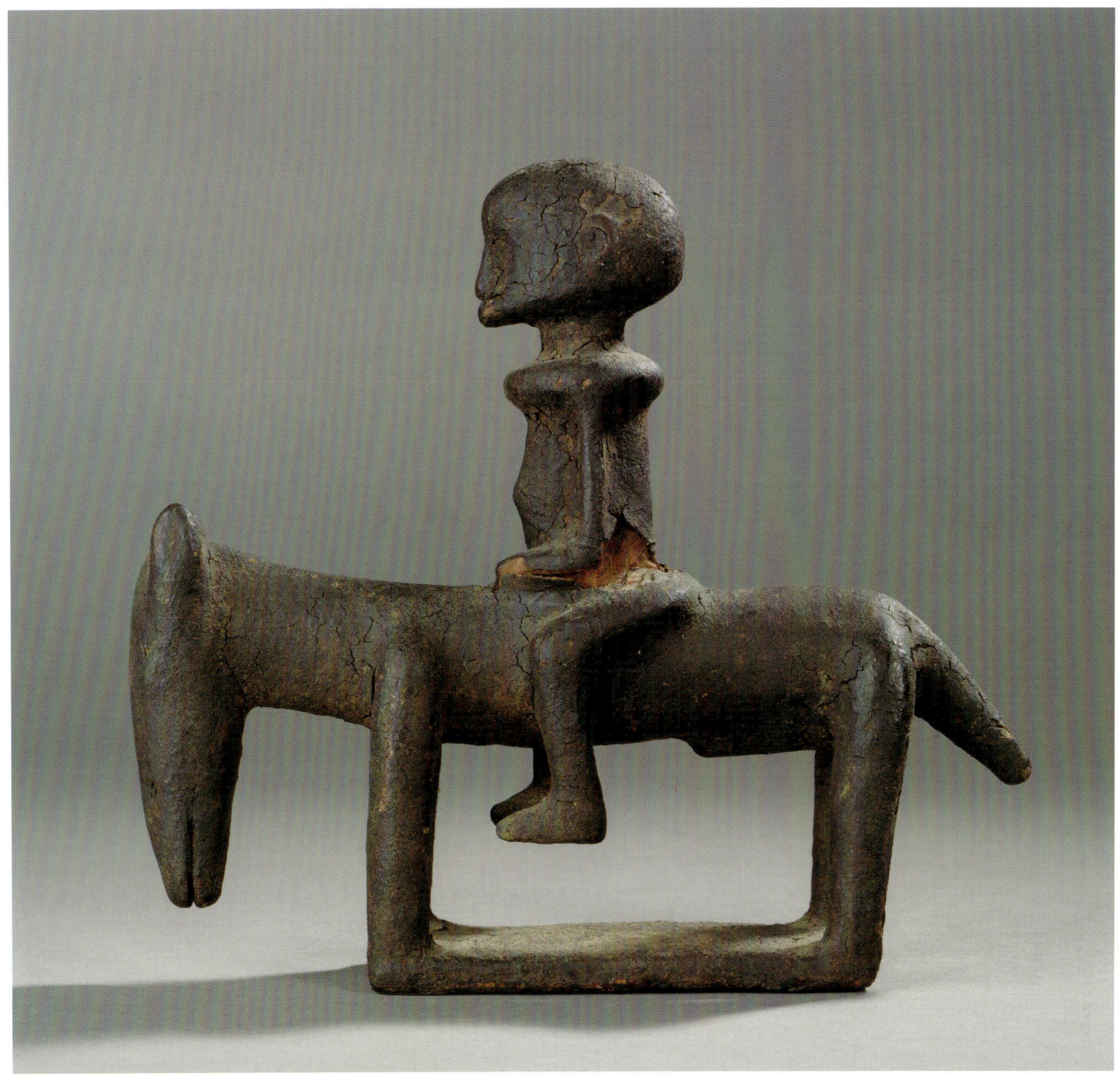

figure 14
Rider figure
Unidentified artist or workshop
Dogon style
Wood
Purchased from an African dealer in Montreal in 1987
Height: 22 cm, WidthL: 5 cm, Depth: 25.5 cm
ROM 2009.126.279

Scholar Jacqueline Fry was another key figure who shaped the reception of African art in Canada during this period. In addition to knowing Murray Frum, she socialized with Leon and Louise Lippel, knew Esther Dagan from her time in Paris in the late 1950s, and was an intimate friend of Justin and Elisabeth Lang. Fry was an anthropologist, curator and critic who wrote broadly on non-Western and modern art. Trained as a specialist in African ethnology, she was the head of the Black Africa section at the Musée de l'Homme in Paris from 1960 to 1970. In May 1968, during the student revolts in Paris, Jacqueline Delange met Philip Fry, a Canadian who had recently finished his doctorate in Paris. They were both heavily involved in the protest movement of 1968 and shared an interest in African art. The two married, and in 1970, they moved to Winnipeg where Fry worked as the curator of Non-Western Art at the Winnipeg Art Gallery. She remained in that position from 1970 to 1973, when the couple moved to Ottawa. Between 1973 and 1976, and again in 1980, Jacqueline Fry was a lecturer in the Department of Anthropology at the Université de Montréal. She later became a lecturer at the University of Ottawa and continued in that position from 1976 until 1991.[49] Throughout the seventies and eighties, Fry curated exhibitions of African art for Dalhousie University (*Masks without Masquerades*, 1974) the National Gallery of Canada (*Twenty-Five African Sculptures*, 1978) and the Agnes Etherington Art Centre (*Visions and Models*, 1985; *Visual Variations*, 1987; and, *Heroic Figures*, 1988), where she was affiliate curator for the Lang Collection after its donation. In her various capacities, Fry was responsible for producing the majority of institutional African art shows that occurred in Canada between the 1970s and the early 1990s.

The publications and exhibitions Fry produced in Paris and Canada offer insight into her approach to African art. In 1967 she co-authored *Afrique Noire, La Création Plastique* with Michel Leiris.[50] Leiris was an anthropologist connected to the Parisian Surrealist movement in the early twentieth century. He was friends with a number of the avant-garde artists who proclaimed the aesthetic value of Primitive arts, including Pablo Picasso.[51] Fry and Leiris developed a strong friendship through which she became connected to the avant-garde literary and visual arts community in Paris.[52] In their publications, both Fry and Leiris made a point of acknowledging the difficulties of understanding African art in the Western context and provided detailed information about the original contexts of art objects as much as possible. Yet despite her scholarly attention to context, Fry privileged a strong aesthetic approach in her displays, which were meant to emphasize the form of the artworks. When discussing her curatorial practices at the Agnes Etherington Art Centre, Fry emphasized the importance of displaying African objects as aesthetic masterpieces in their own right.[53] Here, there are echoes of the Modernist Primitivist values espoused by the circle of collectors and dealers with whom Fry associated as well as the avant-garde community she was connected to in Paris.

Collections and Institutional Legacies

The Lippels, the Langs, Dagan, and the other Canadian gallerists of the second half of the twentieth century all closed their commercial activities between the late 1980s and early 1990s. While some collections were sold or dispersed, others were eventually donated to institutions.

Justin and Elisabeth Lang donated their collection to the Agnes Etherington Art Centre (AEAC) at Queen's University over a period of five to seven years beginning in the mid-1980s. Their son, Robert Lang, was an alumnus of Queen's, and the Art Centre, as both a regional and university art gallery, offered the combination of public and academic accessibility that was so important to them.[54] For the Langs, it was critical that their collection be used for educational purposes and be made available to both local and national audiences. At the same time, their decision to donate to an art museum was bound up with their desire to see the collection displayed aesthetically. As AEAC Curator Dorothy Farr explained, the Langs "were looking for an artistic approach, so they gave [their collection] to the people who were trained in examining objects from an artistic point of view."[55] To ensure the collection would continue to play a central role in the life of the university and its communities, the Langs provided a modest endowment to cover the costs of research and programming and, in the first years after its donation, they funded a part-time affiliate curator of African Art (held by Jacqueline Fry from 1985 until her sudden death in 1991).[56]

Murray Frum, a strong advocate of the modernist aesthetics of Primitive art, deliberately chose to donate his collection to the Art Gallery of Ontario (AGO) as a way to affirm his focus and interest as a collector. When stating his desire to donate the collection to the AGO rather than the Royal Ontario Museum (ROM) in 1999 he explained that

> the ROM's interest is anthropological. I collected this as an art form. It's a battle that was fought a long time ago. Anthropology doesn't distinguish objects in terms of esthetics, I do. I collected art objects, it's important that be understood.[57]

Frum argued also that his collection belonged in an art gallery because of African art's "profound influence on Western art."[58] He told a journalist that he found the pieces in his collection particularly interesting because of the ways in which their illustrations of the human form affected Western Impressionist, Expressionist, and Post-Impressionist artists.[59] Like many of the other African arts collectors in Canada at this time, Barbara and Murray Frum also collected modern Canadian paintings by artists such as Betty Goodwin, Jack Bush, and Michael Snow[60] and had established a long-term patronage relationship with the AGO which went beyond their African arts holdings.

The Amrad Collection assembled by Esther Dagan, which was donated to the ROM in 2009, reflects a very different sensibility and interest. For Dagan, the objects she acquired were always part of her experience and understanding of the creativity and ingenuity of African artists and dealers. While in many ways she shared with her cohort of collectors and dealers a fascination for the "deep cultural meaning and spirituality" of African art, she was also interested in the creative and adaptive process of the African artists and dealers that she encountered in her numerous travels throughout the continent.[61] Dagan fervently refused the ideal of confining the "authenticity" of African creativity to a traditional past. Nor did she believe in attributing value only to those pieces that could be recognized as masterpieces within the parameters of the scholarly and market canon defined in the West.[62] One of the most enjoyable aspects of her life as a dancer, collector and dealer was the time she spent learning about the creative inspiration of performers and plastic artists that she met in her travels.[63] Dagan considered the African dealers whom she met repeatedly in Dakar, Abidjan, Korhogo, Lomé, Accra, Libreville, and Foumban partners in her discovery of the deep interconnectedness of art and life. Interestingly though, like many of her colleagues and friends in Montreal and beyond, the market interactions through which her knowledge and collections were built were never an important focus of her reflection or her understanding of the creative transformations that she was recording through her acquisitions. Though she travelled for over ten years with explicit intent to purchase the objects that would be featured in her exhibitions, and though she had long-term relationships with a number of dealers in the main city markets that she was visiting, none of these exchanges and people were recorded in her extensive archive, nor were the stories of these acquisitions made part of the narrative informing her exhibitions and catalogues.[64] For Dagan, the objects in her collection were a living testimony to the resilience and creativity of African aesthetics and she wanted to use her resources to promote the understanding of Africa in Canada (Fig. 13). Her plan was to build an independent centre for African art that would serve as a museum and a cultural hub to introduce the broader Canadian public to African art. While the plans for the Amrad Centre for African Arts in Montreal of the mid-1990s—and the successive proposal for a bigger and more elaborate institution to be built in Israel—did not come to fruition, Dagan never ceased to be an advocate for the need to promote a public engagement with the arts of Africa beyond the strict masterpiece approach still prevalent in canonical museum displays.[65]

Though many of the protagonists in this mid- to late-twentieth-century love story with African art shared the desire to make these artworks more broadly understood and appreciated, not many traces of their activity remain in Montreal, where a new generation of high-end art dealers and art collectors promote a much more exclusive and canonical appreciation of the ancient arts of Africa.[66] Yet their legacy remains inscribed in many ways in the collections that have found different institutional homes. As complex "material and social assemblages,"[67] collections may be unpacked to reveal networks that connect objects and people and enable us to learn and understand historical and contemporary processes of creativity, production, circulation and display. Because of the premises on which they were built, not all these elements may always be readable and recoverable. However, because of the profound human interest that motivated these twentieth-century Montreal art lovers, their collections relate as much, if not more, to Africa, its peoples and the collecting experiences than to the abstract aesthetic canonical references that determine value in the high-end market.

1 James Clifford, *The Predicament of Culture: Twentieth-Century Ethnography, Literature, and Art* (Cambridge, MA: Harvard University Press, 1988), 189–214.

2 Marie-Louise Labelle, *Beads of Life: Eastern and Southern African Beadwork from Canadian Collections* (Gatineau, Quebec: Canadian Museum of Civilization, 2005), 7.

3 Shelly Errington has argued that "the author of a work about the primitive and primitivism needs some devices to show ironic distance from terms that could be misinterpreted as being uttered in the author's own voice." We have chosen to capitalize the terms "Primitive," "Primitivism" and "Modernist Primitivism/ist" to indicate that these labels are constructs of Western culture, embedded in the specific ideologies that we are analyzing, and do not reflect our own perspectives on the cultures or art forms being discussed. In some cases, we have qualified the terms with words such as "so-called" and "supposedly" to reinforce this position. Where we quote someone else's opinion, we have not capitalized or otherwise changed their terminology. For Shelly Errington's discussion of this topic, see Shelly Errington, *The Death of Authentic Primitive Art and Other Tales of Progress* (Berkeley: University of California Press, 1998), xxv–xxvii.

4 A trend towards viewing non-Western arts from an aesthetic perspetive was reflected in Chinoiserie and Japonisme. These began to develop as early as the seventeenth century but will not be addressed within the scope of this discussion.

5 For examples of these perspectives, see Robert John Goldwater, *Primitivism in Modern Art*, rev. ed. (New York: Vintage Books, 1967).

6 Ronald W. Hawker, "Northwest Coast Art as National Heritage: Two Federal Projects of the Late 1920s," chap. 4 in *Tales of Ghosts: First Nations Art in British Columbia, 1922–61* (Vancouver: UBC Press, 2003).

7 Ann Duncan, "Lippel a Pioneer in Promoting Africa in the West," *Montreal Gazette*, December 14, 1991.

8 Ibid.

9 Ibid.

10 Ibid.

11 Philip Fry, personal communication to Catherine Hale, June 13, 2006.

12 Ibid.

13 Philip Fry, "The Lang Collection," Series 4: Other Professional Papers: Box 20, File 2 [Correspondence—Lang Collection—Museology Course, 1977; 1980–1982], Jacqueline Fry fonds, Library and Archives, National Gallery of Canada.

14 Robert Lang, personal communication to Catherine Hale, June 30, 2006.

15 "Gallery Owner Elisabeth Lang was Lover of Art," *Montreal Gazette*, February 1, 1990.

16 Elisabeth Lang, introduction in *Héritage Africain = African Heritage: Galerie Des 5 Continents, Montréal, 10e Anniversaire, Septembre 1988 = 10th Anniversary, September 1988*, by Elisabeth Lang, Normand Biron, and Galerie des 5 continents (Montreal: Galerie des 5 continents, 1988), 3.

17 Robert Lang, personal communication to Catherine Hale, June 30, 2006.

18 Clarence Epstein, foreword to *Max Stern, Montreal Dealer and Patron*, by Michel Moreault (Montreal: Montreal Museum of Fine Arts, 2004), 9.
19 Ibid.
20 Édith-Anne Pageot, "A Dealer of 'Living' Art," in *Max Stern, Montreal Dealer and Patron*, ed. Michel Moreault (Montreal: Montreal Museum of Fine Arts, 2004), 15.
21 Ibid., 16.
22 Ibid., 17.
23 Ibid., 27–28.
24 Ibid., 23.
25 Ibid., 17.
26 "Bruno Cormier," Institut Philippe Pinel de Montreal, accessed July 10, 2006, http://www.pinel.qc.ca/cormier/bruno_cormier.html.
27 J. Arboleda-Flórez, "Breaking the Chains: Bruno M Cormier and the McGill University Clinic in Forensic Psychiatry [Book Review]," *Canadian Journal of Psychiatry*, March 2011, https://ww1.cpa-apc.org/Publications/Archives/CJP/2001/Mar/Reviews3.asp
28 Canadian Broadcasting Corporation, "Launching of Le Refus Global," CBC Digital Archives website, 2006, accessed July 18, 2006, http://www.cbc.ca/archives/entry/1948-launching-of-le-refus-global.
29 Dorothea Rockburne, "Resplendent Anarchy," *Time*, August 24, 1998, 45–46.
30 Esther Dagan, personal communication to Silvia Forni, December 6, 2008.
31 Mel Solman, "Israeli Authority on African Culture Awakens to her own Spiritual Roots," *Canadian Jewish News*, September 29, 1978, 7.
32 Esther Dagan, personal communication to Silvia Forni, July 15, 2009.
33 Sarah Scott, "Search for African Art Took Many Strange Roads," *Montreal Gazette*, July 27, 1981, 47.
34 Esther Dagan, personal communication to Silvia Forni, June 30, 2009.
35 Linda Stodola, "Demystifying African Art," *101 Decorating Ideas*, February 1982, 5.
36 After closing her gallery in 1992, Esther Dagan devoted herself full time to her publishing house Galerie Amrad African Art Publications. The first book resulting from this shift in focus and scope is Bogumil Jewsiewicki's 1995 book *Cheri Samba: The Hybridity of Art = l'hybridité d'un art*. Another manuscript by Olu Oguibe on the art of El Anatsui remains unpublished in her archive.
37 Victoria Henry, personal communication to Catherine Hale, July 11, 2006.
38 Ibid.
39 Ibid.
40 Nancy Gall, "Exotic Ethnic Jewellery," *Ottawa Citizen*, February 2, 1989.
41 Victoria Henry, personal communication to Catherine Hale, July 11, 2006.
42 Nancy Gall, "Exotic Ethnic Jewellery."
43 Robert Barde, introduction to *Bruce Onobrakpeya: Nigeria's Master Printmaker* (Toronto: The Best of Africa, 1978), accessed July 15, 2006, http://staff.haas.berkeley.edu/barde/_public/african%20art/onobrakpeya/text.pdf.
44 Victoria Henry, personal communication to Catherine Hale, July 11, 2006.
45 Ibid.
46 Robert Fulford, "How Africa Taught Us to See," *National Post*, December 14, 1999.
47 Philip Fry, personal communication to Catherine Hale, June 13, 2006.
48 William J. Withrow, foreword to *African Majesty: From Grassland and Forest*, by William Fagg (Toronto: Art Gallery of Ontario, 1981), 7–8.
49 Biographical Sketch, Jacqueline Fry fonds, Library and Archives, National Gallery of Canada.
50 Michel Leiris and Jacqueline Delange, *Afrique Noire, La Création Plastique* (Paris: Gallimard, 1967).
51 Marianna Torgovnick, *Gone Primitive: Savage Intellects, Modern Lives* (Chicago: University of Chicago Press, 1990), 105.
52 Philip Fry, personal communication to Catherine Hale, June 13, 2006.
53 Jacqueline Fry, ed., *Heroic Figures: African Sculpture from the Justin and Elisabeth Lang Collection: 12 May–25 September 1988, Agnes Etherington Art Centre, Queen's University, Kingston, Canada* (Kingston, Canada: The Agnes Etherington Art Centre, 1988), 1.
54 Robert Lang, personal communication to Catherine Hale, June 30, 1996.
55 Dorothy Farr, personal communication to Catherine Hale, June 29, 2006.
56 Dorothy Farr, personal communication to Catherine Hale, June 29, 2006.
57 "African Art Belongs in AGO, Frum Says," *Toronto Star*, December 10, 1999.
58 Ibid.
59 Dan Brown, "Murray Frum Donates $12-Million Art Collection," *National Post*, December 8, 1999.
60 Fulford, "How Africa Taught Us to See."
61 Esther Dagan, personal communication to Silvia Forni, June 30, 2009.
62 Esther Dagan, personal communication to Silvia Forni, July 1, 2009.
63 Esther Dagan, personal communication to Silvia Forni, June 30, 2009.
64 Alongside her gallery, Dagan ran the Galerie Amrad African Arts publishing house. Through this she published thirteen books on African art, most of them catalogues accompanying her exhibitions, and three fiction books. Though many critics have pointed out the lack of in-depth scholarship characterizing her art publications, often too broad and general, many are still remembered as somewhat groundbreaking in their thematic approach. After closing her gallery in 1992, Dagan took up publishing as her main professional activity and commissioned a few manuscripts on contemporary African art.
65 Plans and correspondence relative to the project of creating the Amrad African Art Centre in Montreal (1996) and Israel (1998) are found in the Amrad Africana Archive at the ROM. Dagan's

views vis-à-vis the need for a broader public promotion of African art in Canada are expressed in several interviews, and in particular in Dorota Kozinska, "A Passion for Africa," *Montreal Gazette*, February 14, 1998, J1–J2.

66 See Jacques Germain, "African Art in Canadian Collections," *Tribal Arts* 74 (Winter 2014): 102–109.

67 Sarah Byrne, Anne Clarke, Rodney Harrison, and Robin Torrence, "Networks, Agents and Objects: Frameworks for Unpacking Museum Collections," in *Unpacking the Collection: Networks of Material and Social Agency in the Museum* (New York: Springer, 2011), 4.

Bibliography

Arboleda-Flórez, J. "Breaking the Chains: Bruno M Cormier and the McGill University Clinic in Forensic Psychiatry." Book Review. *Canadian Journal of Psychiatry*, March 2011. Accessed July 10, 2006. http://www.cpa-apc.org/Publications/Archives/ CJP/2001/Mar/Reviews3.asp.

Barde, Robert. Introduction to *Bruce Onobrakpeya: Nigeria's Master Printmaker*. Toronto: The Best of Africa, 1978. Web version accessed July 15, 2006. http://staff.haas.berkeley.edu/barde/_public/african%20art/onobrakpeya/text.pdf.

Byrne, Sarah, Anne Clarke, Rodney Harrison, and Robin Torrence. "Networks, Agents and Objects: Frameworks for Unpacking Museum Collections." In *Unpacking the Collection: Networks of Material and Social Agency in the Museum*, 3–26. New York: Springer, 2011.

Canadian Broadcasting Corporation. "Launching of Le Refus Global." CBC Digital Archives website, 2006. Accessed July 18, 2006. http://archives.cbc.ca/IDC-1-68-260-1299/arts_entertainment/refus_global_launch/clip1.

Clifford, James. *The Predicament of Culture: Twentieth-Century Ethnography, Literature, and Art*. Cambridge, MA: Harvard University Press, 1988.

Duncan, Ann. "Lippel a Pioneer in Promoting Africa in the West." *Montreal Gazette*, December 14, 1991.

Epstein, Clarence. Foreword to *Max Stern, Montreal Dealer and Patron*, edited by Michel Moreault, 9–10. Montreal: Montreal Museum of Fine Arts, 2004.

Errington, Shelly. *The Death of Authentic Primitive Art and Other Tales of Progress*. Berkeley: University of California Press, 1998.

Fry, Jacqueline, fonds, Library and Archives, National Gallery of Canada. http://www.gallery.ca/english/library/biblio/ngc020.html#a0.

Fry, Jacqueline, ed. *Heroic Figures: African Sculpture from the Justin and Elisabeth Lang Collection: 12 May–25 September 1988, Agnes Etherington Art Centre, Queen's University, Kingston, Canada*. Kingston, Canada: The Agnes Etherington Art Centre, 1988.

Germain, Jacques. *"African Arts in Canadian Collections." Tribal Arts* 74 (Winter 2014): 102–109.

Goldwater, Robert John. *Primitivism in Modern Art*, rev. ed. New York: Vintage Books, 1967.

Hawker, Ronald W. "Northwest Coast Art as National Heritage: Two Federal Projects of the Late 1920s." Chap. 4 in *Tales of Ghosts: First Nations Art in British Columbia 1922–61*. Vancouver: UBC Press, 2003.

Institut Philippe Pinel de Montreal. "Bruno Cormier." Accessed July 10, 2006. http://www.pinel.qc.ca/ContentT.aspx?NavID=105&CultureCode=fr-CA.

Labelle, Marie-Louise. *Beads of Life: Eastern and Southern African Beadwork from Canadian Collections*. Gatineau, Quebec: Canadian Museum of Civilization, 2005.

Lang, Elisabeth. Introduction in *Héritage Africain = African Heritage: Galerie Des 5 Continents, Montréal, 10e Anniversaire, Septembre 1988 = 10th Anniversary, September 1988* by Elisabeth Lang, Normand Biron, and Galerie des 5 continents. Montreal: Galerie des 5 continents, 1988.

Leiris, Michel and Jacqueline Delange. *Afrique Noire, La Création Plastique*. Paris: Gallimard, 1967.

Pageot, Édith-Anne. "A Dealer of 'Living' Art." In *Max Stern, Montreal Dealer and Patron*, edited by Michel Moreault, 15–31. Montreal: Montreal Museum of Fine Arts, 2004.

Rockburne, Dorothea. "Resplendent Anarchy," *Time International*, August 24, 1998. Accessed July 10, 2006. http://www.time.com/time/magazine/1998/int/980824/the_arts.art.resplenden6a.html.

Stodola, Linda. "Demystifying African Art." *101 Decorating Ideas*, February 1982.

Torgovnick, Marianna. *Gone Primitive: Savage Intellects, Modern Lives*. Chicago: University of Chicago Press, 1990.

Withrow, William J. Foreword to *African Majesty: From Grassland and Forest*, by William Fagg. Toronto: Art Gallery of Ontario, 1981.

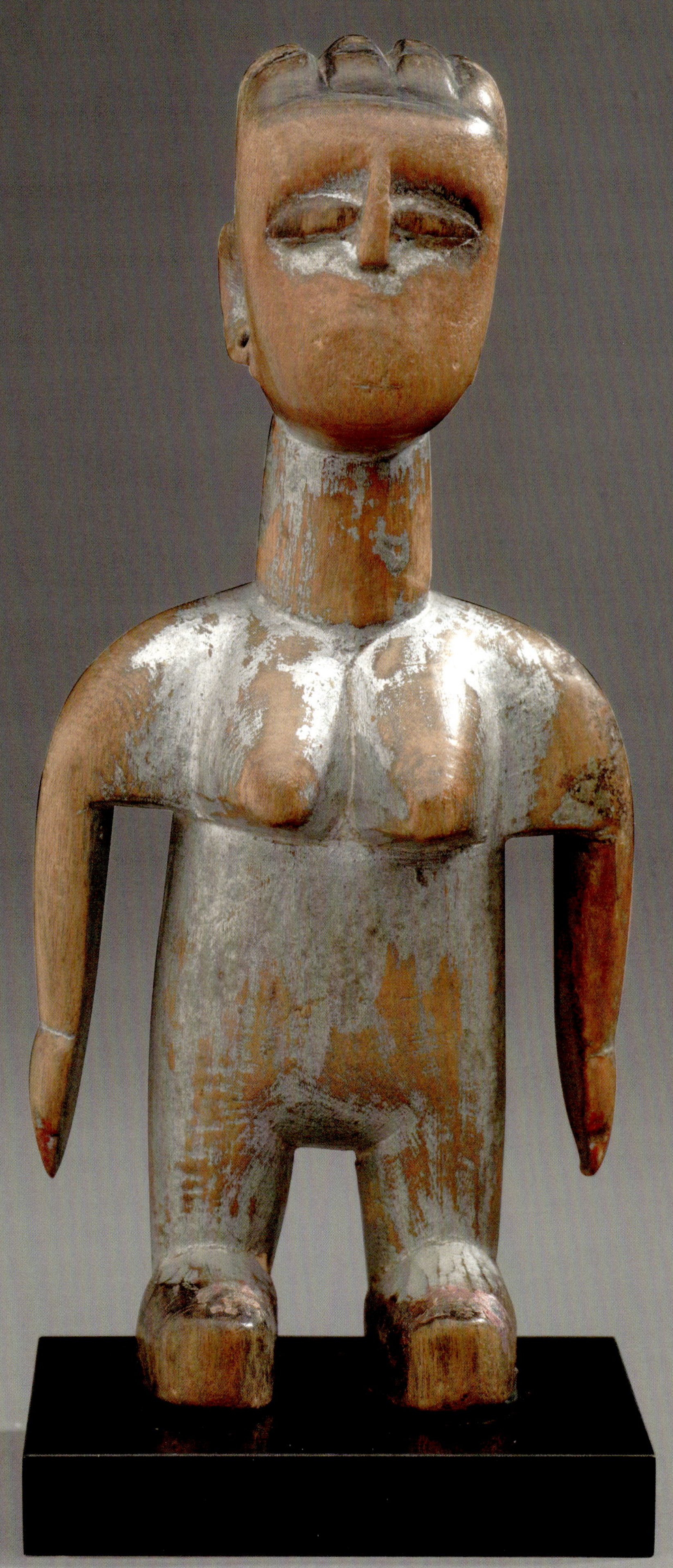

plate 3

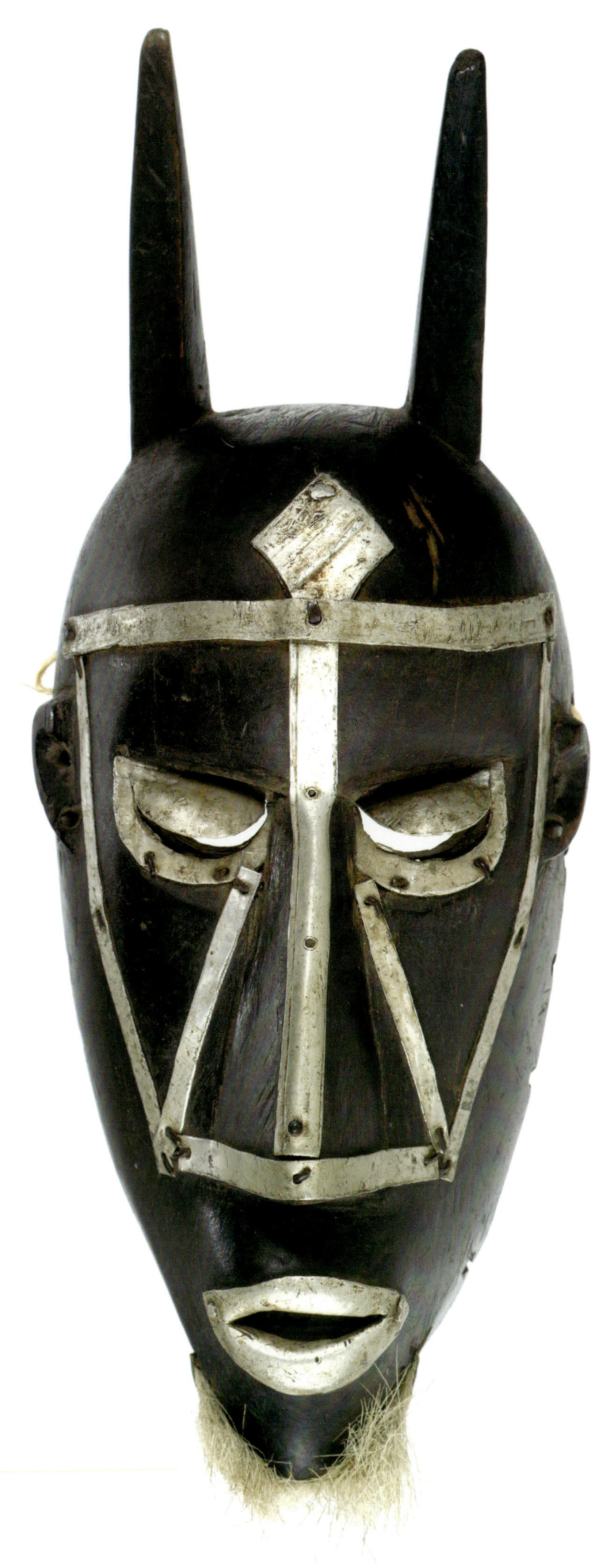

plate 4

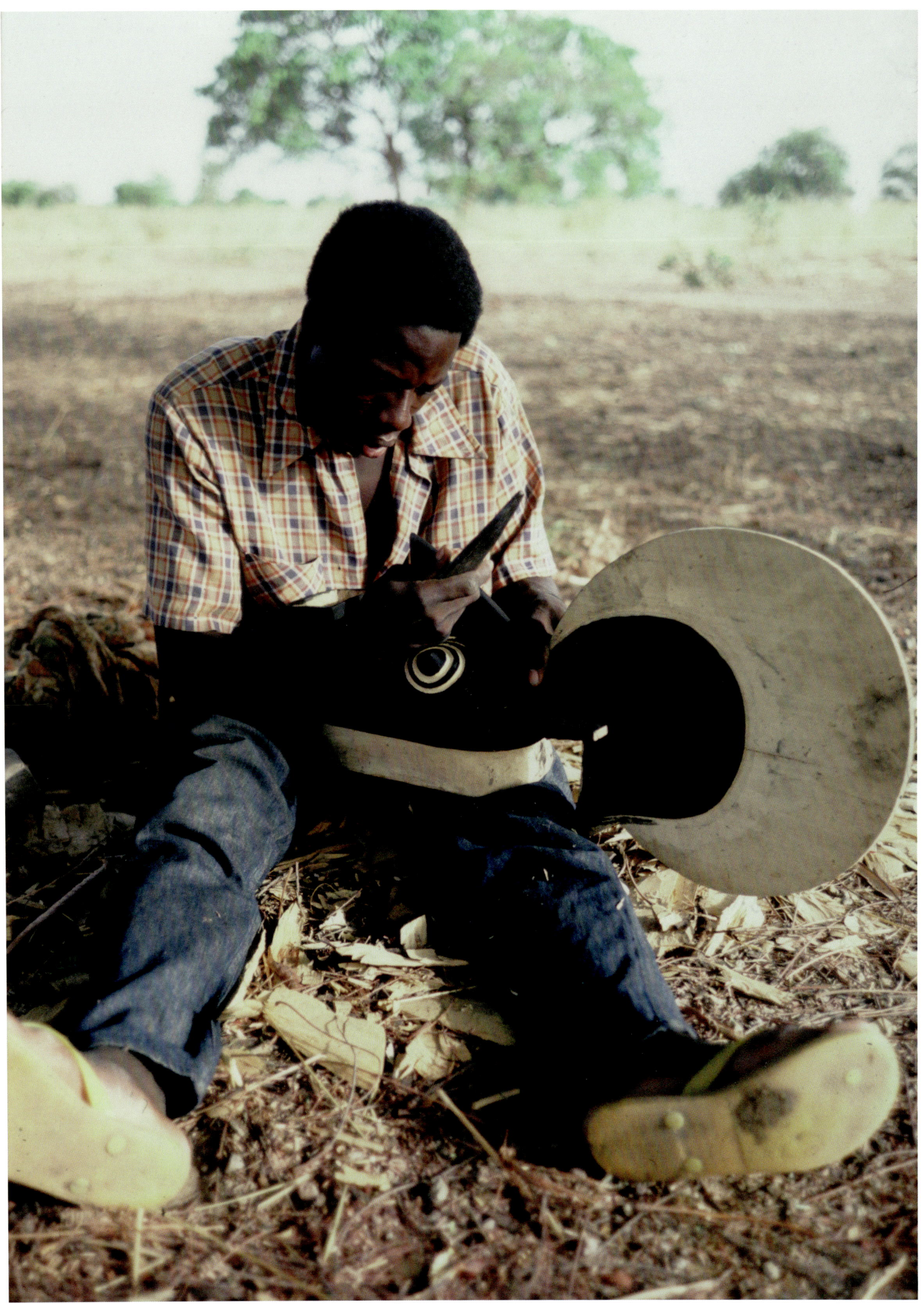

CHAPTER 3

THE ART MARKET IN BURKINA FASO: A PERSONAL RECOLLECTION

CHRISTOPHER D. ROY

Thirty years ago, Burkina Faso was considered to be the end of the earth. It is only in the past twenty years that significant numbers of tourists have begun to visit this small, very poor country. Many tourists have been attracted by the spectacular mask performances that are held in rural villages. Many tourists purchase souvenirs in the capital city to take home with them when they leave. At the same time, Burkina Faso continues to be a source for valuable "artifacts" for the art market as objects are made, used, broken, replaced, and discarded before being shipped to France, London, or New York.

I have been familiar with the art market in Burkina Faso and especially in the capital, Ouagadougou, since 1970, when I began to work at the national art centre in Ouagadougou as a Peace Corps volunteer. I had studied art history and pottery at St. Lawrence University, and I spoke fluent French because I had attended the Sorbonne for a year, and so when my wife Nora and I applied for the Peace Corps they assigned us to what was then called Upper Volta (Haute-Volta) and is now Burkina Faso. I was one of five Peace Corps volunteers who were recruited to work at the Centre Voltaique des Arts, an art centre that had been established by a French artist named Louis Laouchez. Just before we arrived in Burkina Faso, the French director was fired and expelled from the country (it seems he had had an argument with the minister of education), and because I spoke French well they asked me to take over temporarily as director.

The other Peace Corps volunteers were specialists in such things as batiks, macramé, sculpture and weaving. They were Frances Burckhard, Josh Hoffman, Gene French, Alfred Mock and Robert Carvuto. We all worked at the art centre for a very pleasant two years. When we began, there were about thirty African artists working there. When we left, there were seventy-five artists from Burkina Faso employed at the art centre.

The Centre Voltaique des Arts is now the Centre National d'Artisanat d'Art (CNAA),[1] but it remains on Avenue Dim Delobsom, near the central post office. It is still a very lively place, full of productive artists who continue to create objects to sell to tourists. Unfortunately, land speculators have had their eye on the property for years and today it is under threat of being expropriated to build banks or government buildings.

In the late 1980s the chamber of commerce constructed the Village Artisanal de Ouagadougou[2] on the *route circulaire* (Boulevard Tengsoba). This project began in about 1971 or 1972 with a meeting in Ouagadougou of a large number of French expatriates (a meeting I attended and for which I purchased an administrator's suit, a "tenue de fonctionnaire"). The group was intent on creating a site that would attract more tourists to Burkina Faso, and among the proposals was the creation of a living history museum similar to the one for which the city of Niamey, Niger, is famous. The current *village artisanal* is quite large and well set up, although it is a little bit less lively than the old art centre where

detail
A carver of the Konaté family carving "sun" masks for the tourist market
Village of Ouri, Burkina Faso, 1985
Photo by Christopher D. Roy

I served as a Peace Corps volunteer. The village produces lots of very good quality materials to be sold to visitors to the country, including excellent textiles, leather work, basketry, brass casting and a variety of other art forms. Every fall there is an international art and craft fair at the *village artisanal*, which I have never been able to attend because it is always held in the fall semester when I must be teaching. It is called the Salon International de l'Artisanat de Ouagadougou (SIAO).[3] The most recent was held in November 2014 with the theme "Artisanat africain: entreprenariat feminin et protection sociale."[4]

One of my responsibilities at the Centre Voltaique des Arts was to export as much of the art from the centre as possible. The intention was to bring hard currency into the economy of Burkina Faso. We regularly received very large orders from major department store chains in France and the United States. I remember filling orders for hundreds and hundreds of baskets, and hundreds of pounds of brass castings. The kinds of objects that our artists made at the art centre included a lot of very good quality brass casting, and especially handmade wax-resist batiks. There were a number of other kinds of art that sold well locally but did not export well. These included large-scale stone sculpture and most of the pottery. The artists had never made batiks before and so Gene French, Robert Carvuto and Alfred Mock taught them how to do it. The art form took off so quickly that before long we were selling thousands of CFA francs worth of batiks every day. The other major source of income was the brass casting, which had been an important art form in Burkina Faso for centuries: Mossi brass casters had been making equipment for horses since at least the sixteenth century.

Batiks were the major contribution made by volunteers Robert Carvuto, Gene French and Alfred Mock. The technique was totally unknown in Burkina Faso until 1970 when Robert, Gene and Alfred began to train a group of twenty apprentices at the art centre. Within a year, their apprenticeship had been completed and they were replaced by twenty new apprentices. Within two years, there were several dozen skilled batikers working in Ouagadougou and selling their work in many of the capital cities in West Africa. That technique has since spread all across Africa and has become a ubiquitous and popular art form. Twenty years ago a group of African students who were studying at the University of Iowa invited me to an exhibition of art from their home countries. Among the objects displayed from Burkina Faso were batiks like those that Robert, Gene and Alfred had taught the apprentices at the art centre. The students were very proud of their cultural heritage in the form of batiks that, unknown to them, did not exist before 1970.

During the two years of our Peace Corps service, Nora and I often looked at objects that had been made out in rural villages by practicing carvers and then brought into Ouagadougou by art dealers to sell. The dealers brought these objects to our home in Ouagadougou where they laid them out on our front porch. Some were old and already damaged, and would have been replaced at home by new carvings and the originals sent to the capital city to sell. There were rarely some very fine quality pieces that would perhaps benefit a museum either in Burkina Faso or in America. Most of the objects were much more recently made by artists in the rural towns who were carving figures and masks in large numbers with the express intent of sending them to Ouagadougou to be sold by art dealers. Almost all of these objects had been artificially aged to make them appear older than they really were. I don't recall any of the techniques that the carvers used being very sophisticated. They simply smoked the objects in the rafters of a woman's kitchen for a period of time to give them the appearance of age. They all smelled strongly of wood smoke. It was not very hard to tell that the objects were fairly new, and that they had a thin, recent patina of soot. One of the Peace Corps volunteers who taught sculpture was from Chicago, Illinois, and was intent on acquiring large numbers of good-quality sculptures to take back home with him. He stayed in Ouagadougou for only one year and then left. Many years later I had a chance to see the objects that he had purchased when he offered them for sale, and they were the very same sort of new copies that the artists in the rural villages had been making to send off to the art dealers in Ouagadougou. I don't recall any of them being of "museum quality."

The principal place to buy art in Ouagadougou in the early 1970s was an extensive market in front of the railroad hotel called the Régie Abidjan Niger (RAN). The market was a long series of stalls with thatched roofs, and underneath were tables on which were piled vast quantities of brass and wood objects. There were a large number of masks and figures carved of wood in the styles of different peoples in Burkina Faso, as well as large quantities of brass bracelets that had been discarded in the previous decades and were being sold almost for scrap. The brass casters at the art centre and I would regularly go to the stalls and purchase brass bracelets by the sack full to take back to the art centre, where they were heated and broken up to cast figures to sell to tourists. There was very little imported art from such places as Conakry, Guinea, in the stalls in front of the hotel, but there were quite a large number of Chiwara crests from Bamako, Mali. I think that the artists in Burkina Faso were so prolific that few of the art dealers felt much need to purchase objects from as far away as Guinea. Almost all of the objects were gray and dusty and badly eroded from careless handling. Many had been displayed for sale for decades and had suffered as a consequence. None resembled in the least the sorts of objects that were being used by people in rural villages.

In the mid-1980s the entire city of Ouagadougou was surveyed officially and new streets were cut with bulldozers. All of the old shops disappeared and were moved to a series of brand new, beautifully constructed shops alongside the Place d'Armes (Army Plaza) which is across from several big banks and from the major army barracks in Ouagadougou. This large square is the site of a spectacular crafts market every second year

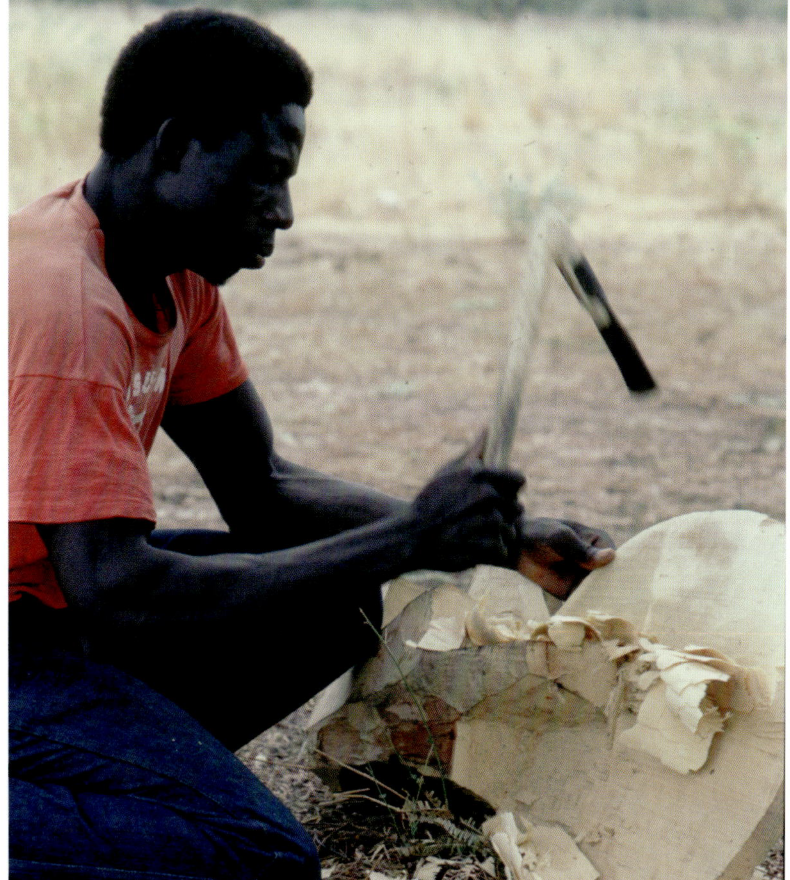

figure 1
Poboye Konaté, in the early stages of carving a "hombo" mask
Burkina Faso, 1985
Photo by Christopher D. Roy

during the Pan-African film and television festival FESPACO.[5] Those stalls are still there and are thriving. They continue to sell very much the same kinds of things that were being sold in the 1970s, although in the past twenty years they have begun to sell other more exotic and interesting objects, including costumes from the Fulani people. Larger and larger numbers of brass castings are being made by casters in the city who do not work at the art centre. Many of these are extraordinarily large, and I often wonder how anybody gets them back home to Europe or America.

The key player in the art market in Ouagadougou from 1960 to 1980 was the director of the national museum, Toumani Triandé. He had been trained as a young man before independence by the great French anthropologist Guy Le Moal, who was a scholar of the Bobo people. Triandé had been a devout Muslim all of his life, and in 1984 Le Moal told me that he was very worried that Triandé would systematically sell all of the objects in the museum. Le Moal proved to be correct. When I first visited the museum in 1970, at its old location at the Centre National de la Recherche Scientifique et Technologique (CNRST; formerly IFAN), across from the main hospital, most of the collection was still intact and contained many superb objects that Le Moal had collected before 1960. Soon after, it was moved to the Hotel Independence on the main avenue downtown. It was still there in the mid-1980s when I was doing research as a faculty member at the University of Iowa. Between 1970 when I first saw the collection and 1985 when I last visited at the Hotel Independence, large numbers of objects disappeared and were replaced by copies that had clearly been carved recently. A decade or so ago a brand new art museum was built at the edge of the city near the *village artisanal* which was established by the Chamber of Commerce. Triandé is long since deceased and the new art museum is professionally staffed by a very competent director. They do their very best to display what few objects survive in the museum, and often have to make do with photo displays. They are struggling mightily to acquire some objects for their permanent collection and they are making steady progress.

Triandé hired a number of artists from rural villages, including and especially a young artist from the village of Ouri named Poboye Konaté (Fig. 1), to come to Ouagadougou and copy objects in the museum as closely and carefully as possible. These new objects were then put on display, and the original objects disappeared—I can only imagine to make their way quickly to Paris. I am sure that none of those objects was ever offered for sale locally for fear that someone might recognize that they had come from the museum. Poboye Konaté died of HIV/AIDS in the late 1980s. He is still known in the village of Ouri as a *voleur des masques*. His younger brother is currently one of the art dealers who travels frequently to Ouagadougou to offer objects for sale. I have no indication that this younger brother ever steals anything from the village.

One of the volunteers at the art centre until 1969 was a young man named Norman Stokstad. He returned to the art museum as a Peace Corps volunteer in the mid-1970s and made a photographic record of everything in the art museum. Norman recently sent me copies of the photographs he took, and I intend to post them on the Internet in an effort to locate some of the objects that were sold from the museum during this sad period. I also photographed a large number of the objects in the museum, at least the ones that were on public display, between 1976 and 1977 (Fig. 2). I am tempted to post the photos online as evidence of objects that were stolen from the museum.

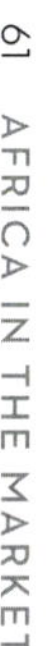

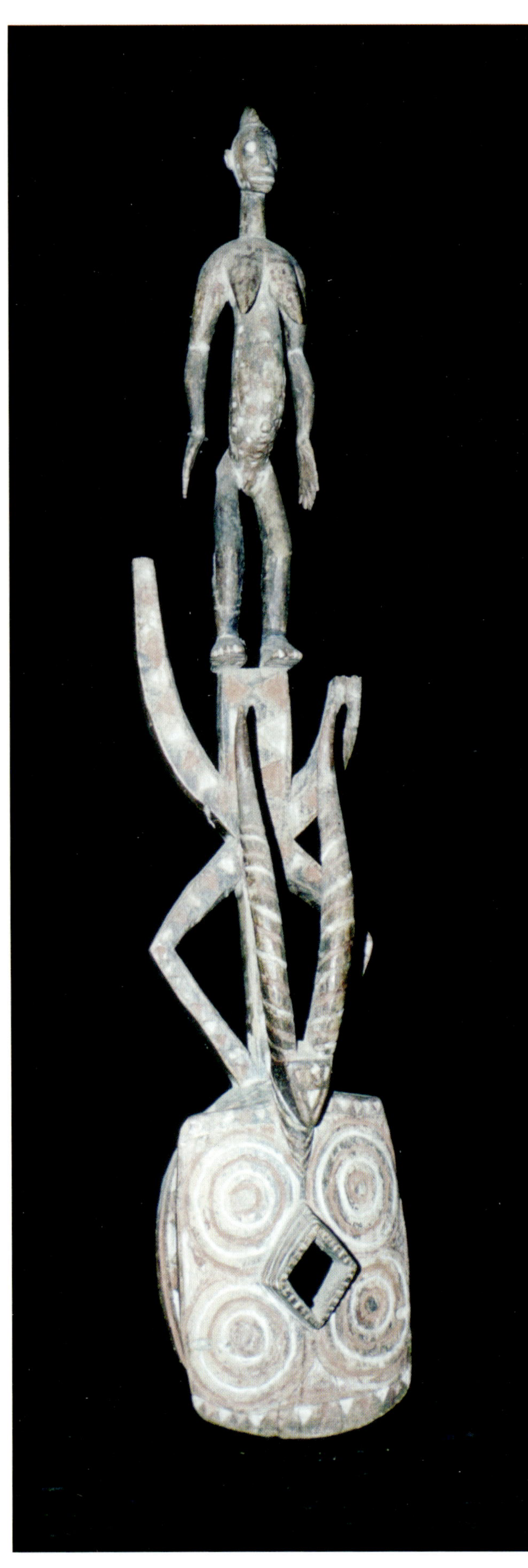

figure 2
A mask by a Mossi artist in the village of Kirsi in the national museum in Ouagadougou, Burkina Faso, 1976
The mask has since been stolen and sold into a private collection
Photo by Christopher D. Roy

Triandé was also involved in the visits to Ouagadougou of a number of important personalities in the world of African art in the 1960s and 1970s. I believe he hosted William Fagg at some point, although I don't know exactly when Fagg visited Ouagadougou. It must have been before I began graduate studies at Indiana in 1973 because one of the first books I found in the Indiana library was by Fagg, in which he wrote that "the Mossi no longer make art and most of them have become Muslim." I am quite sure that he got this drivel from Triandé. Triandé was the head of the Muslim League in Ouagadougou before he died. I am also convinced that Triandé was involved in the purchase of several very beautiful Gurunsi figures which are now in public and private collections in France and Switzerland. I suspect, but I don't know for sure, that the dealer involved was Henri Kamer. I don't imply that anything was done illegally; after all, anything could be exported with the permission of the museum director. Nothing important ever left Burkina Faso without Triandé's knowledge. Whenever I exported the production of the art centre, I was required to go to Triandé's office with a list of the objects, in triplicate, that he could sign and stamp for customs at the airport.

Triandé was also very much in control of the art dealers in Ouagadougou, who either carried objects around to the villas of European expatriates or flew with them to Paris. He made very sure that all of the art dealers showed him important objects before they left the country. The principal dealer whom I knew was named Mamadou Diarra. He was not a native of Burkina Faso (he was either from Mali or Guinea) and knew very little about what objects were used for in rural villages or what they meant. Occasionally I would engage him in conversation about where objects came from, who had owned them, how they had been used and what they meant. It was immediately obvious that he made up everything that he told me, and that he in fact knew absolutely nothing about art in rural villages. However, he could tell the difference between an old and authentic piece and a brand new copy. He was an extremely unpleasant and disreputable person. There was another very important dealer in Bobo-Dioulasso named Harouna, whom I met in 1977, and from whom I purchased a few small objects. There were also two important dealers in Ouagadougou named Issa and Bernard. I have not seen any of these people since the mid-1980s.

For at least forty years, the laws of Burkina Faso have stated that any cultural objects must be approved for export by the museum director. For decades, art dealers would fill a crate with all of the "copies" that they could find and haul it off to

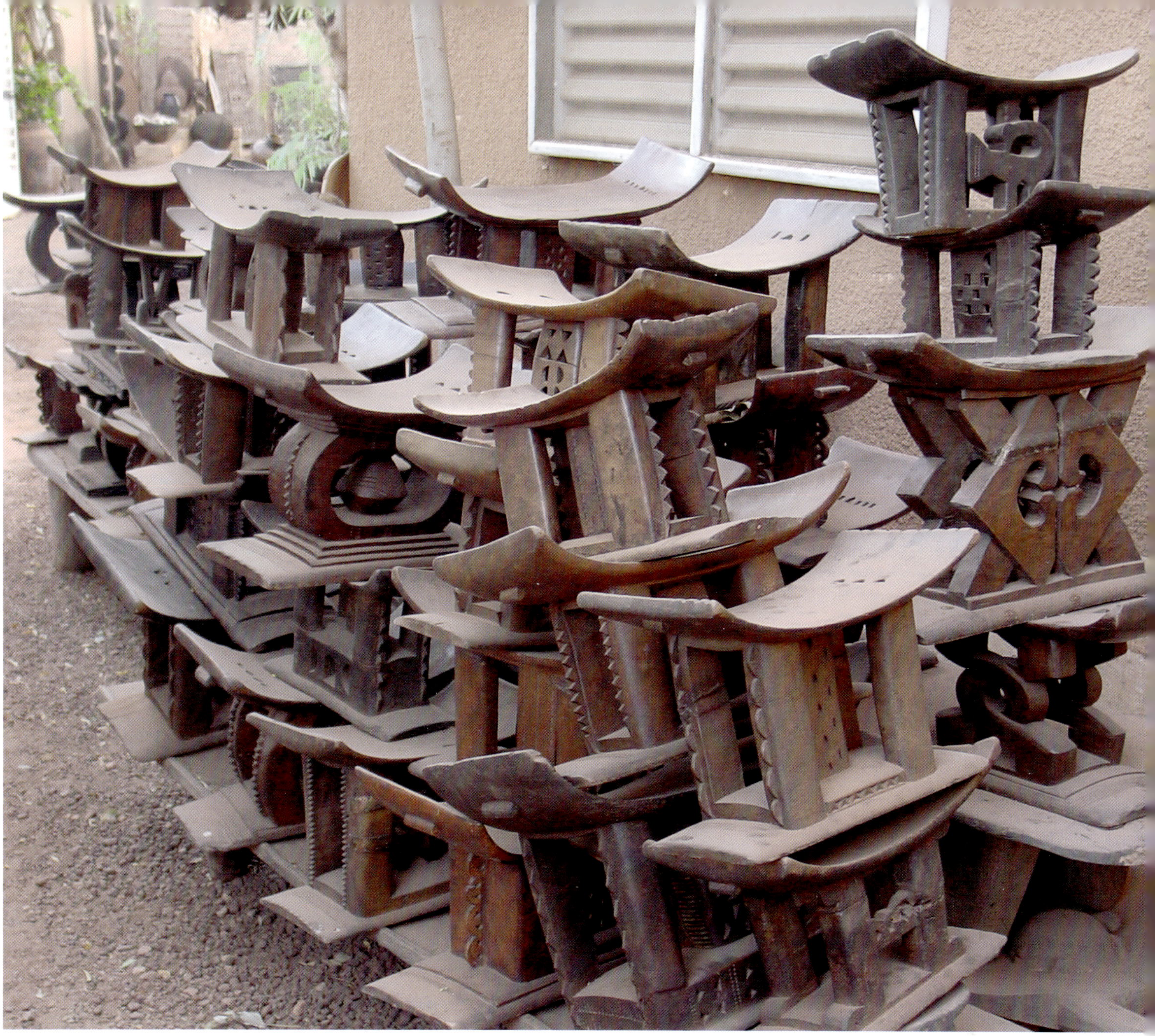

figure 3
Asante stools stacked for shipment in the courtyard of an art dealer in Ouagadougou, Burkina Faso, 2014
Photo by Christopher D. Roy

the art museum, where the director looked at it and signed an inventory saying that the items were all approved for export. The art dealers then substituted very valuable, high-quality cultural treasures for the old copies, submitted the list to customs at the airport, where the customs official merely counted to make sure that the number of objects in the crate matched the number on the inventory, and shipped them out of the country. This is how so many objects of value left the country so easily.

Today in Ouagadougou, there is an excellent shop, in a private home right next to the radio station, which was owned by a former pilot for Air Afrique and is now owned and run by his son.[6] These men are quite knowledgeable, and they sell both old and heavily worn but authentic objects such as stools, as well as hundreds of other kinds of objects from all over West Africa. In some cases, these have obviously been purchased in bulk and they are stored outside the house (Fig. 3). In other cases, the objects are quite beautiful, in good condition, and valuable; these are displayed inside the home. The men also sell new objects they have commissioned, including beautiful Tuareg

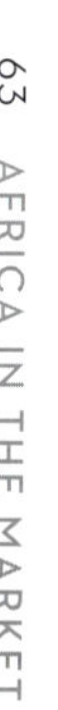

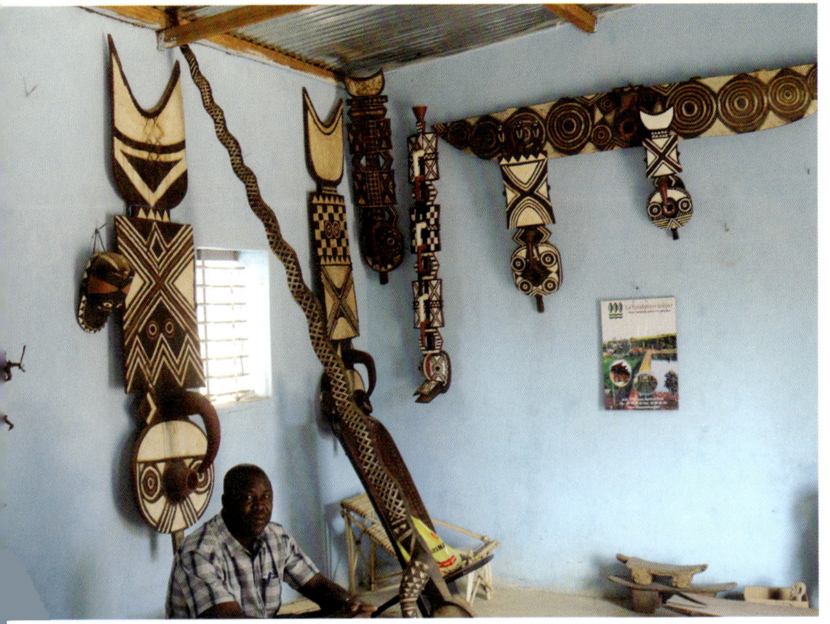

figure 4 (top)
The sales gallery of Yacouba Bondé, with several Bwa masks for sale
Village of Boni, Burkina Faso, 2012
Photo by Christopher D. Roy

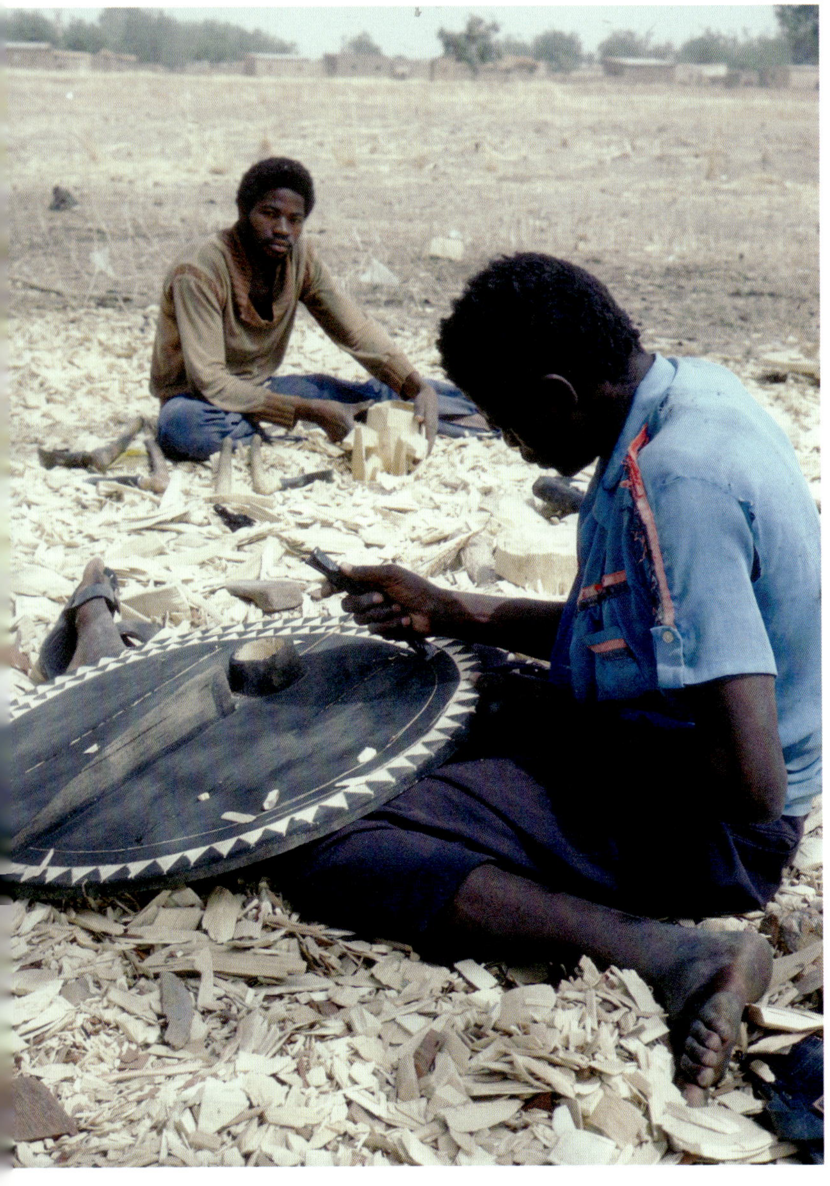

figure 5 (bottom)
Two carvers of the Konaté family carving "sun" masks for the tourist market
Village of Ouri, Burkina Faso, 1985
Photo by Christopher D. Roy

jewelry made of silver. There is a wonderful mix of valuable, high-quality, authentic pieces and blatantly "decorative" tourist objects ("copies"), but most of the latter are of good quality, and if you can recognize the difference, it is worth a visit. The sellers are both professional and ethical, and I think that their shop has become the place Ouagadougou expatriates go to today for good-quality objects. I am quite sure that whenever they export, they do all of the paperwork required. Every time I go to Ouagadougou I stop at their shop and purchase jewellery for my wife and daughter. I once purchased a Senufo *kpelie* mask that is either authentic or has been so perfectly faked that it is difficult for me to detect how it has been done, even after having seen a thousand fakes offered by art dealers. It is an excellent testament to the skills of the dealers in Korhogo, Côte d'Ivoire, in aging art.

The major source of most of the objects carved for export and sold in Ouagadougou and Bobo-Dioulasso are the families of artists in such towns as Boni and Ouri. There are many, many others throughout the country but these are the two that I know best. There are still hundreds of extremely skilled and talented artists all over Burkina Faso who regularly carve excellent objects to be used in a traditional village context. The principal characters are Yacouba Bondé in the Bwa village of Boni (Fig. 4), and the several carvers of the Konaté family in the Winiama village of Ouri, north of Boromo (Fig. 5). All of these artists are quite legitimate and are doing nothing at all illegal. They are extremely creative, and I have enjoyed many years of visiting them and speaking with them about the objects they carve that are used in their villages. I wrote an extensive article for the second edition of the catalogue titled *Art and Life in Africa: Selections from the Stanley Collection* (1991) in which I talked about the fact that the Konaté carvers are able to carve objects in several different styles for all of the people who live in the region (a direct attack on the idea

figure 6
Bomavé Konaté with a Bobo-style mask he has carved
Ouri, Burkina Faso, 1985
Photo by Christopher D. Roy

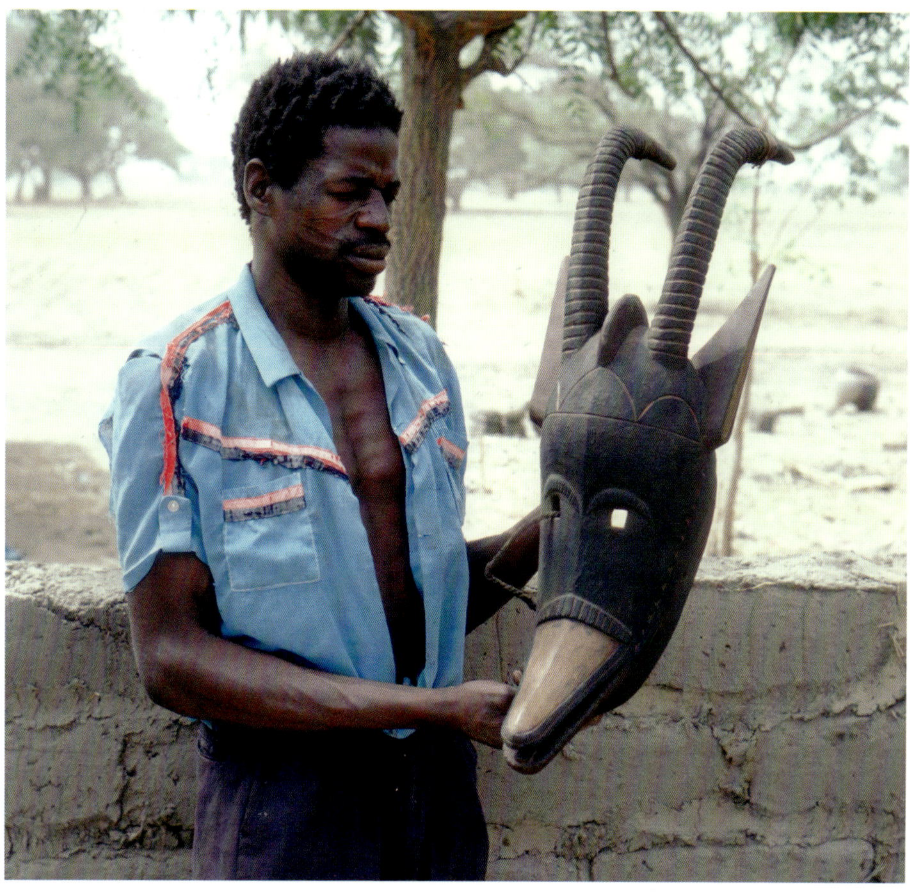

of "one tribe, one style"). They are by no means limited to the styles of their own group of people, but can and do carve in at least five other ethnic groups' styles (Fig. 6). The very first time I visited them in 1983, there was an enormous pile of brand new carved "sun" masks of the type that have been illustrated in European catalogues (Fig. 7). These had been stacked up ready to be sent off to Ouagadougou. I was told that one of the men in the family would load them on his moped and take them to Ouagadougou the next day. The numbers of these objects and the income they generate are so small that the carvers cannot possibly survive just by carving objects for traditional use. All of them carve large numbers of what they call "copies" to be sold in Ouagadougou. The Konatés have a sales shop in the roadside town of Boromo, and Yacouba Bondé has a sales shop right next to the main highway in Boni. Tourists regularly stop at both places to look at objects and to make purchases. I think they feel reassured that they are getting authentic things because they are buying them in rural towns instead of in the capital city.

In 2006 Nora and I visited the village of Gorom-Gorom, north of Dori in the Sahel. There were two young Peace Corps volunteers there, a married couple, who had been given the task of organizing craftwork by local Fulani and Tuareg artists. They had done an excellent job of cataloguing the individual artists and their work, and they were providing expert advice to the artists on the export and sale of their work. They were extremely knowledgeable about the excellent artistic creativity of the people in the area. I think that this couple had a very positive impact on the art market in that part of Burkina Faso. Unfortunately the young couple suffered in the summer of 2006 when terrible rainstorms flooded the area and destroyed much of their home. I have no idea if that project has been continued. It would be wonderful if the Peace Corps saw the benefit to the economy of Burkina Faso and to the well-being of the artists, and continued to staff such helpful projects.

I have been pleasantly surprised over the years at the fine-quality objects current artists produce in Burkina Faso. These objects include everything from wooden masks to brass castings, printed and woven textiles, excellent leather work and outstanding pottery. On several occasions I have had the opportunity to purchase new masks, just carved, that had been commissioned by rural villagers but then never paid for. These are skillfully carved and essentially indistinguishable, except by age, from objects in important public and private collections. I remonstrate with the dealers who subject such fine objects to elaborate processes, especially smoking, to make them appear old. I try to explain that the objects are wonderful even if they are not old. They respond by telling me that tourists will never purchase even an excellent object if it does not look ancient. One of the better objects that Esther Dagan collected is an

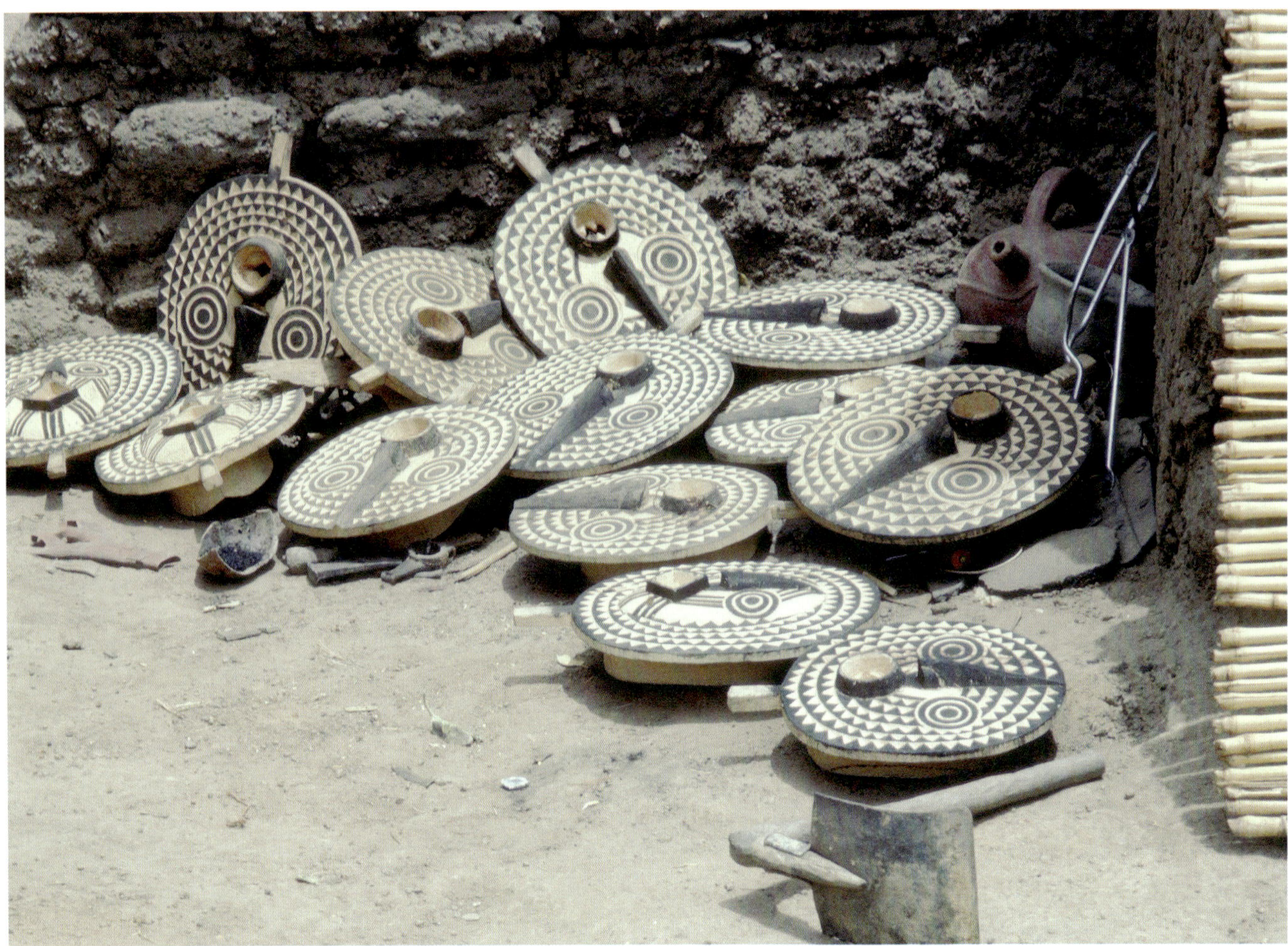

figure 7
Several "sun" masks, carved by the Konatés for the tourist market, ready for shipment to Ouagadougou, Burkina Faso, 1983
Photo by Christopher D. Roy

excellent Nouna mask representing a large beaked bird. It is by the same artist as, and virtually indistinguishable from, one that I purchased in the mid-1980s (Fig. 8). This is an excellent example of the quality of objects being carved to this day by sculptors in rural towns. The object now in the ROM seems to have been lightly smoked, but it does not appear to have been spoiled by art dealers the way so many others have been.

The objects in the collection of Esther Dagan include both "authentic" pieces and "copies." The stools are especially good (Fig. 9), and the Mossi dolls are quite typical of the kinds of objects little children play with in villages. Many of these are dusty and broken because children play with them and then neglect them, leaving them outside in all kinds of weather. In the mid-1980s I purchased several brand new, beautifully carved Mossi dolls in the Ouagadougou market for twenty-five cents each. One fine example is currently on public display in the Smithsonian Institution. Some of the Lobi figures are authentic and old, if not terribly well carved. Most Lobi men feel qualified to carve figures, whether they are talented or not, and so there is a great range in expertise and quality. Several of the masks show clear evidence of having been used in rural villages in a "traditional" context. The Kurumba antelope crest (Fig. 10) is among my favourites because it is very similar to several that were displayed at the Ouahigouya regional fair in 1971. The Kurumba artist brought several of these to the fair to display, and I was about to purchase some or all of them for the art centre when Toumani Triandé suddenly appeared and bought them all to take to the art museum in Ouagadougou to sell himself. I am convinced that it was from conversations with Triandé about this experience that William Fagg got his mistaken impressions of the creativity of Kurumba artists. Fagg wrote very condescending and dismissive comments about contemporary Kurumba sculpture that have unfortunately persisted to the present. The Kurumba mask in the ROM is beautifully carved, and could easily have been used by a performer in Arabinda (Fig. 11).

figure 8
Bird mask
Unidentified artist or workshop
Nouna style
Wood, pigment
Purchased in 1981 from a dealer at the market of Ouagadougou, Burkina Faso
Height: 22.7 cm, Length: 99 cm, Width: 25 cm
ROM 2009.126.156

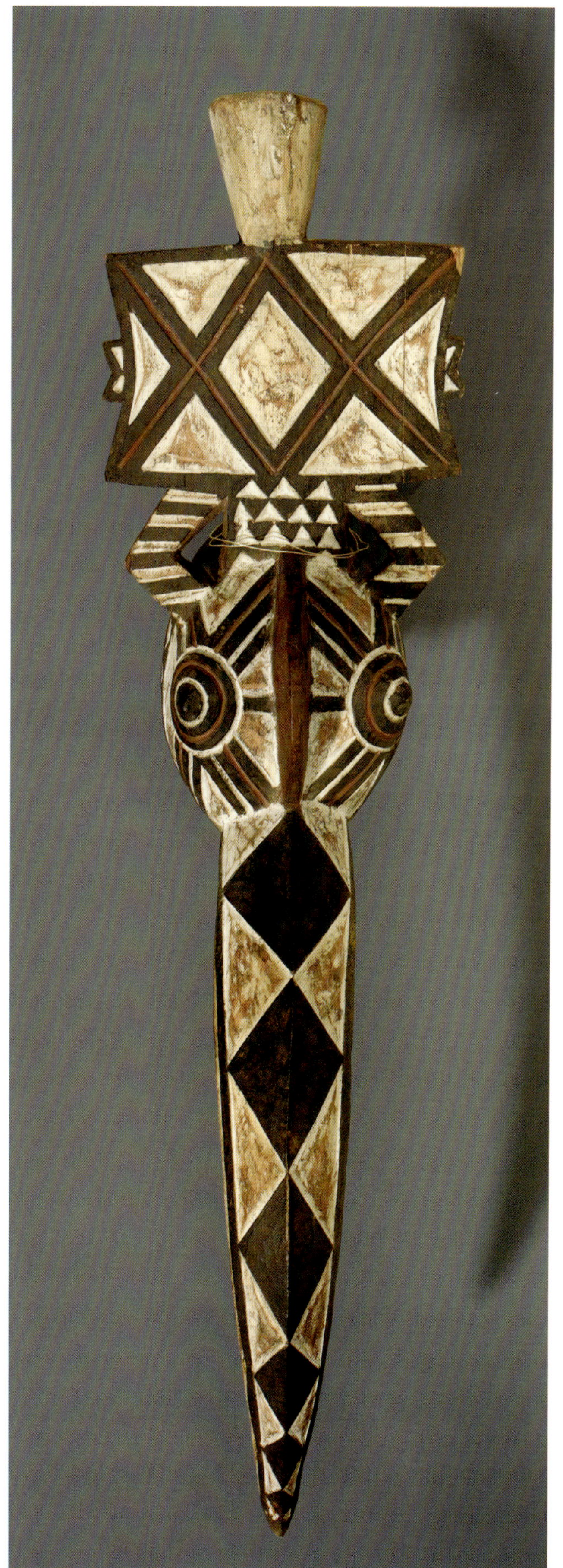

The Amrad Collection also includes several staffs from various peoples in Burkina. The staffs are all perfectly authentic, extremely old and excellent examples of the sorts of staffs that are used by diviners throughout central Burkina Faso. I own several such myself. On the other hand, there are a significant number of masks that are completely typical of the sorts of tourist objects that are sold in the stalls near the Place d'Armes or in front of the Hotel Independence.

As Christopher Steiner has correctly pointed out in *African Art in Transit*, African art dealers are extremely adept at making new objects appear to be old. In Burkina Faso masks and other objects of wood are often stored in the rafters of kitchens where the soot from the cooking fires keeps them free of insect damage. Dealers try to reproduce the dark surface by "smoking" new masks. For many years collectors and tourists inspected the backs of masks to see if there were signs of sweat stains where the mask rested against the cheeks and forehead of the performer. It wasn't long before African dealers began to bleach the wood with common household bleach to reproduce the effect of sweat stains. When dealers in Burkina Faso noticed that clients inspected the holes pierced around the edge of the mask to see if there were signs of wear that results when the fibre costumes are attached, the dealers began to rub and abrade the wood to imitate the signs of years of use.

It is a mistake to make too many assumptions about the history of an object based on its appearance after it has left Africa. I had a remarkable experience in 1977 in the Mossi village of Seguenega. I was attending a funeral in a very conservative *sukwaba* community. Among the last masks to appear was a red, black and white mask with a black fibre costume and two broad horns. The mask was called *katre*, the hyena. It was a red, black and blue Guro *zamble* mask that had been repainted in the colours red, black and white that are traditionally used by Mossi families. The mask had been purchased in one of the tourist art stalls in Abidjan, Côte d'Ivoire, by a young man of the family who was working in the bicycle factory there. He wrapped the tourist piece up in a burlap bag and carried it with him on the train back to Ouagadougou. He gave it to his father and grandfather, who repainted it and named it after their sacred protective spirit. The senior elders of the family were quite happy to have such an object because they thought that it was beautifully carved and would serve their purposes quite well. They were not at all concerned about where it had been carved or by whom.

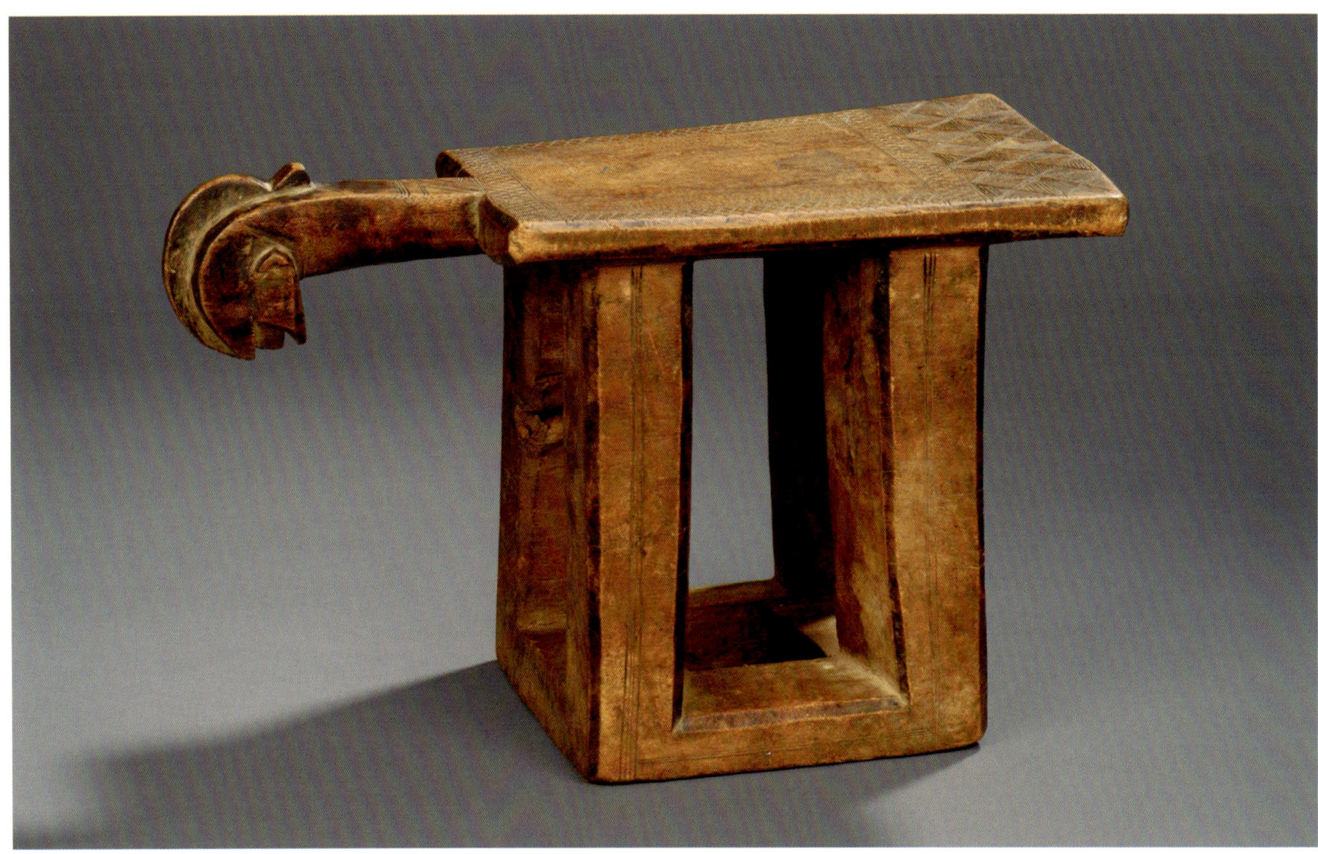

figure 9
Stool
Unidentified artist or workshop
Bwa style
Wood
Purchased in 1981 from a dealer at the market of Ouagadougou, Burkina Faso
Height: 21.6 cm, Width: 35 cm, Depth: 17 cm
ROM 2009.126.10

figure 10 (opposite)
Antelope headcrest
Unidentified artist or workshop
Kurumba style
Wood, pigment
Purchased in 1981 from a dealer at the market of Ouagadougou, Burkina Faso
Height: 83 cm, Width: 9.5 cm, Depth: 31 cm
ROM 2009.126.147

And so an object carved for the tourist market in Côte d'Ivoire became a "traditional" Mossi mask. I think that this example is particularly important, because it addresses the whole issue of authenticity. The piece was perfectly authentic at least as far as the senior Mossi elders who used it were concerned. Do we decide that an object is authentic if it has been used by a rural African community to represent their beliefs? A curator like me might look at such an object and wonder how a Guro mask came to be painted red, black and white, and dismiss it out of hand as some sort of a fake or tourist object. But that would be a terrible mistake. If the mask ever turns up in a Western collection, I wonder what the collector or curator will make of it.

In 2010 I visited Ouri again as I have tried to do almost every year. I visited the Konatés and spent a couple of pleasant afternoons talking with them and with a good friend of mine who is a senior elder of the Winiama community. He had just had a brand new bush buffalo mask carved to replace an older one that was damaged and worn. He had given the old mask to a Konaté carver to take to Ouagadougou to sell. The new mask was very large and looked like it was old because it had been smoked (Fig. 12). I had seen the mask perform and I was able to inspect the mask up close myself. I said to him, "But this looks older than it really is, it has been smoked." His response was, "But Chris, I wanted it to look like the one in your book." He clearly respected me as much as I respected him, and he could see from my book what it is that I valued. He could see from the illustrations in my book that the older objects showed some signs of use and wear, including smoke. He lives right across the road from a major carving family, and understood very well that old objects often showed signs of storage in the rafters of women's kitchens. And so he chose to emulate those important masks that he saw illustrated in my book.

I enjoy commissioning new masks from the carvers in the villages I know. My office at the University of Iowa is cluttered with masks that I've purchased directly from the artists over the years. The traditional pigments—which include a brick red made from ground hematite, a glossy black made from the boiled seed pods of the acacia tree, and a bright white that is made from the excrement dug from the burrows of small lizards (or sometimes from classroom chalk)—are all clear and bright. Of course it is very difficult for most tourists to do as I do and visit the workshops of these carvers in remote rural villages.

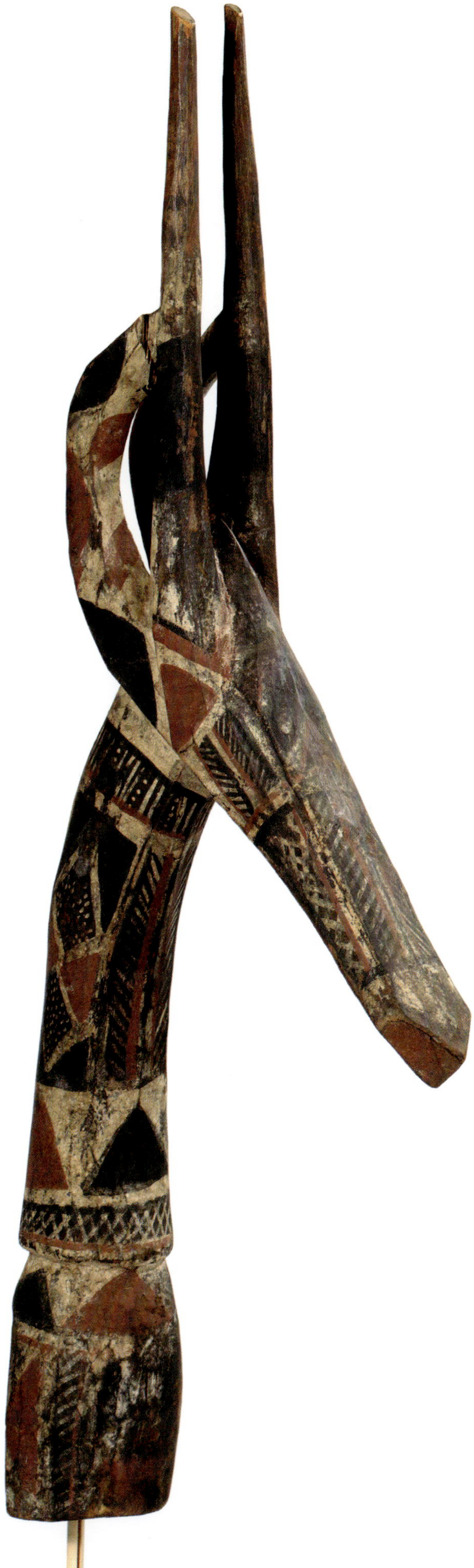

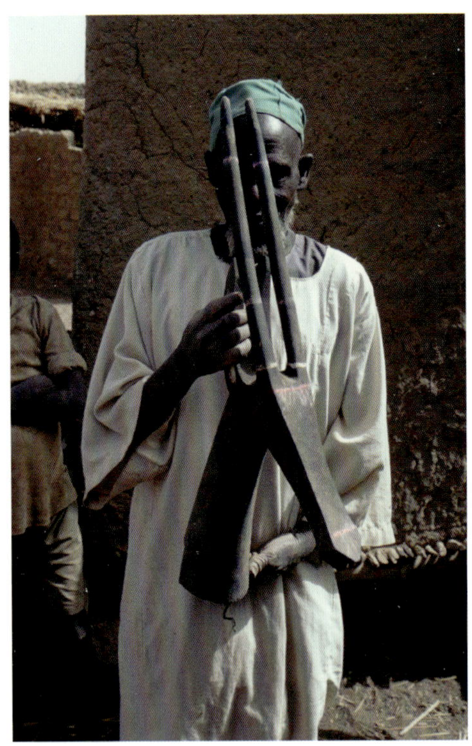

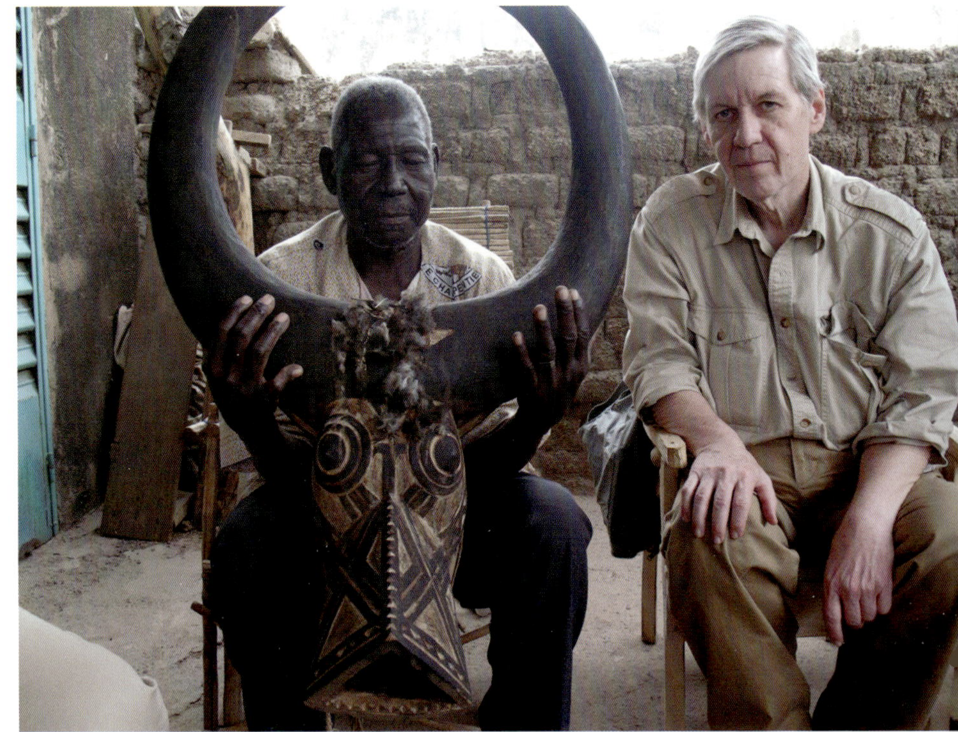

It is important to understand that all of the peoples of Burkina Faso repaint their masks each year before they are used for the first time. The masks that appear in performances in villages all are brightly painted in red, white and black, or in the case of the Bobo, with a broader palette of colours. The only peoples I have ever known who allow active masks to become darkened with age or sooty and black with patina are the Winiama in central Burkina Faso. Many of the artists who carve these masks now paint them with bright enamel paints rather than the more traditional red and white mineral pigments, and with the sticky, glossy black created by boiling down acacia seed pods. It is true that many of the very old masks that are owned by senior elders and are stored in their bedrooms become darkened with age, but these masks rarely if ever appear in public performances. Unfortunately, these old masks are frequently the targets of thieves.

Without a doubt the major development in the art of Burkina Faso in the past thirty years has been the dramatic increase in the number of public mass performances that are organized either by the government or by local communities. In the 1970s masks only performed outside of the village for the occasional regional fairs that the government organized every year in different towns and cities around Burkina Faso. During the period from 1970 to 1972, these regional fairs were held in Ouahigouya, Po, Bobo-Dioulasso and Koudougou. I don't recall having seen any masks in Ouahigouya, but I do distinctly remember seeing performances in the southern city of Po. While I was director of the art centre in Ouagadougou, I was invited to a conference at the town hall where a group of expatriate French administrators talked about the needs that Burkina Faso (then Upper Volta) had for the tourist industry. One of the things they mentioned was creating a living history museum and the other was organizing more regional fairs where the arts and crafts of the country could be displayed. This was in the very early stages of the organization of the film festival FESPACO. I think in the early years, FESPACO included some performances by masks that were invited to come in from rural villages. Because FESPACO was only organized every second year, people in Bobo-Dioulasso began to organize a different cultural festival called the annual week of culture, Semaine National de la Culture (SNC). This included large numbers of mask performances. In addition, the association for the preservation of masks, or ASAMA, in the town of Dédougou began to organize a mask festival, Festival des Masques (FESTIMA) that takes place every second year. Masks from all over the northern part of Burkina Faso attend and perform at FESTIMA, and masks from outside the country were also occasionally invited. When I attended this festival in 2006, there were masks from Switzerland, Côte d'Ivoire, Mali and the country of Benin (Fig. 13). There are similar public mask performances now in several towns across Burkina Faso. One of the best is in the central town of Pouni. There may be others in the northwest that I have not visited, but I certainly would enjoy doing that.

FESPACO is a major international cultural event. It is to be taken seriously. Large numbers of filmmakers from all over Africa, large numbers of tourists who are interested in cinema, and significant numbers of non-African filmmakers attend the event. There are many excellent theatres in Ouagadougou in which the films are shown. Ouagadougou has been a centre for African filmmaking for decades. Many of the most prominent filmmakers in Africa are from Burkina Faso (Gaston Kaboré, Idrissa Ouédraogo, Annette Danto, Haile Gerima, Fanta Régina Nacro, S. Pierre Yameogo). Prize-winning films by Africans are often shown in Ouagadougou, and films shown at FESPACO for the first time sometimes receive prizes outside of Africa.

The film and craft festivals in Ouagadougou (FESPACO

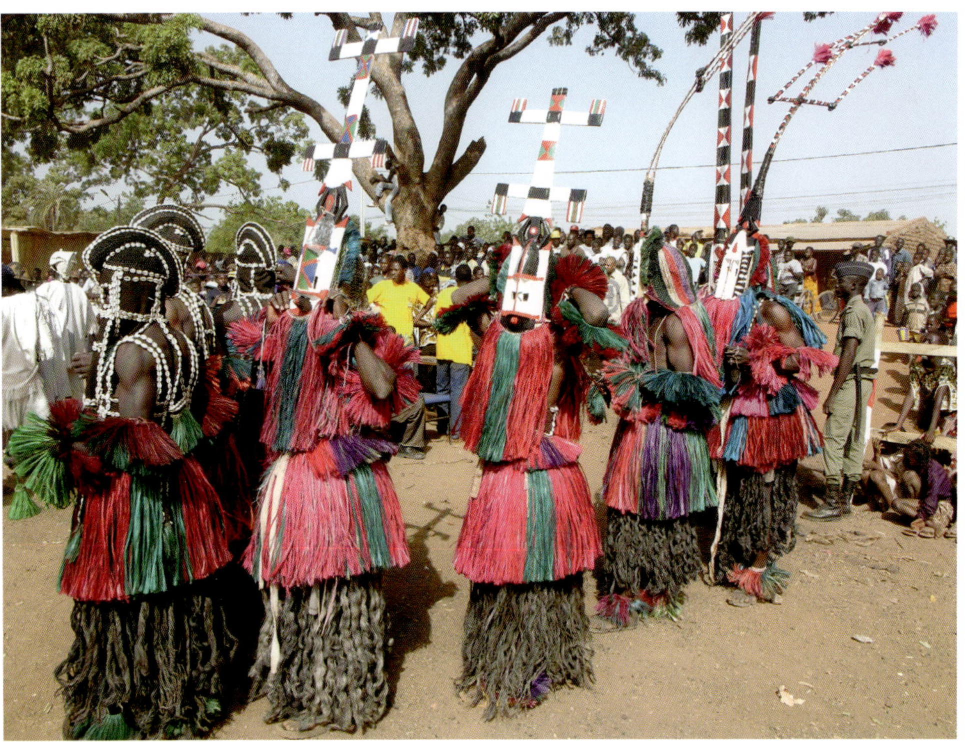

figure 11 (opposite left)
A Kurumba artist in the village of Arabinda holding an antelope mask he has carved
Burkina Faso, 1985
Photo by Christopher D. Roy

figure 12 (opposite right)
Yiriko Gnamou and Christopher Roy with Gnamou's "old" bush buffalo mask, recently carved
Ouri, Burkina Faso, 2014
Photo courtesy of Christopher D. Roy

figure 13
Dogon masks at the FESTIMA festival in Burkina Faso, 2006
Photo by Christopher D. Roy

and SIAO), and the regional mask performance festivals in towns such as Dédougou (FESTIMA) have contributed enormously to an increase in the income from tourism in Burkina Faso in the past thirty to forty years. Very large numbers of Europeans and Americans attend FESPACO. Significant numbers of strangers as well as buyers for retailers attend SIAO. Quite a few intrepid travelers go to Dédougou every second year to attend the mask festival. Unfortunately, Dédougou is quite typical of most rural towns in Burkina Faso in that there is almost no infrastructure for tourism. The two hotels in town are rundown and certainly not very comfortable. There is one good restaurant in town that serves clean and tasty food. The road from Koudougou to Dédougou was bad clay washboard (*tole*) in 2006, but it has since been paved. I once dreamed of constructing an inexpensive earth brick (*adobe*) hotel in the village of Boni that could house tourists in clean and inexpensive surroundings, but I have never been able to raise the necessary funding. Once upon a time (the mid-1980s) there was an absolutely delightful hotel in the town of Markoye, in the far northern part of Burkina at the south edge of the Sahara, that was maintained by the French magazine *Le Point*. The hotel was provided for tourists who flew on *Le Point* charter flights from Paris. It was picturesque, tidy, clean, efficient and built inexpensively with local materials. I visited it in 1985 but I have not been back since. It would contribute enormously to the tourism income in Burkina Faso were some investor, government agency, or NGO to invest in a string of small, clean, attractive hotels in some of the cities and towns outside the capital and outside Bobo-Dioulasso. In conversations with current and former ministers of tourism, I have been told that to construct such hotels would contribute in very important ways to the economic well-being of the entire country. Perhaps Donald Trump or Sir Richard Branson would be interested in investing in a chain of hotels across rural Burkina Faso.

I have enjoyed working in Burkina Faso for well over forty years, in great part because so many people continue to make and use wonderful art. In spite of serious development, health and education deficits, this small country has not suffered many of the problems of neighbouring countries such as Mali and Niger, where the dramatic increase in the spread of Islam has led to a decline in the visual arts; or Ghana and Nigeria, where Christianity has had such a negative impact on "traditional" culture. Certainly there has never been any attempt to emulate Côte d'Ivoire or Guinea-Conakry and establish government-sponsored secular dance programs that bear no relation whatsoever to ancient African religion and art. Even in the most difficult period, from 1984 to 1987, Burkina Faso was, and still is, a country in which it is very easy to travel and to do research, relatively free of the violence, crime, bribery, kickbacks and corruption that plague other West African countries. The result is that Burkina Faso continues to be a wonderful place to visit and a very rich field for research in the visual arts.

---

1 "Le Centre national d'artisanat d'art: point de mire de le filière artisat au Burkina," lefaso.net, last modified October 14, 2004, http://www.lefaso.net/spip.php?article4508.

2 "Editorial," Village Artisanal de Ouagadougou, last modified 2009, http://www.villageartisanal-ouaga.com.

3 "Report de la 14e édition du Salon," Salon International de l'Artisanat de Ouagadougou, last modified 2014, http://www.siao.bf/.

4 Ibid.

5 "Panafrican Film and Television Festival of Ouagadougou," http://www.fespaco.bf/en/.

6 "The Art Gallery," Arts and Craft of Africa, last modified 2010, http://www.africartisanat.com/index.php.

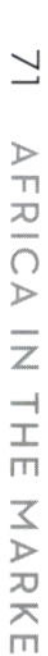

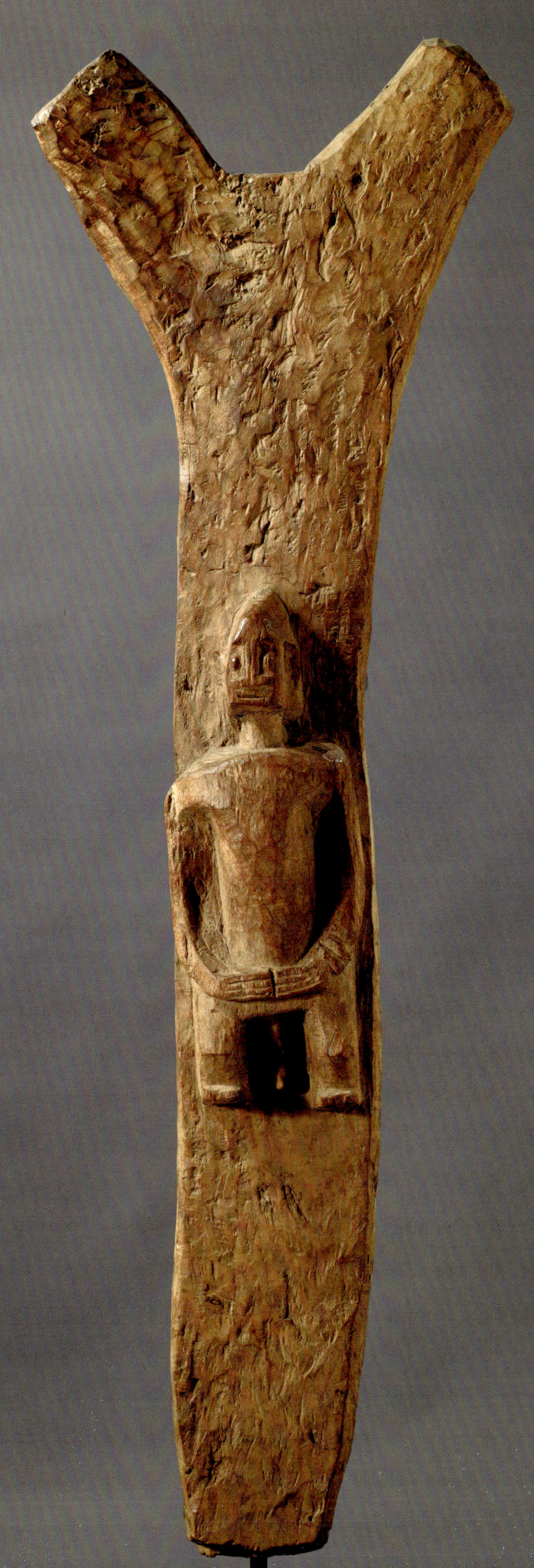

plate 5

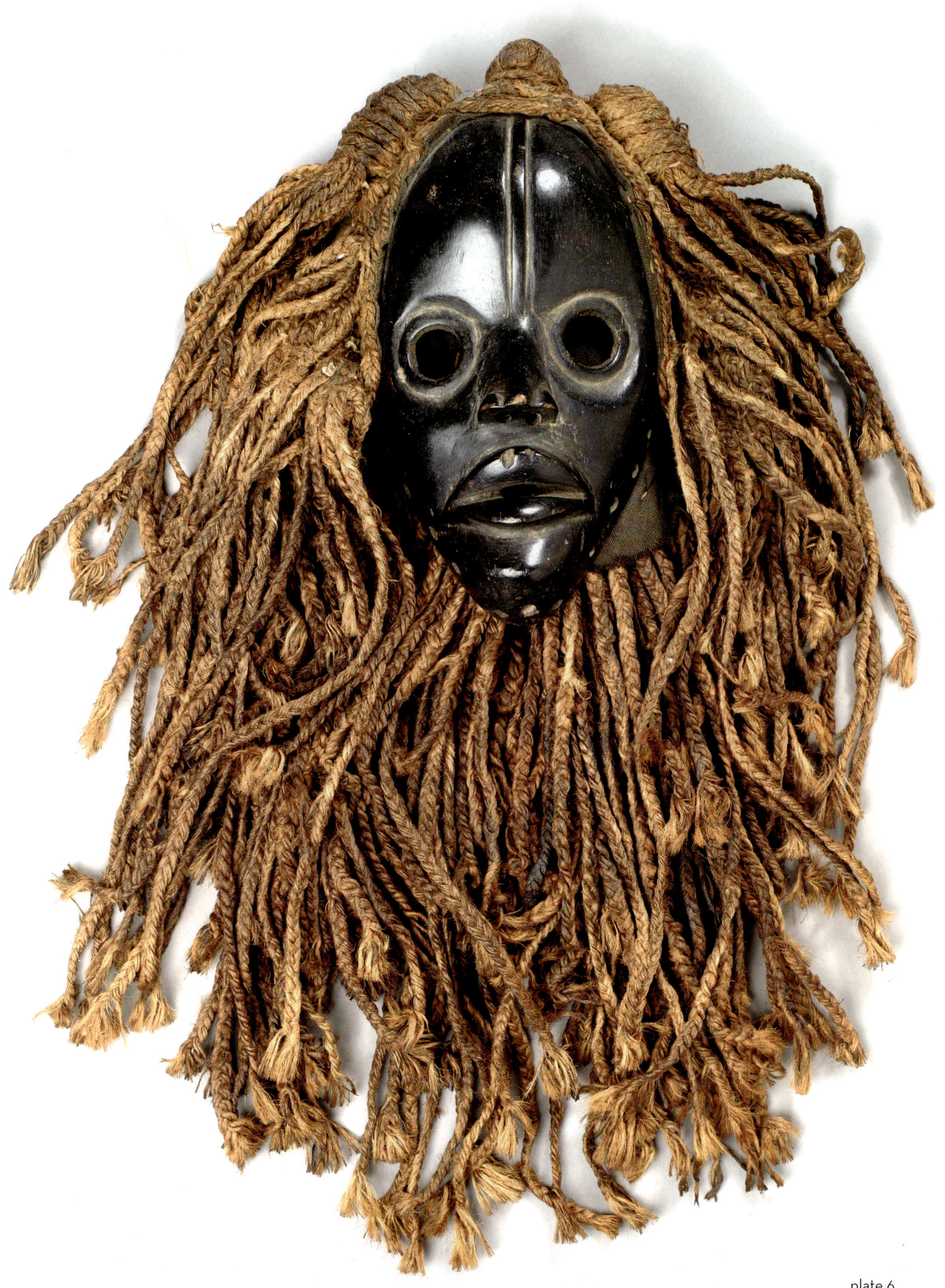

plate 6

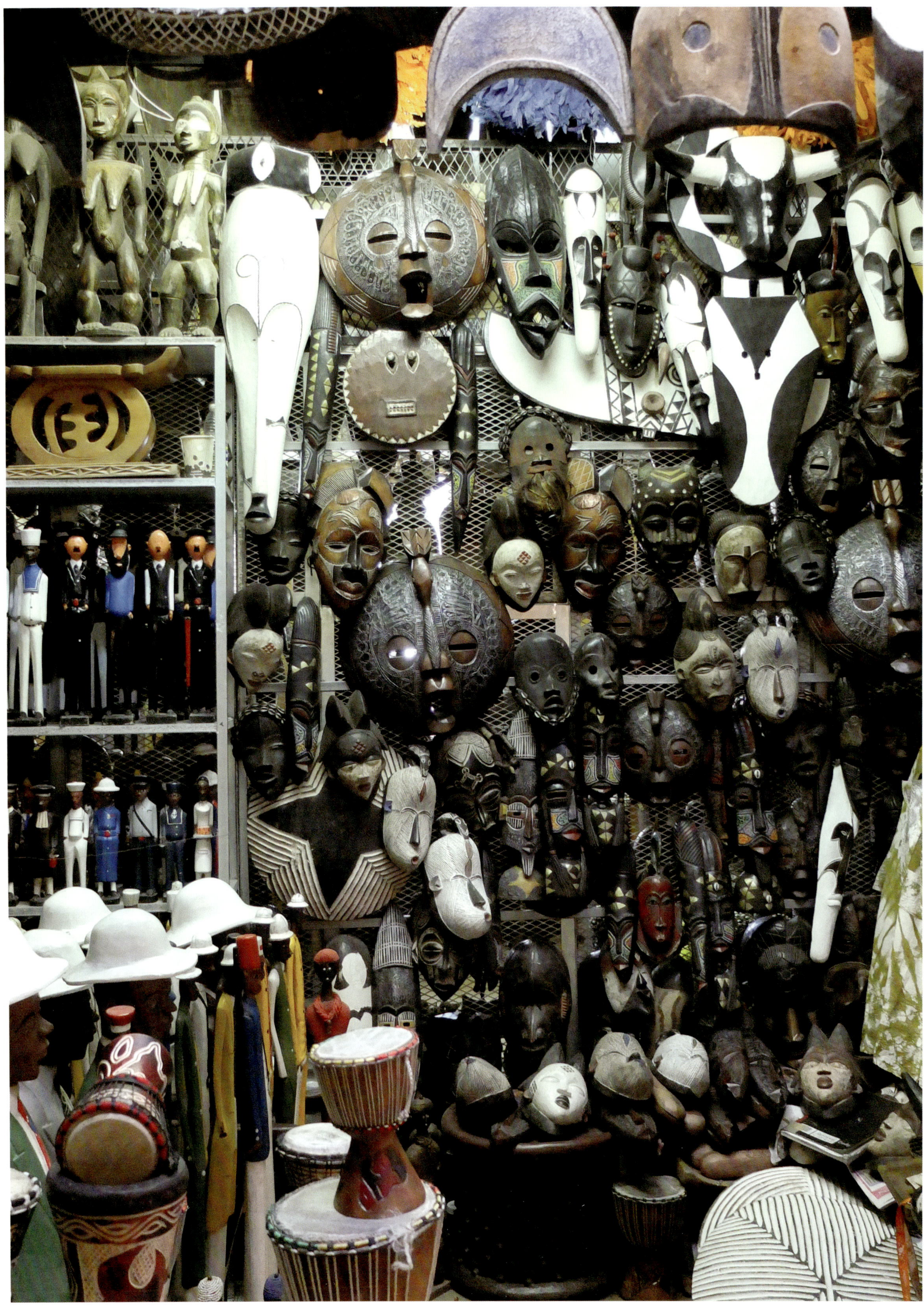

CHAPTER 4

NEW MARKETS, NEW PATRONS: WORK-TRADE RELATIONSHIPS IN A WEST AFRICAN ART MARKET

TILL FÖRSTER

Many African artworks collected over the past 120 years reflect transformations of work and trade induced by the colonial penetration of the continent. The colonial powers built roads and railways, which facilitated long-distance transport, stimulated the emergence of urban settlements and enabled a division of labour that did not exist in most rural societies. Many artisans, among them sculptors, weavers, and others, made use of the new opportunities and profited from such transformations. In addition, the emerging communities of civil servants, missionaries and their visitors changed art patronage profoundly. During the period of decolonialization and the first two or three decades of independence, tourism and the international networks of the art market led, for the first time in West Africa's history, to an intensified manufacturing of masks and figures that comes close to mass production.

The changing relationship among work, consumption and trade often becomes manifest as changing style and genre. My essay tries to trace this transformation over the past hundred years. More than other West African countries, Côte d'Ivoire, with its once comparatively successful economy, lends itself to such an analysis. I look at four periods that were characterized by specific configurations of artisanal work and trade. Though related to specific moments in history, these configurations, or figurations,[1] overlapped and at times existed parallel to each other. Pre-colonial times, and later the more local interactions parallel to the emerging overland art market, were characterized by separation of work in workshops and trade or barter. This figuration led to fairly stable genres and styles. Under colonial domination, it transformed into a market-driven figuration.

After independence, the country's strong economic growth—*le miracle ivoirien* (the Ivorian miracle)—attracted art and curio dealers from many other parts of Africa and also from Europe. From the early 1950s, and more so after independence, Hausa and Senegalese traders served as intermediaries, linking local networks to the wider curio and art market. When Côte d'Ivoire increasingly slid into an economic and later a political and military crisis, these figurations of work and trade changed again. Under rebel domination, patronage by "big men" (rebel leaders) replaced most other forms of interaction. It led back to stable genres sustained by local patronage under the umbrella of rebels and their leaders. Finally, after the end of civil war in 2011, very little was left of the existing, older relationship between work and trade. Many artisans and local artists complained about the collapse of the art market and gave up their workshops in favour of other business.

At a more theoretical level, this essay links Arjun Appadurai's concept of the social life of things and Igor Kopytoff's cultural biography of things to a classical, art historical understanding of genre and a sociological conceptualization of agency and action.[2] I argue that the transformations described in this essay pushed older genres into an accelerated articulation of difference, while the actors increasingly depended on foreign markets, which finally led to a deadlock when the patronage associated with these markets was no longer accessible to them.

detail
Selection of art from all over the continent in the market stall of an Ivoirian art dealer in Rosebank market Johannesburg, 2013
Photo by Till Förster

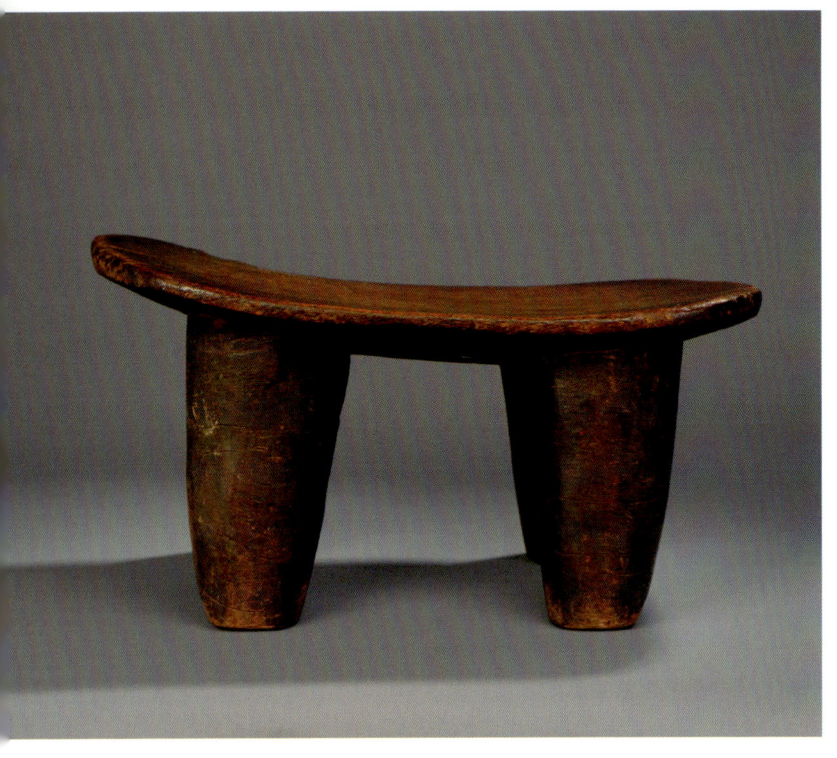

figure 1
Stool, *kul*
Unidentified artist or workshop
Senufo style
Wood
Purchased in 1981 from a dealer at the market of Korhogo, Côte d'Ivoire
Height: 23.5 cm, Width: 48 cm, Depth: 31.5 cm
ROM 2009.126.15

Artisanal Life and Barter in Pre-Colonial Times

Since at least the eighteenth century, long-distance trade routes have linked old trade centres of Manding-speaking people along the Middle Niger River to the fringes of the rainforest, where slaves, ivory, cola nuts and other commodities were exchanged for cloth, salt and some precious metals. The savannah that lies between the former empire of medieval Mali, its successor states in the North and the rainforest in the South was mainly inhabited by subsistence farmers who had no central political institutions and spoke another language. The colonial conquerors later labelled them as Senufo, a corrupted version of what they had heard from their interpreters: "those who greet by saying *syene*."[3]

The Manding-speaking interlocutors of the French saw the Senufo as *bamana*—peasants that "did not believe in God."[4] Among the farmers lived a number of artisanal groups. With few exceptions, these groups were neatly integrated into the acephalous society of the Senufo and shared the farmers' local religion. They also practiced the same rites and ceremonies. Like the farmers, the artisanal groups participated in the cycle of *poro*, a so-called secret society. The biggest artisanal group were the *fonobele*, the smiths, as all farmers needed the tools they were producing. Besides forging the blades of hoes, smiths also sculpted the appropriate handles and other household items such as spoons and stools (Fig. 1). Some smiths developed more skills and carved masks and statuettes for ritual purposes. The experts in these genres, however, were the *kulibele*, another artisanal group that specialized exclusively in carving and did not work iron.

Strictly speaking, there was no long-distance trade in wooden objects in pre-colonial times. Such objects were too heavy and their value was too low to make them worth carrying over long distances, compared to the rare and precious commodities that accounted for most of the inner West African trade. Smaller objects, such as household utensils and the few pieces of furniture that an ordinary Senufo compound owned, were produced ahead of demand by less-skilled carvers, often by apprentices, and offered on local markets. The customers came usually from the same village or rarely from a neighbouring village. This sort of petty trade made use of habitual tools of measurement. Hollow moulds were filled with corn or other aliments, for instance chilli pepper, and exchanged for the desired items. To buy a spoon, for instance, meant to fill it with millet or some other grain before it changed hands. The buyer received the spoon, the seller kept the grain.

Many *kulibele*, seeing themselves as the true professional carvers, adapted to the market by travelling to villages where no carver or smith settlement existed and where they could expect, and satisfy, a demand for household objects. Such journeys could take many months if not a year or two. They were part of the life cycle of a carver: When coming of age, carvers left their homes and spent some time in distant villages, where they met other people and experienced their way of life. The young carvers thus enlarged their lifeworld—and replaced broken or rotten objects, including smaller statues (Fig. 2). After having worked far from home for some time, and when they became older, the carvers usually returned to their own villages where they reintegrated into the workshop where they had learned to carve as children.[5]

The market for prestigious, ritual objects was different. Young carvers spending their youth on the road were seldom experienced in these genres, which required more aesthetic competences and artisanal skills. Such objects were generally produced on commission, and most often only in *kulibele* colonies that had one or two bigger workshops. Because of the *kulibeles*' small numbers, such workshops did not exist everywhere. The farmers often had to purchase the masks and statues for their paraphernalia of *poro* in other, sometimes distant, villages. The customers knew where such workshops existed, and they also knew that these workshops were commissioned by *poro* lodges from afar.[6] Not being familiar with the internal organization of faraway *kulibele* settlements, farmers usually ordered such objects through the spokesperson of the carvers' lineage, the Old Carver.

figure 2
Standing figure, *tugu*
Unidentified artist or workshop
Senufo style
Wood
Purchased in 1981 from a dealer at the market of Korhogo, Côte d'Ivoire
Height: 16.5 cm, Width: 5 cm, Depth: 4.5 cm
ROM 2009.126.91

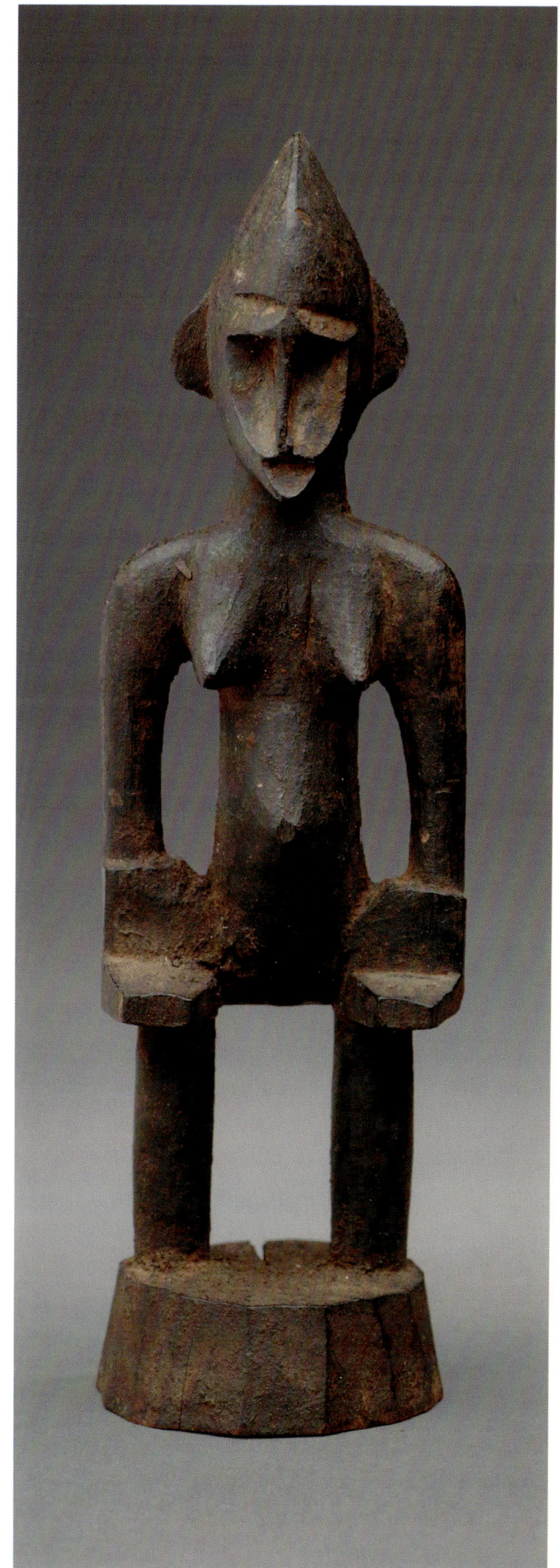

They would travel one or two days (but never as far as the Jula traders on their journeys between the Middle Niger and the fringes of the rainforest in the South).

Masks and other paraphernalia of the *poro* society were no ordinary goods of trade. Unlike household objects, ritual objects had no set price. Customers had to negotiate with the Old Carver of the *kulibele* colony that produced the objects. Customers who were members of a *poro* lodge commissioned mostly masks or statues to replace damaged or rotten older ones, or, as the market for "traditional" art increasingly penetrated the interior of Africa, objects that had "disappeared." They told the Old Carver what they wanted by referring to a standard genre, say a *kponyugu* (head of poro) mask. After having clarified whether such a mask could be carved in that *kulibele* colony, they specified which type of kponyugu they wanted. These indications most often concerned the iconography of the mask because the new mask had to replace an older one and should not look too different—it should remain recognizable as the mask of a particular *poro* lodge.

The Old Carver negotiated the price of the work. After having reached an agreement, the Old Carver decided who among the members of the workshops in the village would do the work. He also collected the advance payment, which was usually calculated in cowrie shells.[7] The carver who would later do the work was not involved. This gave the Old Carver some room to manoeuver, so that he could satisfy the customers' notion of a fair price, his own interest in keeping a little for his brokerage, and the younger carver's interest to make a living. As there was no need to apprise customers of who would execute the work, the customers, who would come back later to buy the work, were often unaware of the Old Carver's choice. Very rarely did they search for a particular sculptor to execute their order.[8]

It took little time to transform the wooden object into a commodity and later into a ritual object. The Old Carver expected an advance payment and received the remaining amount when the work was completed and had finally changed hands. This was often when disputes arose. The customers either could not pay the full amount that they and the Old Carver had agreed upon, or they were not willing to pay it. The reasons put forward were often the quality of the wood, but sometimes also the execution of the work by the carver. As they had not seen the object before coming back to the *kulibele* settlement, there was very little they could do. The work was done, and they as customers could only accept it or reject it.

As paraphernalia of *poro* were most often replacing older pieces, the representatives of the respective *poro* lodge were mainly concered with the iconography and sometimes criticized the completed artwork because it did not reproduce one or another other iconographic element that they had wanted and asked for when commissioning the work. Such disputes were, however, extremely rare, said my interlocutors among the *kulibele*.[9] Most often, the money was handed over to the Old Carver who then forwarded a part to the artist.

Workshops were social spaces separated from the exchange or trade of the masks and statues that they produced. The cultural knowledge about style and authorship were confined to the membership of the workshop. Only very rarely did it penetrate the barriers supervised by the elders of the lineage. Genres and their iconography were, however, related to the ritual use of the object. Information about the future use of a commissioned object was therefore channelled by the elders towards the carvers who would execute the work.

The "Olden Days": Art Trade under Colonial Rule

The specific figuration of work and exchange between workshops of *kulibele* settlements and *poro* lodges set the stage for the emergence of market-driven genres and the commercialization of art. It began rather slowly under colonial domination but accelerated during the decolonization period of the 1950s and '60s. Objects that emerged out of the older, specific context of work and exchange, soon labelled as "traditional," easily fulfilled the criteria of authenticity; the artworks were produced and consumed locally, or so it seemed.[10] Most important was that they were not made for commercial purposes, though the carvers, of course, produced these objects to make a living and sold them against the most widespread medium of exchange of the time: cowries.

In the memory of most elder carvers, art trade in a narrower sense began some time in the 1920s, when the French administration had firmly established their facilities and offices. Because of its administrative functions, Korhogo had grown into a town of almost 5,000 inhabitants. In 1922, Korhogo was home to sixteen Europeans that either belonged to the civil administration of the county or served as missionaries or teachers in the catholic primary school, the first school in the north of the country. Besides Korhogo, catholic missions were founded in a few bigger villages that had served as trading posts in pre-colonial times; for instance, Kouto, on the trade route that linked the Middle Niger to the South. Sinématiali, a powerful chiefdom east of Korhogo,[11] was also selected as appropriate for a mission station. Such mission stations were rather small in terms of European staff. They usually consisted of one or two priests and sometimes one or two nuns, who in addition to their religious functions often also served as nurses, as the missions provided basic health services in their fiefdoms.[12]

figure 3
Adama Coulibaly was one of the most successful carvers in the Korhogo. Here, he is carving a kneeling madonna for the catholic church
Photo by Till Förster (2014)

Besides the permanent staff, the administrative and mission stations hosted, more or less regularly, visitors from the central colonial bureaus in Bingerville and later Abidjan. The colonial administrative staffs, the missionaries and their visitors eventually became the first foreign customers to local artisans. Very few of the carvers I met in the 1970s still had firsthand knowledge of these exchanges, but many told me what they had heard from their forefathers. According to them, a wide network already existed in the period between the two World Wars. However, it was not run by intermediary traders; it was the carvers themselves who sustained it.

The *kulibele* were, as in pre-colonial times, a small artisanal group living in segregated neighbourhoods in Senufo villages. These colonies were scattered over Senufoland, often a day's journey from each other. The older regime of work and exchange largely persisted and was sustained parallel to the emerging art trade. Building on existing ritual ties, in particular within the cycle of the rites of *poro*, *kulibele* carvers were able to exchange more or less regularly with their peers in other villages. During the 1920s and 1930s, these ritual ties were increasingly used to send and receive goods and services. *Kulibele* neighbourhoods that were closer to European settlements adopted the role of intermediaries. They kept objects that they had received from other colonies, and they tried to sell them to the new patrons. In particular, the *kulibele* settlement in Koko, a neighbourhood of Korhogo, became a hub for such trade. Though still few in number overall, the Europeans were more numerous in the growing town. Because of its role as an administrative centre, Korhogo attracted higher-ranking civil servants from the coast and to some degree the French mainland. These visitors were the first clientele with money to spend in their pockets. They would, the older sculptors said, stay for a month, at times two, before they travelled back to what became known as *la basse* Côte (d'Ivoire), the lower (Ivory) Coast. And they were interested to take something home that reminded them of the remoteness of the place. The term they used was still known to most carvers half a century later: *l'Afrique profonde* (deep Africa).[13]

The image of the northern territories of Côte d'Ivoire as "deep Africa" was immensely powerful. While the presence of the French was characterized as the driving force of *l'oeuvre civilisatrice* ("the civilization" of the local population), many visitors also wanted to display the imagined ambivalent character of the local culture when they were back home—that is, the "superstition" and the "artistry" of the Senufo as two sides of the same coin. Because the foreigners had almost no knowledge of the rites of *poro* and its female counterpart, the

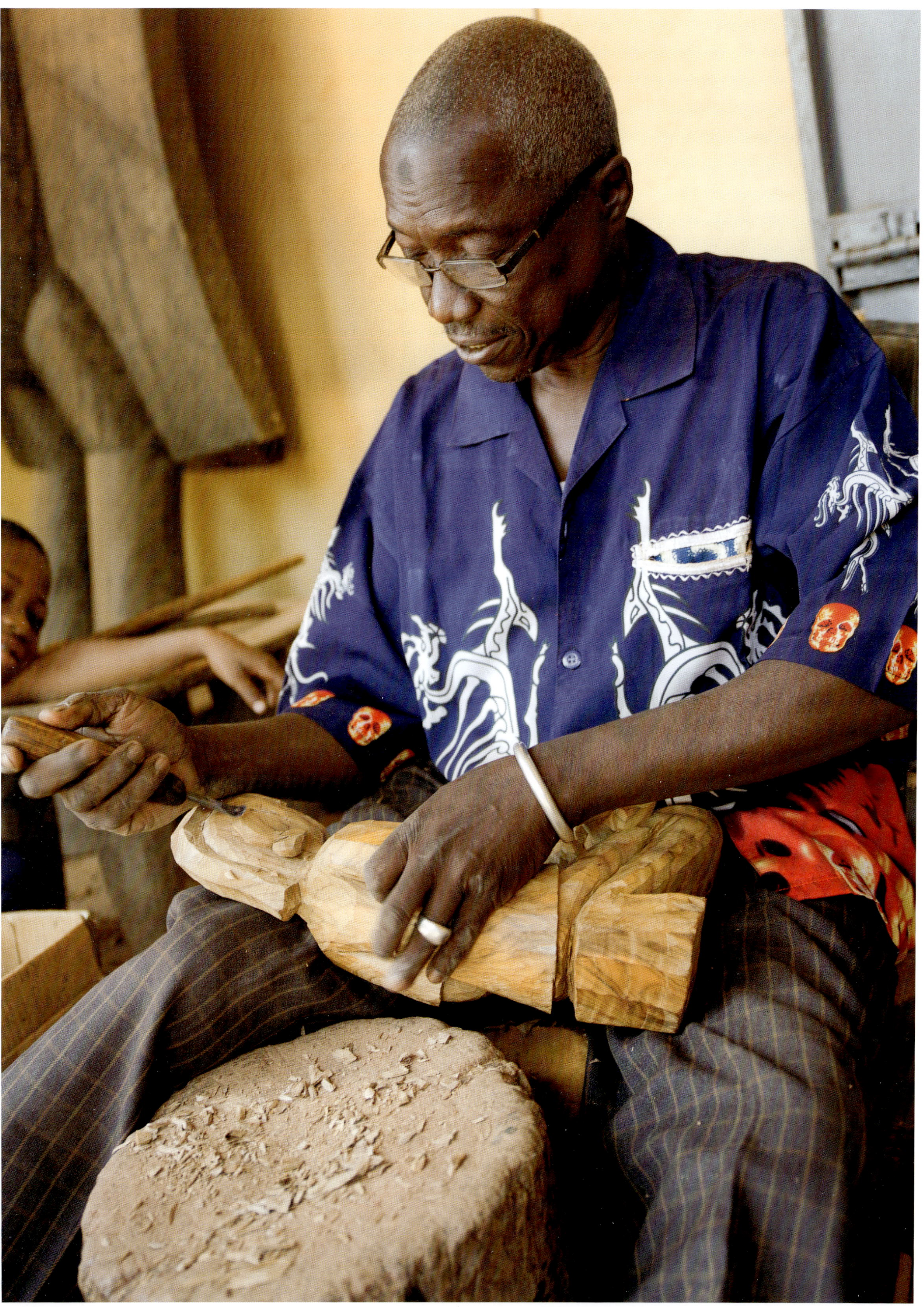

sādo'o society, they did not know of the ritual value of specific masks and statues either.[14] In addition, many of the visitors did not have the means to transport the bulky helmet masks or the tall and heavy standing couples that were at the centre of the arts associated with the secret societies.[15]

The *kulibele* soon became aware of the new clientele and tried to satisfy the small but growing demand for "traditional" sculpture. The older sculptors remember that this was the time they started to produce face masks in big numbers. These masks, which later became known as *kpelie*, had no ritual function in the farmers' *poro* societies, and they were rather small and easy to carry. They showed a human face at approximately natural size. The first items that were collected before World War I showed a simple iconography: the faces were adorned with small horns on the forehead and sometimes with one or two decorative projections or rectangles on the cheeks. Often, but not always, they had wooden extensions at the chins that aesthetically balanced the horns on top of the mask (Ch. 2, Fig. 7). Among the Senufo farmers, these masks were known under the generic name of *kodali*, which stood for any mask that could be seen by uninitiated children and women and that performed "to entertain" the public.

Among the *kulibele*, this mask had a completely different role. It was the central mask of their *poro* society and hence the counterpart to the big helmet masks of the farmers' *poro*. As did the latter, it performed on the occasion of funerals for initiated elders, and it did so as a pair of two masks. One was considered to be ugly, while the mask of the initiation centre of the deceased carver had to be to most beautiful one of all masks performing.[16] These face masks looked like those of the farmers with the exception of a tiny but important iconographic detail: between the two horns on the forehead, the carvers' masks showed the seed pods of the kapok tree (*Ceiba pentandra*). This element made them visibly different from the ordinary entertaining masks of the same genre (Fig. 4).

During the 1930s but particularly in the 1950s, the *kodali ye'e*, "the (wooden) face of the entertainment mask," was developed into a model that served the emerging European market. These masks were relatively small and could be packed into any suitcase, and because their iconography was not strictly bound to ritual use, the carvers were free to test forms and iconographies that would sell better than the usual ones. However, the carvers' own masks, which were still produced for their rites, would not change as quickly as the ones sold to Europeans. The name of the mask changed to *kpelie*, which meant "jumper" or "jumping."[17] It was a reference to the artistic performance of the entertaining mask among the Senufo farmers. The demand for such masks rose so quickly that it became *the* Senufo mask par excellence. Despite its ritual marginality, it was depicted in many of the first exhibitions of Senufo art as an example of outstanding craftsmanship, and often placed beside the big standing statues.[18] The iconographic flexibility of the model

figure 4
Kodali ye'e mask
Unidentified artist or workshop
Senufo style
Wood
Purchased in 1970 from a gallery in Paris
Height: 32.5 cm, Width: 14.7 cm, Depth: 7.2 cm
ROM 2009.126.184

was, and still is, related to its subordinate position in the ritual spectrum of Senufo culture—but by the same token, it was a precondition of its success as a commodity in the newly emerging art trade (Fig. 5).

Besides the increasing numbers of visitors, a few civil servants and missionaries began to collect the arts of central and northern Côte d'Ivoire. Missionaries in particular, who usually stayed longer than the French administrators, became interested in the full spectrum of sculpture. The most prominent was Pierre Knops, who lived in Senufoland, mainly in Sinématiali, from 1923 through 1935. After he had retired and returned to his native Belgium, he published a series of articles on various aspects of Senufo society and culture, including a paper on Senufo artists in their West African setting,[19] and late in his life a monograph about how he had experienced Senufo society and culture in the 1920s and '30s.[20]

Like other missionaries, Knops had collected "ethnographic specimens," which included all sorts of objects from ordinary household utensils through works labelled as fine art. With the co-operation of the colonial administration in Korhogo, some of these collections were later transferred to museums. Knops' collection was donated to the Afrika Museum in Berg en Dal in the Netherlands, which also received objects from other missionaries.[21] These collectors had an interest in the local society and its arts and were stimulating the emergence of another art trade that complemented the first. Here, the focus was much more on artworks and their presumed "authenticity." The *kulibele* colony in Koko became an important intermediary for this trade, too. They sold objects that they had received from other, remote *kulibele* settlements. When the demand was high and they could not find appropriate objects in the vicinity of the city, they began to send younger men to their relatives to find out whether they had such artworks at hand. According to my interlocutors, this internal trade must have started before World War II, but it intensified immensely after the war when more and more Europeans travelled through Senufoland. Among them was Esther Dagan, whose collection largely mirrors the market for African art in northern Côte d'Ivoire during the 1970s and '80s.

The trade in "traditional" or old art was fuelled much more by the events that followed the war. In particular, the new French Constitution of 1946, which brought an end to forced labour, had a direct impact on the societies under French colonial

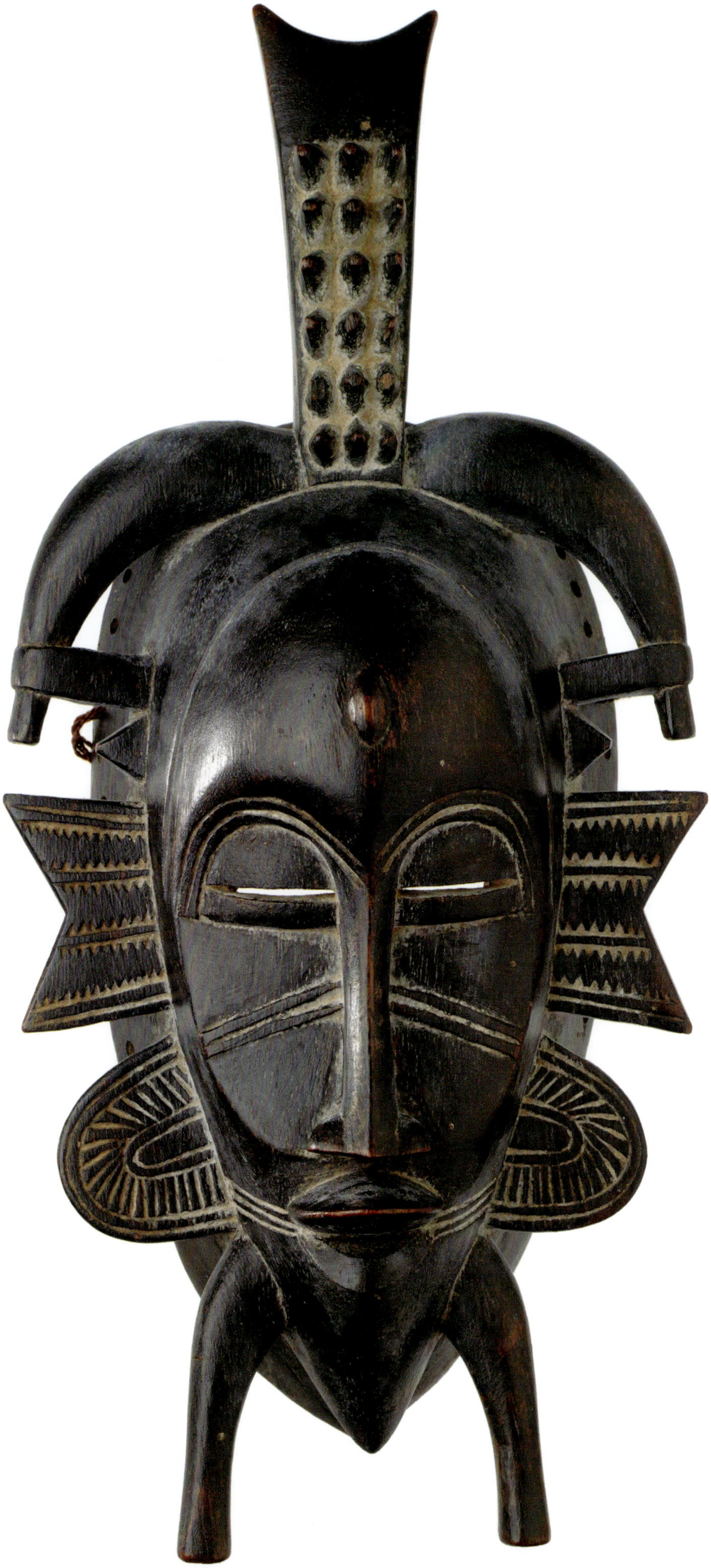

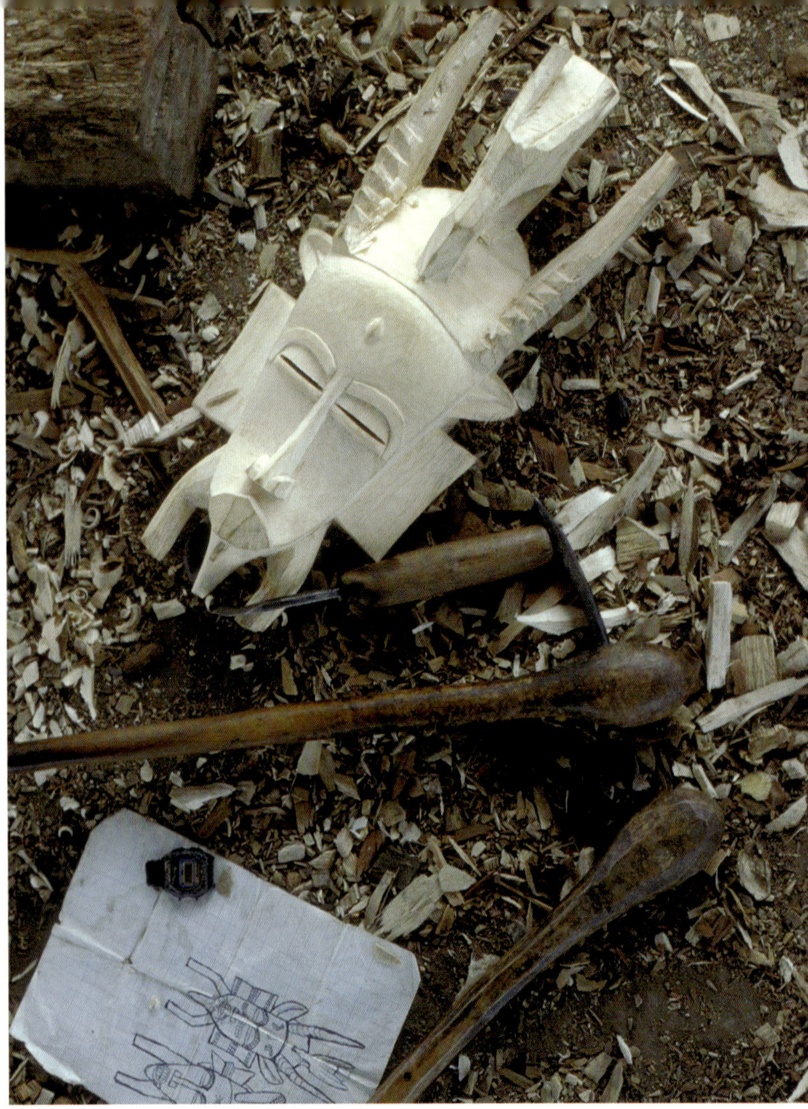

figure 5
A *kodali ye'e* or *kpelie mask* produced for the tourist market in 1991. A Hausa trader had ordered 200 masks of this kind and provided the sketch (bottom left) as template
Photo by Till Förster

figure 6 (opposite)
Painted cloth, *toile de Fakaha*
Unidentified artist or workshop
Cotton
Purchased in 1981 from a dealer at the market of Korhogo
Length: 287 cm, Width: 176.5 cm
ROM 2009.126.231

domination.[22] The memories of this time were still vivid in northern Côte d'Ivoire in the 1970s and '80s. Most elderly people remembered that they did not believe the French would ever give up this instrument of domination. Many thought that the abolition of forced labour was a precursor to much deeper revolutions in social life. Revivalist movements emerged in various French colonies.

The north and the centre of Côte d'Ivoire were in particular affected by the cults of Massa and Moussa.[23] Both movements aimed at restoring the social order. Both were based on the assumption that the people had neglected the values of a just and reciprocal society, and both claimed that they would exorcise witches and other malevolent beings from the villages that adopted their remedies. These consisted mainly of the distribution of "magical medicine" to the shrines that would be erected in the villages adopting the new cult. But before the new shrine would be erected, the inhabitants had to confess all possible wrongdoings, and they had to destroy all shrines that could have been used with malevolent intentions.

The inhabitants of the villages that adopted Massa, or later Moussa, had to search for objects that the masters of the cults considered capable of being misused. These objects, among them many paraphernalia of *poro* but also sculptures of other rites, were collected and brought to a square where they would be burned by ritual experts of the new cults. Others were built into the walls or roofs of the structures that would later house the substance of Massa or the water of Moussa.

This cataclysm attracted the attention of international art dealers and collectors. Probably for the first time since the beginning of colonial penetration, they travelled to the West African savannah "to save" as many artworks as possible.[24] Many masks, but more so statues and figures, were removed from their shelters and laid on the ground in front of the places where the new shrines would be built. Collecting the artworks, however, was not always as easy as this short description suggests. Most elder carvers remembered that there were attempts to penetrate into the sacred forests where, at the time, artworks were kept. (Not all villages had delivered all the objects of *poro* to the masters of the new shrines. Many were convinced that these objects would not do any wrong and therefore saw no need to hand them over.) But nonetheless, they said, objects "disappeared" during these years. Many suspected young men to have sold them to intermediaries, not directly to the European art dealers. Who they were, they did not know.

Whatever these first art dealers did, their presence in a time of such societal turmoil had an enormous impact on the further development of art trade in the region. The role of intermediary trade became more important than ever, and the *kulibele* were no longer the only ones in the field.

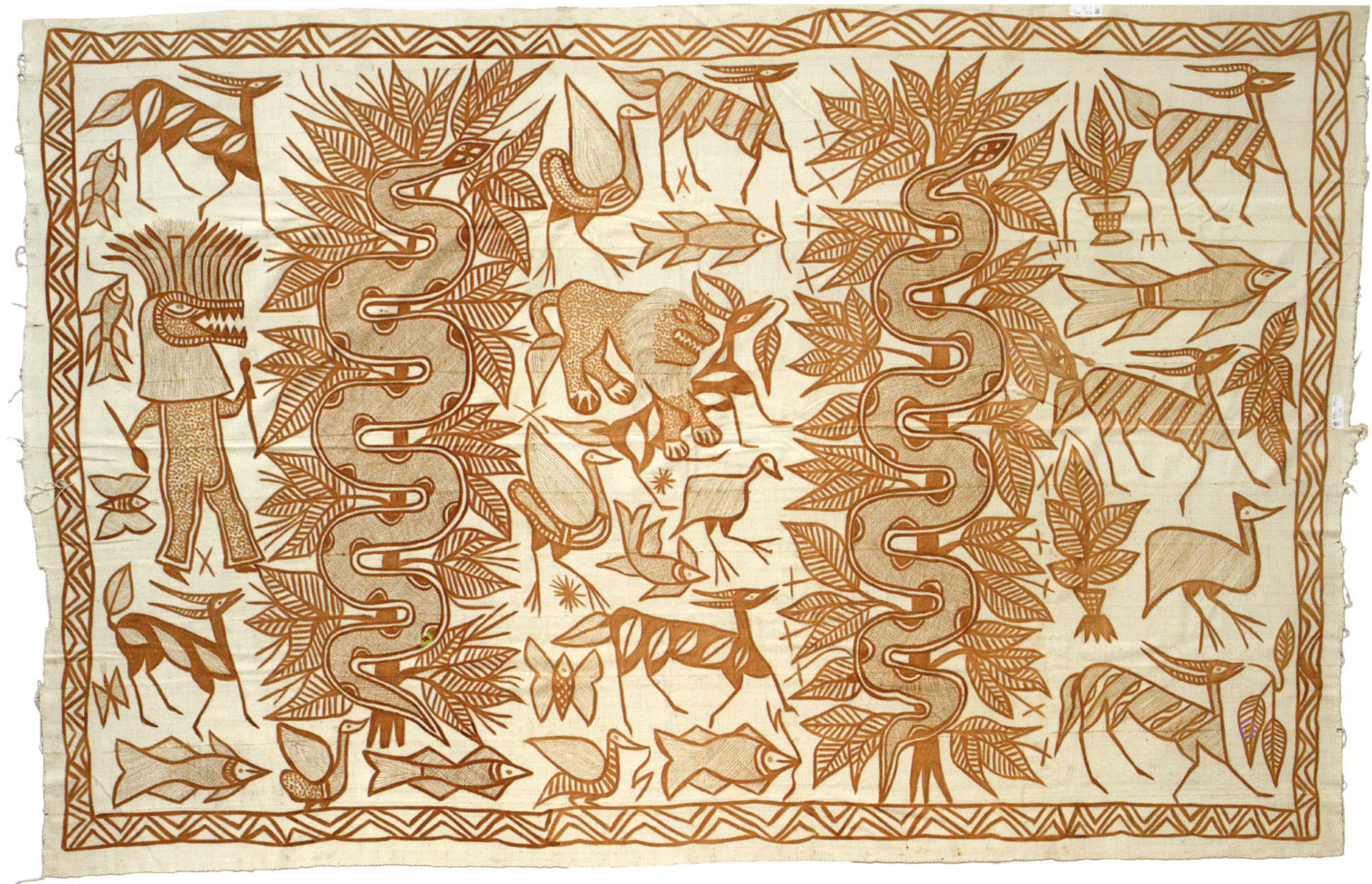

The "Golden Years": Tourists and Wholesale Traders

The years after independence saw a steep rise in tourism in Côte d'Ivoire. Already the last French civil administrators had had an interest in promoting local artisans and their work. Particularly successful were the two co-operatives founded in Fakaha, a small hamlet some 40 km south of Korhogo, and Waraniéné, a bigger village on the outskirts of the city.[25] Artisans soon started to produce for a wider market. First, it was for the foreigners and expatriates living in Côte d'Ivoire, but through the 1970s and 1980s, the artisans worked mainly for an international tourist market.

In Fakaha, artisans were invited to adapt the dyeing and painting of white, cotton wrap skirts to the taste of foreign visitors. The technique had been practiced in many parts of northern Côte d'Ivoire since at least the mid-nineteenth century.[26] The fabric, which is made of narrow cotton strips, is first painted with sap made of a special bark. It is then covered with ferrous mud and washed. The oxidization caused by the reaction of the ferrous ingredients with the sap produces a deep black hue. The older decoration of cotton wraps, trousers and shirts mainly consisted of geometric designs that often picked up the horizontal or vertical structure of the narrow strips. Only rarely did it include figurative elements. For example, the shirts of hunters, with pockets on all four sides of the body, could show a human figure that resembled a stickman, as it was thought to represent a *tugu*, a dwarfish being that lived in the wilderness. It was the subject of many a cock-and-bull story that the hunters would narrate when they came back from their nightly expeditions into the wild space surrounding the villages.

The transformation of the genre was closely related to increasing immersion in the tourist and later the international market. First, the artisans were invited to paint on flat, rectangular fabrics. They served as a sort of canvas and were labelled accordingly as *toiles de Fakaha* (or Korhogo), "Fakaha canvas." European customers could hang the paintings on the walls of their living rooms back home. More important than the change in materials was the transformation of the paintings. Some of them still incorporated the graphic designs that were used for skirts and shirts. But more often, the subject of the paintings had changed. Animals of all kinds surfaced on many canvases, some of them wild animals, such as snakes, leopards, antelopes and fishes (Fig. 6); others, farm and domestic animals, such as fowls and goats.

In other paintings, the artists depicted a collection of masks and members of *poro* in their attire. Such pictures were completely alien to the Senufo. Masks and ritual acts were not meant to be depicted on a two-dimensional surface; they were expected to act and to be seen in action only. Many of

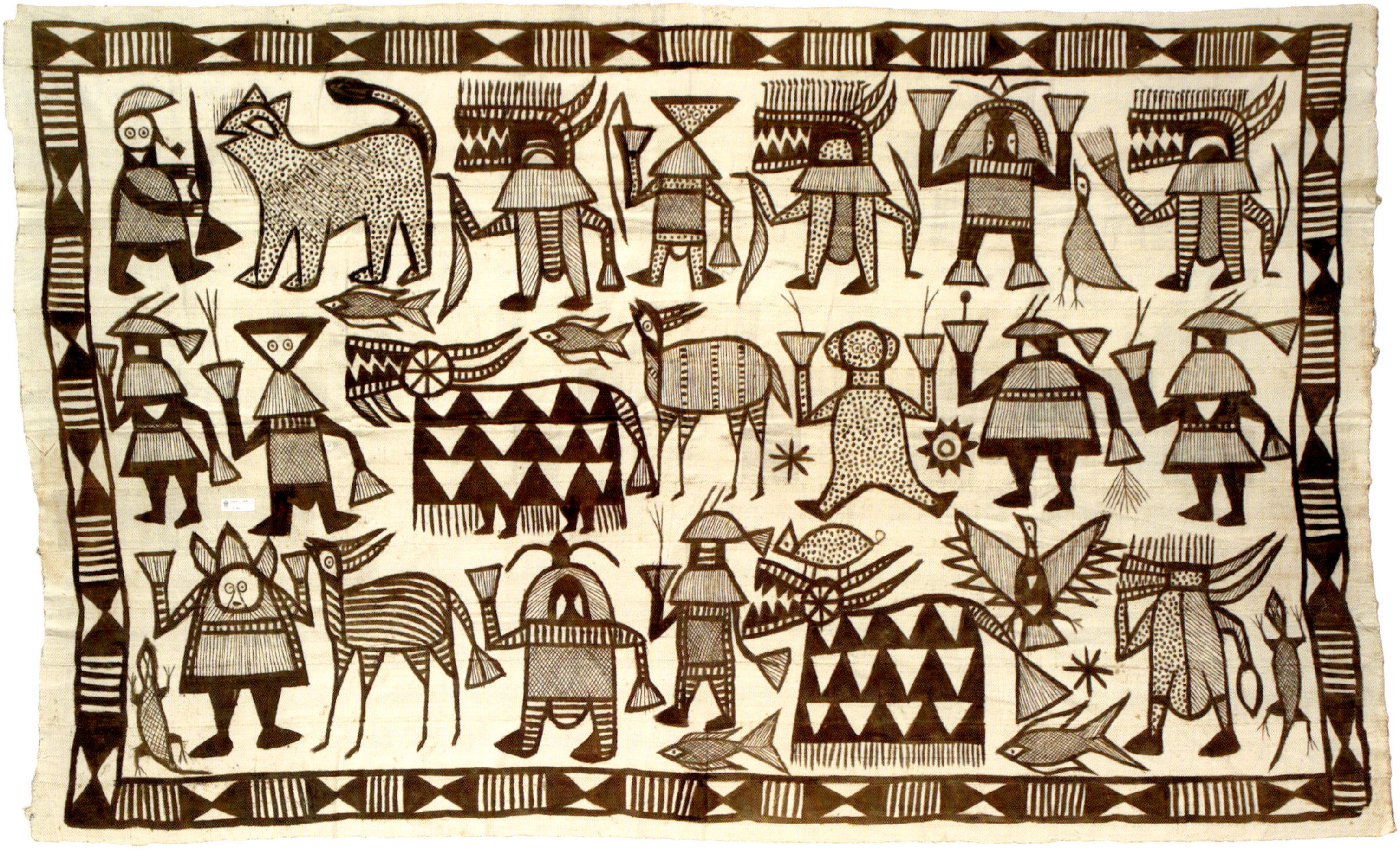

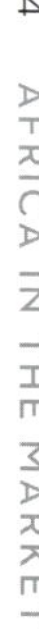

figure 7
Painted cloth, *toile de Fakaha*
Unidentified artist or workshop
Cotton
Purchased in 1981 from a dealer
at the market of Korhogo
Length: 282 cm, Width: 169 cm
ROM 2009.126.232

the prohibitions related to *poro* aimed to produce a particular view and vision of the society's masks, which would feed into the mental image that spectators would acquire over time. A mask should perform as an animated being—it was not meant to be still, as in a photograph. Initiated members of *poro* sometimes accompanied the masks on the canvas, holding branches or sticks in their hands. (The branches were usually used to keep uninitiated spectators at a distance when the masks were performing.) Such figures had never been depicted in Senufo sculpture.

Because their makers were unfamiliar with two-dimensional drawing, the *toiles* of the first generation of painters displayed rather simple designs, accentuating contours and profiles. These pictures were more drawings than paintings. Economic success and rapidly growing production led to more and more elaborate depictions of animals, masks and increasingly also floral elements such as leaves and trees. "Traditional" houses also became a subject. These new themes and subjects certainly attracted the tourists' gaze and satisfied their desire for naïve art, which they believed mirrored a primordial culture and its art. Through their work, the artists actually created a novel genre of painting. The scenes of wildlife and the parades of *poro* masks and figures became so popular among travellers that they were sold first in all major hotels of Côte d'Ivoire, then across the entire continent, and finally in fair-trade shops all over the world (Fig. 7).

In the 1970s, the paintings had become the major source of income for the population of Fakaha. Older members of families were running stands at the main market in Korhogo and along two major streets to circumvent the intermediary traders. One of the stands faced the only big hotel in Korhogo, another was erected on the road that led to Waraniéné, the village where the second co-operative had been founded. But the painters also sold to the intermediary traders, who had more stalls by far in front, to the right, and to the left of the big hotel and along the main street. They were also running shops inside the three tourist hotels in town. Trade between the North and the big tourist resorts in the South was almost entirely in the hands of Hausa and Senegalese traders who also ordered *toiles* in big numbers for the international market.

Most of the Fakaha painters continued to live in their tiny hamlet. Working in such a remote village had a double-sided effect. On the one hand, few tourists were able to visit the artists in the place where they worked. The artists learned about their clients' tastes only through intermediaries. On the other hand, as their work was not constrained by iconographic conventions, the painters were free to experiment with form and, when they became aware of other dyes, also with colour. Various shades of brown and red were used, and the background, which had always been white in the older canvases, was sometimes kept in yellow or red ochre (Fig. 8). Some painters began to see themselves as artists and developed a personal style. The refined ruling of the black contours mirrored their skills.

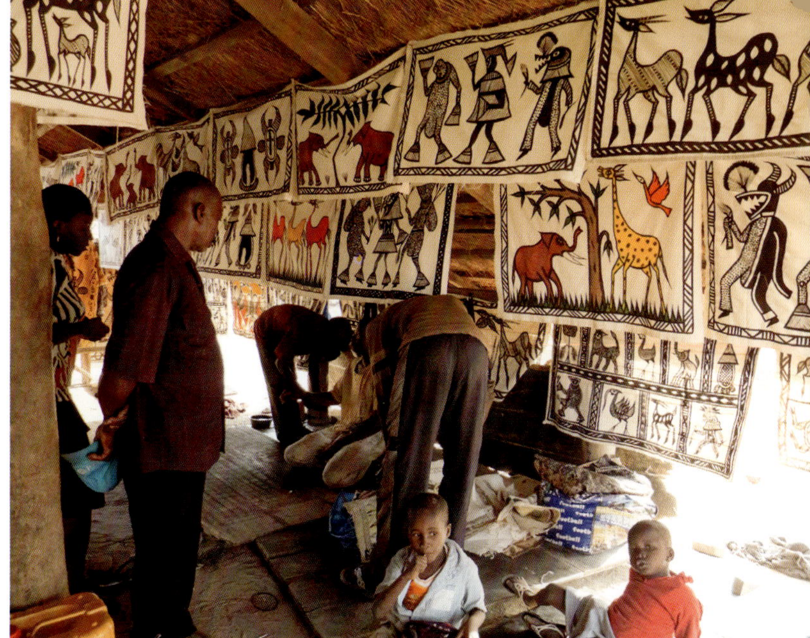

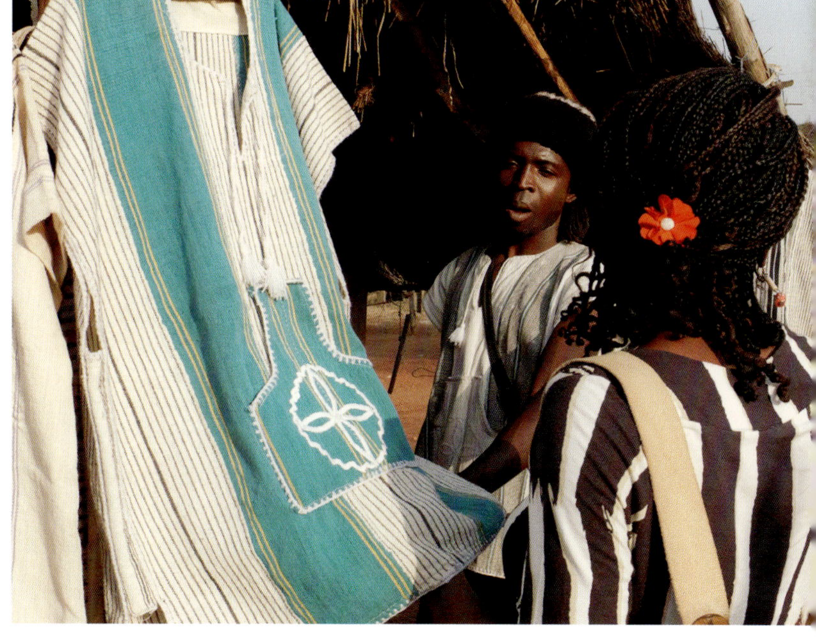

figure 8 (top)
So-called *toiles de Fakaha* in a market stall in Korhogo displaying wild animals and masks of the poro society in 2015
Photo by Till Förster

figure 9 (bottom)
A young trader sells a semi-traditional shirt to a foreign visitor
Photo by Till Förster (2015)

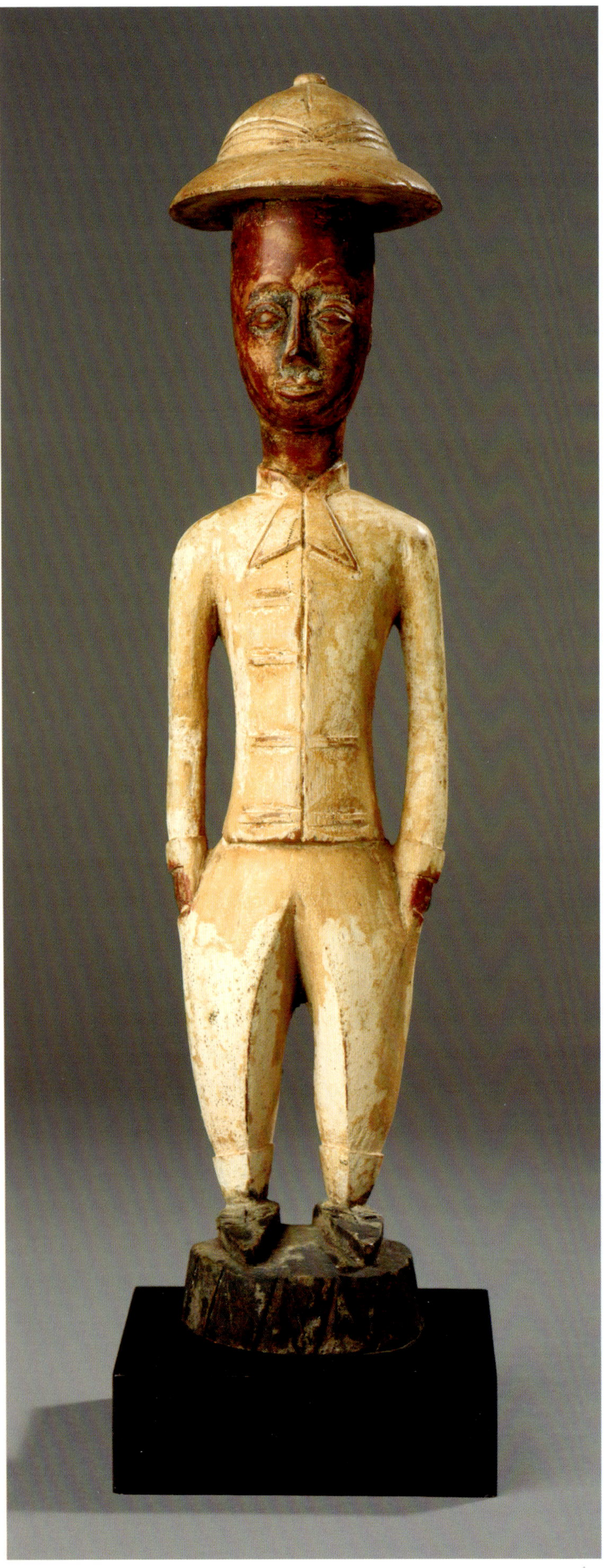

figure 10
Colon figure
Unidentified artist or workshop
Baule style
Wood, pigment
Purchased in 1987 from a dealer
at the market of Bouaké, Côte d'Ivoire
Height: 42 cm, Width: 9.6 cm, Depth: 9.2 cm
ROM 2009.126.287

Waraniéné was a different case. It lay in walking distance to Korhogo, and during high season, no tourist would escape the guides that would take them to the village where in the dozens—at times more than a hundred—were producing tablecloths, napkins, blankets, shirts and other cloth for the new clientele. The artisans all practiced narrow-strip weaving on horizontal looms, thus iterating an old technique into the present. They also made use of supplementary weft floats. The dyes were a mixture of vegetable indigo and industrial dyes. In the 1970s, deep blue was still dominant. Later, more colours were used: light blue and green, brown, yellow and combinations of basic colours were current during the 1980s and through the 1990s.

The continuity of the technique stood, however, in stark contrast to the commodities it produced for the tourist market. Neither tablecloths nor napkins were used by the peasant Senufo, and the shirts produced in Waraniéné followed Western fashion. However, the local "seven streets" shirts served as a model for more fashionable varieties. As their name indicates, they were made by sewing together seven narrow cotton strips. Because the artisans of the co-operative could react immediately to their customers' requests, they produced cloth that largely mirrored Western taste. But unlike the *toiles*, their fashion was, at least among the youth that identified itself as "genuinely African," comparatively well received on the local markets. Shirts adapted to the taste of the foreign clientele were increasingly sold to local customers on the main market of Korhogo (Fig. 9).

The entanglement of local markets with tourist and international markets was fostered by a series of events. The yearly celebrations of independence were related to a big development scheme, which aimed at attracting tourists from the former colonial power and from other northern countries. Every year, a city was selected for the festivities and endowed

figure 11
Standing figure, *tugu*
Unidentified artist or workshop
Senufo style
Wood
Purchased in 1981 from a dealer
at the market of Korhogo, Côte d'Ivoire
Height: 15 cm, Width: 3 cm, Depth: 3 cm
ROM 2009.126.90

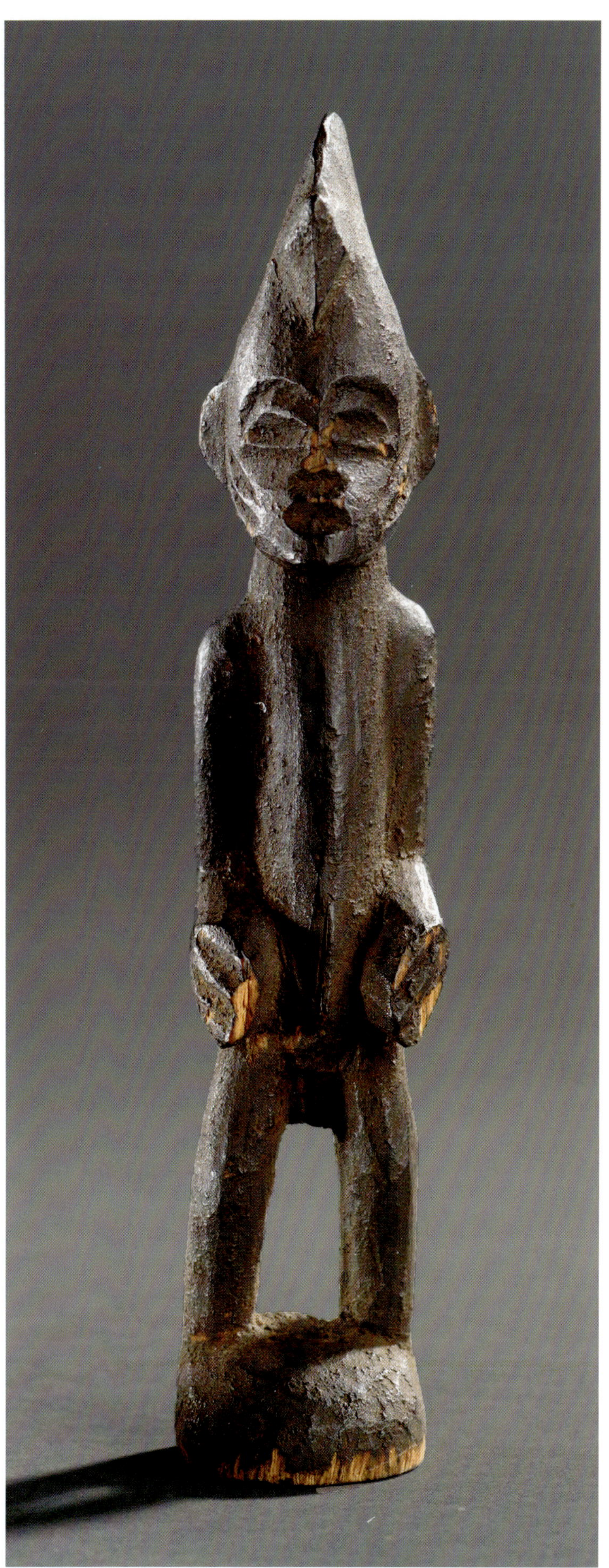

with infrastructure that was labelled as "modern." In 1964, the city of Korhogo was hosting the ceremonies. At the time, it had some 25,000 inhabitants but only a fragmentary street grid. In preparation for the independence celebrations, Korhogo hence received a grid of tarmac streets. A big hotel named Le Mont Korhogo was built on the main street that linked the former colonial offices, which had become the seat of the prefecture, to the central market.

The site where the hotel was built had been a place where funerary rites were conducted until then. Many people in Korhogo saw its debasement as sacrilege—in particular as the hotel's promotion played heavily with "traditional" Senufo culture. Its nightclub was baptized Le Poro after the secret society that governed village life among the peasant Senufo. The hotel also hosted one of the bigger art and curio shops where visitors could buy sculptures from the area and from other parts of Côte d'Ivoire. Some objects even came from neighbouring countries such as Mali and Ghana. In particular, the popular masks and figures, which had become iconic for "traditional" African art, were sold here and increasingly also by the Senegalese and Hausa merchants working under the trees in front of the hotel.

Bamana *chiwara* headdresses, Dogon riders, central African Songye masks and other well-known copies of masterworks of African art were among the replicas for sale. The bulk of sculptures came from the local Senufo carvers. They began to copy the works from other parts of Africa but mainly worked in what would be labelled as "their tradition." Most younger carvers supplied small standing statuettes, usually between 10 and 30 cm high. They resembled the *tugubele* figures of Senufo diviners, and many were carved as such. But carvers also started to reproduce styles from other parts of the country. In particular, the *colon* figures representing white colonial officers were selling well (Fig. 10).

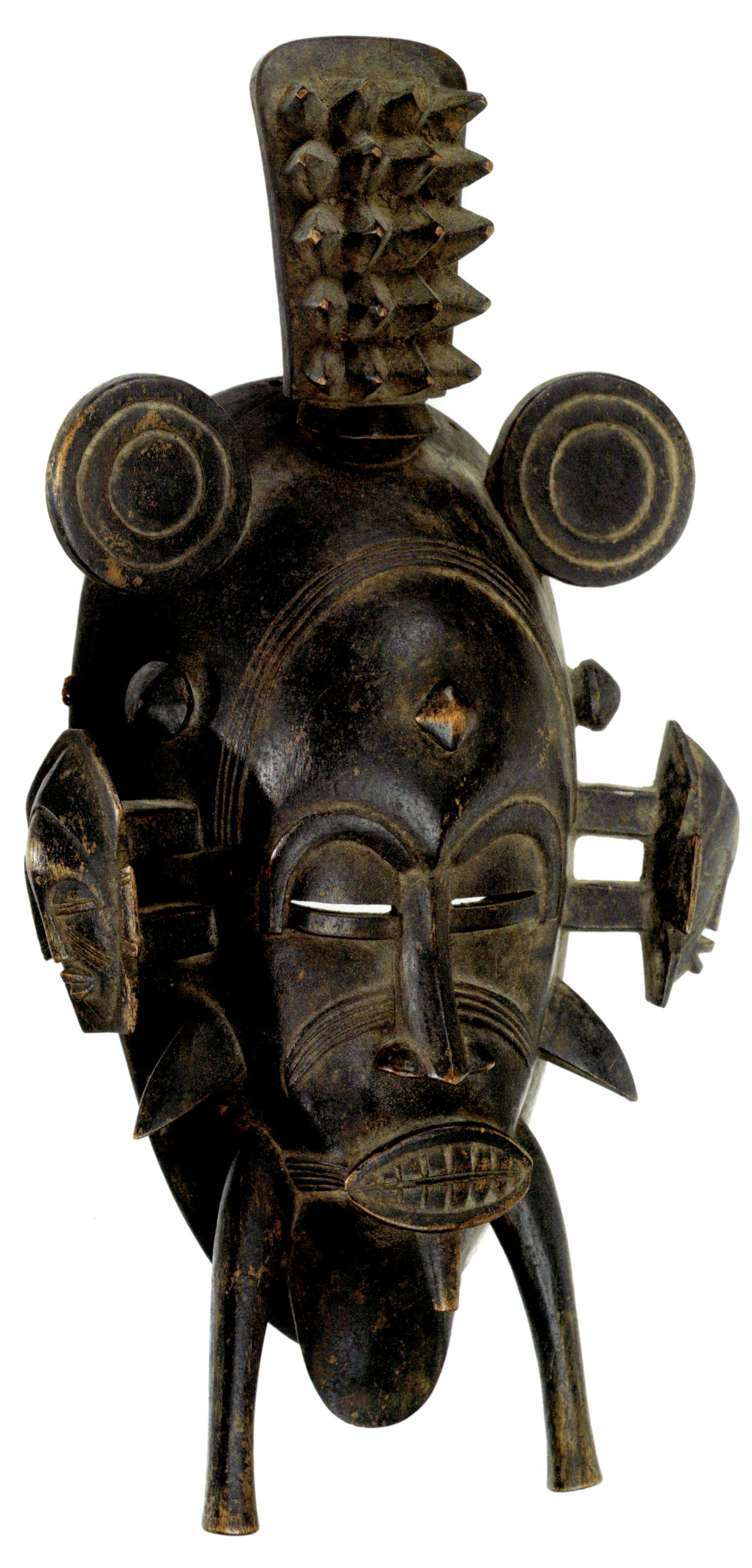

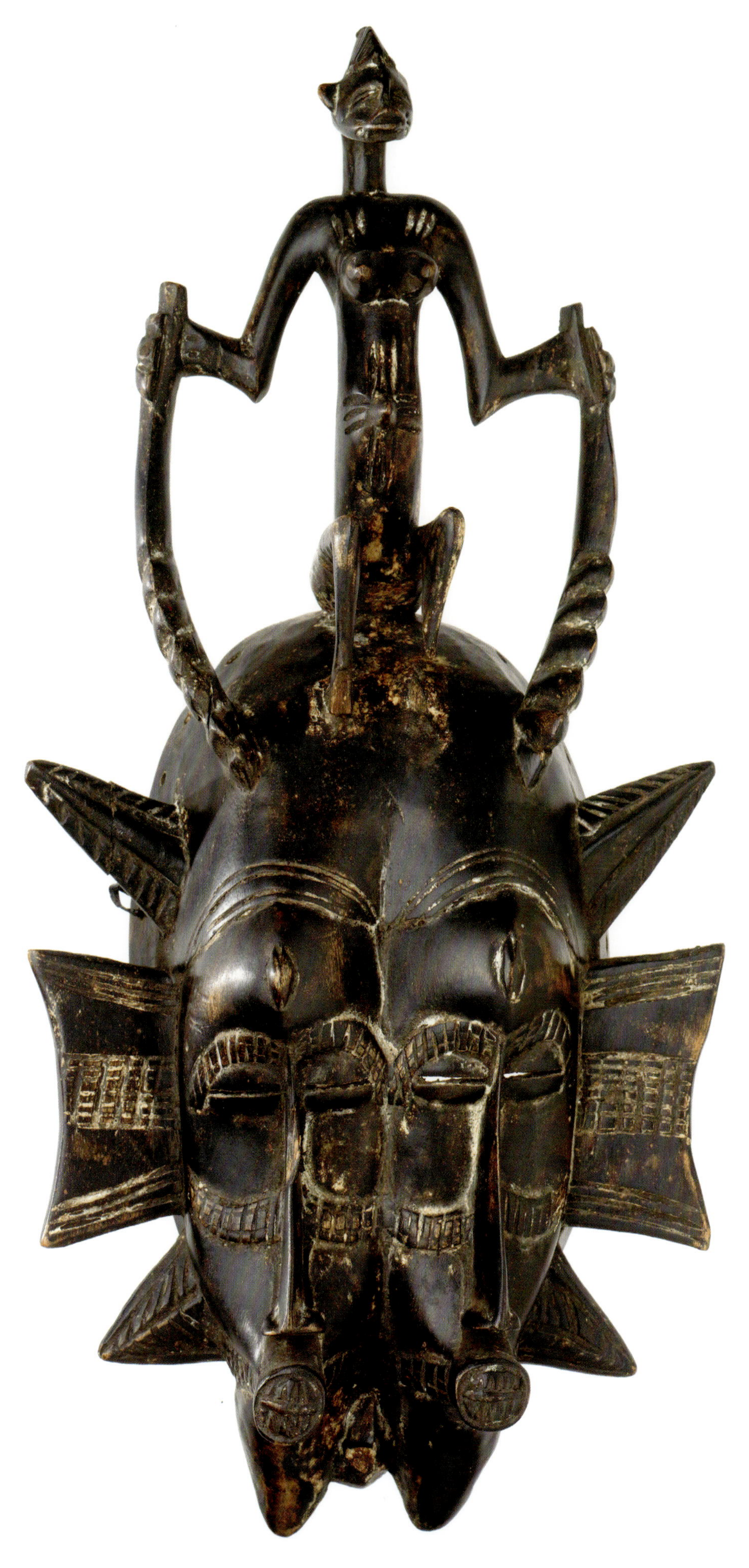

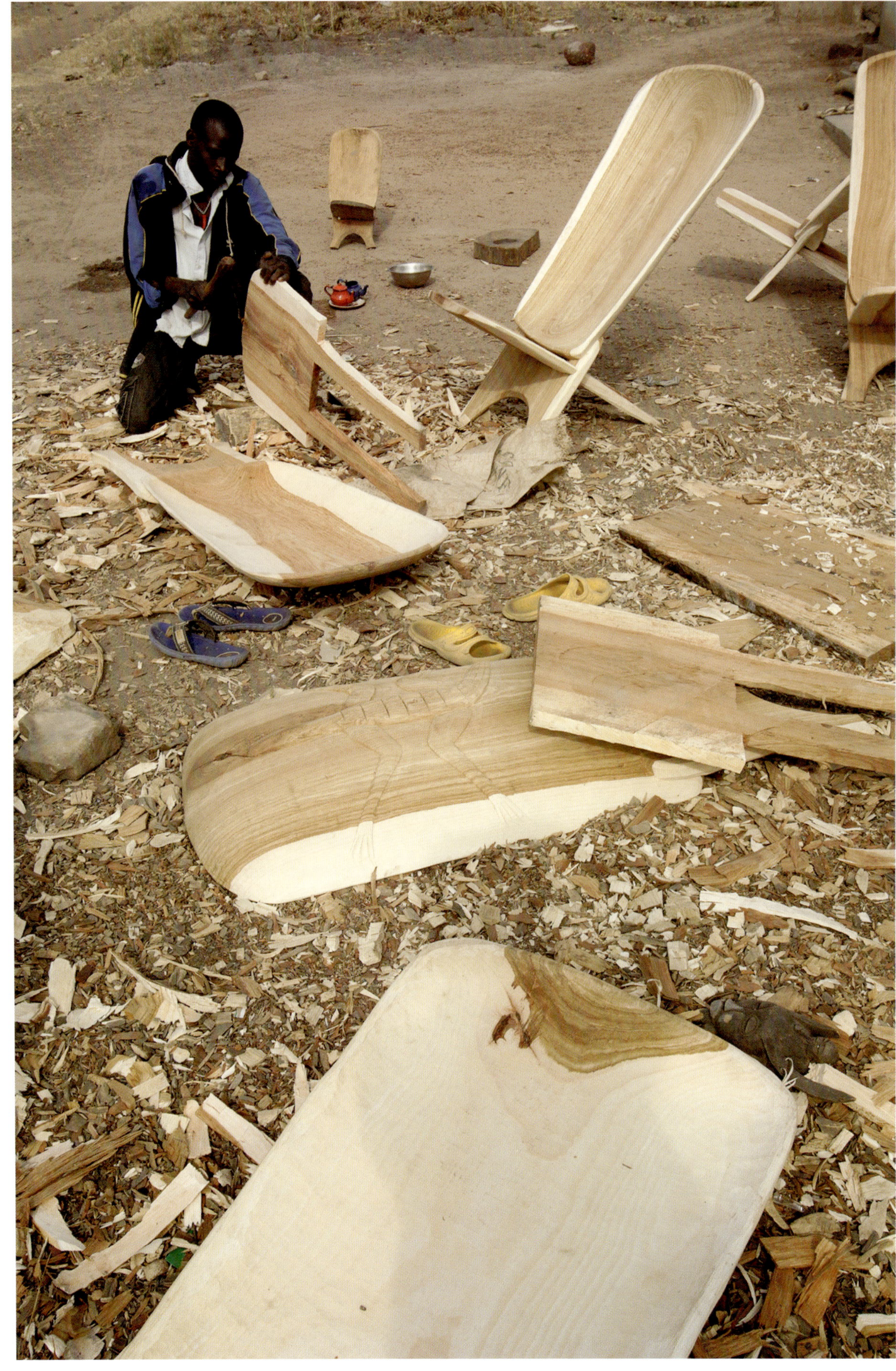

figure 14
Sculptor working on a big chair for rebel leaders in 2009. Such chairs had to be made of huge trees and were mainly produced in rural areas and then brought to urban centres for sale
Photo by Till Förster

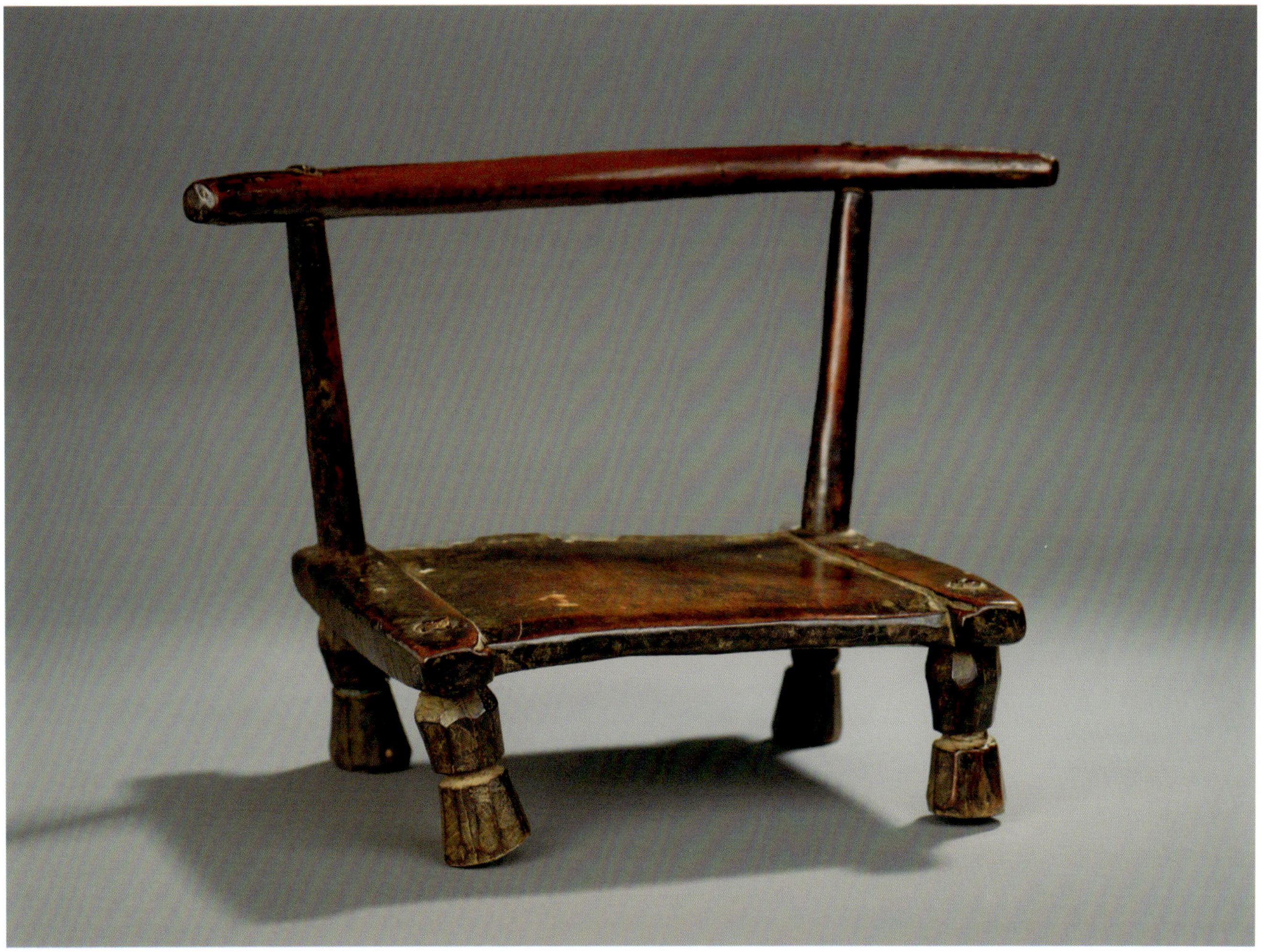

figure 15
Chair
Unidentified artist or workshop
Dan style
Wood, stain, wax
Purchased in the mid 1980s from a gallery in New York City
Height: 28 cm, Width: 44 cm, Depth: 25.5 cm
ROM 2009.126.16

---

figure 12 (page 88)
Kodali ye'e mask
Unidentified artist or workshop
Senufo style
Wood
Purchased in 1970 from a gallery in Amsterdam
Height: 33.5 cm, Width: 18 cm, Depth: 9 cm
ROM 2009.126.186

figure 13 (page 89)
Kodali ye'e mask
Unidentified artist or workshop
Senufo style
Wood
Purchased in 1982 from Tribal Art Gallery in New York City
Height: 40.7 cm, Width: 19.6 cm, Depth: 8.8 cm
ROM 2009.126.187

The Senegalese and Hausa traders sold them together with a narrative, which was at least to some extent constructed in the interaction with foreign customers.[27] The small *tugubele* statues became, for instance, *déesses de manioc*[28]—manioc being a staple food that the Senufo largely ignored and that they considered to be "Southerners' food," which implied for most peasants that it was not healthy (Fig. 11). Other statues were sold as "devils" and, if they were dirty or showed traces of "sacrifices," as "fetishes."

One of the most successful objects was the *kpelie* mask (see Figs. 4 & 5). It became one of the few Senufo artworks that were appropriated by the tourist as well as the connoisseur market as representative of Africa the continent. Today, it is sold on market stands from Senegal to Kenya and from Morocco to Cape Town. During this process of appropriation, the iconography was repeatedly adapted to the changing taste of the international clientele. The decorative elements that protruded from the face became more and more dominant and increasingly related to each other. The hypertrophic style of the masks produced for the alien market influenced to some degree the masks that were carved for the *poro* societies of the *kulibele*. While older carvers I spoke with in the 1980s still remembered that these masks were rather "simple" in their youth, they told me that such masks would no longer draw a crowd and would not win a competition of *kulibele* masks. But all *kulibele* masks still showed, they insisted, the seeds of the kapok tree above the front. Compared with the masks produced for the foreign market, the variation in style and iconography of the *kulibele* masks was limited.

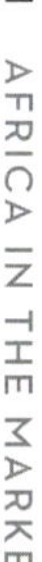

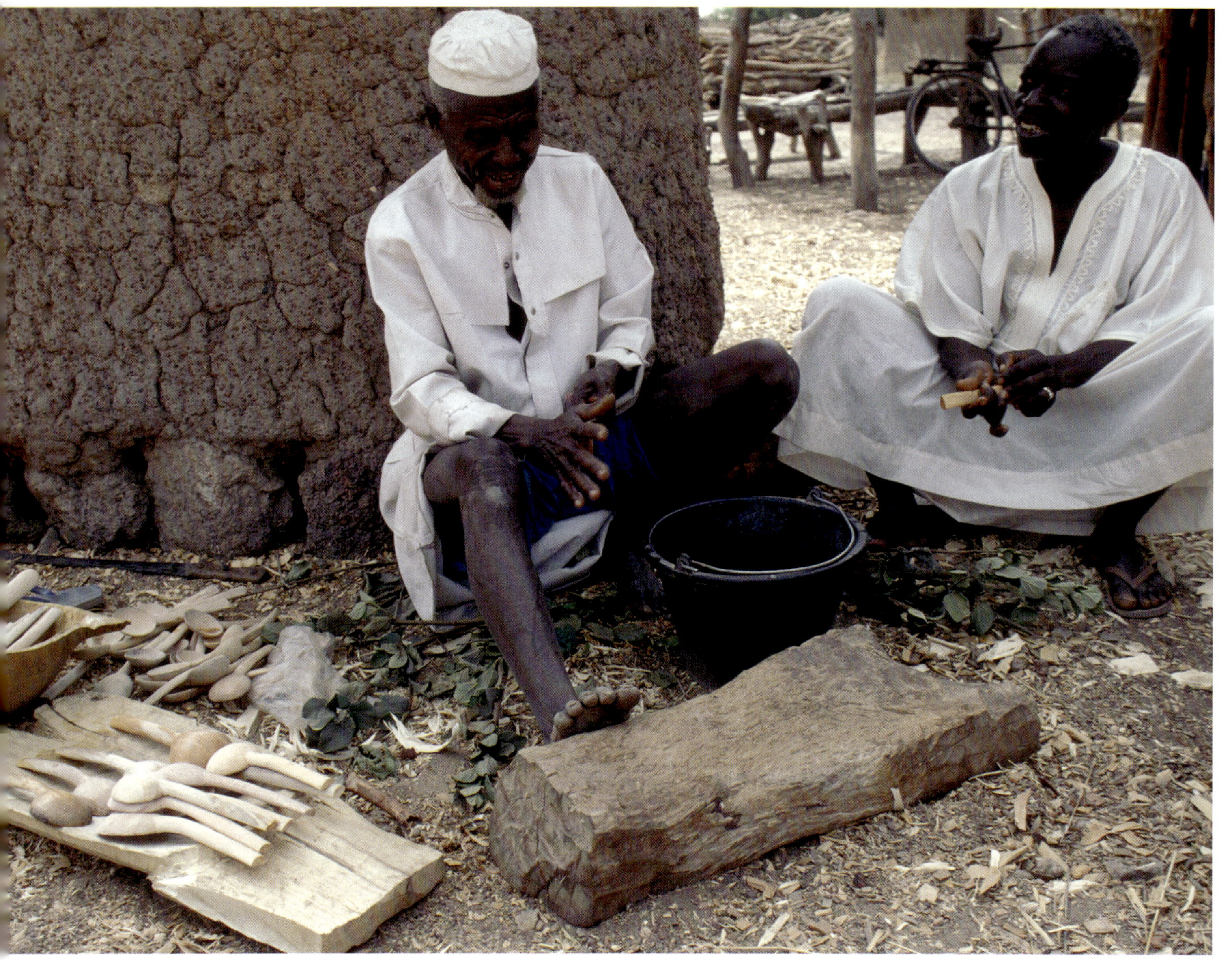

figure 16
The production of household objects for the daily market was carried out by apprentices or by old carvers who could not handle the heavy blocks of wood anymore
Photo by Till Förster (1991)

figure 17 (opposite)
A carver produces a chair of "European" style. Such chairs were, however, introduced by Muslims into the area who carried them over their shoulders when they went to attend a meeting
Photo by Till Förster (1990)

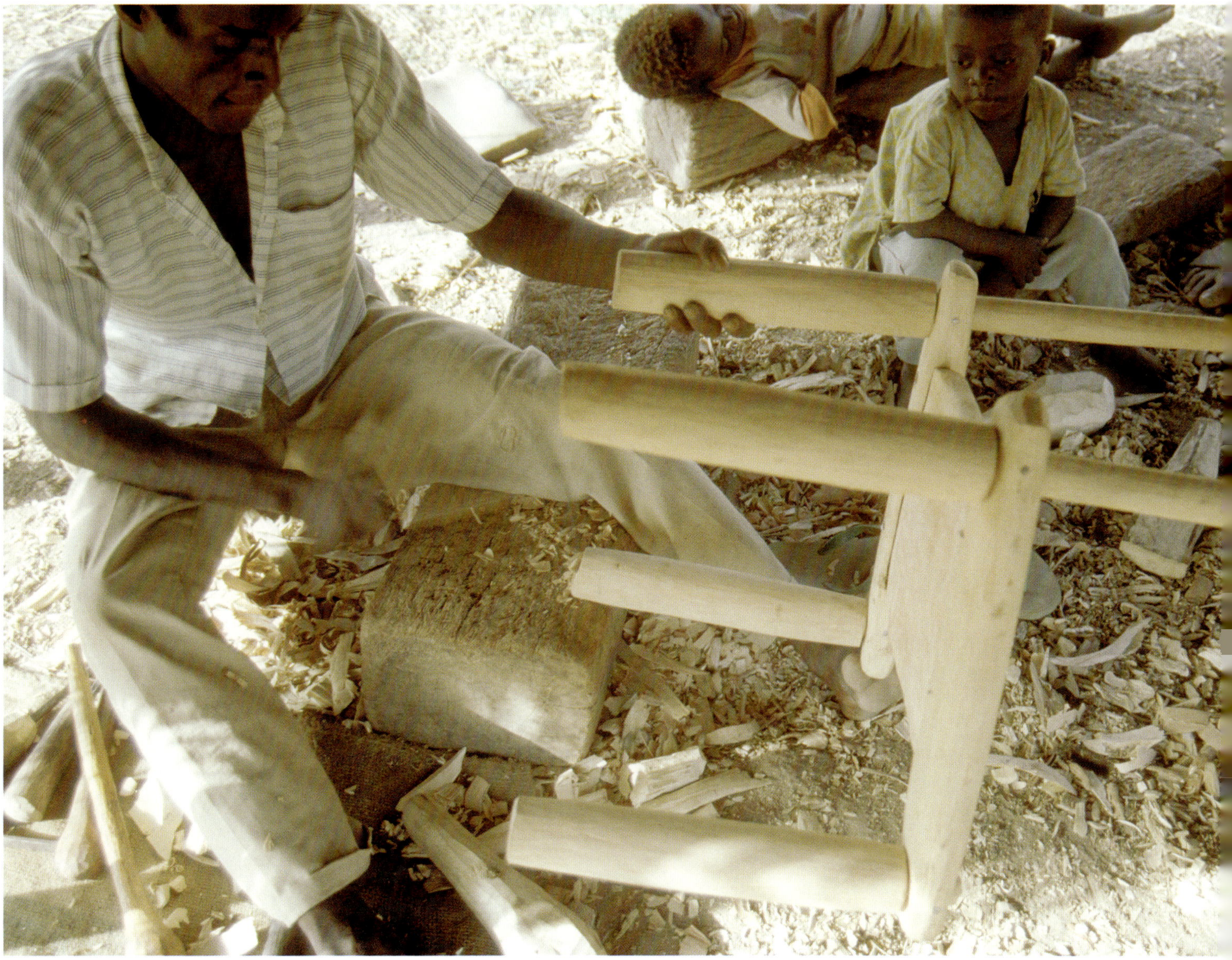

Intermediary traders insisted on the hypertrophic style that would please the customers in the tourist resorts along the coast and the international market. In order to ensure that their customers' expectations were fulfilled, traders came with sketches of models that had been extraordinarily successful (Figs. 12 & 13). They ordered such masks by the hundreds. Usually, they did not ask for a fine quality of wood and a careful execution. Instead, they insisted that carvers' colonies guarantee delivery of the requested number of items and that they resemble the model as closely as possible. As carvers had to work in a hurry, they were unable to select good chunks of wood or to avoid sometimes damaging slim extensions during the carving. Glue hence became indispensible, and many a mask was already repaired once or twice before it was delivered to the traders.

By the same token, many younger carvers quickly became experienced in *kpelie* masks as a genre. For some the process became so routine that they were able to produce several masks a day. In addition, the fact that carvers no longer needed to focus on the more general features of the *kpelie* masks allowed them to focus on novel iconographic elements and, to a lesser degree, on innovative styles. The traders, who usually came back after a fortnight to collect and pay for the objects, were of course aware of such variations, but saw them as deviations from the models they had ordered rather than innovations. Immersion in the international network of trade was a double-sided sword: it contributed enormously to the commercialization of a significant part of Senufo sculpture, but it also fostered innovation—the transformation of older genres and their iconography and style in Senufo sculpture and the emergence of new genres in weaving.

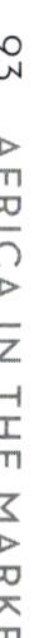

The Rebellion: New Patrons, Old and New Genres

The rebellion that split the country into two halves in 2002 had an immediate effect on artisanal work in the north of Côte d'Ivoire. Though tourism to the savannah areas had already dropped significantly after the coup of December 24, 1999, the rebellion brought it to an end. The tourist hotels along the coast had to temporarily close down. The big resort run by Club Méditerrané in Assinie was closed and remains so until today. All bus lines between the north and the centre on the one side of the country and the south on the other were interrupted, and when they were re-established, few petty traders dared to travel them. The majority were women, as women were less suspected of belonging to the rebel forces and carrying weapons. With the exception of a handful of Hausa art traders who were also engaged in the trade of other commodities to Côte d'Ivoire's northern neighbours, all art dealers had left. Many of them were trying to re-establish their business along the *petite côte* of Senegal and the coast of Gambia, on the island of Gorée or in Mali, which increasingly attracted tourists wanting to visit the Dogon and other peoples that had become icons of "traditional Africa."

In the part of Côte d'Ivoire that was held by the rebels, a new kind of patronage emerged. The big rebel commanders, who were often profiting enormously from the warlike situation and their power to extract money from the old elites, built houses and developed a new sort of conspicuous consumption. To some extent, it built on that of the older, Western-oriented elite, but it also incorporated elements that the commanders considered to be "pure" Senufo or Manding culture. The carvers in particular were able to make a living out of this demand. As new patrons, which the rebel commanders were in both the political and the economic sense of the word, they ordered big chairs that would reflect their position. These chairs were composed of two planks of wood. They had been in use for decades already and had largely replaced older stools that resembled European models but were smaller than their northern counterparts (Fig. 15).[29]

Over the years, rebel commanders developed a taste for big chairs that they proudly displayed under the hangars in their courtyards where they would receive visitors and discuss political and military issues. As the chairs were always composed of two separate, plain planks of wood, a big chair had to be made of a very big tree: a diameter of at least a metre was necessary. An order for such a big chair meant that the sculptors had to search for an appropriate tree deep in the wilderness. It often took them days to find one, my friends remembered. And when they found one, it was not easy to bring the trunk back into the village where they could do the carving (Fig. 14). That such trees were mostly growing in formerly protected forests was an issue that they were not concerned about.

The demand from rebel commanders allowed carvers to fill the gap left by the collapse of the tourist market. From 2007 through 2011, when the fighting resumed again, the *kulibele* were still able to live on their artisanal work. Some *kulibele* settlements were even able to persuade their new patrons that stools alone would not be enough to display their power. They offered them big statues that, the carvers told them, would "look very good" when they were standing close to the chairs during a reception of visitors.[30] These big statues were often carved from the slightly narrower part of the tree trunk from which they had also sculpted the big chairs. These statues were up to 1.5 m high, and they showed a mixture of various styles. Some recognizably picked up the old genre of *poro* statues; others elaborated on this genre and mixed it with elements that came from other, mainly West African peoples.

Though the sculptures would not have found a market among tourists, they also borrowed from what the carvers had learned about tourists' tastes over the past three to four decades. The big statues often displayed exaggerated iconic elements that had their roots in the local sculpture and in the transformations that it had gone through in the golden years after independence.

The End of a Profession?

For the sculptors, the real crisis came when the military crisis ended. After the fall of the Gbagbo regime in April 2011, patrons old and new ceased to exist, or more precisely, they were inaccessible. From the winter of 2011, almost all *kulibele* I met complained bitterly about not being able to sell their work. In rural areas as well as the city of Korhogo, they saw no prospects for their youth. Elder carvers said that they had told their younger siblings to give up their profession and to do something else—anything else. The carvers in Korhogo had ceased to buy objects from the *kulibele* colonies in the rural areas, as their storehouses were full of objects that they could not sell. Virtually no intermediary traders had come back after the end of the rebellion, and the tourist market was still non-existent. The few volunteers of international NGOs had also left, as the north of the country was now considered a "post-conflict" area.

From a more general perspective, the situation is best described as a breakdown of work–market relationships. It is a situation that will certainly be overcome when the country resurfaces as a tourist destination and when intermediary traders start to rebuild their networks. Whether that comes in time for the *kulibele* settlements in the north, however, is another question. Some may give up carving until then; others may stick to their work. What many of the younger carvers do comes close to a practice that is much older than many outside observers realize: they leave their home country and try to find a place where they can work and sell. Senufo carvers become migrants; they spend years far from home, filling the gaps where they can find them. This resembles the practice in olden times, when carvers served the local market of other villages. They now travel hundreds of kilometres, and they have to learn other languages. They also become familiar with the arts of others. This wider horizon of their lifeworld will certainly again affect their work and the artworks that carvers create.

1 I use the term "figuration" as used by Norbert Elias. The term refers to a specific relationship of social practices and institutions that remains stable over some time. See Elias, *Die Gesellschaft der Individuen* (Frankfurt a.M.: Suhrkamp, 1987); Elias, "Figuration," in *Essays III: On Sociology and the Humanities*, vol. 16 of Collected Works (Dublin: UCD Press, 2009); and Johann Arnason,"Figurational Sociology as a Counter-Paradigm," *Theory, Culture and Society* 4, no. 2 (1987), 429–56. Figuration in this sense is comparable to Charles Tilly's concept of regime. See Tilly, *Regimes and Repertoires* (Chicago: University of Chicago Press. 1998), 19.

2 For the social life of things and the cultural biography of things, see Chapter 1 ("Introduction: Commodities and the Politics of Value" by Arjun Appadurai, 3–63) and Chapter 2 ("The Cultural Biography of Things: Commoditization as Procss" by Igor Kopytoff, 64–91) in Arjun Appadurai, ed., *The Social Life of Things: Commodities in Cultural Perspective* (Cambridge: Cambridge University Press, 1986). For two different perspectives on genre, see Jacques Derrida and Avital Ronell, "The Law of Genre," *Critical Inquiry* 7, no. 1 (1980): 55–81; and Clare Beghtol, "The Concept of Genre and Its Characteristics," *Bulletin of the American Society for Information Science and Technology* 27, no. 2 (2001): 17–19. Regarding the sociological conceptualization of agency, see Mustafa Emirbayer and Ann Mische, "What is Agency?" *American Journal of Sociology* 103, no. 4 (1998): 962–1023.

3 See the colonial reports by Maurice Delafosse, then *comandant du cercle de Korhogo* in "Le cercle de Korhogo," in *Gouvernement Général de l'Afrique Occidentale Française La Côte d'Ivoire* (Marseille, 1906), 319; as well as Delafosse "Le Peuple Siéna ou Sénoufo, part 1–6" in *Revue des Etudes Ethnographiques et Sociologiques* 1 (1908): 17. See also Till Förster, *Zerrissene Entfaltung: Alltag, Ritual und künstlerische Ausdrucksformen im Norden der Côte d'Ivoire* (Köln: Köppe, 1997), 92–95.

4 The colonial personnel initially adopted these terms for their own use. See François-Joseph Clozel and Roger Villamur, *Coutumes indigènes de la Côte d'Ivoire* (Paris: Challanel, 1902): 317–23.

5 On the internal organization of these workshops, see Till Förster, "Work and Workshop: The Iteration of Style and Genre in Two Workshop Settings, Côte d'Ivoire and Cameroon," in *African Art and Agency in the Workshop*, ed. Till Förster and Sidney Kasfir (Bloomington: Indiana University Press, 2013): 325–359. The passage through the villages of the region was still practiced in the 1980s and early 1990s. It iterated into the present in other forms, too: young carvers travelled to the few touristic resorts along the coast where they worked for some time before coming back to the north. When, because of the crisis and civil war, tourism had come to an end in Côte d'Ivoire, some were travelling further afar to Senegal and the Gambia, where a tourist market was still flourishing.

6 Susan Vogel has observed a similar relationship among the neighbouring Baoule. See "Known Artists but Anonymous Works," *African Arts* 32 no. 1 (1999): 40.

7 Even after the introduction of the colonial currency, the Franc of the Banque d'Afrique Occidentale (BAO franc), in 1901, and the CFA franc after 1945, the value of such objects was still calculated in cowries and then converted into the equivalent in BAO franc or CFA franc.

8 The very few potential customers living in a village with a *kulibele* colony were an exception as they had firsthand knowledge about the skills of the artisans living among them.

9 During my repeated fieldwork stays of almost nine years, I witnessed only one such case. It was an order of several dozen stools and two types of face masks, fifty pieces each, which was placed by an intermediary Hausa curio trader. He complained that the stools were badly executed and not symmetric but twisted to one side. The masks of one of the two types were, he complained, not reproducing the model that he had wanted. The carvers argued that the Hausa trader had only complained to withhold a part of the money that he still owed them.

10 On authenticity as a modern figure of thought, see Till Förster, "Authentizität: Ein Traum Von Einmaligkeit." In *Afrika Mit Eigenen Augen: Vom Erforschen Und Erträumen Eines Kontinentes*, edited by Matthias Winzen, 85-106 (Oberhausen, 2012). See also Sidney Kasfir, "African Art and Authenticity: A Text with a Shadow," *African Arts* 25, no. 2 (1992): 41–53, 96–97.

11 The Senufo were mainly an acephalous society. The chiefdom of Sinématiali was an exception and probably the most powerful polity headed by a Senufo chief. On this topic in general, see Förster, *Zerrissene Entfaltung*, 1997.

12 Since 1905, the colonial program for the *mise en valeur* of the country envisaged the creation of a public health system, which mainly served the tiny European population. Because of high infant mortality, medical assistance to the "indigenous people" was planned from 1921 onwards, but it consisted mainly of preventive medicine while curing was left to the missionary nurses. Harris Memel-Foté, *Les représentations de la santé et de la maladie chez les Ivoiriens* (Paris: L'Harmattan, 1998).

13 The term refers to *la France profonde*, which connotes the culture of rural, agricultural France that escapes the dominant classes in Paris. It implies a certain backwardness and stubbornness of the population. See the 1973 memoires of Gilbert Bochet, former *administrateur civil* of Korhogo: "En Côte d'Ivoire à six cents kilomètres au nord d'Abidjan, le pays sénoufo a conservé croyances et traditions au sein d'une organisation sociale exemplaire." *Connaissance des Voyages* 15, no. (1973).

14 With one exception, the first empirically based studies of Senufo art and religion were all conducted after World War II. The exception was field research conducted by Albert Maesen in Korhogo from January through September 1939. His dissertation of 1946, *De plastiek in de kultuur van de Senufo van de Ivoorkust (Fransch West Afrika)* (Ghent: Rijksuniversiteit, 1946) was based on this research. For examples of studies conducted after World War II, see Gilbert Bochet, «Le 'poro' des Dieli," *Bulletin de l'institut Francais d'Afrique Noire*, serie B 21, no. 1–2 (1959); «A Propos Des Fondéments Spirituels De La Vie Sociale Sénoufo," *Bulletin de la Société Royale Belge d'Anthropologie et de Préhistoire* 74, no. (1963); and "Les masques sénoufo, de la forme à la signification," *Bulletin de l'Institut Français d'Afrique Noire*, série B 27, no. (1965); as well as Hans

Himmelheber, "Massa—Fetisch der Rechtschaffenheit," *Tribus* 4/5, no. (1954–56).

15 The European visitors also ignored the significance of fibre masks for *poro*, and since these masks did not have a wooden body, they were not considered to be art.

16 On the occasion of funerals, masks from neighbouring *kulibele* settlements came and performed in the deceased's honour. It was a kind of competition, but it was expected that the mask of the *poro* of the deceased carver would win that contest. See Förster, *Zerrissene Entfaltung*, 483–88; and Dolores Richter, *Art, Economics and Change: The Kulebele of Northern Ivory Coast* (La Jolla: Psych/Graphics Publishers, 1980), 49–51. See also Dolores Richter, "The tourist art market as a factor in social change," *Annals of Tourism Research* 5, no. 3 (1978): 323–38.

17 Also spelled *kpeliye'e*, "face of the jumper"; Robert John Goldwater, *Senufo Sculpture from West Africa*, (New York: Museum of Primitive Art, 1964). In the 1970s and early 1980s, the name was unknown to many carvers living and working in settlements that had no direct access to the tourist market.

18 Goldwater, *Senufo Sculpture from West Africa*, 14–16, 30–34.

19 Pierre Knops, "L'artisan Sénoufo dans son cadre ouest-africain," *Bulletin de la Société Royale Belge d'Anthropologie et de Préhistoire* 70, (1959): 83–111.

20 Pierre Knops, *Les Anciens Senufo, 1923–1935*, (Berg en Daal: Afrika Museum, 1980).

21 Other, smaller missionary collections also found their way into museums; for instance, that of Alexandre Gillès de Pélichy, a Belgian missionary like Knops. He had lived among the Senufo in the 1940s and '50s but focused much more on missionary work. See, for example, Alexandre Gillès de Pélichy, "Het "hiernamaals" bij de Senufo,"*Handelingen van het Negentiende Vlaamse Filologencongres 27–29 Maart 1951* (1951). See also the website of the Afrika Museum, www.afrikamuseum.nl (accessed 9.3.2014).
Pierre Boutin traces Knops' (50–51) and other missionary collections in "Comment se constituent les collections: l'exemple sénoufo," *Afrique: Archéologie et Arts* no. 10 (2014): 47–60.

22 Babacar Fall, "Le travail forcé en Afrique Occidentale Française (1900–1946)," *Civilisations* 41, (1993): 329–36.

23 Patrick Royer, "Le Massa et l'eau de Moussa," *Cahiers d'Etudes Africaines* 39, no. 2 (1999): 337–66. Hans Himmelheber, "Massa—Fetisch der Rechtschaffenheit," *Tribus* 4/5, no. (1954–56): 56–62.

24 One of them was Emil Storrer (1917–1989), a Swiss citizen who enrolled in the French Foreign Legion. After having retired as an active soldier by the end of WWII, he became a dealer of Moroccan carpets in Tangier from where he repeatedly explored sub-Saharan Africa, buying artworks to sell later in Europe. In 1951, Storrer travelled together with Elsy Leuzinger to Côte d'Ivoire and Mali (then French Sudan). This journey coincided with the peak of the Massa movement. Both Storrer and Leuzinger collected an enormous number of artworks, some of very high aesthetic quality. Storrer organized the first sales exhibition in Zurich, Switzerland, in 1952–53. In 1956, Leuzinger became director of the Museum Rietberg where many of the artworks are still kept. Jean Gasc, an officer of the French Foreign Legion who owned a hotel in Korhogo until the mid-1990s, participated in the collection of artworks and sold some of them in the reception room and bar.

25 Together with other co-operatives, the two joined the Union des Groupements à Vocation Coopérative des Artisan du Nord (UGAN) in 1983. Supported by a French organization of volunteers for development, this association built an artisanal centre with an exhibition hall in Korhogo in 1986.

26 The technique is known today as *bògòlanfini* or simply as *bogolan*, a Manding word signifying "(black) mud cloth." See Pascal James Imperato and Marli Shamir, "Bogolanfini: Mud Cloth of the Bamana of Mali," *African Arts* 3, no. 4 (1970); and Victoria Rovine, "Bogolanfini in Bamako: The Biography of a Malian Textile," *African Arts* 30, no. 1 (1997).

27 Christopher B. Steiner's work describes and analzes such interactions in great detail: see "World Together, Worlds Apart: The Mediation of Knowledge by Traders in African Art," *The Society for Visual Anthropology Review* 6, no. 1 (1990); and *African Art in Transit* (New York, Cambridge: Cambridge University Press, 1994).

28 Till Förster, "Eine andere Perspektive: Senufo zum Weg ihrer Kunst in die Fremde,"*Trickster* 14, no. (1985): 4–11.

29 These chairs had existed among the Manding in pre-colonial times already and belonged to a noble's furniture. The photos taken by General Joseph Gouraud on the occasion of Samori Touré's arrest in 1898 already depict such chairs. See Gouraud, *Souvenirs d'un Africain: Au Soudan* (Paris: Pierre Tisné, 1939).

30 Korona Yéo, personal communication to author, January 20, 2009.

Bibliography

Appadurai, Arjun, ed. *The Social Life of Things: Commodities in Cultural Perspective*. Cambridge: Cambridge University Press, 1986.

Arnason, Johann. "Figurational Sociology as a Counter-Paradigm." *Theory, Culture and Society* 4, no. 2 (1987): 429–56.

Beghtol, Clare. "The Concept of Genre and Its Characteristics." *Bulletin of the American Society for Information Science and Technology* 27, no. 2 (2001): 17–19.

Bochet, Gilbert."A propos des fondéments spirituels de la vie sociale sénoufo." *Bulletin De La Société Royale Belge d'Anthropologie et de Préhistoire* 74, no. (1963): 5–31.

———. "En Côte d'Ivoire à six cents kilomètres au nord d'Abidjan, le pays sénoufo a conservé croyances et traditions au sein d'une organisation sociale exemplaire." *Connaissance des Voyages* 5 (1973).

———. "Le 'poro' des Dieli." *Bulletin de l'Institut Français d'Afrique Noire*, série B 21, no. 1–2 (1959): 61–101.

———. "Les masques sénoufo, de la forme à la signification." *Bulletin de l'Institut Français d'Afrique Noire*, série B 27, no. (1965): 637–77.

Boutin, Pierre. "Comment se constituent les collections: l'exemple sénoufo." *Afrique: Archéologie et Arts* no. 10 (2014): 47–60.

Clozel, François-Joseph and Roger Villamur. *Coutumes indigènes de la Côte d'Ivoire*. Paris: Challanel, 1902.

Delafosse, Maurice. "Le cercle de Korhogo." In *Gouvernement Général de l'Afrique Occidentale Française* (ed.) *La Côte d'Ivoire*. Marseille: 1906, 312–422.

———. "Le Peuple Siéna ou Sénoufo, part 1–6" *Revue des Etudes Ethnographiques et Sociologiques* 1 (1908): 16–32, 79–92, 151–9, 242–75, 448–57.

Derrida, Jacques and Avital Ronell. "The Law of Genre." *Critical Inquiry* 7, no. 1 (1980): 55–81.

Elias, Norbert. *Die Gesellschaft der Individuen*. Frankfurt a.M.: Suhrkamp, 1987.

———. "Figuration." In *Essays III: On Sociology and the Humanities*. Vol. 16 of Collected Works, 1–3. Dublin: UCD Press, 2009. Originally published in Norbert Elias, *In Quest for Excitement: Sport and Leisure in the Civilizing Process* (Oxford: Basil Blackwell, 1986).

Emirbayer, Mustafa and Ann Mische. "What is Agency?" *American Journal of Sociology* 103, no. 4 (1998): 962–1023.

Fall, Babacar. "Le travail forcé en Afrique Occidentale Française (1900–1946)." *Civilisations* 41, (1993): 329–36.

Förster, Till. "Authentizität: Ein Traum Von Einmaligkeit." In *Afrika Mit Eigenen Augen: Vom Erforschen Und Erträumen Eines Kontinentes*, edited by Matthias Winzen, 85–106. Oberhausen, 2012.

———. "Eine andere Perspektive: Senufo zum Weg ihrer Kunst in die Fremde." *Trickster* 4, (1985): 4–11.

———. "Work and Workshop: The Iteration of Style and Genre in Two Workshop Settings, Côte D'Ivoire and Cameroon." In *African Art and Agency in the Workshop*, edited by Till Förster and Sidney Kasfir. Bloomington: Indiana University Press, 2013, pp. 325–359.

———. *Zerrissene Entfaltung: Alltag, Ritual und künstlerische Ausdrucksformen im Norden der Côte d'Ivoire*. Köln: Köppe, 1997.

Gillès de Pélichy, Alexandre. "Het "hiernamaals" bij de Senufo." *Handelingen van het Negentiende Vlaamse Filologencongres 27–29 Maart 1951* (1951).

———. "Prières païennes d'Afrique Noire." *Rythmes du Monde* (1959): 1–24.

———. "Qu'est-ce qu'un pays de missions." *Bulletin des Missions* 26, no. 1–2 (1952): 1–11.

Goldwater, Robert John. *Senufo Sculpture from West Africa*. New York: Museum of Primitive Art, 1964.

Gouraud, Joseph. *Souvenirs d'un Africain: Au Soudan*. Paris: Pierre Tisné, 1939.

Himmelheber, Hans."Massa—Fetisch der Rechtschaffenheit." *Tribus* 4/5, (1954–56): 56–62.

Imperato, Pascal James and Marli Shamir. "Bogolanfini: Mud Cloth of the Bamana of Mali." *African Arts* 3, no. 4 (1970): 32–41, 80.

Kasfir, Sidney. "African Art and Authenticity: A Text with a Shadow." *African Arts* 25, no. 2 (1992): 41–53, 96–97.

———. "L'artisan Sénoufo dans son cadre ouest-africain." *Bulletin de la Société Royale Belge d'Anthropologie et de Préhistoire* 70, (1959): 83–111.

Knops, Pierre. *Les Anciens Senufo, 1923–1935*. Berg en Daal: Afrika Museum, 1980.

Maesen, Albert. *De plastiek in de kultuur van de Senufo van de Ivoorkust (Fransch West Afrika)*. PhD dissertation, Rijksuniversiteit, 1946.

Memel-Fotê, Harris. *Les représentations de la santé et de la maladie chez les Ivoiriens*. Paris: Harmattan, 1998.

Richter, Dolores. *Art, Economics and Change: The Kulebele of Northern Ivory Coast*. La Jolla: Psych/Graphics Publishers, 1980.

———. "The Tourist Art Market as a Factor in Social Change." *Annals of Tourism Research* 5, no. 3 (1978): 323–38.

Rovine, Victoria. "Bogolanfini in Bamako: The Biography of a Malian Textile." *African Arts* 30, no. 1 (1997): 40–51, 94–96.

Royer, Patrick. "Le Massa et l'eau de Moussa." *Cahiers d'Etudes Africaines* 39, no. 2 (1999): 337–66.

Steiner, Christopher B. *African Art in Transit*. New York, Cambridge: Cambridge University Press, 1994.

———. "World Together, Worlds Apart: The Mediation of Knowledge by Traders in African Art." *The Society for Visual Anthropology Review* 6, no. 1 (1990): 45–49.

Tilly, Charles. *Regimes and Repertoires*. Chicago: University of Chicago Press, 1998.

Vogel, Susan. "Known Artists but Anonymous Works." *African Arts* 32 no. 1 (1999): 40–55, 93–94.

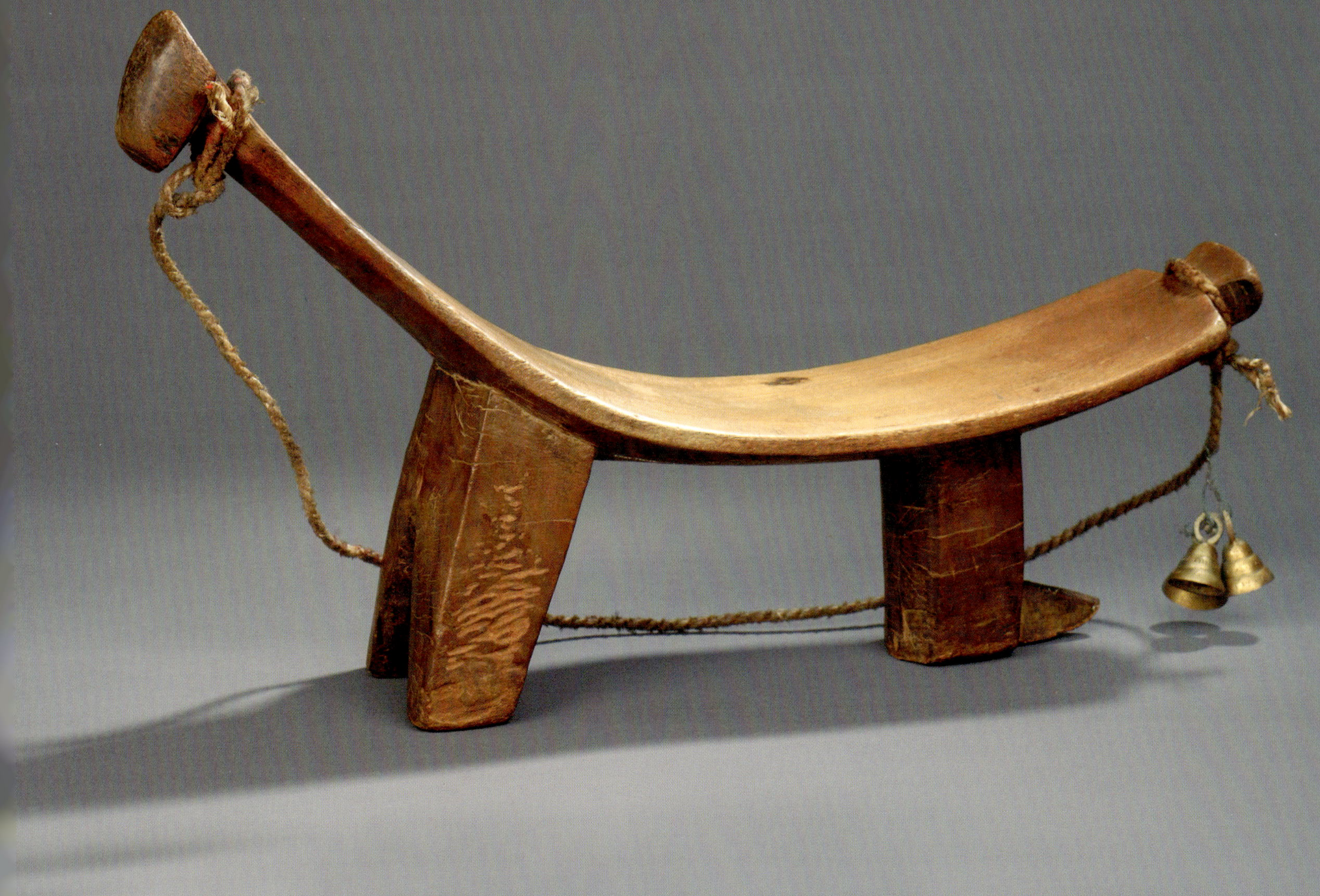

plate 7

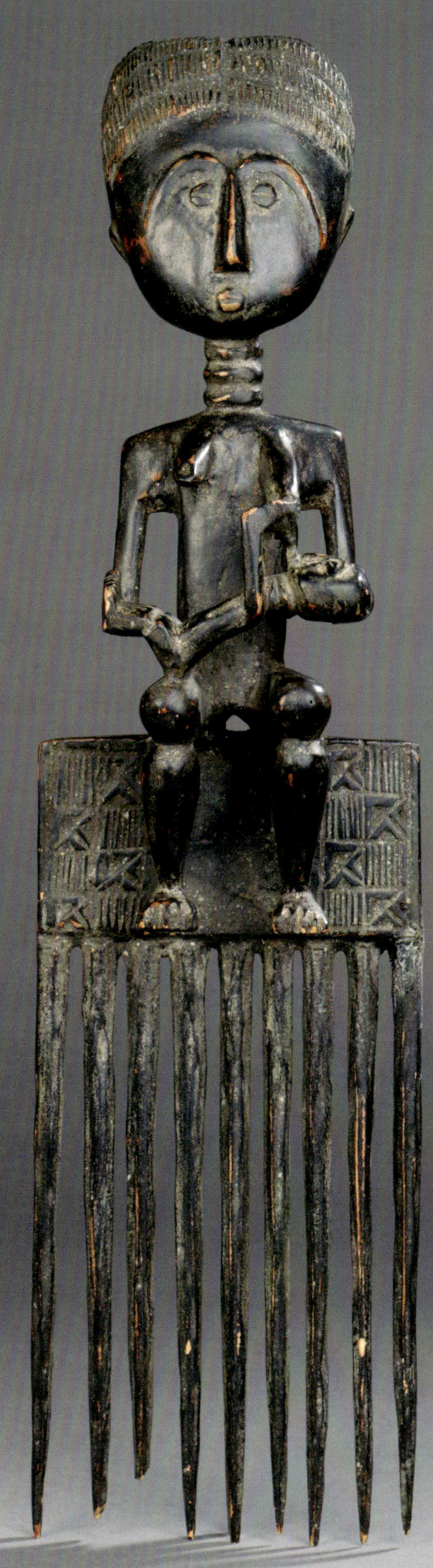

plate 8

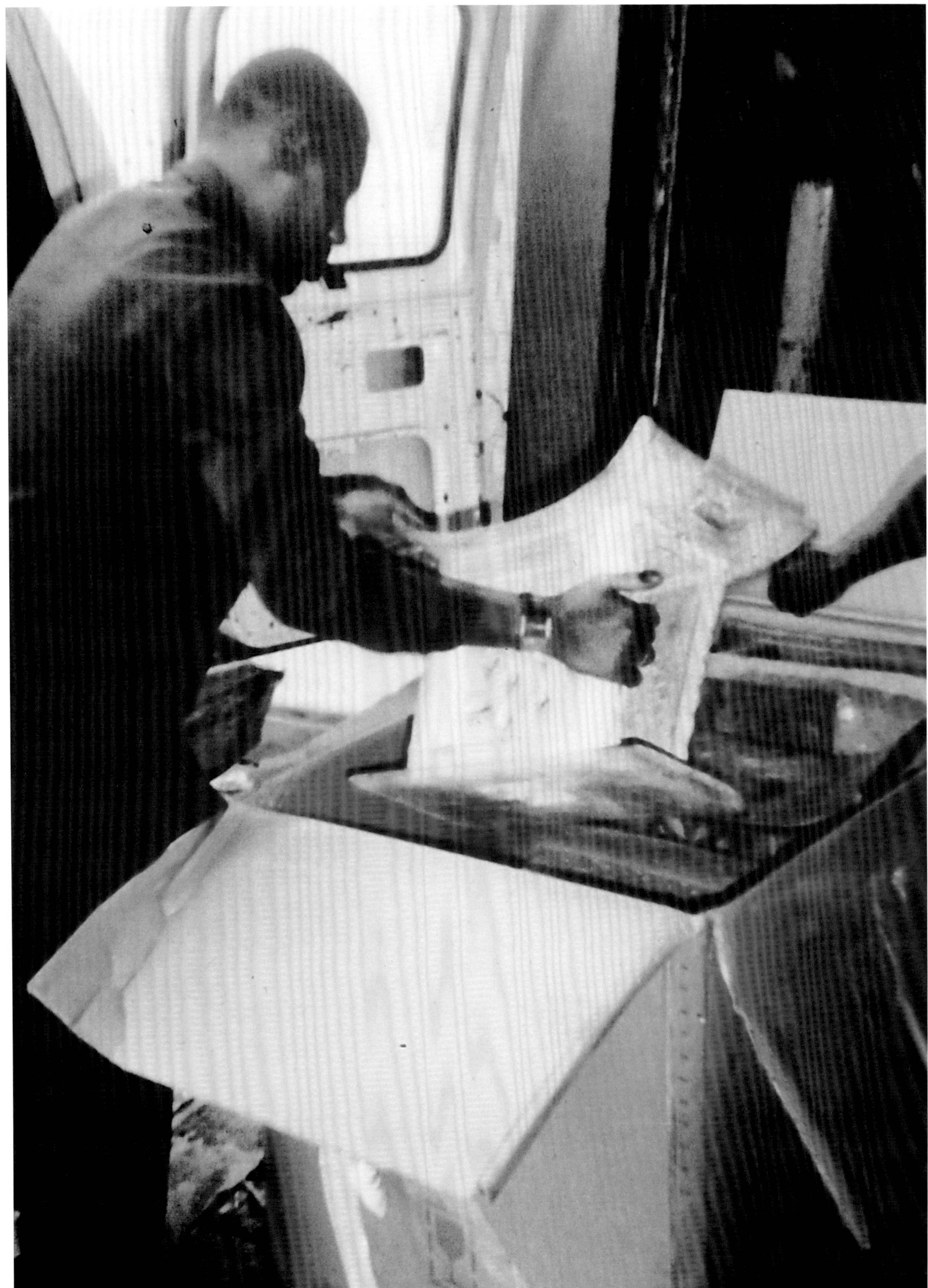

CHAPTER 5

MARKETS AND MATRILINEAGES: ASANTE STOOLS IN THE TWENTIETH CENTURY

CATHERINE M. HALE

In the summer of 2007, a billboard for SG-SSB International Business Centre, a majority European-owned financial services company based in France, dominated one of the busy roundabouts in Kumase, Ghana (Fig. 1). The advertisement featured an image of a freshly carved stool with the hands of the carver still applying the finishing touches. The slogan next to the image read "Carve a Strong Niche on the International Market," and a list of services, in areas such as foreign accounts and import assistance, appeared in smaller print above it. What caught my attention at the time, and continues to resonate with me, is the way the billboard so neatly encapsulates the complex issues at stake in navigating the market of Asante stools and understanding their dynamic relationships, in both local and global contexts, over the course of the twentieth century.

For the Asante of Ghana, stools are integral components of social and political life. In their most critical functions, they are vital identity markers and sacred mediums for honouring and communicating with ancestors. The paramount political symbol of the Asante peoples is the Golden Stool or *Sika Dwa Kofi* ("Golden Stool born on Friday") and stools are frequently mobilized to suggest Asante identity more broadly. In the political hierarchy, each chief and queen mother has a stool or set of stools that are symbolic of their respective roles. These objects are so central to their positions that when a chief or queen mother takes office, he or she is said to have been "enstooled." In these key socio-political settings, stools—referenced here interchangeably as *asese dwa* (sing. *sese dwa*)—share a conventional form. As illustrated by two examples from the Dagan collection (Figs. 2 & 3), they have a rectangular base with incised "steps" on either side of the central support structure (which is usually abstract but may incorporate figural representations), a curved seat with geometric "cut-outs" running linearly at the base of each curve, and a shape (usually square, sometimes carved in concentric repetition) carved into the underside of the base at its centre. Almost always, these stools are used in a "raw" state (no varnishes or lacquers are added) and their custodians maintain them by mixing sand and water that they rub onto the stool using a rough leaf (from the *nyankyerene*, which is a common tree). Lime juice may be used in their cleaning, and on some occasions white clay is added to make the stool even "brighter."[1]

Historically, very extravagant stools made for high-ranking individuals were "smoked." These stools, which are not represented in the Dagan collection, have a richer brown hue, and as the smoking was a form of pest protection, they rarely show signs of infestation. Because the same smoking process—which traditionally involves placing the stool on the roof of a dwelling over top of the area where the stove or fire is located—can take months to complete, it is much less common in contemporary practice. Nowadays, only stools made for the Asantehene or Asantehemaa (king and queen mother of Asante, respectively) are likely to get this kind of treatment.[2] Depending on the owner's status and other factors,

detail
Hausa art dealer Aladji Baaré unloading Asante stools
Kennedy Airport, New York
Photo by Christopher B. Steiner (1991).

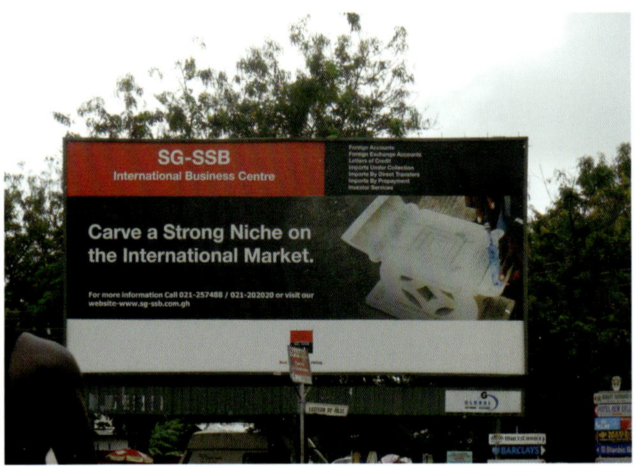

figure 1
SG-SSB billboard
Kumase, Ghana, June 2007
Photo by Catherine Hale

figure 2 (opposite, top)
Conventional stool, *sese dwa*
Unidentified artist or workshop
Asante style
Wood
Purchased in 1986 from Arouna, a dealer in Lomé, Togo
Height: 26.5 cm, Width: 40.5 cm, Depth: 17 cm
ROM 2009.126.19

figure 3 (opposite, bottom)
Conventional stool, *sese dwa*
Unidentified artist or workshop
Asante style
Wood
Purchased in 1986 from Arouna, a dealer in Lomé, Togo
Height: 34 cm, Width: 50 cm, Depth: 23 cm
ROM 2009.126.22

---

the complexity of the design of each stool may be more or less elaborate and could include such things as metal plating.

This common stool type certainly predates the confederation of the Asante kingdom at the end of the seventeenth century and, according to most royals with whom I spoke, is understood to have existed from the very beginnings of the lineages that now compose the Asante peoples.[3] The conventional stool type is differentiated from other kinds of stools by the term *sese dwa*, which refers to the high-quality *sese* wood used to make them. Raw *asese dwa* are frequently termed "white" stools to distinguish them from the "black" stools of ancestors. Regular household stools made from inexpensive wood and available at most shops are called *nyame dwa*.

It was not until the latter half of the twentieth century that the type of stool pictured on the billboard emerged. It draws on the conventional Asante stool shape but is less finely hewn, has a more block-like structure, and displays significantly less curvature in its seat (Fig. 4). Stools of this type are frequently varnished and feature *adinkra* symbols (visual representations of concepts or proverbs) as a central design motif, rather than being left unfinished and/or boasting the more abstract geometric patterns common to conventional stools in the Ashanti region. The incised steps on top of the base (on either side of the central support) and the concentric shapes carved into the underside of the stool that are hallmarks of tradition and prestige on conventional stools are also absent from this new design.

According to Nana Frempong Boadu, chief carver to Asantehene Otumfuo Osei Tutu II (the current king or ruler of the Asante peoples), carvers developed this new stool type in response to a combination of factors, including reduced supplies of the traditional *sese* wood used to carve stools, increased costs of tools required for carving, and the rising demands of the foreign market.[4] These new stools require much smaller pieces of wood from which to carve and craftsmen often replace *sese* with a cheaper or more readily available wood such as mahogany. Because of the uneven and darker colouring of cheaper woods, the stools made from them are sometimes referred to as "red" stools. The new stool type can be carved in a matter of days rather than the weeks, months or, in some exceptional cases, years necessary to create conventional stools. Unlike *sese dwa*, the new stools' designs do not have gendered and hierarchical ownership prescriptions—anyone can own and use any style of the new stool, but how they do so differs dramatically from how they do conventional stools.

The most popular new stool type features the *Gye Nyame adinkra* symbol, which refers to the proverb "I fear nothing except God" (Fig. 4). S. F. Adjei, current director of the Centre for National Culture–Kumase (formerly the Asante Cultural Centre), and Nana Sarfo Kantanka, the institution's deputy director, credit Dr. A. A. Kyerematen, founder and first director of the Centre, with the conception of this now ubiquitous design. Adjei and Kantanka explained that Kyerematen asked the carvers at Ahwiaa (the village in the Ashanti region where carvers are centralized) to create a stool that would represent the Asante Cultural Centre in its role as protector and promoter of Asante culture.[5] The selected design, with its reference to God, mediated between indigenous spirituality and the Christian belief systems that were adopted by the majority of the Asante population by the mid-twentieth century. In 1963, after a visit by Dr. Kwame Nkrumah, first president of the newly independent Ghana, the Asante Cultural Centre was renamed the Ghana National Cultural Centre, and its symbols and strategies were adapted into a larger nationalist agenda.[6] Since that time, the *Gye Nyame* stool has become the most frequently produced and

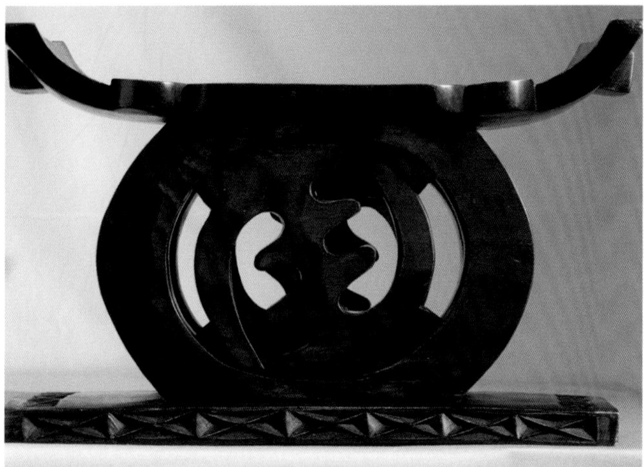

figure 4
Example of the new stool type with *Gye Nyame* design
Collection of the author
Photo by Catherine Hale

purchased form of the new stool type. It is readily available in markets from Accra in the south to Tamale in the north and appears in tourist shops in other West African nations. For example, I observed the *Gye Nyame* stool in Burkina Faso and Mali during fieldwork in 2009.

Carvers in Ahwiaa and at the Centre for National Culture–Kumase report that the market for the new stool type is primarily foreign. Promoted as the quintessential souvenir of Asante and, more broadly, Ghanaian identity, it comes in a variety of sizes and finishes that facilitate cross-border portability. (Smaller stools not only fit in luggage better, the varnish that is applied to most of them helps alleviate any concerns international border agents have about transmission of insect infestations.) Locally, Asante buyers also may purchase these stools as decorative features for their homes, but most queen mothers and chiefs with whom I spoke declared that it would be entirely inappropriate to use them in any kind of official political or ritual capacity.[7]

Of all the queen mothers I interviewed, only one, Nana Ama Agyeman (the Kodiehemaa, or queen mother of Kodie), had one of the new stool types in her possession. It was covered in a dark brown varnish and featured the *sankofa adinkra* symbol (a bird with its head turned back towards its tail, representing the proverb "go back and pick," which makes reference to the idea that one should learn from the past in order to move forward). Nana Ama Agyeman explained that she received the stool as a gift from a friend and, although she appreciated its aesthetic appearance, she would never use it for official purposes. Instead, it was integrated into her living room as an ornament. The information that royals would never use the new stool type in ritual is, of course, rarely shared with overseas customers, who are often regaled with stories about stools' roles in chieftaincy and ancestral veneration in the process of a sale. Product descriptions on websites such as eBay and Overstock.com include numerous references to "Asante royal stools" in their promotion of stools that conform to this new type.

Although the new stool type proliferates in the shops that line the main road running through Ahwiaa and can be found in almost every tourist outlet across Ghana, it did not replace the conventional style, but emerged in parallel as a solution to the growing problem of reduced resources and increased demand from global markets. At the same time as carvers create these new stools for foreign buyers, they are still actively creating the more conventional stool type or *asese dwa*. Tourists are welcome to purchase a variety of *asese dwa* that are for sale in Ahwiaa, but the carvers report that most foreigners opt for the new type, which is cheaper and almost always varnished. Several shops also sell varnished stools of the new type that have been made to look old through the addition of dust, mud and wear marks.

Located on the spectrum between conventional stools used in official capacities by Asante royalty and the new stool type predominantly sold to outsiders are higher-quality commemorative stools carved to honour important moments in history. These stools share formal similarities with conventional stools, including such things as carefully hewn seats (rather than the more "block-like" structure of the new stool type) and "cut-outs" that run along the base of the seat's curve. Like conventional stools, they are finely carved from good-quality wood and attract local as well as international consumers. An example in the Dagan collection (Fig. 5) features an adaptation of the Ghanaian coat of arms as its central design motif. While the four supporting columns that frame the design on either side as well as the four semicircular "cut-outs" on the top of the seat are characteristic of many conventional stools, the coat of arms motif, emblazoned with "Ghana" above, mark this as a commercial stool. Members of Asante elite society might own a high-quality stool of this type as a showpiece but, like the new stool type, royals would use it for ritual purposes. A limited number of stools such as the one in the Dagan collection were produced to celebrate Ghana's independence from Britain in 1957. The Fowler Museum at the University of California, Los Angeles, possesses a stool with striking similarities to the one now in the collection of the Royal Ontario Museum.

Adom Gyamfi Richard, secretary of the Ahwiaa Wood Carvers

figure 5
Commemorative stool celebrating Ghana's independence from Britain in 1957
Unidentified artist or workshop
Asante style
Wood
Purchased in 1986 from Arouna, a dealer in Lomé, Togo
Height: 40 cm, Width: 57 cm, Depth: 25 cm
ROM 2009.126.21

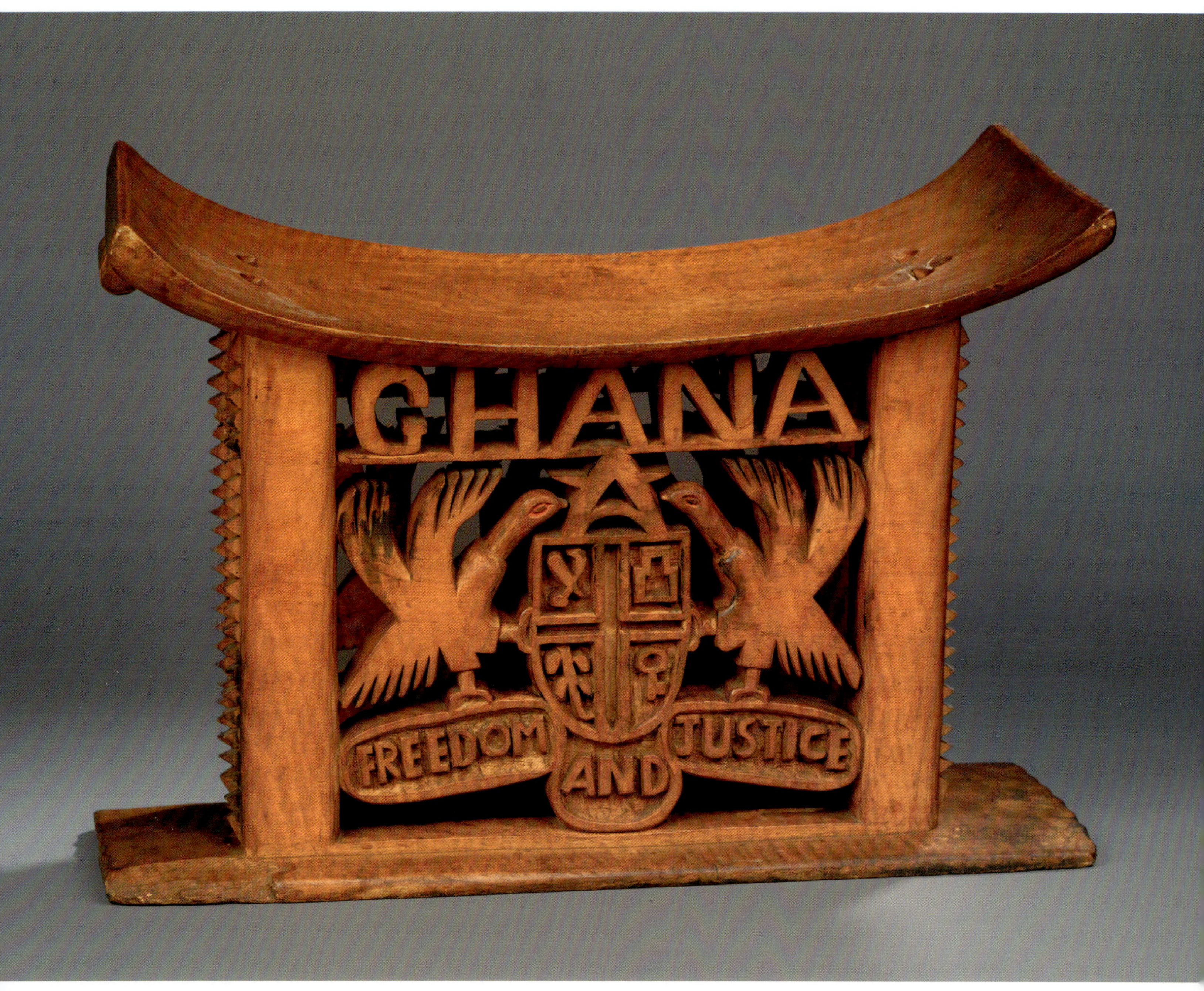

Association, informed me that, next to foreign visitors, queen mothers have been the stool carvers' most frequent customers throughout the twentieth century.[8] Depending on their rank and financial resources, queen mothers purchase ready-made conventional stools of a standard design or commission more elaborately embellished ones (at greater expense) to use in their official capacities, which include such events as judging disputes, attending durbars and presiding over female puberty rites (Fig. 6). When they are enstooled, queen mothers inherit all of the stools belonging to the previous queen mothers from that line. They also may choose to have a new stool made to suit their tastes, or they may select one of the inherited ones for regular use. All these objects fall under the heading of "Stool property" (a term that is comparable to "Crown" property in its reference to an official political division), and when a queen mother chooses to have a new stool made, it becomes part of this archive. If she chooses to leave her post or passes away, each stool, including any newly made ones, is transferred to the next queen mother.

These stools, which might be called "archival" stools, differ from the blackened stools of ancestors that have been a frequent subject of discussion in the literature on Asante culture. While blackened stools are sacred objects not meant for practical use as seating, archival stools are often presented to queen mothers to sit on during their visits with one another or with chiefs.[9] Chiefs also maintain archival stools that are part of their stool property but their own uses of the stools differ from those of queen mothers.[10] The bulk of the stools in European and North American museum collections are archival stools.

Queen mothers, rather than chiefs, have been the largest local consumers of Asante stools since at least the early twentieth century. Yet for the most part, existing discussions of stools have centred on their roles in (male) chieftaincy traditions and ancestral veneration; in turn, queen mothers' roles are largely presented as a female equivalent to male chieftaincy.[11] Both are problematic because the positions of Asante queen mothers and the related engagement with stools are distinct from those of men. Museum records in Europe and North America, when they exist, generally reinforce false assumptions about the male identity of stools by making exclusive mention of chiefs, even though this reference is frequently inaccurate or misleading.

The origins of these ideas are traceable to the period of active collecting of Asante stools, which took place in the late nineteenth and early twentieth centuries. Prevailing Euro-American ideas about stools in the early twentieth century are clearly evident in the newspapers from that period, and especially in editorial sections. The content of articles from the *London Times* reveals the pervasiveness of Euro-American peoples' understanding of Asante stools through equations of the British Throne with male chieftaincy or kingship, as well as their general confusion regarding the role of the Golden Stool and *asese dwa* more broadly. An article from September 21, 1921, provided by the newspaper's Dunkwa correspondent, explained that "the Golden Stool of Ashanti is the symbol of sovereignty corresponding to the Throne and a Monarch in Ashanti was not enthroned but enstooled."[12]

figure 6
Nana Kwartemaa Nyiano Ababio, Wadie Adwumakasehemaa, sitting on her *mmaa dwa* stool next to her *nyansapo* stool
Photo by Catherine Hale

Not only was the Golden Stool equated with the Throne, stools in general were often conflated with the Golden Stool. For example, in the follow-up to his initial article concerning the Golden Stool, the Dunkwa correspondent offered further details about the stool and then launched into a discussion of "true Ashanti stools," explaining that

> [t]hey are rectangular and oblong in plan with a flat solid base carrying a column at each corner and a larger central upright, which may be circular or square but is, in the best kinds, hollowed out and pierced with rectangular holes. The columns are also embellished by scalloping, etc, cut out of the stolid. The top or seat is curved downwards from the ends to the centre, the design as whole being simply severe and pleasing, and the proportions always good.[13]

Shortly after the article was published, a woman by the name of Lucy C. F. Cavendish wrote in to announce that she was aware of "three copies of the Golden Stool" that were in the possession of her family. She explained that two of the stools, both covered in "Native Silver," were brought home by Sir Owen Lanyon after the Kumase campaign and one was given to her with her initials carved into it. According to Cavendish, the stools "tall[ied] exactly, except as to size, with the description given lately by your Ashanti correspondent."[14] Cavendish recalled "Sir Owen telling [her] that no one was allowed to sit on the stool except the King and that it was always kept lying on its side to prevent any devil sitting on it."[15]

These Western articles reveal confusion about Asante stools on a number of levels. First, the Golden Stool is not the same shape as that described by the Dunkwa correspondent and it is covered in gold, not silver. Thus, Cavendish's stools clearly were not copies of it. Second, the Golden Stool does not belong to the "King" or Asantehene, nor is it a throne. Considered a living being, the Golden Stool is enthroned on an *asipim* (a high-backed European-style chair) with its own set of royal regalia. Finally, even in the late nineteenth and early twentieth centuries, it was primarily queen mothers, not chiefs, who used stools as a type of "throne," in the sense of a "seat" that expresses power.

Articles from the American popular press during the nineteenth and early twentieth centuries reveal a similar

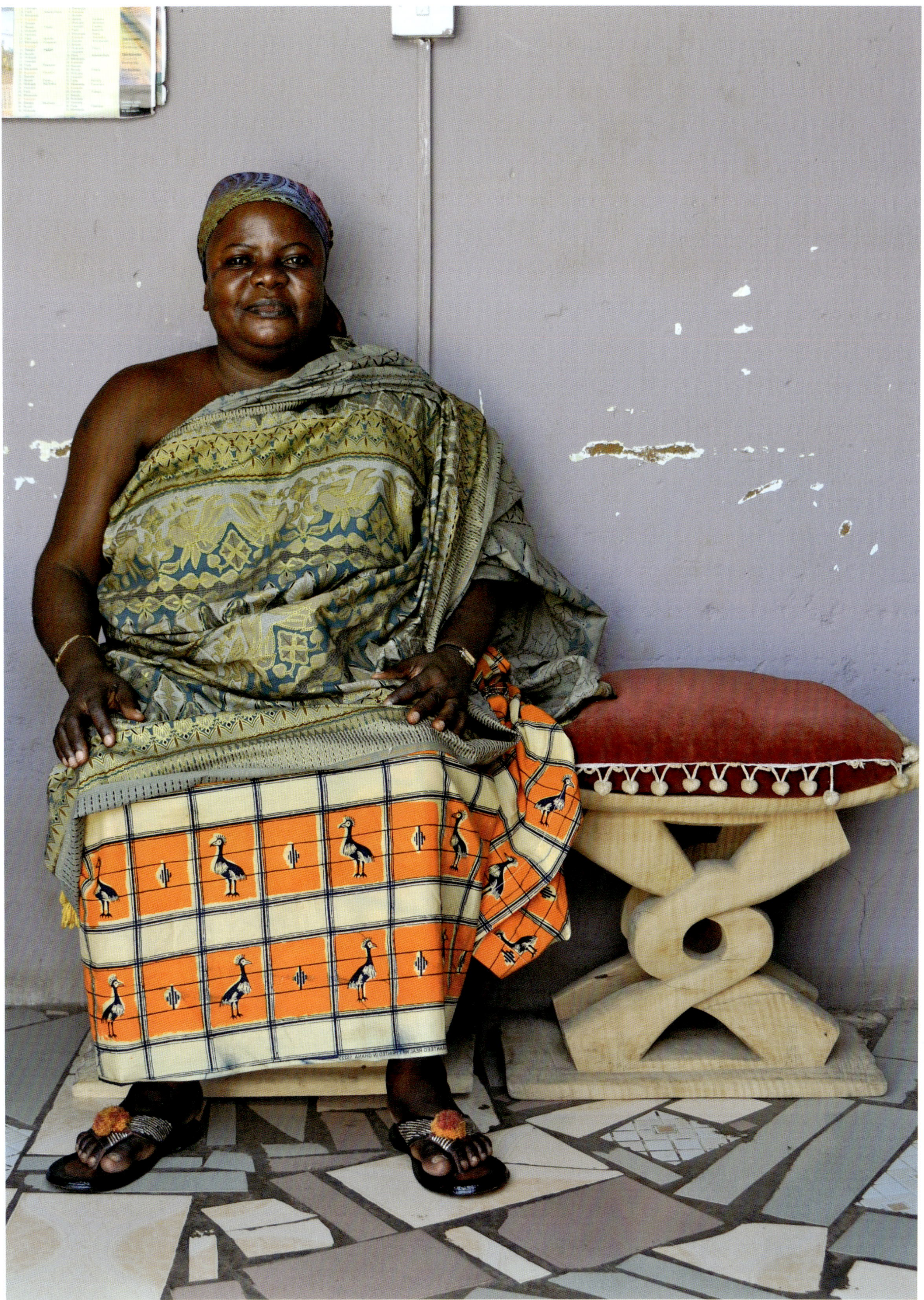

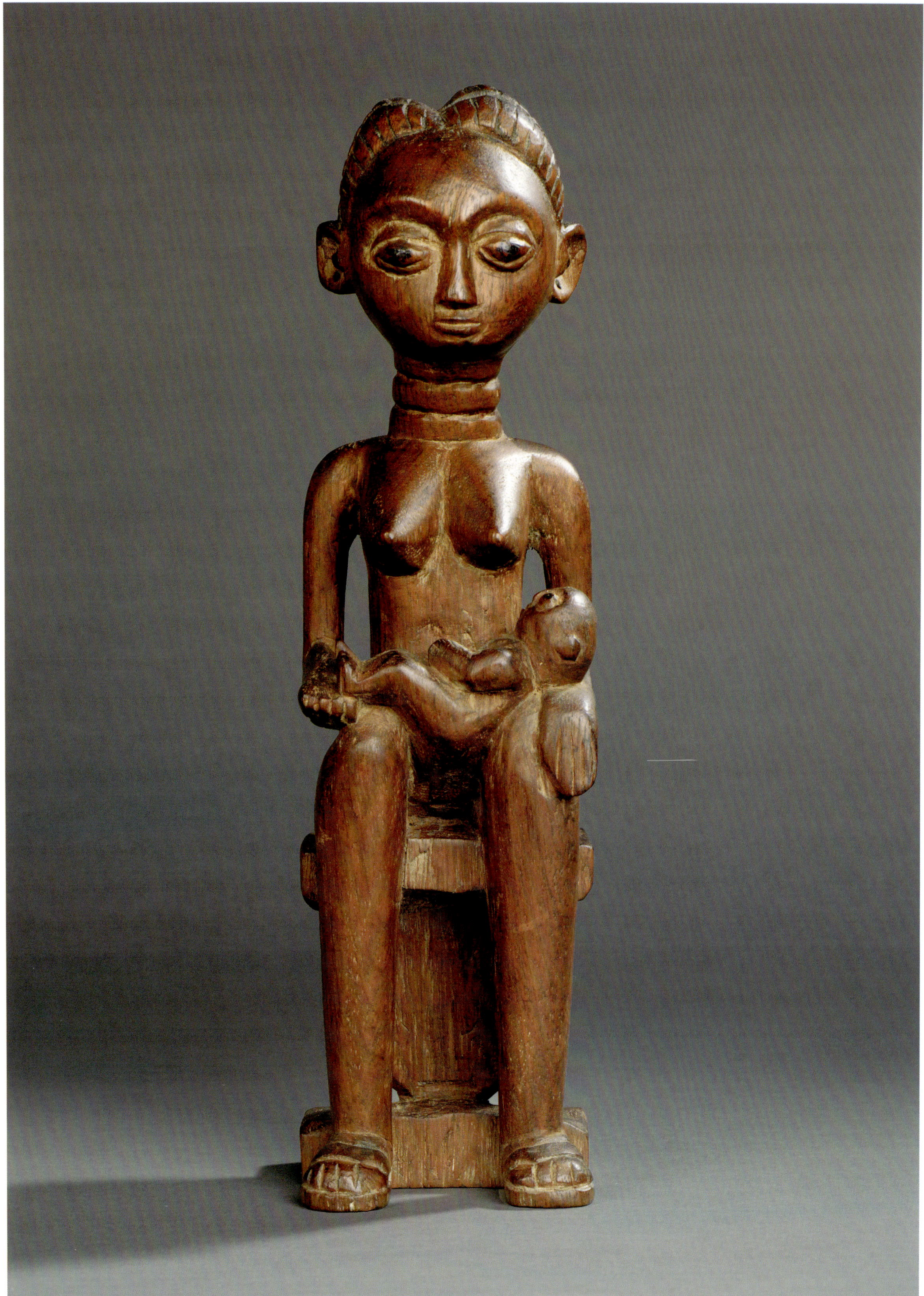

tendency to conceive of Asante stools, and the Golden Stool specifically, in terms of British coronation symbolism. Male chieftaincy narratives reached well beyond England's borders. An article from the *Dallas Morning News* in April 1900 refers to "the Gold Stool of the Ashanti, the royal throne."[16] Around the same time, a news brief about the Asante from the *Philadelphia Inquirer* mentions the "ancestral golden throne."[17] An 1899 story from the *San Jose Mercury News* talks about "Ashanti kings ... and treasures attached to the royal stool, or throne."[18]

The degree to which the Golden Stool was conceived as a male coronation seat or throne, and the problematic nature of this belief, is best evidenced by the story of Sir Frederick Hodgson. In late March of 1900, Hodgson, Governor of the new Gold Coast Colony, met with Asante leaders in Kumase to discuss their petition for changes in the British occupation. After demanding that the Asante pay interest on an old war indemnity, Hodgson concluded his speech by proclaiming:

> ...once and for all that Prempeh will never again rule over this country of Ashanti.... The paramount authority of Ashanti is now the great Queen of England whose representative I am at the moment.... Where is the golden stool? Why am I not sitting on the golden stool at this moment? I am the representative of the paramount power, why have you relegated me to this chair? Why did you not take the opportunity of my coming to Kumase to bring the golden stool and give it to me to sit upon?[19]

When Sir Frederick Hodgson demanded to sit on the Golden Stool, the Asante peoples were so offended that they resolved to defend the Golden Stool, the soul of their nation, by waging war against the British.

The campaign that ensued, which Nana Yaa Asantewaa, the queen mother of Ejisu, is credited with instigating, is acknowledged as one of the "most determined resistance movements of the colonial era."[20] The British eventually overcame the Asante when reinforcements arrived with new weaponry, but not before lives were lost on both sides as a result of Hodgson's demands. In his arrogance, the Governor failed to understand that no one sits on the Golden Stool, not even the Asantehene or Asantehemaa. Even after the nine months of war that followed the British Governor's politically motivated assertion, calls for the Golden Stool did not cease. Authorities continued to search for it throughout the Asante region during the next two decades. As Pamela McClusky has explained, the British mistook the Golden Stool for a coronation seat and saw it as a prize that they should capture and own.[21]

Museum records in Europe and North America indicate that conventional Asante stools continued to be understood in terms of coronation symbolism throughout the twentieth century. While some aspects of this comparison are accurate—such as referring to the political office of a chief as a "Stool" in the same way that one refers to the "British Throne" or the "Crown" to indicate such things as property ownership—the equation contributed to many misconceptions about stools, about the Asante political system more generally, and about the gendered history of both. What is particularly remarkable is that stools were envisaged as "seats" of power used by male chiefs, with little or no mention of their principal users, and specifically the place of queen mothers (*ahemaa*, the important female rulers who appoint chiefs) within this process.

One of the most striking features of Asante stools is that queen mothers are the most important leaders in society permitted to sit on them in public, and their use by queen mothers expresses the official power and importance of these women. In my interviews with chiefs, queen mothers and other members of Asante royal lineages, the resounding consensus is that a (male) chief only sits on a *sese dwa* very briefly (lowering himself upon it three times) during the enstoolment process, when he is bathing (a traditional practice that has become somewhat less common over time as domestic washroom facilities have changed) and, in some instances, before approaching the ancestral stools in the *nkonnwafieso* (stool house). Additionally, certain male office holders may sit on small stools while serving the Asantehene in a specific capacity, as is the case of the *okyeame* (orator or linguist). In these roles, the men are generally perceived as attendants to the ruler, not as chiefs in their own right.

Although my interviews on this topic took place in 2012, I believe it is not likely that the differences I witnessed between women's and men's uses of stools changed much over time and with respect to status. In other words, it seems highly unlikely that (male) chiefs in the late nineteenth century or early twentieth century sat on stools in public, or that chiefs of higher rank sat on stools while those of lower rank sat on chairs (or vice versa). Interviews with queen mothers and chiefs of all ages and at all levels of the political hierarchy, including Nana Yaa Birago Kokodurofo, the Adumasahemaa or queen mother of Adumasa, who has been on the stool since 1928 (she was enstooled at the age of six), made it clear that chiefs appear not to have used stools other than in the very limited contexts I outlined above for at least a century.[22] Stools here remained largely the privileged object of female historical agency and political power.

Historical photographs in the Basel Mission Archives that date as far back as the 1880s as well as anthropologist R. S. Rattray's

figure 7
Mother and child figure
Unidentified artist or workshop
Akan style
Wood
Purchased in from dealer Arouna in Lomé, Togo, in 1983
Height: 35 cm, Width: 10 cm, Depth: 10 cm
ROM 2009.126.60

early twentieth-century photographs of Asante corroborate this information. For example, a photograph titled "Yaw Sapong, Asante Chief" taken by Frederick A. L. Ramseyer sometime between 1888 and 1895 shows the young leader sitting in state on a European-style *asipim* chair, not a stool.[23] Another image taken by Ramseyer during the same period, titled "The indigenous chief of Obomeng," shows the chief sitting in state with his entourage. He wears a top hat and the finial of an *asipim* is visible above his left shoulder.[24] Similarly, in a photograph taken by a Mr. Berger between 1903 and 1912 of the "Chief of Kokofu," the armrests of an *asipim*, as well as its upper rail, are visible behind the seated leader.[25]

In Rattray's images, too, it is clear that chiefs sit on chairs and queen mothers sit on *asese dwa* (stools). This is perhaps best exemplified in the image of the model court scene Rattray asked carvers to create for him. Significantly, the figure of the chief or Asantehene is seated on a chair, while the queen mother and *okyeame* are both seated on *asese dwa*.[26] Another image taken by Rattray showing the Juabenhene and Juabenhemaa sometime before 1929 includes the Juabenhene sitting on an elaborate *asipim* beside an *akonkromfi* chair that supports the Juaben Stool (Fig. 8).[27] On the other side of the Stool, the female leader here, the Juabenhemaa, is seated on what appears to be the *mmaa dwa* ("woman's stool") style of *sese dwa*, which is decorated with metallic strips. I am unaware of any historical images or documents that present an Asante chief sitting in state on a *sese dwa*. As is the case today, and as has been since at least the late nineteenth century, it appears that Asante chiefs sit on chairs and queen mothers sit on traditional stools when acting in official capacities publically.

What, then, accounts for the fact that early twentieth-century collectors did not mention queen mothers in their documentation of Asante stools, despite the fact that these women were their primary users? There are many possibilities. Writing in 1923, after finally learning about the vital roles of queen mothers in the matrilineal society of the Asante, R. S. Rattray gave on explanation:

> [he] asked the old men and women why [he] did not know all this—[he] had spent very many years in Ashanti. The answer is always the same: "The white man never asked us this; you have dealings with and recognize only the men; we supposed the European considered women of no account, and we know you do not recognize them as we have always done."[28]

That an early twentieth-century African trader might mislead a Western collector into thinking that a stool belonged to a (male) chief rather than a female ruler because he thought it would be more highly valued is a distinct possibility. Christopher Steiner's research into the African art market reveals that it was, and still is, a common tendency for African traders to alter the histories and forms of objects to suit the perceived tastes of

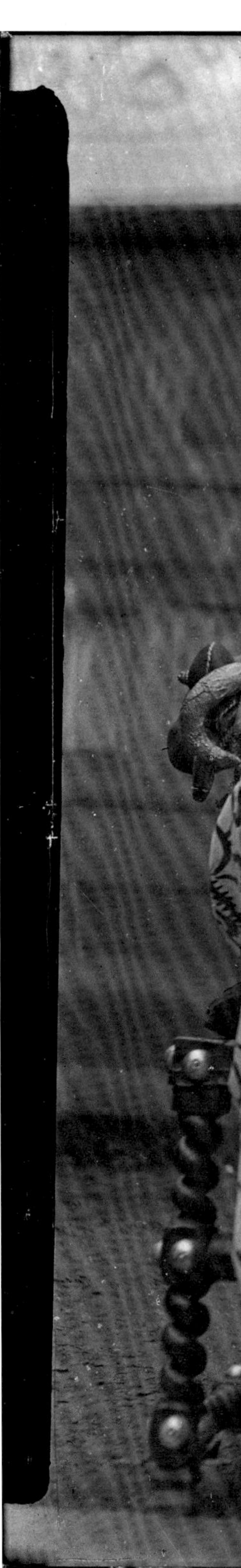

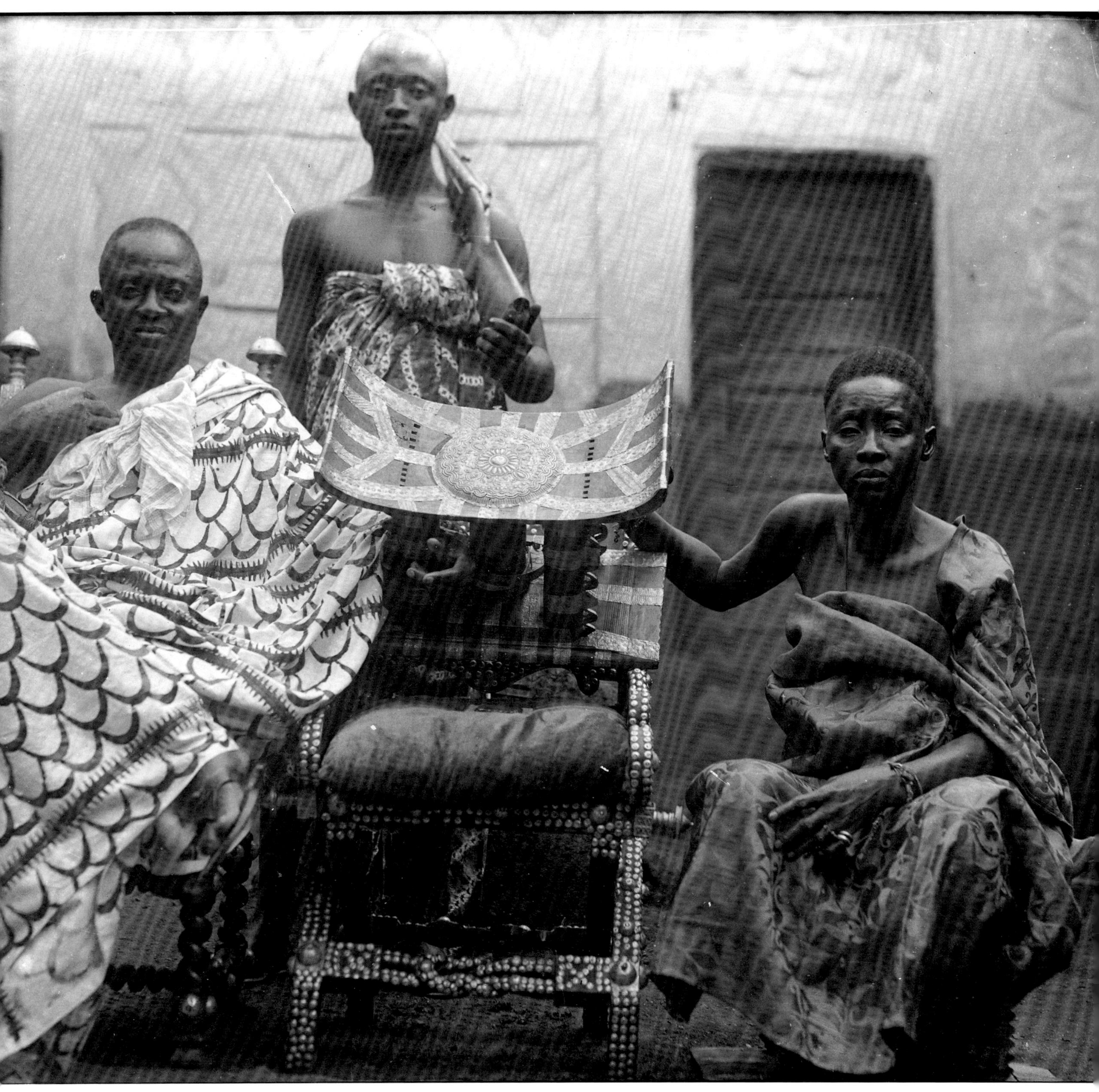

figure 8
"Juaben Hene and Ohema with stool"
Photograph by R. S. Rattray, ca. 1921–1929
(Pitt Rivers Museum, University of Oxford,
Acc. Number: 1998.312.529.1)

Western collectors. For example, Steiner quotes the experience of the American scientist, Frederick Starr, who travelled through the Belgian Congo to collect specimens and artifacts for the American Museum of Natural History in the early twentieth century. In December 1905, Starr reported the following:

> Yesterday a well-carved wooden figure was offered. I refused it because it was rather new and empty [of medicine] in its stomach hole. Today it appeared again, this time with a fat round belly neatly sewed up and well smeared with cam and oil. I agreed to the price, getting it down to 1.50 francs.[29]

Steiner explains that Starr's sources eventually became so familiar with his tastes that they only offered him objects they knew would meet his criteria. The pervasiveness of this kind of scenario, particularly in West Africa, means that the objects that have come to represent "Africa" in European and North American museums tend to be selected and framed by specifically Western perspectives.

This problem imposed by the colonial reconstruction of knowledge is exacerbated by the ways in which later scholars have used early sources, and inaccurate taxonomies perpetuated by them. In 1927 R. S. Rattray published photographs of thirty-one conventional Asante stools. He explained that the list was not necessarily exhaustive of all the possibilities but felt that it was "sufficient to show their graceful lines and the technique and beauty of their design."[30] For each stool, he listed information such as its title and the member or members of society who had permission to possess it. For example, he described the *esono 'gwa* or "the elephant stool," which could only be used by the "King of Ashanti," and the *sakyi dua koro 'gwa* or "the stool with the single centre support," which was used "only by the priesthood."[31] Among the stools he mentioned were three that he claimed were exclusive to women: the *ahema 'gwa* or "The Queen's stool," which is the stool of "Nyako Kusi Amoa, one of the early Queen Mothers of Ashanti"; the *mma 'gwa* or "the woman's stool," which "a man, when he marries, generally presents his wife with this stool;" and *Me fa asa 'gwa* or "my half is finished," which he explained meant "half my clan is dead."[32] Rattray's outline, with its tidy descriptions of users and meanings, promoted a picture of Asante stool designs and functions as being static, clearly defined and rigidly hierarchical.

This idea has been replicated in the majority of the literature on Asante stools produced in the twentieth century. For example, Peter Sarpong, in *The Sacred Stools of the Akan*, appears to draw the bulk of his examples of stool owners and stool designs and symbolism from Rattray's early account.[33] M. D. McLeod, in *The Asante*, devotes most of his discussion of Asante stool types and uses to a reiteration of the content of Rattray's compilation.[34] Sharon Patton's unpublished 1980 dissertation, "The Asante Stool," strives to categorize stools and hierarchies in an approach that draws on Rattray's framework, too. As not many substantial studies of stools were published during the twentieth century, most other publications and catalogues also espouse Rattray's framework in their brief discussions.

These early twentieth-century categories are inscribed similarly in the tourist sphere, where a poster that outlines stool types, their meanings, and ownership limitations has been circulating in various forms since at least the 1970s.[35] Although different variations exist, the fundamental structure of each poster includes black and white outlines of multiple conventional stools, their identifying features emphasized for easy recognition. Every stool silhouette is paired with a description of its meaning and/or the individual in society permitted to own it; most pairings are drawn directly from Rattray's account, and in some cases, the author has added a few more recent examples to the illustration. Many shopkeepers and carvers keep the posters on hand and/or have them available for purchase. They use them readily as a way to explain the cultural importance of the stools they have for sale, relying on the clearly delineated rules to communicate their value and meaning to outsiders. On more than one occasion, carvers presented me with the poster as a kind of menu from which to choose the design that was most suitable or desirable for my purposes.

Yet, Rattray's own language suggests that even as he was writing in the late 1920s, the cogent categories he described were not so exclusively demarcated as his catalogue may have implied. Specifically, he opens his discussion of stools by saying that "a generation or so ago, every stool in use had its own particular significance and its own special name which denoted the sex, or social status, or clan of the owner."[36] Such an observation suggests that, although he believed stringent rules regarding ownership existed previously, they may not have been employed so rigorously at the time of his observations.

When Sharon Patton undertook a study of the stools of the chiefs of the Kronti political division in the late 1970s, she also noted that individuals in possession of stools did not necessarily follow the policies outlined by Rattray or the carvers with whom she spoke. For example, contrary to Rattray's assertion that only women could own the *mmaa dwa*, and that a husband gave it to his wife, Patton documented multiple chiefs who possessed this design.[37] She also observed that despite the carvers' insistence that chiefs' stools should have black designs painted on the bottom, most of the stools of the chiefs she viewed did not incorporate this feature.[38] Although Patton noted the disconnect between the "rules" and practice, her study did not penetrate more deeply into the ways in which stools were used in different contexts: she noted that certain chiefs possessed the *mmaa dwa*, but did not comment on how or why these chiefs were using these specific stools.[39]

My own research in Asante reveals that although many of the carvers and shopkeepers at Ahwiaa and elsewhere continue to promote the structured framework for stools established by Rattray (particularly when they are trying to appeal to a foreign buyer), the queen mothers who are the primary local users of conventional stools employ and think about them in very different ways. Specifically, hierarchical prescriptions are highly relative and context is a crucial component of how a leader chooses which stool to employ at a given moment. Contrary to the guidelines that Rattray claimed governed who could own which stools, every queen mother with whom I spoke declared that she could own any design or size she wished. What was of critical importance was where and when she chose to present a particular stool publically. She had to ensure that whichever stool she selected would not be more elaborate than the ones used by queen mothers (in attendance) whose ranks were above her own. Such a decision would necessarily shift and change with each event—its nature, purpose, and guest list. While some discrepancies can indeed be attributed to "rule breaking" and/or changes that have occurred over time, at least in the case of queen mothers, there is also an important sense in which Asante stools and their uses are fluid and dynamic and have been since at least the early part of the twentieth century.[40] In other words, the rules that apply to an individual's use of stools in one situation may not be equally relevant under a different set of circumstances.[41]

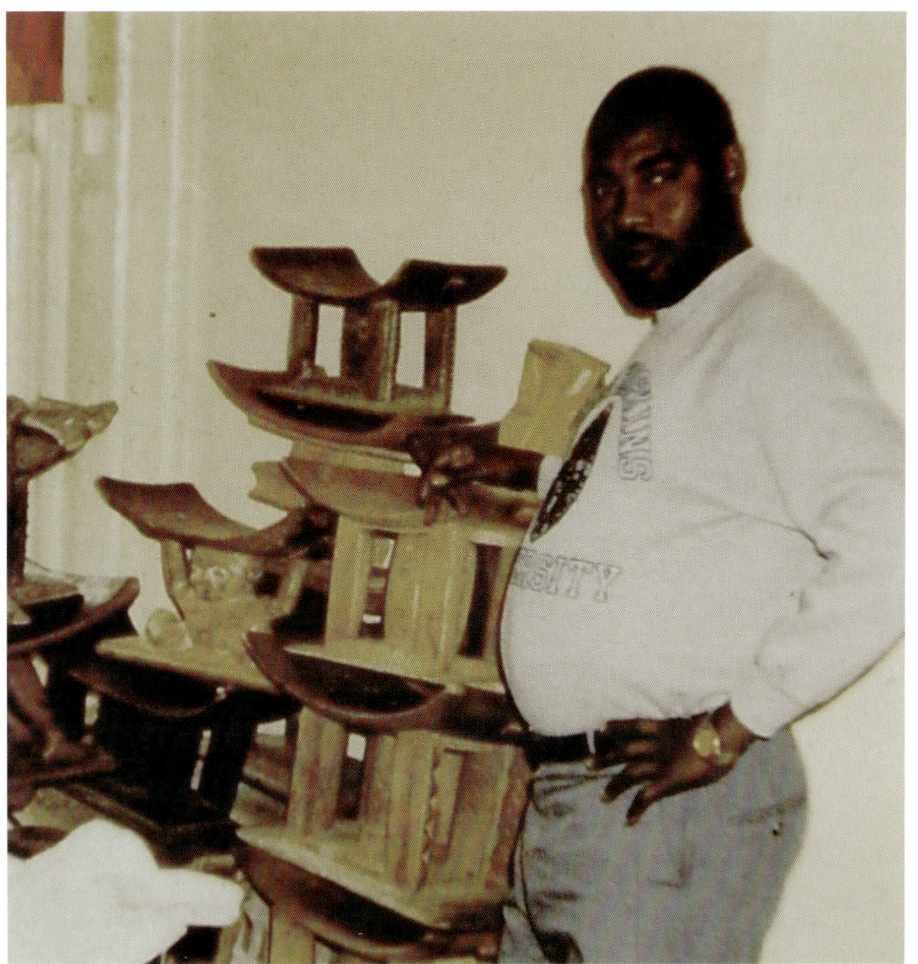

figure 9
Hausa art dealer Aladji Baaré
with Asante stools for sale
Hotel Belleclaire, New York City
Photo by Christopher B. Steiner (1991)

This idea plays out more broadly in the contemporary market at Ahwiaa, where carvers produce stools that are readily available to anyone interested in making the purchase. Acquiring a ready-made stool was a common practice among the queen mothers I interviewed at all levels of the hierarchy. Several of them shared with me warm memories of travelling to Ahwiaa, or having a family member go on their behalf, to select a stool after they learned they would soon be appointed. It was rare even for very high-ranking women to commission a new stool. In many cases, going to the market to purchase a stool was an important part of the ritual of taking on a new leadership position. As previously mentioned, although international tourists tend to favour the new stool type, they are not prohibited from purchasing the conventional stools used by queen mothers in their official political and ritual capacities. What matters most is not whether tourists (or anyone else) purchase conventional stools but how they make use of them. Here, again, context is crucial. As Nana Afia Serwaa (the queen mother of Aputuogya, or the Aputuogyahemaa) explained to me, "You can buy one and put it in your room for decoration's sake but not to sit on it as traditional authority permits."[42] As a foreigner, I can take a conventional stool home to North America and keep it in my house but it would be a great offence for me to sit on it openly in Ghana.

The realities of this market scenario are, of course, much more opaque than the unambiguous parameters of Rattray's categories and the prevailing narratives of male chieftaincy that have dominated twentieth-century literature, museum records and auction catalogues. Framed in these terms, the histories of the conventional stools in Western collections are much more elusive. For example, if read according to Rattray, the stool from the Dagan collection illustrated in Figure 3 could be deemed a *mmarima dwa*, which he defines as "the man's stool."[43] Yet it shares significant features with the type I saw for sale in large quantities at Ahwiaa and that was represented widely in the stool collections of queen mothers throughout Asante. As this example illustrates, the fixed, gendered categories that have been used to interpret Asante stools in the global marketplace over the course of the twentieth century fail to capture the complex and nuanced uses of their primary local customers, queen mothers.

Returning once more to the billboard I mentioned at the outset of my discussion, the incorporation of the new stool type, rather than the *sese dwa* used most frequently by queen mothers, is significant. At first assessment, the pairing of an Asante stool with the slogan "Carve a Strong Niche on the International Market" appears to suggest the promotion of a uniquely Asante identity within the global sphere. Yet, as the preceding discussion illustrated, the new stool type is more closely associated with broader notions of Ghanaian nationalism and external perceptions of Asante identity (as the most popular item in tourist markets) than it is with local politics and ritual.

It is worth noting that the billboard was located in one of the most affluent areas of the city, where hotels and banking institutions abound and expats from around the world frequently stay for extended periods of time. This begs the question: Who is the advertisement's intended audience? Although it is tempting to hypothesize about the intentions of the advertiser, the main point I want to focus on here is that this marketing strategy exemplifies the larger phenomenon that has impacted Asante stools and African material culture in the course of cross-cultural exchanges throughout the twentieth century—namely, framing them in terms of vocabulary, ideas and concepts that are professed to be local or "authentic" but more often than not reflect the perceptions and/or misperceptions of external agents. Here, it is particularly salient that the *adinkra* symbol depicted on the stool on the SG-SSB billboard appears to be an abbreviation of *kintinkantan*, which is a warning against arrogance.

Collectors in the late-nineteenth-century and early-twentieth-century appear to have understood the Asante stools they acquired primarily through the lens of male chieftaincy and equations with British monarchical symbols. At the same time, Rattray's widely cited but significantly flawed system of ownership prescriptions further complicated this history. Both narratives, which together established the dominant framework for thinking about Asante stools for much of the twentieth century, largely overlooked the critical connections among women, queen mothers and stools. As is the case with much African art housed in museums and circulating in the international market, global understandings of Asante stools have been mediated through the perspectives of outsiders with varying biases, levels of familiarity with Asante culture, and access to information. It is only in retrospect that scholars, museum professionals and other stakeholders are now able to start unravelling information and seeking out additional perspectives to develop more comprehensive understandings of these unique objects.

---

1 Nana Afia Serwaa, Aputuogyahemaa (queen mother of Aputuogya), in conversation with the author, June 4, 2012.

2 Nana Frempong Boadu, Otumfuonkonnwasenefuohene (Otumfuo Chief Carver), in conversation with the author, June 14, 2012.

3 This information was gathered during fieldwork in the Ashanti region between 2007 and 2012.

4 Nana Frempong Boadu, Otumfuo Chief Carver, in conversation with the author, June 14, 2012.

5 S. F. Adjei, Director of the Centre for National Culture–Kumase and Nana Sarfo Kantanka, Deputy Director of the Centre for National Culture–Kumase, in conversation with the author, June 2012. It is worth noting the parallels between Adjei and Kantanka's account of Kyerematen's conception of the *Gye Nyame* stool and the well-known story of the birth of the Golden Stool, which is said to have come into existence around the beginning of the eighteenth century when Osei Tutu asked his chief priest and

advisor, Okomfo Anokye, to create a symbol that would represent the Asante nation.

6 Nana Sarfo Kantanka, Deputy Director of the Centre for National Culture–Kumase in conversation with the author, June 2012.

7 This information was gathered during fieldwork between 2007 and 2012.

8 Adom Gyamfi Richard, Secretary of the Ahwiaa Wood Carvers Association, in conversation with the author, May 26, 2012.

9 For a discussion of blackened stools, see Peter Sarpong, *The Sacred Stools of the Akan* (Accra-Tema: Ghana Publishing Corporation, 1971); and A. Kyerematen, "The Royal Stools of Ashanti," *Africa: Journal of the International African Institute* 39, no. 1 (Jan. 1969): 1–10.

10 The preceding information about Asante queen mothers' uses of stools is based on interviews I undertook with fourteen queen mothers in the Ashanti region of Ghana in May and June of 2012.

11 See R. S. Rattray, *Religion and Art in Ashanti* (Oxford: Clarendon Press, 1927); A. Kyerematen, "The Royal Stools of Ashanti," *Africa: Journal of the International African Institute* 39, no. 1 (Jan., 1969): 1–10; Peter Sarpong, *The Sacred Stools of the Akan* (Accra-Tema: Ghana Publishing Corporation, 1971); and Sharon Patton, "The Asante Stool," (PhD diss., Northwestern University, 1980).

12 "The Golden Stool Found: Ashanti Symbol of Sovereignty," *London Times*, September 21, 1921.

13 "Golden Stool of Ashanti: Mystery of Its Fate," *London Times*, October 14, 1921.

14 "The Golden Stool of Ashanti," *London Times*, November 11, 1921.

15 Ibid.

16 "Golden Stool War," *Dallas Morning News*, April 10, 1900.

17 "Is Ashanti's throne found? Discovery of the Golden Stool May be the Cause of Trouble," *Philadelphia Inquirer*, April 8, 1900.

18 "The Coast of Blood and Gold," *San Jose Mercury News*, June 24, 1899.

19 Quoted in Pamela McClusky, *Art from Africa: Long Steps Never Broke a Back* (Seattle: Seattle Art Museum in association with Princeton University Press, 2002): 91.

20 Pamela McClusky, *Art from Africa*, 91.

21 Pamela McClusky, *Art from Africa*, 92.

22 Nana Yaa Birago Kokodurofo, Adumasahemaa, in conversation with the author, June 15, 2012.

23 "Yaw Sapong, Asante Chief," record I.D.: impa-m38378, Basel Mission Image Archive, University of Southern California Libraries.

24 "The indigenous chief of Obomeng," record I.D.: impa-m38338, Basel Mission Image Archive, University of Southern California Libraries.

25 "Chief of Kokofu," record I.D.: impa-m25845, Basel Mission Image Archive, University of Southern California Libraries.

26 R. S. Rattray, *Religion and Art in Ashanti* (Oxford: Clarendon Press, 1927): fig. 188.

27 R. S. Rattray, *Law and Constitution in Ashanti* (Oxford: Clarendon Press, 1929): fig. 29.

28 R. S. Rattray, *Ashanti* (Oxford: Clarendon Press, 1923): 84.

29 Christopher B. Steiner, "The Taste of Angels in the Art of Darkness: Fashioning the Canon of African Art," in *Art History and Its Institutions*, ed. Elizabeth Mansfield (London: Routledge, 2002): 142.

30 Rattray, *Religion and Art in Ashanti*, 273.

31 Ibid, 272–73.

32 Ibid, 272.

33 The examples cited by Sarpong are the same stools listed in Rattray's account. See Peter Sarpong, *The Sacred Stools of the Akan* (Accra-Tema: Ghana Publishing Corporation, 1971): 19–25.

34 M. D. McLeod, *The Asante* (London: British Museum Publications, Ltd., 1984): 114–15.

35 The most recent poster I encountered was attributed to Prof. Ablade Glover and listed a first publication date of Feb. 1971 and a subsequent (revised) edition date of Feb. 1992.

36 Rattray, *Religion and Art in Ashanti*, 271.

37 Sharon Patton, "The Asante Stool" (PhD diss., Northwestern University, 1980), 66.

38 Patton, "The Asante Stool," 108.

39 A number of people I interviewed provided reasons that the "woman's stool" may have been in these chiefs' possession. Among other things, they speculated that the chiefs might have had them to provide to queen mothers to sit on when they came to visit.

40 I suspect that the fluid and dynamic character of stool rules and hierarchies is applicable to chiefs' and other users' engagement with them, but I cannot comment in more depth as my investigation focused on queen mothers. This is an area that would be fruitful for future study.

41 The most elderly queen mother I interviewed was Nana Yaa Birago Kokodurofo, who was enstooled in 1928 (at the age of six), the year after Rattray published *Religion and Art in Ashanti*. Her experience with stools has been as dynamic as more recently appointed queen mothers, which suggests that this kind of fluidity was operational even at the time that Rattray was writing.

42 Nana Afia Serwaa, in conversation with the author, June 4, 2012.

43 Rattray, *Religion and Art in Ashanti*, 272.

Bibliography

Kyerematen, A. "The Royal Stools of Ashanti." *Africa: Journal of the International African Institute* 39, no. 1 (Jan. 1969): 1–10.

McClusky, Pamela. *Art from Africa: Long Steps Never Broke a Back*. Seattle: Seattle Art Museum in association with Princeton University Press, 2002.

McLeod, M. D. *The Asante*. London: British Museum Publications, Ltd., 1984.

Patton, Sharon. "The Asante Stool." PhD diss., Northwestern University, 1980.

Rattray, R. S. *Ashanti*. Oxford: Clarendon Press, 1923.

———. *Law and Constitution in Ashanti*. Oxford: Clarendon Press, 1929.

———. *Religion and Art in Ashanti*. Oxford: Clarendon Press, 1927.

Sarpong, Peter. *The Sacred Stools of the Akan*. Accra-Tema: Ghana Publishing Corporation, 1971.

Steiner, Christopher B. "The Taste of Angels in the Art of Darkness: Fashioning the Canon of African Art." In *Art History and Its Institutions*, edited by Elizabeth Mansfield, 132–45. London: Routledge, 2002.

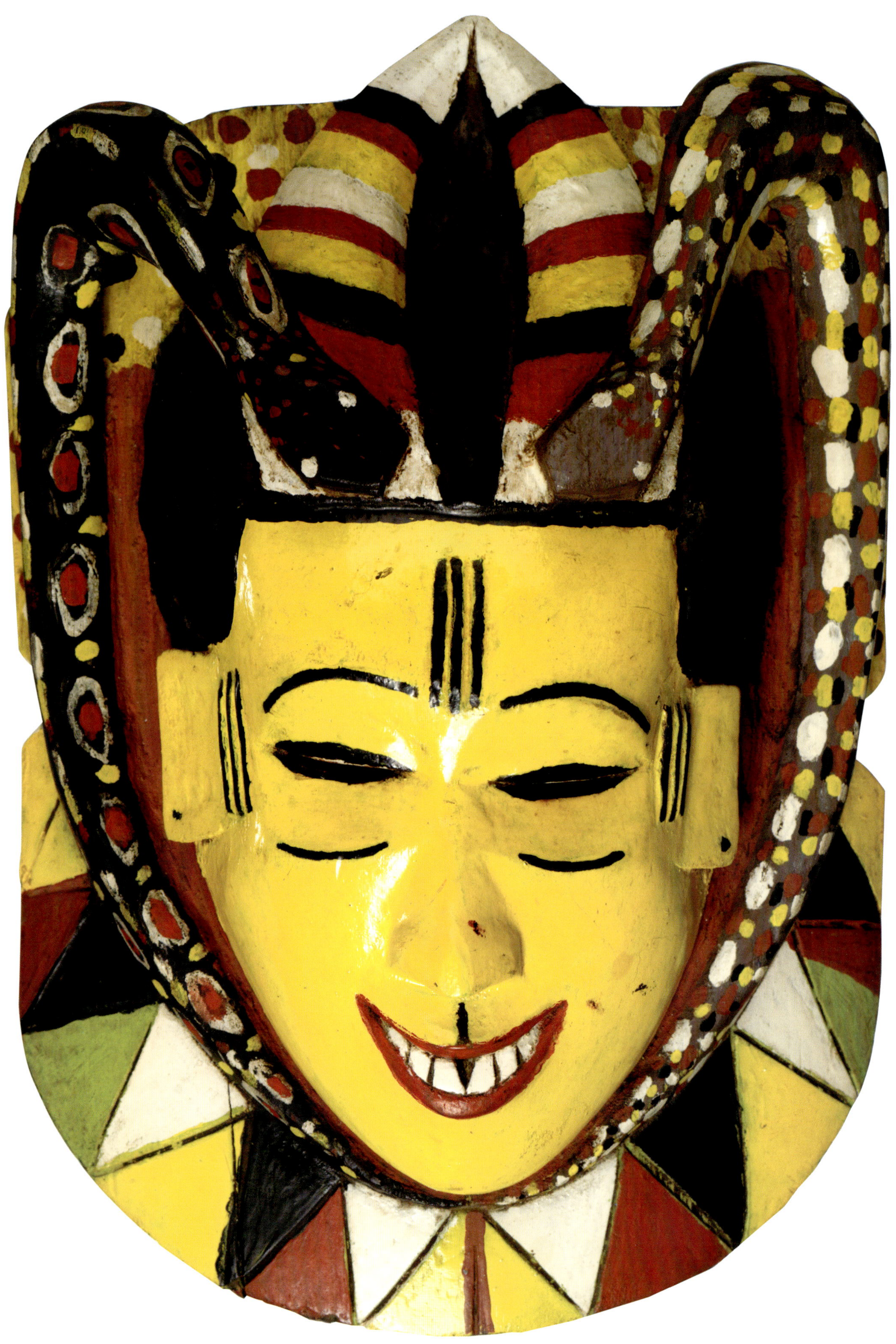

plate 9

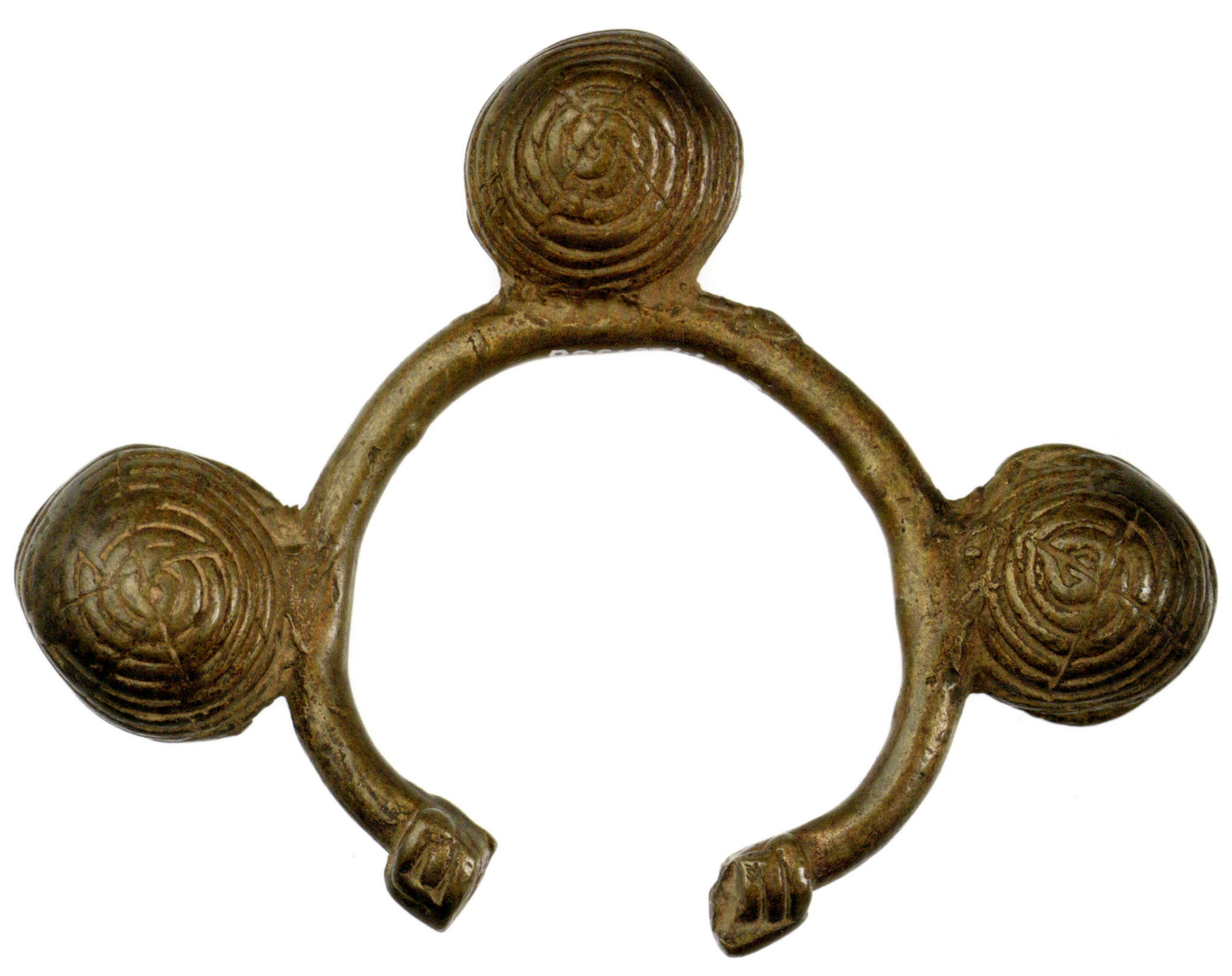

plate 10

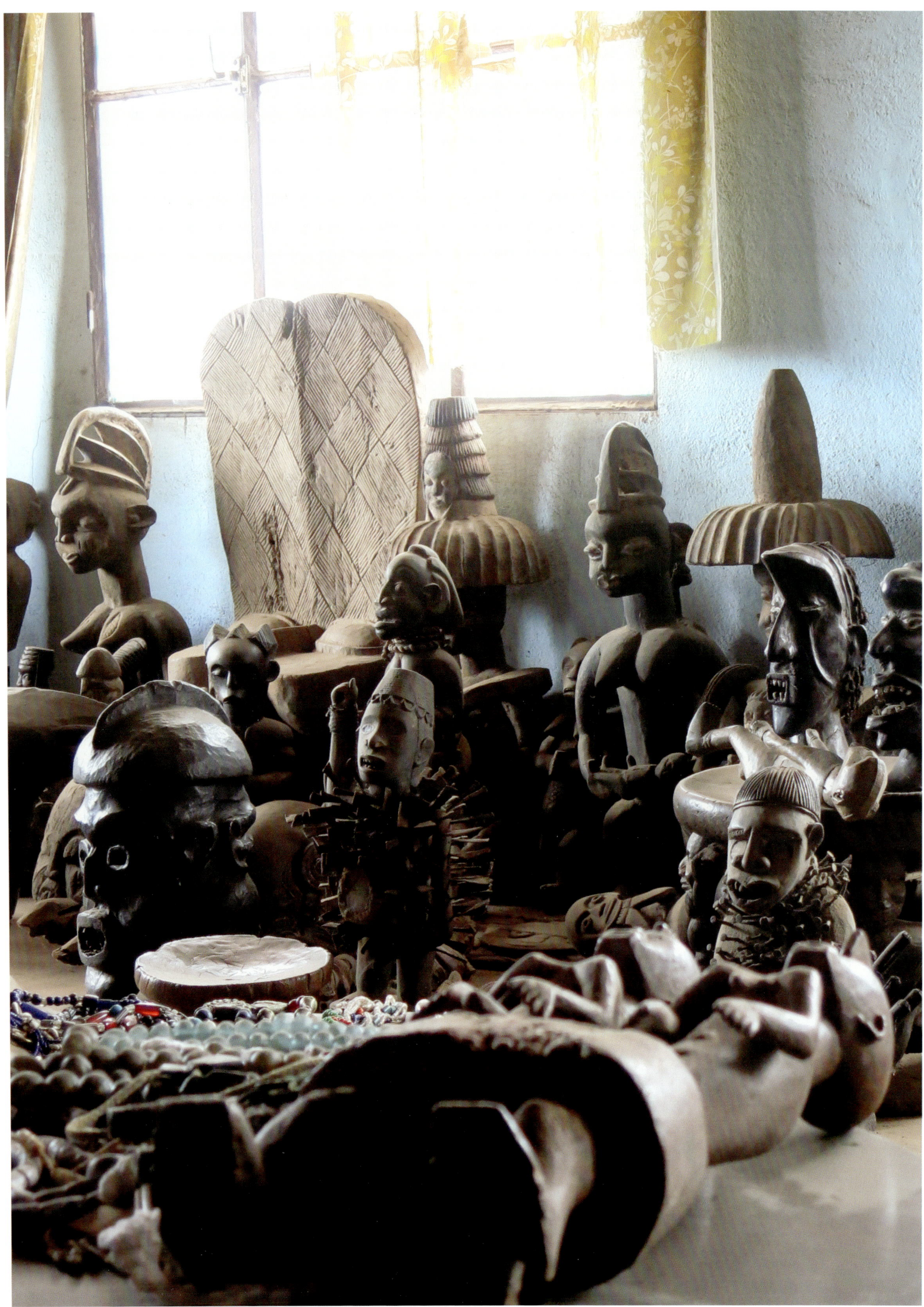

CHAPTER 6

CANONICAL INVENTIONS AND MARKET KNOWLEDGE IN THE GRASSFIELDS OF CAMEROON

SILVIA FORNI

The Amrad African Art Collection includes more than thirty pieces that were made or purchased in Cameroon. By the mid-1980s, when Esther Dagan collected her pieces in Douala, Yaoundé and Foumban, Cameroon was a politically troubled country with a relatively stable economy—its currency was secured to the French franc and its relatively large middle class had yet to be hit by the economic measures imposed by the World Bank's structural adjustment plan. At the time, the art market was mostly controlled by Bamum dealers, as it is still today. Foumban, the capital of the Bamum kingdom, was broadly recognized as the main art market in the country with hundreds of merchants specializing in art from the Grassfields and beyond. Many Bamum traders worked as middlemen collecting art from the West, North West and North regions of Cameroon, Nigeria and Gabon, and procuring old and new artworks for art dealers based in Yaoundé, Douala, Europe and the United States. The works that fascinated Esther Dagan during her 1985 and 1987 trips were mainly in Grassfields style and they were quite typical of the production for local use and the international market circulating in the mid-to-late twentieth century.

This chapter analyzes some of the historical developments and contemporary trends in the production and circulation of art in the Grassfields. It shows how broad exchange networks, diplomacy, and market consciousness on the part of local producers and dealers have been important influences in the shaping of regional aesthetics and creativity for well over a century.

Exchange and Regional Identity

Within Cameroon's broad geographical, cultural and linguistic diversity, the Grassfields have long been referred to in colonial and scholarly literature as a distinctive region. Crossing over many local political and linguistic divides, the region appears culturally and geographically different from the forest region of the south or the Adamawa plateau in the north. Today, this area covers the anglophone North West Region—especially the kingdoms of the Bamenda plateau and the Ring Road—and a great part of the francophone West Region, which corresponds to the territories of the many Bamiléké kingdoms and the larger Bamum kingdom. While many polities in the Grassfields have a similar political structure and social organization and are governed by a sacred king, a council of notables, and a male regulatory society in which membership is restricted to individuals who are not part of the royal family, each kingdom has been marked by its own language, as well as a number of specific and idiosyncratic cultural and political characters.

The Grassfields have been a somewhat elusive entity, whose boundaries and distinctiveness have been premised on the intersection of different characteristics whereby each kingdom in the area resembles its neighbours more than it does other cultural and political groups in

detail
Display of antiquities in
a private dealer's residence
Foumban, July 10, 2013
Photo by Silvia Forni

the country. Many scholars have remarked on the key role art has played in reinforcing the perception of cultural unity throughout this region. The architectonic and aesthetic consistency that struck the first European visitors to the region formed a visual texture reflective of the centuries of commercial exchanges, warfare and alliances that characterized the relationship between polities in this densely populated area.[1]

It is quite fitting that the Grassfields were one of the two examples of complex and open regional artistic systems chosen by René Bravmann for his seminal essay "Open Frontiers." Bravmann questioned the effectiveness of studying African cultures and expressive traditions through a model that isolates people and art within "tribal" and stylistic boundaries. The Grassfields, he argued, could not be equated in any way to a "tribe" given that it was a region composed of a number of independent polities speaking different languages and claiming different origins and migration histories.[2] Yet, this diverse area also appeared quite integrated thanks to the extensive network of commercial exchange through which metal, oil, livestock, agricultural products and other goods circulated from one kingdom to the other. Jean-Pierre Warnier convincingly demonstrated how centuries of cohabitation in a relatively densely populated territory, local specialization, a high level of multilingualism, and well-developed regional and long-distance trade routes resulted in the distinctive regional character which clearly sets this area apart from its neighbours.[3]

Art was also part of regional commercial networks. While carvers, weavers and potters were active in virtually every kingdom of the Grassfields, few centres were recognized widely for their exceptional production, which was exchanged and exported throughout the region.[4] This circulation was not limited to objects. Artists would move from one kingdom to the other, working for the court and producing high-quality regalia that could be used as insignia or diplomatic gifts.

The importance of art-making and of the visual affirmation of a polity's political influence was confirmed by the attribution of important bodies of sculpture to specific kings such as King Yu of Kom (1865–1912) or more recently King Zofoa II of Babungo, who reigned until 1999.[5] Whether or not the so-called "sculptor kings" actually produced much of the artwork that has been attributed to them, it is clear that several monarchs were heavily involved in the aesthetic direction of the royal workshops and carefully controlled the visual production that defined local royal style.

The elaborate decor which characterized the king's palaces and the ceremonies of the kingdom constituted a striking visual vocabulary aimed at affirming the status and relevance of senior individuals within the political structure and of a polity *vis-à-vis* its neighbours. Although, as pointed out by Warnier, the formation of Grassfields political hierarchies predated the Atlantic trade by several centuries, the increased wealth accumulated through regional and long-distance trade from the eighteenth century onward stimulated the production of a sophisticated material culture of power.[6] This highlighted social and spiritual distinctions that suggested to the Europeans who travelled through the region at the turn of the twentieth century that there was a degree of cultural uniformity in spite of political and linguistic divides.[7] Warnier, Fowler, Tardits and many others demonstrate how this impression was mostly a consequence of the high degree of mobility of people and goods via the well-developed exchange networks of the region.[8] Within this highly selective hierarchical structure, only one of the sons of a titleholder inherited the compound's wealth and came to control the productive and reproductive power of the family women and his juniors. Trade and exchanges were controlled by a relatively small number of individuals who benefited greatly from the expansion of the trade routes and the intensification of the slave trade from the mid-eighteenth century.[9]

Colonial Rule and the Art Market

The arrival of German colonial officers and missionaries at the beginning of the twentieth century added a new component to the circulation of artworks in the region. Christraud Geary analyzed the competitive nature of early colonial collecting practices aimed at gathering an extensive material record of the material culture of the region.[10] Objects were destined for the ethnographic museums of the main German urban centres and they competed for the best pieces. Missionaries, military personnel, dealers, scholars and curators all contributed to the systematic appropriation of objects of daily life, insignia of power and ceremonial pieces that were collected through looting, as diplomatic gifts and quite often through purchase.[11]

The economic component of the collecting enterprise emerged quite clearly in the correspondence between collectors and museum administrators. Geary quoted a 1906 letter to the director of the Leipzig Museum für Völkerkunde, in which merchant Adolf Diehl urged the museum to send generous funding to secure the most spectacular pieces and pay for the high cost of transport.[12] Diehl stressed the competitive nature of field collecting by highlighting Captain Hans Glauning's exploits on behalf of the Berlin Museum für Völkerkunde. In 1908 Bernhard Ankermann, curator of Africa and Oceania at the Berlin Museum, travelled to the Grassfields for his own collecting expedition, during which he acquired over 1,500 objects for this museum. Although he collected extensively throughout the region, he was particularly impressed by the high quality of the objects found at the court of King Njoya in Foumban. In a letter to the museum's administration in late March 1908, he reported:

> Bamum has by far surpassed my expectation; as a town it is extraordinarily rich in really splendid pieces fit for collecting. Naturally they are more expensive than anywhere else and many of them one can only get for cash. But one can get almost anything for cash, different from Bali.[13]

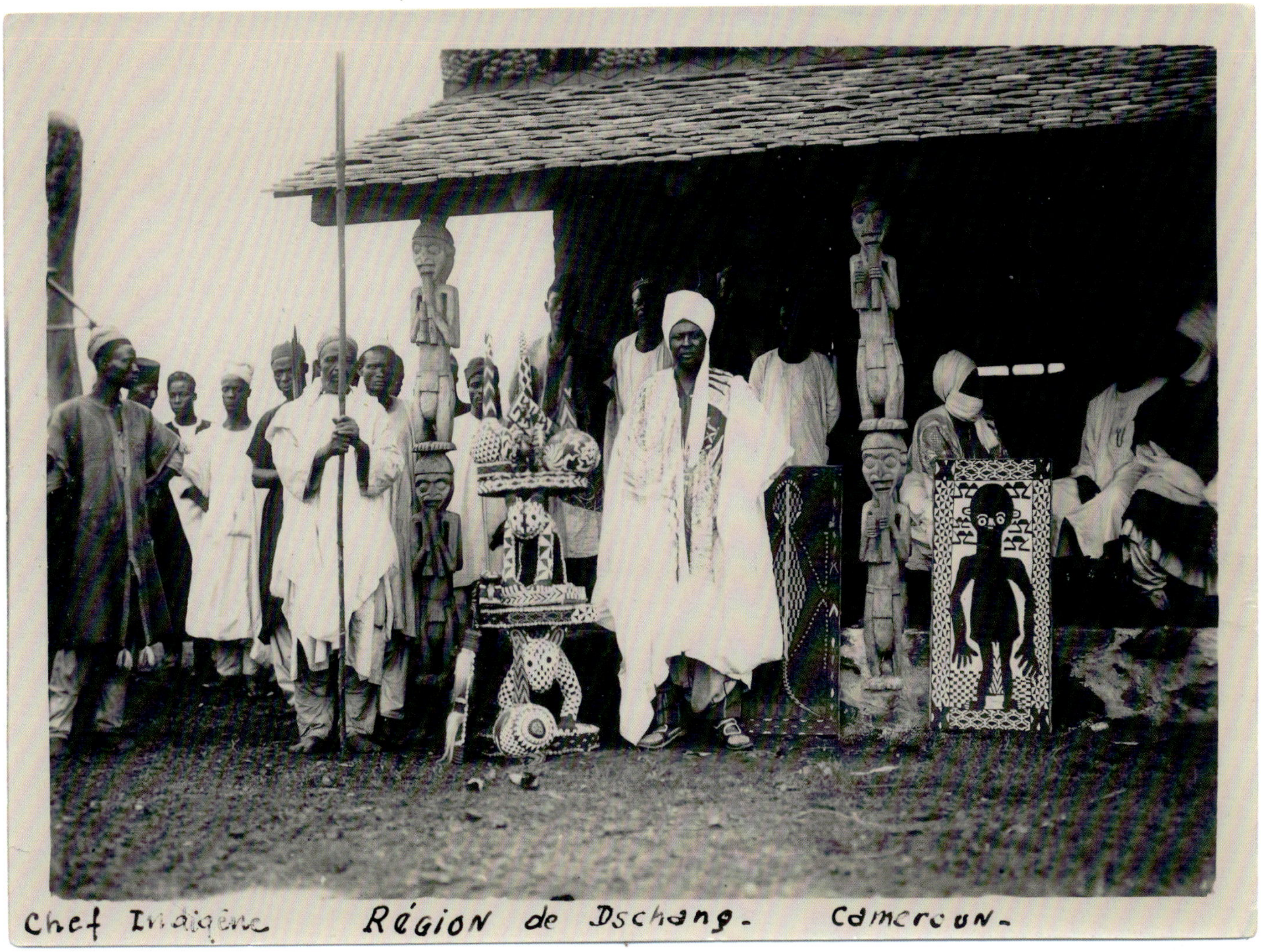

figure 1
Mose Yéyab with his collection of regalia and commercial objects in front of the museum he established in Foumban
Photo courtesy of Christraud M. Geary

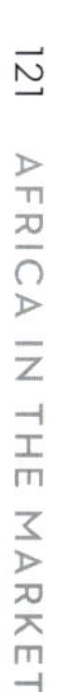

At the time when Ankermann was collecting and writing, sales to foreigners were still regulated by the king and the palace authorities, who had control over the relationship with the foreign newcomers and an economic and symbolic hold over what could be sold or donated. However, by the mid-1920s the situation in Foumban had became quite different. The French colonial administrators, who had replaced the Germans in the control of the region after 1916, were far more active in challenging the structure of traditional kingship. As a consequence, the strict sumptuary laws regulating access to prestige objects produced by artists working exclusively for the king and the hierarchy of notables were progressively undermined. Under German colonial administration, King Njoya, a great promoter of the arts and an entrepreneurial and inventive king, had been treated as a respected ruler and politician. The French did not share this positive opinion of the monarch; they saw him as a great African despot.[14] In establishing their government, the French worked closely with Mose Yéyab, a titleholder who had converted to Christianity and who served as interpreter for the new colonial administration.

Art was one of the domains through which the competition between King Njoya and Yéyab unfolded publicly in the 1920s. In defiance of the courtly control over the production and consumption of prestigious objects (Fig. 1), Yéyab started his own collecting and patronage.[15] He then proceeded to establish a museum not far from the Protestant Mission and encouraged the foundation of an artist colony catering to a different clientele than that of the royal court. This open challenge to the court's authority induced the politically weakened king to change the sumptuary laws, thereby sanctioning the opening up of production to a much larger group of artists and the art market to any willing buyer.[16]

The progressive diminishment of royal and hierarchical patronage in Foumban affected the art production of the entire region, in varying degrees. If kings and titleholders expanded the range of sought-after prestige items to include many imported items of foreign manufacture, the increased number of Europeans living in the Grassfields as missionaries, colonial officers, technicians, doctors, volunteers, curators, dealers and collectors provided a new type of clientele for the workshops and dealers.

The social and political transformations that took place in the first three decades of the twentieth century deeply influenced the creativity of workshops in Foumban and in other regional art-producing centres. Since their early contacts with foreign collectors, cultural brokers such as Njoya and later Yéyab understood the potential that artistic innovation had in sustaining a regional and international art market and strengthening the relevance of Foumban as an art-producing center. In a letter to the director of the Peabody Museum sent on January 5, 1930,[17] missionary George Schwab recounted the Yéyab's critical role in facilitating his collecting activity on behalf of the museum. Schwab also reported his collaborator's requests for a book "with plenty plenty pictures" on African art. While it is not clear whether or not any book was sent, museum director Dr. Earnest Hooton selected twenty-five images of African artworks from the Peabody collection, which were sent on March 15 for Schwab to share with his "native friend." Right at the time when the concept and market of African art emerged in Europe and the United States, these were equally absorbed and acted upon by the African agents who collaborated with foreign collectors in the field.

In Foumban, the colonial dismantling of exclusive hierarchical control over high-quality art production enabled a larger number of enterprising dealers to use their access and knowledge of local arts and their awareness of foreign aesthetic tastes and trends to influence and promote local artistic production. Up until the 1930s, it was mostly the palace that could gift or trade objects as a way of establishing alliances; now, the creation of independent artist colonies such as la Rue des Artisans allowed artists and workshops in the Grassfields a higher degree of freedom and formal experimentation.

Workshops, Traders and the Expansion of the Market

The expansion of patronage and aesthetic influences shifted the relative balance of regional artistic production: while certain regional centres saw a substantial reduction in artistic activity, others thrived over the decades and continued producing artworks for traditional use, urban elite consumption and foreign markets. Places like Oku, Babanki, Babungo (Fig. 2), Bamessing, Bandjoun or Foumban, to name just a few, are known to this day for their carvings, pottery, weaving, metalwork or bronze castings, and are regularly visited by local and international dealers.

Today, most towns and villages in the Grassfields have market areas dedicated to ceremonial wares and other types of locally produced artworks for local and regional customers. Annual ceremonies and celebrations still require appropriate "traditional" attire, and notables and members of the urban elite are also likely to have a few carvings, clay objects or brass objects in their homes. Many urban centres throughout Cameroon have art galleries or craft co-operatives that sell the products of Grassfieds workshops and items traded from neighbouring countries.[18] The main customers for these outlets are foreigners, both tourists and resident expatriates, as well as international fair trade organizations. However, these centres also cater to some urban middle-class Cameroonians who choose to add some "traditional" flair to their home decor.

In the large cities of Yaoundé and Douala one can find large specialized art and craft markets and a few higher-end galleries located close to prestigious hotels or city landmarks (Fig. 3). Many of the dealers in these main urban centres are either from the Grassfields and invariably from Foumban, or

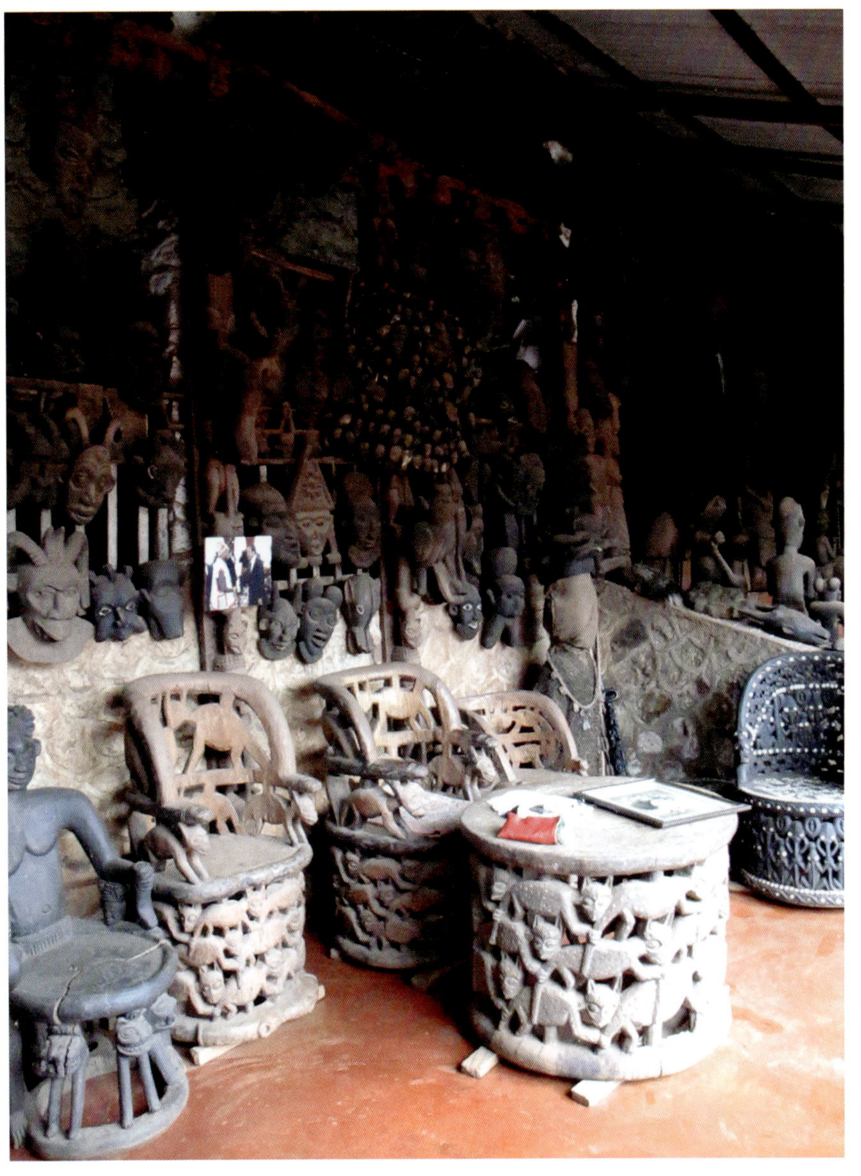

figure 2
Public reception room in the Palace of Babungo
August 6, 2011
Photo by Silvia Forni

have close business relations with Bamum traders, who are still the main middlemen between rural kingdoms and urban centres. Thus, even the large cities do not have the same volume of art circulation that one may find in the relatively small town of Foumban.

Continuing the commercial tradition noted by early collectors, Foumban is known in Cameroon as the main market for both antiquities and contemporary artworks. Many Bamum merchants have borne a largely unrecognized responsibility in building important Western collections and have held long-term relationships with art dealers all over Europe and the United States. Often, antiquaries and art dealers are the descendants of important artist lineages, whose members settled in Foumban at the beginning of the twentieth century, from different conquered villages, to work at the court of King Njoya.

The connection between royal patronage, workshops and galleries is still visible in the landscape today. About thirteen commercial galleries catering to foreigners and urban elites are concentrated around the palace, where many dealers seem to have close ties with the local hierarchy. More than twenty other important outlets are clustered along the Rue des Artisans, where Mose Yéyab established his museum and an artist colony in 1925. More recently, a new cluster of about fifteen commercial spaces called Artisanat du Centre has been established between these two historical sites and offers a more contained market setting for a number of newer galleries. While these public outlets are the most visible manifestations of the town's thriving art market and are likely shared by different dealers, most high-end art dealers sell out of their private residences, often large multi-level mansions located on the hillsides of the densely populated quarters of Njinka and Njiyouom (Fig. 4).

Many of these dealers have been in the business for several decades and have built substantial fortunes thanks to long-lasting relationships with collectors and gallerists. While all of them welcome foreign visitors and potential customers to their homes, many also travel abroad and, over the years, have exported large numbers of artworks now in important collections in Europe and the United States.

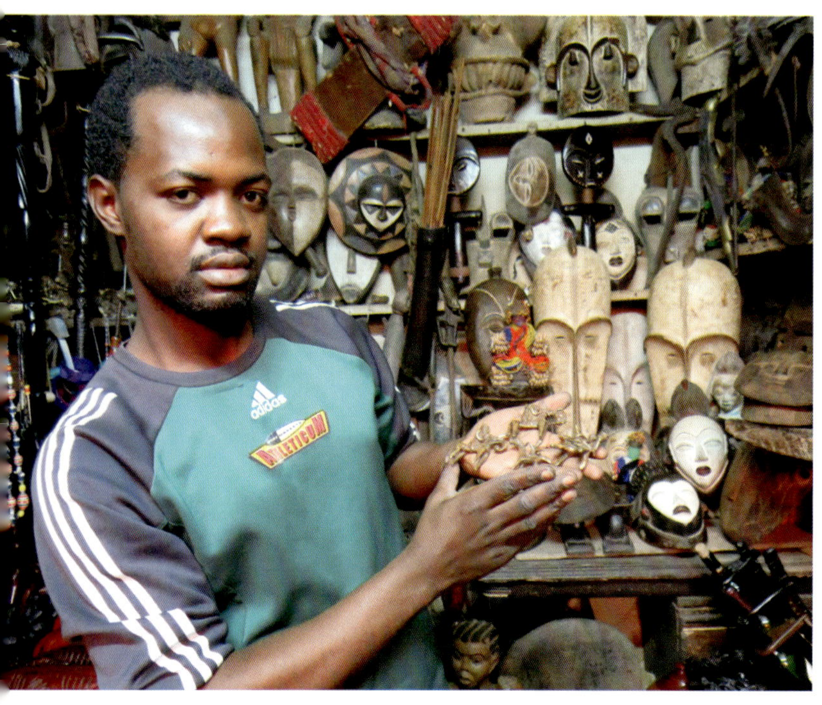

figure 3
Arouna Njoya Bobo in his boutique at the Marché des Fleurs
Douala, July 30, 2013
Photo by Silvia Forni

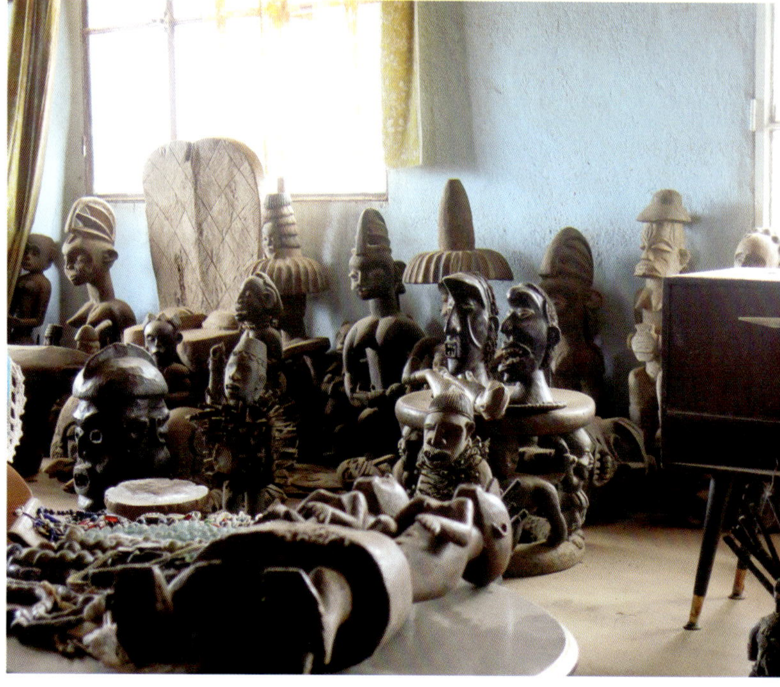

figure 4
Display of antiquities in a dealer's private residence
Foumban, July 10, 2014
Photo by Silvia Forni

figure 5 (left)
Carved architectural post
Unidentified artist or workshop
Northern Grassfields style
Wood
Purchased in 1987 from a dealer
in Foumban, Cameroon
Height: 270 cm, Outside diameter: 22 cm
ROM 2009.126.314

figure 6 (right)
Carved architectural post
Unidentified artist or workshop
Northern Grassfields style
Wood
Purchased in 1987 from a dealer
in Foumban, Cameroon
Height: 269 cm, Outside diameter: 17.7 cm
ROM 2009.126.315

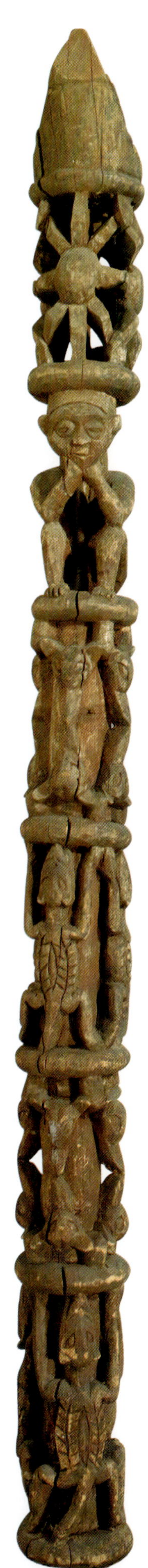

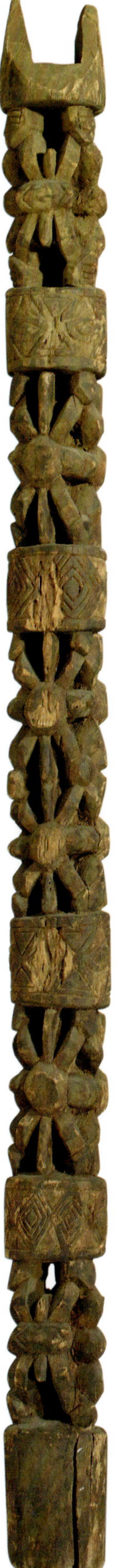

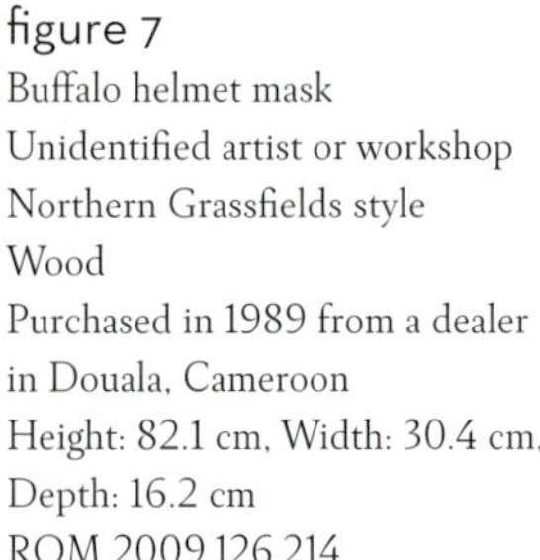

figure 7
Buffalo helmet mask
Unidentified artist or workshop
Northern Grassfields style
Wood
Purchased in 1989 from a dealer in Douala, Cameroon
Height: 82.1 cm, Width: 30.4 cm, Depth: 16.2 cm
ROM 2009.126.214

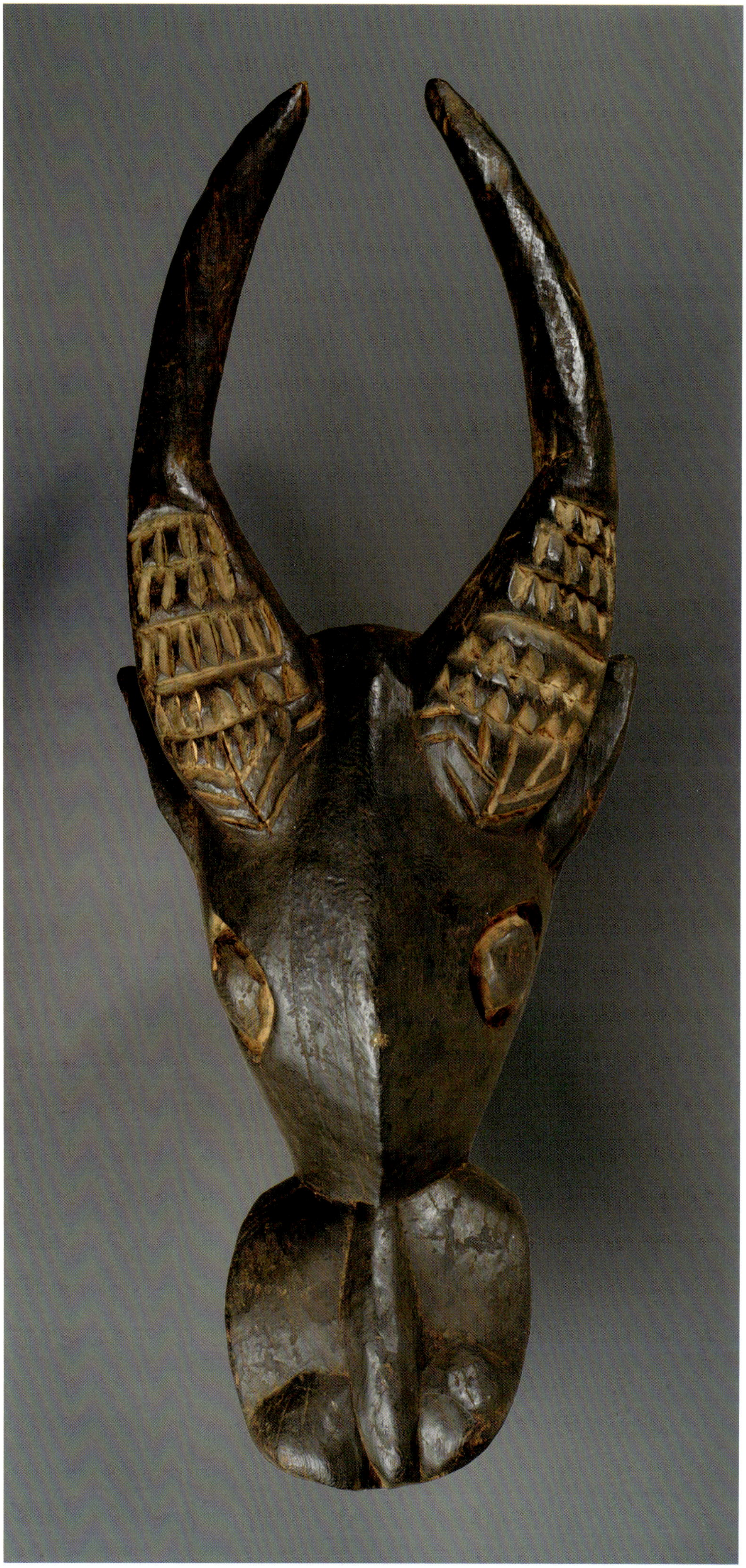

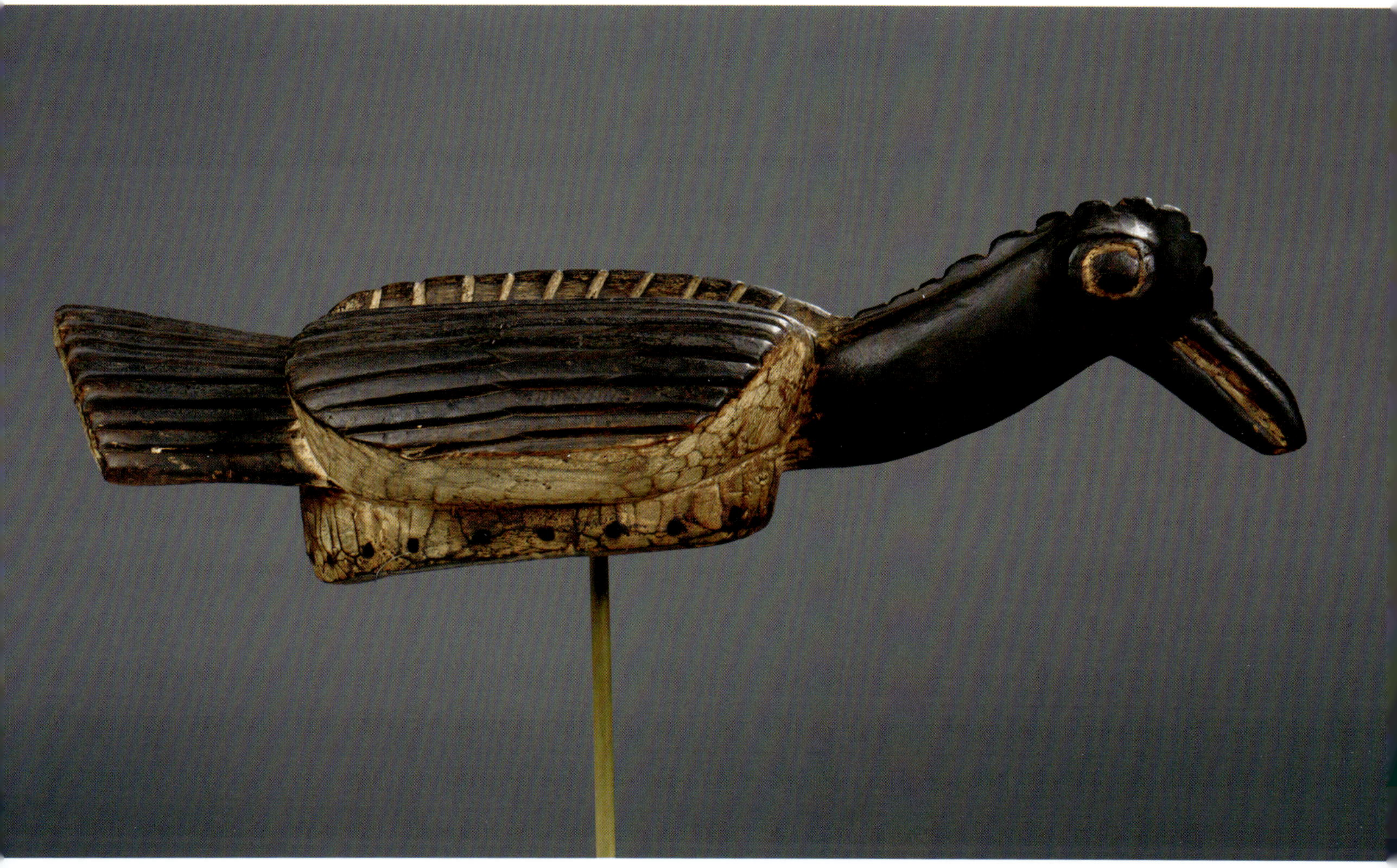

figure 8
Bird helmet mask
Unidentified artist or workshop
Northern Grassfields style
Wood
Purchased in 1989 from a dealer in Douala, Cameroon
Height: 15.3 cm, Width: 27.5 cm, Depth: 61.1 cm
ROM 2009.126.213

One of the most prominent dealers to this day is El Hadji Nji Salifou Njikomo, the descendant of an important family of brass casters, originally from Nguot, who settled in Njinka, very close to the royal palace, to work for the court of King Mbuombuo at the beginning of the nineteenth century. Members of this family are also responsible for the founding of brass-casting workshops in Nkwen, near Bamenda, where they moved because of political pressure in the 1920s. In the 1940s the young Salifou was the master of his own brass-casting workshop in Nkwen, where he met Paul Gebauer who greatly admired his artistic skill and creativity and became a collector of his work.[19]

After returning to Foumban, as head of the family's compound, Nji Salifou Njikomo became increasingly involved in the sale of artworks. Although he defines himself as an antiquities dealer and has, throughout the decades, provided artworks to many important commercial galleries in Paris, Brussels and other European centres, the artworks displayed in different rooms of his large three-storey home range from well-made contemporary commercial pieces on the first floor to selected "antiquities" on the third floor and in his personal apartment.[20] While today it is mostly his many children and younger relatives who accompany prospective buyers to see the collection, prices are always determined by Njikomo himself. At times, Njikomo may even refuse to sell specific pieces, enacting a well-rehearsed performance which aims to underline the value and cultural significance of the artworks in his possession.

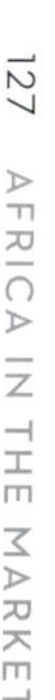

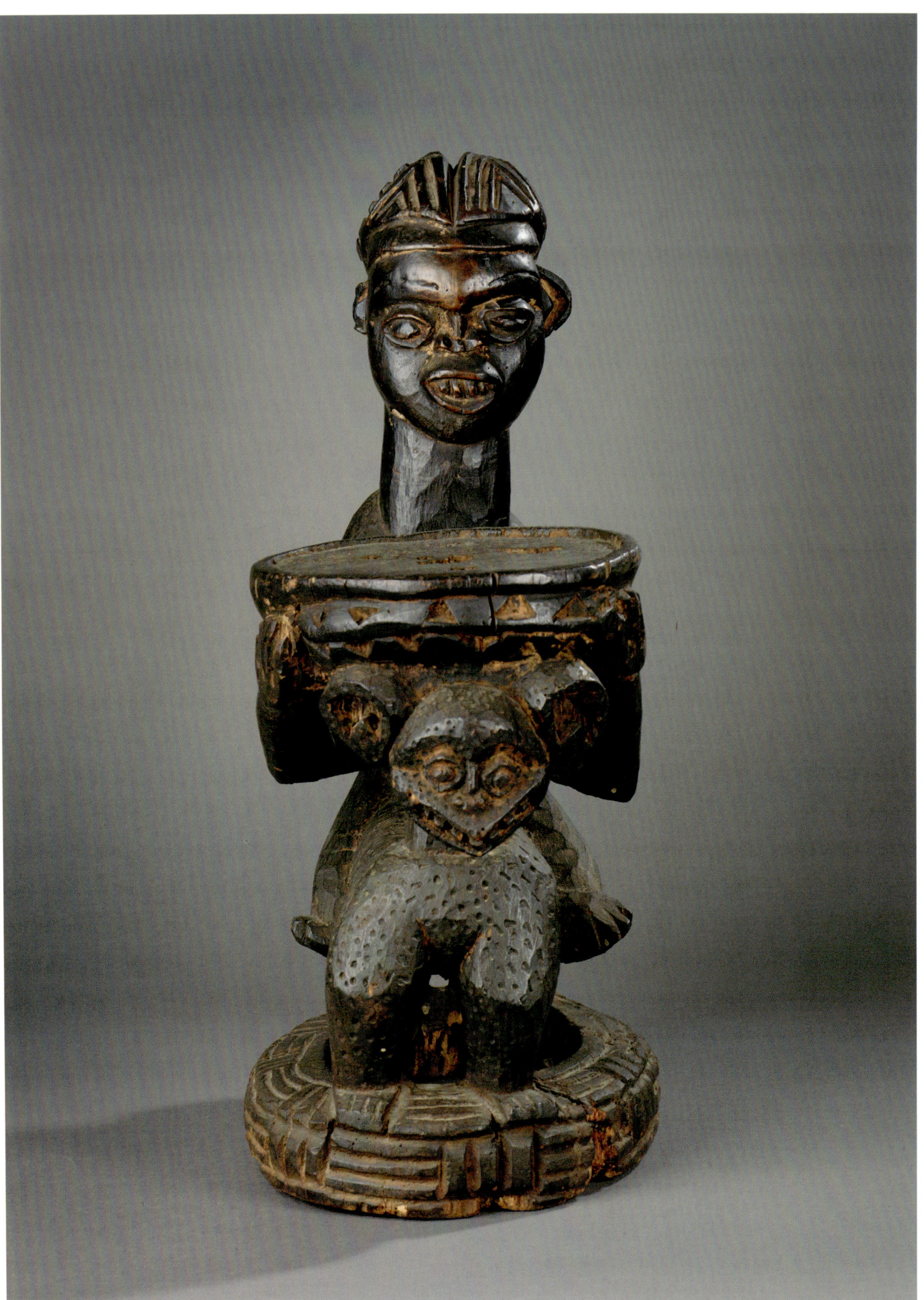

figure 9 (opposite)
Royal stool
Unidentified artist or workshop
Northern Grassfields, Babungo style
Wood
Purchased in 1986 from a dealer in Foumban, Cameroon
Height: 61 cm, Width: 26.5 cm, Depth: 36 cm
ROM 2009.126.293

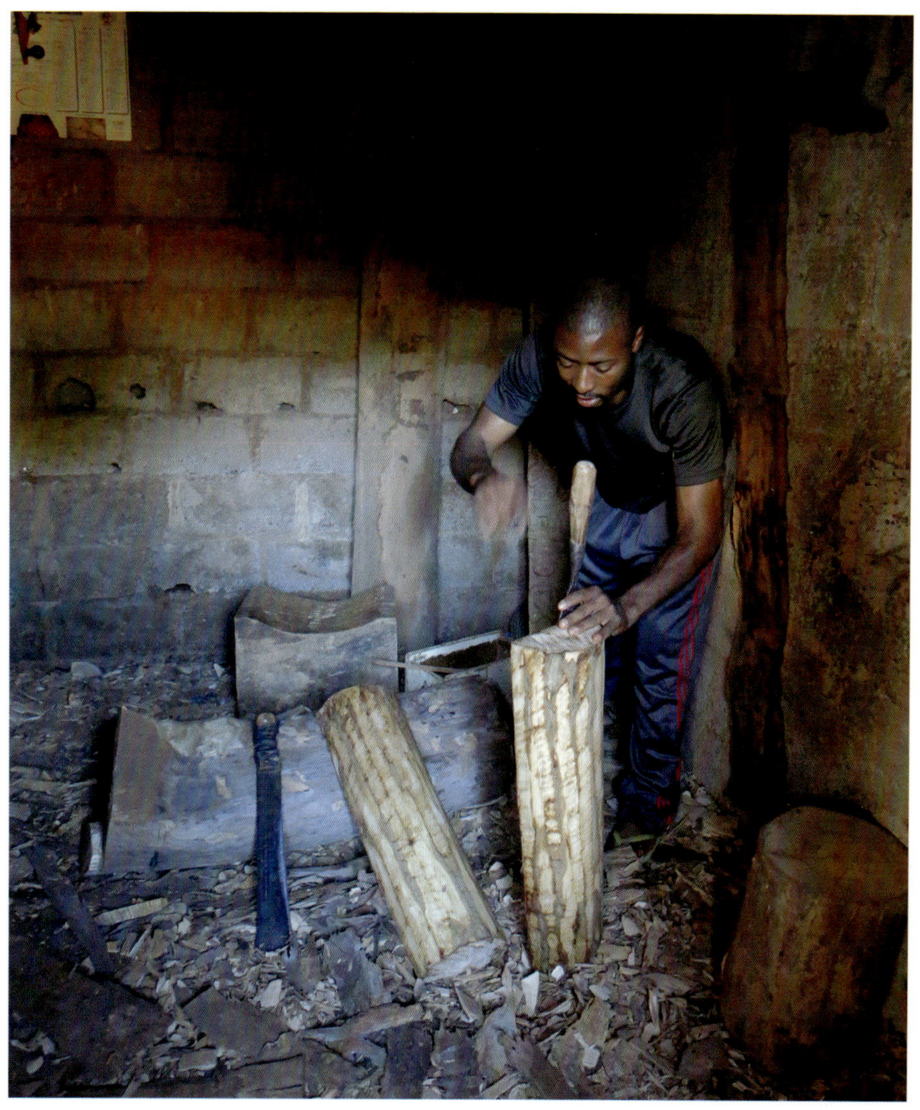

figure 10
Carver Ibrahim in his workshop at the entrance of the Batufam palace and museum
July 10, 2014
Photo by Silvia Forni

The narration of stories that refer to the traditional importance of a piece is a common selling strategy for all art dealers, whether in a Foumban mansion, a stall at the Marché des Fleurs in Douala, or a "Tribal art" fair in Europe or North America. Yet, while most merchants selling standard commercial replicas recycle identical and somewhat general stories for almost identical pieces, antiquaries are usually able to provide a more detailed narrative of the function or acquisition process of specific artifacts. When, in 2011, I met Alahmadou Njitari—a dealer in his late seventies who still travelled frequently to Nigeria to acquire pieces for foreign collectors—he showed me a video illustrating the process of community negotiations and compensation for two brightly coloured Cross River headdresses that he had acquired a few months before. Such smartphone videos are, on the one hand, documentation that may interest a future customer, and on the other, proof that the objects were willingly sold and not stolen and as such a possible defense against harassment by border officers.[21]

The interest of Bamum dealers in the arts of Nigeria is not a recent development. It is a known fact that dealers from Foumban were instrumental in the sale of large numbers of pieces illegally exported from Nigeria in the second half of the 1960s, during

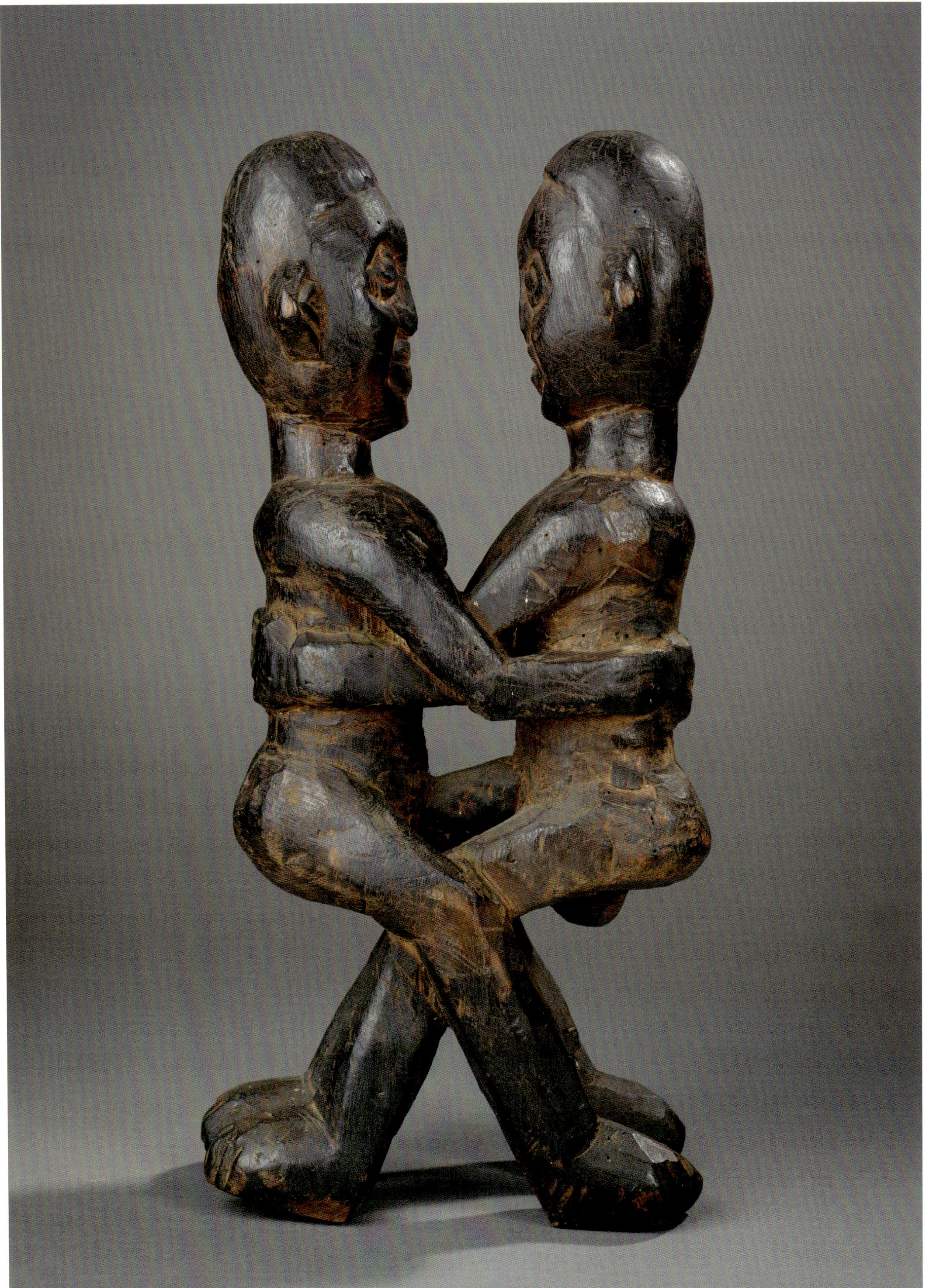

figure 11
Embracing couple
Unidentified artist or workshop
Northern Grassfields, Babungo style
Wood
Purchased in 1986 from a dealer in Douala, Cameroon
Height: 49 cm, Width: 24 cm, Depth: 14 cm
ROM 2009.126.261

the period of the Biafra War (1966–1970). At that time, many artworks were stolen or had to be sold to sustain livelihoods during the conflict and in its aftermath. Bamum traders such as Nji Yende Amadou, the owner of a long-established gallery on the Rue des Artisans, started travelling in the 1960s to the North West Region and across the Nigerian border to look for antiquities for his many European and American customers. Many of the pieces he collected were exported to Europe via Brussels by Philippe Guimiot,[22] who in the 1960s established a high-end gallery in Douala mostly stocked by Bamum antiquities dealers.[23] Indeed, many dealers in Foumban have tales of pieces acquired by prestigious institutions or published in glossy catalogues, and some, like Mama Mbehou Moustapha, can claim to be virtually the sole provider for a number of Swiss and German collectors with whom they have established long-lasting relations of mutual trust.

In recent times, gallerists with public outlets have usually acquired their pieces directly from the workshops dispersed throughout Foumban and in many of the smaller villages of the Bamum kingdom, or through exchange with other dealers. Antiquaries claim to deal exclusively in "authentic" pieces[24] and usually negotiate the acquisitions of used objects from chiefs, notables or communities, or rely on the assistance of local intermediaries to replenish their stock. Antiquaries are the main customers for objects that, for various reasons, have ceased to be used, such as carved poles belonging to buildings that have been replaced by cement structures (Figs. 5 & 6). They also purchase carved masquerade headpieces, which are still quite commonly carved and used (Figs. 7 & 8) but may be sold by dance groups to finance common projects. While architectural elements are usually relinquished in return for monetary compensation, more portable and still culturally relevant objects such as masks or stools are usually exchanged for both money and replacement carvings.

Ideally, the decision to sell an old object should be taken collectively by members of a specific association or family; yet, in certain cases, objects are sold directly by family heads or kings for their own personal gain. While the head of a family is *de facto* in charge of the family wealth, from a normative point of view, the material culture of the palace is not to be considered a king's personal possession and should be inalienable. Undeniably, many palaces in the Grassfields have been progressively emptied of all their treasures, sometimes to the great dismay of local communities. In the last century, thousands of objects and architectural elements from Grassfields palaces, compounds, shrines, and the houses of masquerade and secret societies have been exported and sold abroad. Despite being the fifth state to ratify the UNESCO 1972 World Heritage Convention, Cameroon has not mounted a serious attack against the illegal export of artworks and ethnographic objects. Even though protective laws have been in place since the 1960s, it was only in May 2013 that the government approved broad and comprehensive

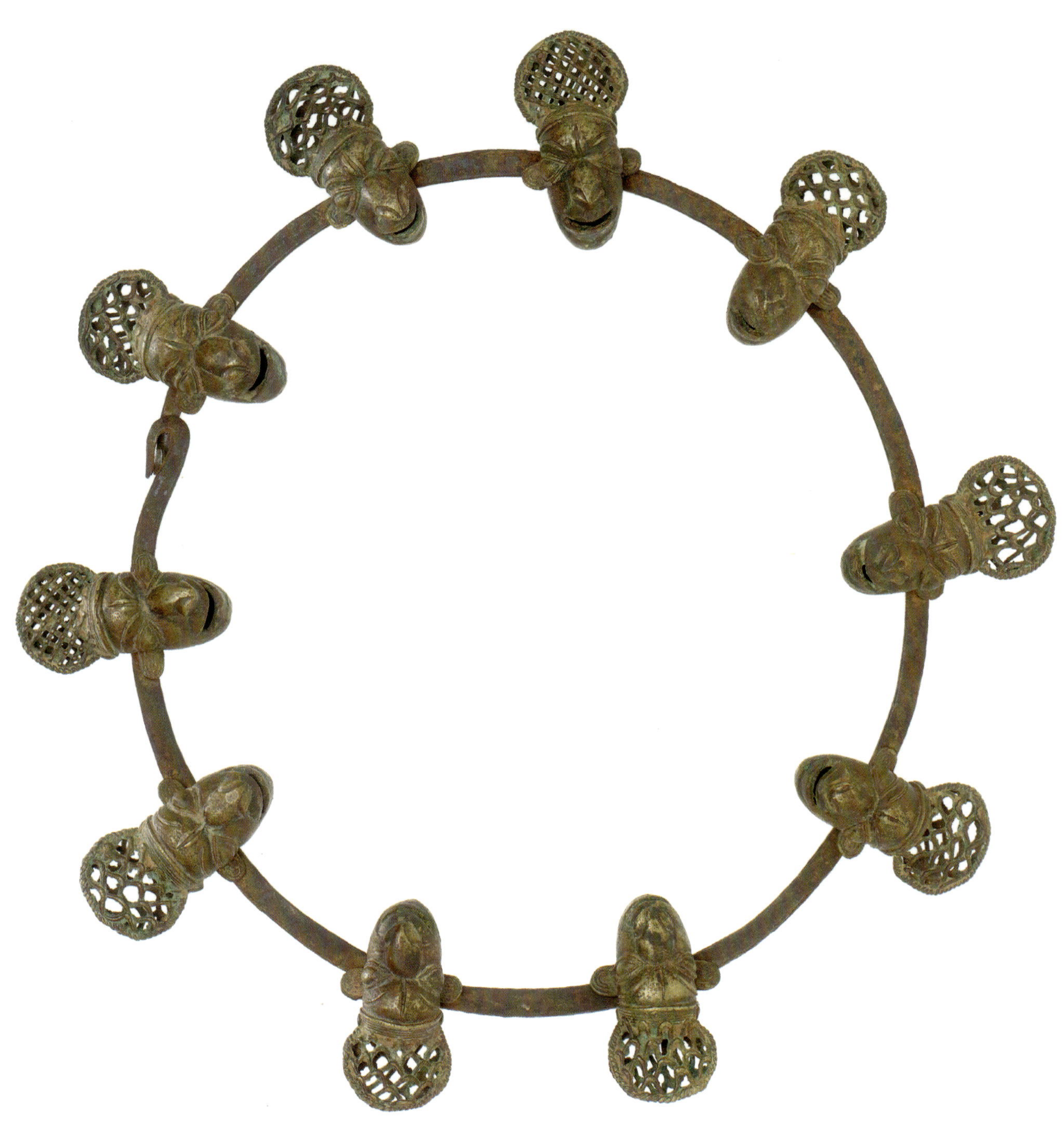

figure 12
Neck ring with heads
Unidentified artist or workshop
Bamum style
Brass
Purchased in 1966 from a private collector in Libreville, Gabon
Height: 3.5 cm,
Outside diameter: 36 cm
ROM 2009.126.299

figure 13 (opposite)
Headcrest
Unidentified artist or workshop
Bamum style
Brass
Purchased in 1986 from a private collector in Yaoundé, Cameroon
Height: 27.8 cm, Width: 20.7 cm,
Depth: 21 cm
ROM 2009.126.298

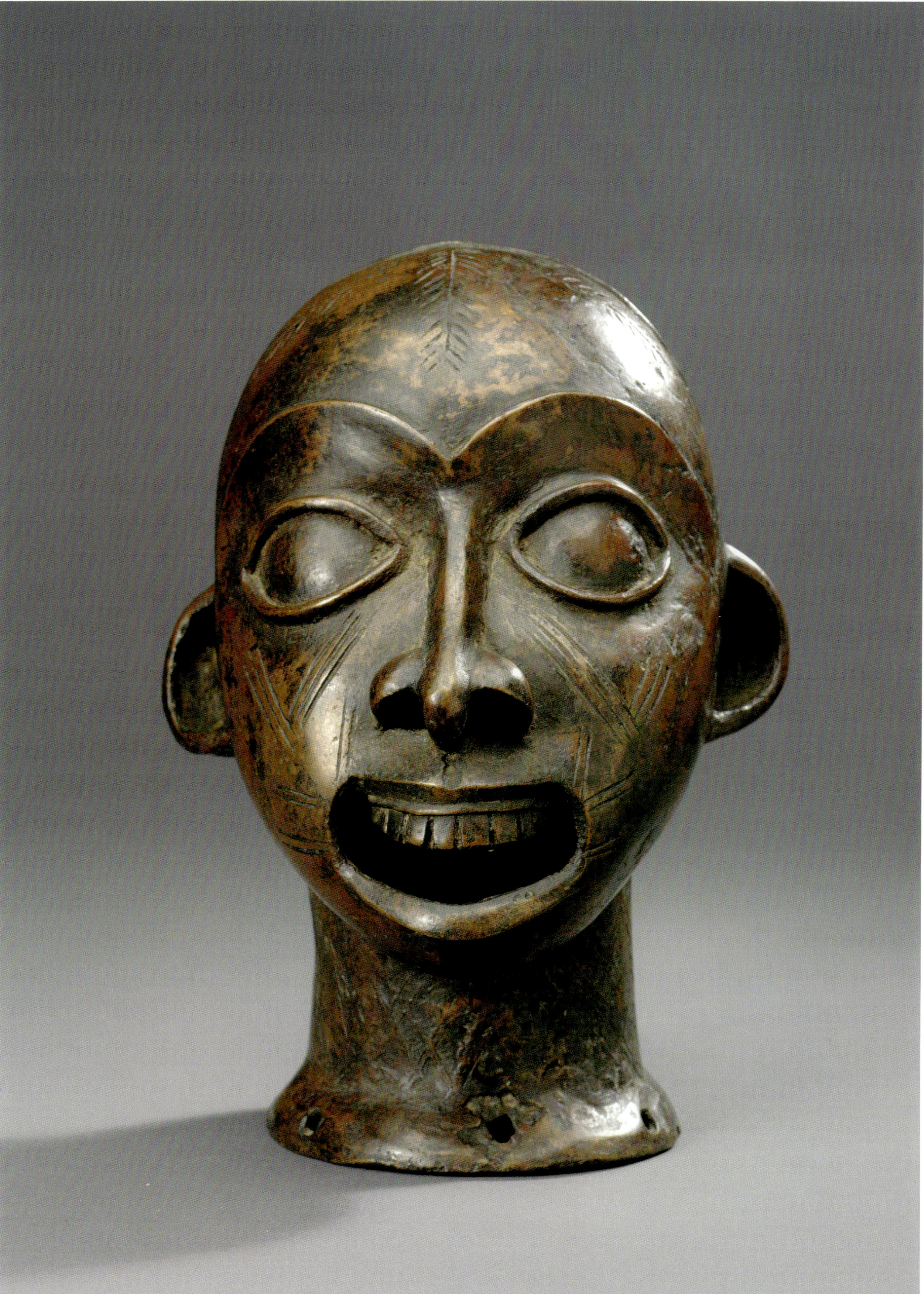

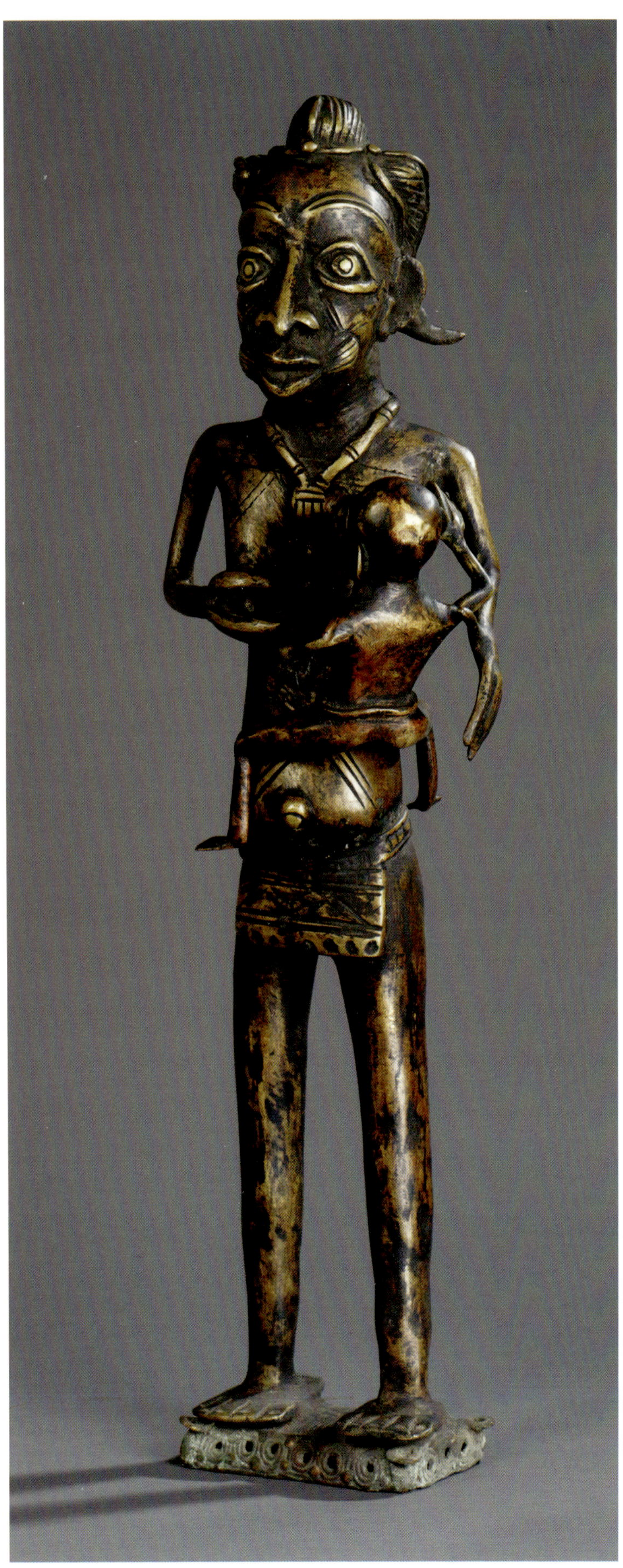

figure 14
Mother and child figure
Unidentified artist or workshop
Bamum style
Brass
Purchased in 1986 or 1987 from a dealer in Douala, Cameroon
Height: 64 cm, Width: 20 cm, Depth: 15 cm
ROM 2009.126.64.1–2

figure 15 (opposite)
Warrior figure
El Hadji Ali (d. 2008)
Bamum style
Aluminum
Purchased in 1986 from a dealer in Foumban, Cameroon
Height: 36.5 cm, Width: 20 cm, Depth: 20 cm
ROM 2009.126.345

---

legislation for the protection of cultural heritage, modelled on heritage laws found in Western countries and particularly the legislation of Quebec, Canada.[25] For its full implementation, however, this law requires a rather extensive and detailed inventory of national heritage, which despite the long history of heritage legislation and the financial support of international funding agencies has not been accomplished so far. A great quantity of old and newer elements of the local material culture of religion, political display, hierarchical status and community affiliation have thus left the country in containers, crates and the suitcases of foreign and local dealers. While it is undeniable that older pieces are often deceptively declared contemporary artworks to obtain the necessary customs clearance,[26] it is also true that very few customs officers and museum functionaries have enough familiarity with the artworks to be able to determine whether a piece is truly old or just a well-made and artificially aged commercial replica.

This hemorrhage of historical pieces seems at odds with the increased interest in museum building that has characterized the Grassfields in the last three decades. Since the 1990s, thanks to a number of international and local initiatives, palaces have increasingly been identified and promoted as places of memory, conservation, and tourism. Yet, when looking at what is actually preserved and displayed in the palace museums, it is clear that kings have done more than preserve effigies of the past—in most cases, they have strategically employed their regal aura to attribute value and cultural significance to recently made carvings produced and aged in the palace's workshops (Fig. 10).

One well-known example is in Babungo, where King Zofoa II, himself a knowledgeable carver, made strategic use of the prolific production and ageing skills of the palace carvers. As illustrated in the catalogues of some of the region's palace museums, Babungo objects are found in many of those palaces,

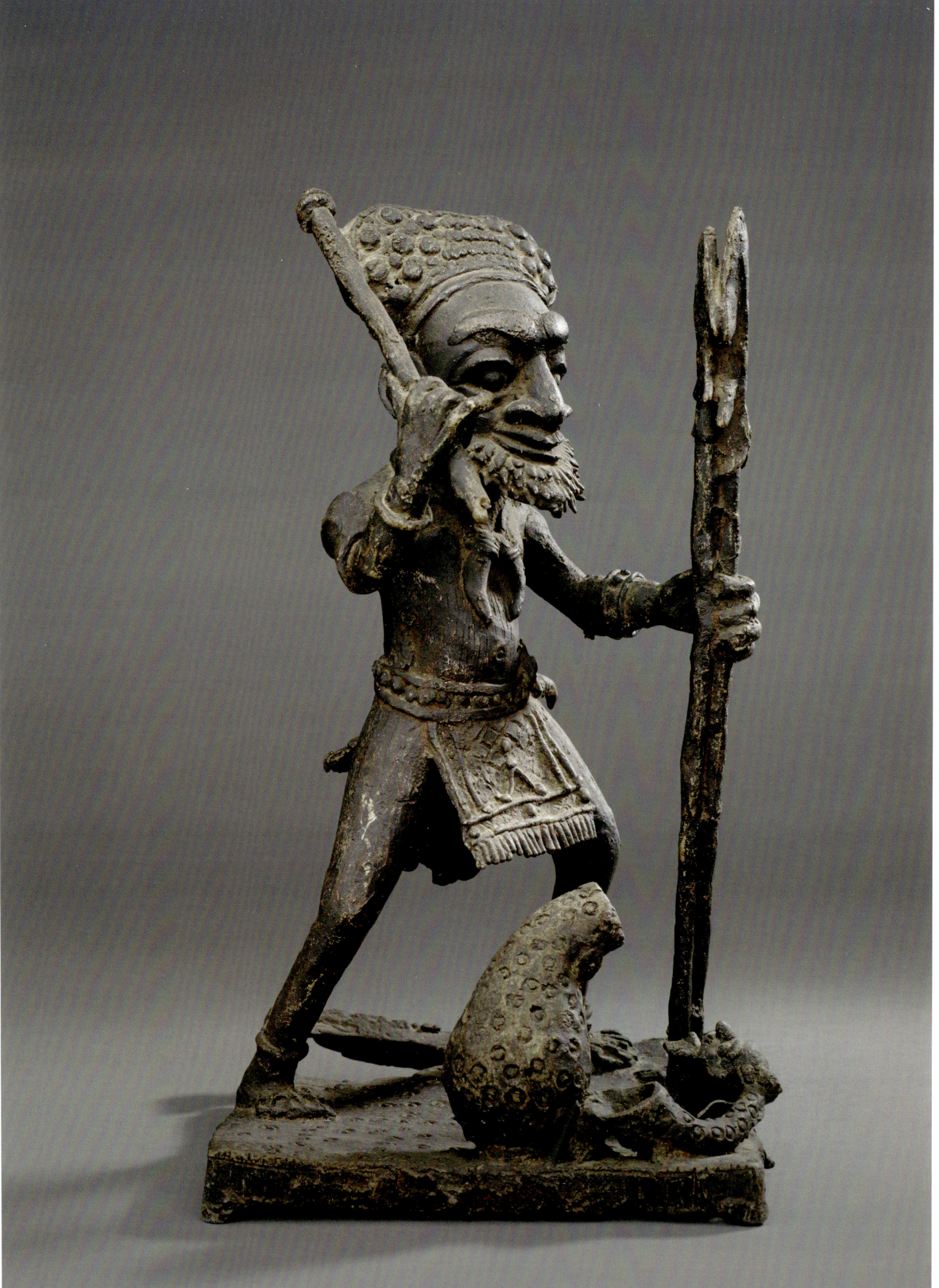

as well as in Western collections and Foumban warehouses. The stool in the Amrad African Art Collection (Fig. 9), which is almost identical to one found in the palace of Mankon,[27] is an example of this mid- to late-twentieth-century royal production, sustaining both the material expression of local cultural values and the regional art market. Other pieces, such as a rather unusual embracing couple (Fig. 11), may also have come from a Babungo workshop, where King Zofoa II often encouraged the exploration of unconventional themes and forms. In the 1970s, the king travelled to India, and this trip had a discernible and lasting influence on his workshop's aesthetics. It is not uncommon for figures, stools and other carvings from the royal workshop to make explicit reference to South Asian iconography.[28] While explicitly sexual imagery is not usually part of the Grassfields carving repertoire, it is quite likely that this piece represents a playful attempt to translate in Grassfields-style imagery inspired by Indian art, to create a novel and attractive form likely to arouse the curiosity of foreign buyers.

Twentieth- and Twenty-First Century Market Trends: Inventions, Antiquities and *Belle* Copies

Just as in Babungo, new and unconventional forms are important products for commercial workshops in other Grassfields towns and villages. Brass casting is another realm in which innovations in traditional and foreign styles are major sources of income for a large number of artists. While prestige objects used as insignia for notables and dignitaries (such as the large-scale pipes or the ornate neck rings given by the king to the members of the great council of notables) have been replicated for the market throughout the twentieth century (Fig. 12), other pieces have been invented as a form of gift for important foreign visitors and, with time, have become iconic examples of twentieth-century commercial production. The bronze headcrest in the Amrad Collection (Fig. 13) is quite typical in this regard. Although it is modelled like a headcrest mask and even has holes at the base suggesting some sort of fibre costume attachment, this piece was never a masquerade component. Most likely, its form was inspired by the Ife bronze heads that more skilled Bamum brass casters started making in the late 1940s.[29] Other twentieth-century inventions are the brass figurines of various sizes representing "traditionally" clad men and women, village scenes or, more recently, Benin-style leopards, kings and warriors. Small- to mid-size works, such as the mother and child figure in the Amrad Collection (Fig. 14), were, until a few decades ago, quite commonly found in galleries all over Cameroon.

While these figures were usually cast in some sort of copper and zinc alloy, by the 1960s some artists had also started to experiment with other metals. The warrior figure in the Amrad Collection (Fig. 15) is a good example of this material experimentation. Cast in aluminum, this figure is a very typical

figure 16
Doll
Unidentified artist or workshop
Namji style
Wood, leather, shell beads, bone beads, seed beads
Purchased in 2004 from Hamill Gallery, Boston
Height: 27.1 cm, Width: 12.8 cm, Depth: 10.8 cm
ROM 2009.126.111

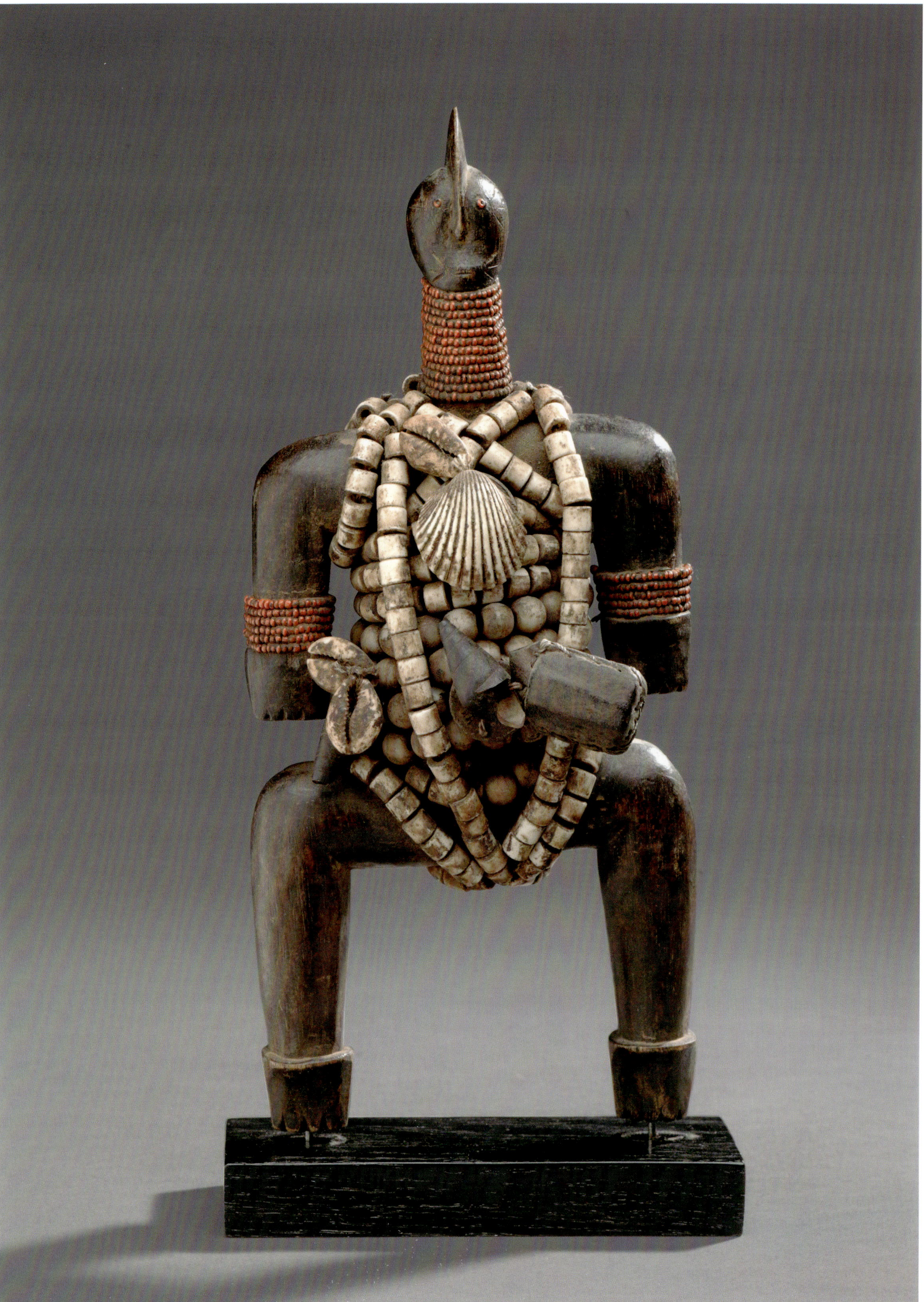

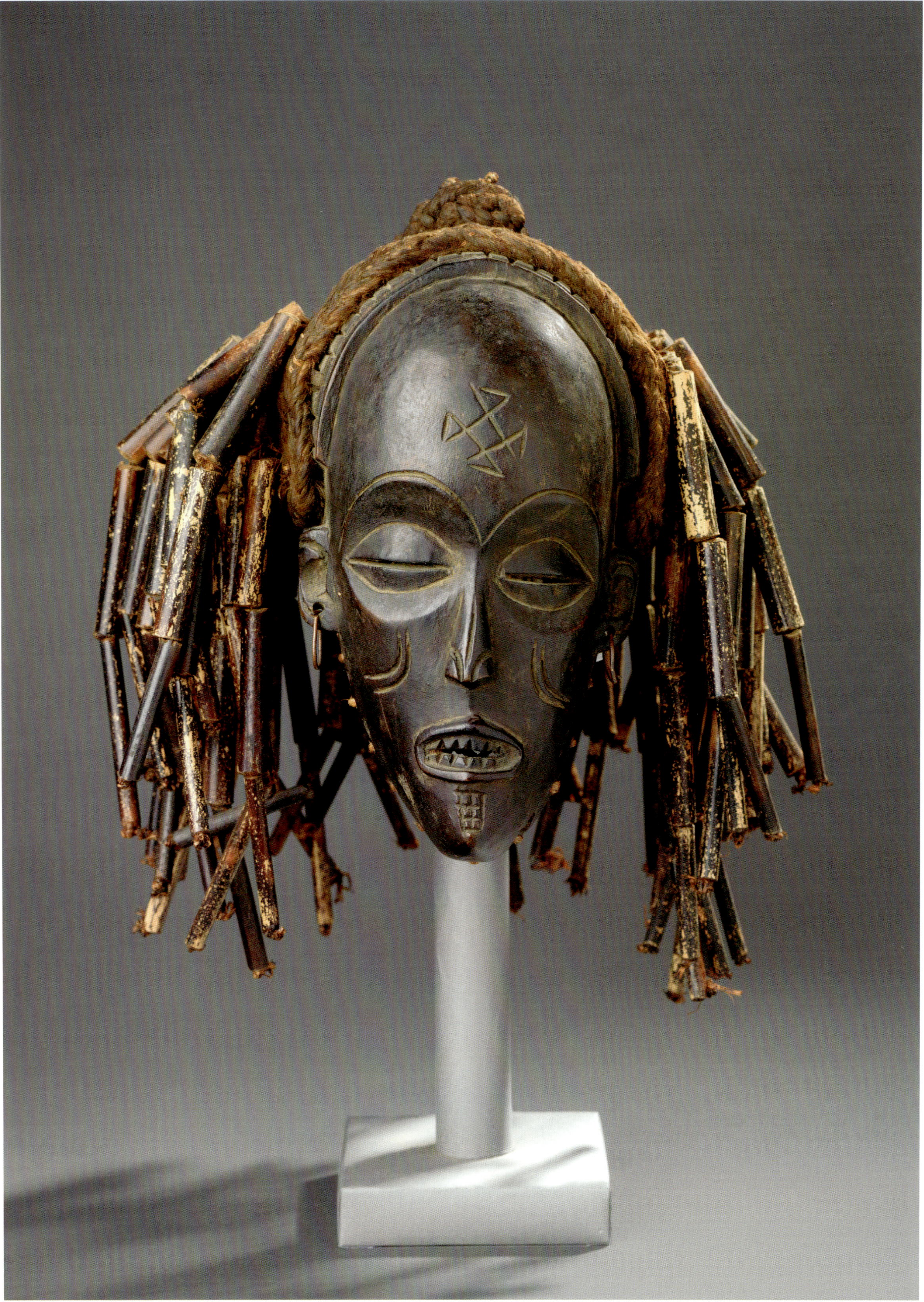

example of the work of El Hadji Ali, a caster who died in 2008.[30] El Hadji Ali was known for his great modelling skills and for experimental aluminum creations that were often commissioned by dealers selling abroad because the pieces were more lightweight and easier to carry. El Hadji Ali was one of the many artists producing traditionally inspired artworks for the market. His work did not replicate forms of the past but recreated an idealized image of tradition for consumption in local and foreign markets. These are figures that usually elicit rather nostalgic comments on the part of local interpreters, who read them as iconic representation of a historical past untainted by colonial rule or the post-colonial state. Interestingly, such figures are quite popular with middle-class Cameroonian elites, who select these modern renditions of a romanticized traditional past as decorations for their urban parlours.

The bronze and aluminum figures represent recently developed interpretations of tradition conceived for the global market. Yet, these art forms have become quite important and iconic in their own right as artists working in this style are commissioned to complete large-scale and monumental works for a number of official settings, including ministerial buildings and presidential residencies. Notwithstanding, the real driving force of the market in Foumban is without a doubt the production of replicas and artworks in a variety of canonical styles, sold as new or old works depending on the setting and the status of the dealer. While the market for *belle copies* (beautiful copies) of artworks in Grassfields style has shrunk considerably in the last three decades, Bamum artists have become increasingly versed in a variety of canonical styles of foreign origin that are now a common feature in the production of local workshops. A walk through the carving, casting and pottery workshops located throughout town provides an instructive overview of the relative popularity of specific stylistic traditions on the international art market: Benin-style plaques, figures and leopards are the most prominent brass-casting production of Bamum foundries; carvers tend to specialize in Mumuye, Kota, Chokwe, Kongo, Yoruba, Punu and Ibo styles; and potters alternate between Mangbetu, Nok, Djenne and Mambila.

The extent of experimentation in different styles seems to have increased considerably in the last couple of decades. In the 1980s, Bamum workshops seemed to privilege the production of copies and thematic variations of works in a Cameroonian style (Fig. 16) or occasionally styles from Gabon or Congo, such as the Chokwe mask in the collection (Fig. 17). Today, the stylistic variations from workshop to workshop, and sometimes within the production of the same workshop or artist, are staggering. Many artists proudly relate their ability to create artworks using different stylistic registers. Salifou, a ceramic artist working behind the Rue des Artisans, told me, "I make Djenne, Yoruba, Mangbetu, Mambila, I can make any style. My favorite though is Mangbetu. I like to think of the container, and of the people who inhabit it. I shape my ideas in that style. I create my own stories."[31]

While style preferences and the range of work produced by artists vary greatly depending on an individual's talent and skill, overall the stylistic distribution found in Foumban commercial galleries is quite consistent with the trends in auction sales. In his recent analysis of African art sales based on a decade of Sotheby's auction results, Eric Nemeth reported a noticeable increase of average sale price, and a marked market preference, for objects from the Democratic Republic of the Congo, Côte d'Ivoire, Nigeria, Mali and Gabon.[32] And while the customers who purchase the works of Bamum workshops are in all likelihood not the same high-end buyers who frequent the prestigious auction houses, their stylistic preferences appear to be not so different.

While *belle copies* offer a somewhat credible version of known canonical styles celebrated in high-end markets, Foumban workshops also produce a fairly large range of original decorative pieces that have become quite popular over the years and have come to define new forms of traditional Bamum productions. This is the case of the painted clay passport masks (which supposedly identified people belonging to different Tikar groups); of the clay and wooden "pigmies" now produced in a broad range of sizes and positions; of the colourful "Fang" masks loosely inspired by the elongated face masks of the Fang

figure 17 (opposite)
Mask
Unidentified artist or workshop
Chokwe style
Wood, fibre, bamboo, metal
Purchased in 1989 from a dealer in Douala, Cameroon
Height: 35 cm, Width: 30 cm, Depth: 31 cm
ROM 2009.126.221

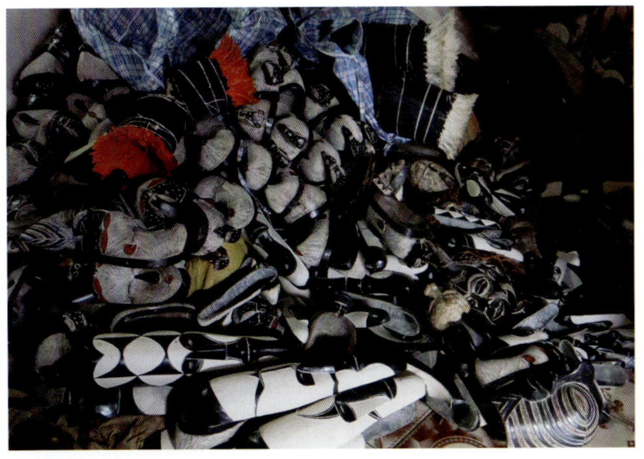

figure 18
Stock being assembled for shipment to South Africa, includes the typical Foumban-style "fang" mask and some "kifwebe" and "tikar" variations
Foumban, Cameroon
July 12, 2014
Photo by Silvia Forni

of Gabon but carved and painted in very distinct Bamum style (see Ch. 1, Fig.7); and, more recently, of the "Tikar" masks, smaller and slightly angular decorative masks painted in bright red, white, blue and yellow fields. These colourful modern productions seem to be quite popular as trade items and are frequently purchased in large quantities by traders selling in South Africa (Fig. 18). Today, there are about one hundred Bamum traders making regular trips to South Africa, with stalls in the major art markets in Johannesburg, Cape Town and important tourist destinations. In general, South Africa seems to be a rather favourable market for Cameroonian products and in particular the "Tikar" masks, which in South Africa are strategically sold as "Freedom Masks," thus fulfilling many tourists' desire to acquire a souvenir that is both quintessentially African (a mask) and distinctively "South African."[33]

Value and Entrepreneurship

In the last three decades, many scholars and cultural critics have pointed to the historical fictiveness of the category of African art—a concept created in the early twentieth century through the artificial grouping of artworks from a variety of places and aesthetic traditions in exhibitions and publications. According to the reading proposed by Valentin Mudimbe, this is the end result of a long process of appropriation and resignification:

> What is called African art covers a wide range of objects introduced into a historicizing perspective of European values since the eighteenth century. These various "objects" which, perhaps, were not "art" at all, became art by being given, simultaneously, an aesthetic character and a potentiality for producing and possibly reproducing artistic forms.[34]

Yet, the fundamentally commercial and economic potential of this framing has usually been kept out of the epistemological definition of African art and, most importantly, alienated from the context of production. Paradoxically, those who could benefit from the recognition of the artistic value and the aesthetic potential of the arts of the African continent were, and in large measure remain, the white collectors and connoisseurs who "discovered" and introduced these foreign artworks in the art-culture system of the West.[35] In this way, the beauty of African art was projected in a fictive world protected from market interference, and cast as radical otherness that ultimately denied any kind of awareness and agency to the producers and the original sellers of these valuable objects of pure beauty.

Since its very inception, art collecting, enmeshed in the unequal and exploitative colonial encounter, has been framed as an active effort carried out almost exclusively by European explorers, functionaries, missionaries, scholars and collectors. In this stereotypical and limited portrayal, Africans are either absent from the picture or appear as passive sources. A look at the historical and contemporary trajectory of artistic production in Foumban—one of many artistic centres on the continent—clearly demonstrates the illusory nature of a simple object trajectory and the significant influence of collaboration, intellectual exchanges and economic transactions since the very beginning of the "scramble for art in Africa."[36] In the 1930s, Mose Yéyab was requesting pictures of African art along with other forms of compensation in return for his services as a cultural broker in the market transactions that enabled Schwab to acquire objects for the Peabody Museum. Likewise, many other African art dealers and producers have been active in the commercial exchanges from which collections all over the world originated. Shifts in collecting agendas throughout the twentieth century have certainly influenced the approach of both European collectors and their African partners. For the most part, early collectors were charged with acquiring regionally and culturally focused collections that would enrich ethnographic and missionary museums and garner support for the civilizing enterprise of colonialism. By the middle to late twentieth century, when several objects had unambiguously moved into the domain of Art, the focus shifted to the recovery of the material and aesthetic testimonies of a non-commercial past that embodied the purest expression of African aesthetic as defined by the canon.[37] What is interesting to assess from the perspective of the dealers and producers working in Africa is the effective feedback of this shift in focus and aesthetic. By the second half of the twentieth century, Western collectors and institutions, which now included art museums, were competing with one another for what were perceived to be finite resources necessary to achieve a higher level of representativeness and inclusiveness in their collections, thus driving the prices of African art to record-breaking highs. At the same time, the production and market offers found in the main art-producing centres in Africa became at once increasingly diverse and more canonically consistent.

Foumban offers a compelling vantage point from which to look at the varying collecting and commercial strategies of workshops and dealers. The Cameroonian pieces in the Amrad African Art Collection, acquired from Bamum dealers in the 1980s, are quite representative of the range of objects offered for sale at the time. The collection includes architectural elements of old buildings that were being replaced by modern, unadorned constructions, furniture, pieces produced and artificially aged, traditional artworks, as well as experimental forms, decorative pieces illustrating essentialized images of the past, *belle copies* of artworks from neighbouring areas (such as Namji-style dolls and Chokwe-style masks likely made in Foumban) and new commercial inventions for both local and international markets. This mix of old and new but mostly Cameroonian styles is very different from what one can find in the same location today. Esther Dagan followed her own thematic exhibition agendas and aesthetic preference when collecting. At the same time, despite her profound admiration

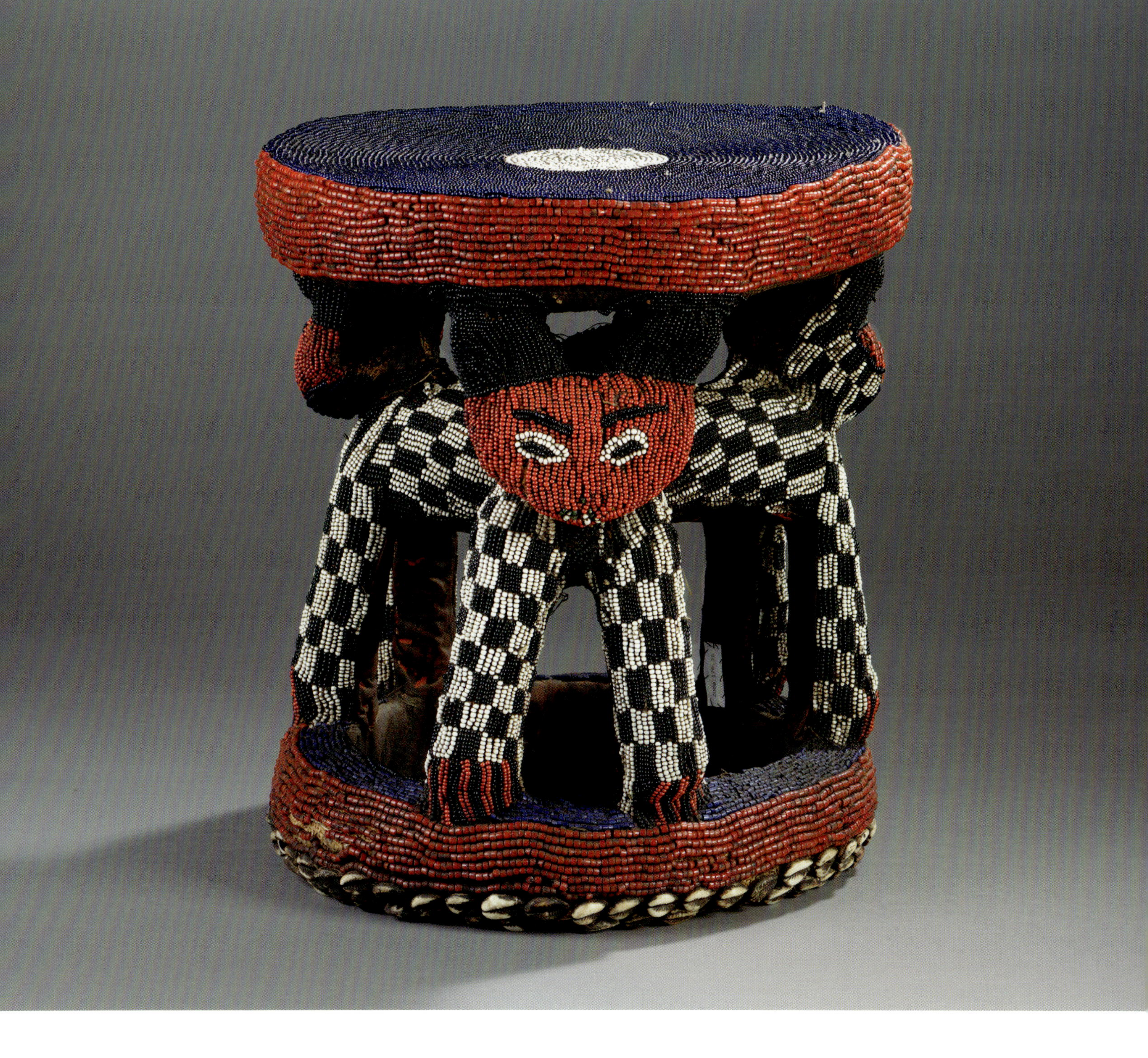

for African creativity, she relied heavily on Bamum dealers to source the material she was interested in, without investigating in detail the provenance and the makers of the pieces that she was acquiring as cultural artworks more than as objects made by an individual. Although she was fully aware that she was not acquiring masterpieces, Dagan still sought to include in her collection objects that would embody some form of "authentic" creative expression, despite the fact that they were sold and purchased in a marketplace. In this sense, this collection is the product of a dialogue informed by knowledge exchange, market research, aesthetic consciousness and canonical inventiveness on the part of Bamum artists, antiquaries and commercial art dealers, and by Dagan's own quest to purchase and collect non-commercial authenticity.

figure 19
Stool
Unidentified artist or workshop
Bamiléké style
Purchased from a private collector in Montreal in 1983
Wood, glass beads, cowrie shells, burlap
Height: 36 cm, Diameter: 33 cm
ROM 2009.126.25

1 Ian Fowler, "Tribal and Palatine Arts of the Cameroons Grassfields: Elements for a 'Traditional' Regional Identity," in *Contesting Art: Art, Politics and Identity in the Modern World*, ed. Jeremy MacClancey (New York: Oxford, 1997), 66.

2 René Bravmann, *Open Frontiers: The Mobility of Art in Black Africa* (Seattle: Henry Art Gallery by the University of Washington Press, 1973).

3 Jean-Pierre Warnier, *Échanges, développement et hiérarchies dans le Bamenda pré-colonial (Cameroun)* Studien zur Kulturkunde 76 (Stuttgart: Steiner-Verlag, 1985).

4 Ibid.

5 Tamara Northern, *The Art of Cameroon* (Washington: Smithsonian, 1984), 61.

6 Jean-Pierre Warnier, "The Grassfields of Cameroon: Ancient Center or Recent Periphery?" *Africa Today* 53, no. 3 (2012).

7 Fowler, "Tribal and Palatine Arts."

8 See Warnier, *Echanges, développement et hiérarchies* and "The Grassfields of Cameroon"; Fowler, "Tribal and Palatine Arts"; and Claude Tardits, *Le royaume bamoun* (Paris: A. Colins, 1980).

9 Warnier, Echanges, *développement et hiérarchies*, 297–301.

10 Christraud M. Geary, *Things of the Palace* (Wiesbaden: Franz Steiner Verlag, 1983), 85–94.

11 For a detailed overview of early twentieth-century collecting practices, see M. Oberhofer, "Die Wiederentdeckung und Reinterpretation einer verloren geglaubten Afrika-Sammlung aus Bamum (Kamerun)" *Mitteilungen der Berliner Gesellschaft für Anthropologie, Ethnologie und Urgeschichte* Bd. 31 (2010): 73–88.

12 Geary, *Things of the Palace*, 86–87

13 Quoted in Christaud M. Geary, *Bamum* (Milano: 5 Continents, 2011), 55.

14 Accounts of the significant shift in approach towards the Bamum Kingdom between the German and French colonial administration may be found in Geary, *Things of the Palace*; Geary, *Bamum*; and Alexandra Loumpet-Galitzine, *Njoya et le royaume bamoun* (Paris: Karthala, 2006).

15 Geary, *Bamum* (Milano: 5 Continents, 2011), 56–59

16 Sultan Njoya and Pasteur Henri Martin, "Histoire et coutumes des Bamum. Rédigées sous la direction du Sultan Njoya," *Memoires de l'Institut Français d'Afrique Noire*, no. 5 (1952): 129.

17 Epistolary exchange between Schwab, the Peabody Museum's director Dr. Hooton and his assistant Donald Scott [PM} 30–2. I owe this find to Jonathan Fine, who very generously shared this correspondence with me.

18 The largest and best know craft co-operative active in the region is Prescraft, founded in 1961 as the Presbyterian Handicraft Centre by Reverend Hans Knöpfli, which has strong ties with Mission 21 in Basel. Prescraft has its main outlet in Bamenda and sells to a broad international clientele. Another fairly large, but not as successful, outlet for local artists is the Handicraft Cooperative in Nkwen, a non-religious organization currently managed exclusively by Cameroonians. See also H. Knöpfli, *Crafts and Technologies: Some Traditional Craftsmen of the Western Grasslands of Cameroon* (British Museum, 1997).

19 Paul Gebauer, *Art of Cameroon* (Portland: Portland Museum of Art, 1979), 121–2.

20 Chris Geary, who lived in Salifou's household for a few months, provides a vivid account of his activity as a dealer in C. M. Geary and S. Xatart, *Material Journeys: Collecting African and Oceanic Art, 1945–2000* (Boston: Museum of Fine Arts, 2007), 141.

21 Conversation with Alahmadou Njitari, July 21, 2011.

22 For a biography of this important dealer and collector, see Sotheby's,"Philippe Guimot and Domitilla de Grunne Collection d'Art Premier," Sotheby's, Paris, June 17, 2009.

23 Conversation with Nji Yende Amadou, July 23, 2011.

24 Antiquaries consistently define authenticity with the most common definition of this term in relation to African artworks: objects made by local artists for local use. While most of the pieces available for sale today by Foumban antiquaries were probably made in the 1970s or later, many of them have been collected in the field through often complicated and lengthy negotiations.

25 Personal communication with Mme Medou, Director of Cultural Heritage, Cameroon, July 23, 2013.

26 Sometimes pieces are also altered so they may look newer than they actually are. Chris Geary (personal communication, January 2015) mentioned having seen older pieces covered with new beads so that they would pass customs inspection. In another instance, while at the home of Souleman Njankuo, I saw an older beaded artwork emerge from the fragments of a contemporary clay sculpture in which it had been encased.

27 Jean-Paul Notué and Bianca Triaca, *Mankon: Catalogue of the Mankon Museum* (Milano: 5 Continents, 2005): 226.

28 One of the most striking examples of this Indian-inspired production is a throne currently on display in the Mankon Museum which features on the back a Grassfields-style representation of an Indian divinity. See Notué and Triaca, *Treasures of the Sculptor Kings in Cameroon: Babungo* (Milano: 5 Continents, 2005): 161.

29 Gebauer, *Art of Cameroon*, 122.

30 Information about El Hadji Ali was provided by Soulemanou Njankuo in July 2013.

31 Interview with Salifou N., potter, July 13, 2012.

32 Erik Nemeth, "Art Sales as Cultural Intelligence: Analysis of the Auction Market for African Tribal Art," *African Security* 4, no. 2 (2011): 132.

33 Conversation with Moussa, trader in his thirties, Rue des Artisans, July 15, 2012.

34 V. Y. Mudimbe, "African Art as a Question Mark," *African Studies Review* 29, no. 1 (1986): 4.

35 James Clifford, "Histories of Tribal and the Modern," in *The Predicament of Culture: Twentieth-Century Ethnography, Literature and Art* (Cambridge, MA: Harvard University Press, 1988).

36 Other compelling examples of agency and strategic adaptation to market demnd in early encounters may be found in Schildkrout, Enid, and Curtis A. Keim, *The Scramble for Art in Central Africa*. (Cambridge, UK: Cambridge University Press, 1998).

37 For a discussion of the criteria of formation and definition of the canon and the challenges posed by contemporary productions, see

amongst others Christopher B. Steiner, "Can the Canon Burst?," *The Art Bulletin* 78, no. 2 (1996); Christopher B. Steiner, "The Taste of Angels in the Art of Darkness: Fashioning the Canon of African Art," in *Art History and Its Institutions: Foundations of a Discipline*, ed. E. Mansfield, (London and New York: Routledge, 2002); and Silvia Forni, "Ambiguous Values and Incommensurable Claims: The Canon, the Market and Entangled Histories of Collections and Exhibits," *Critical Interventions: Journal of African Art History and Visual Culture* 4, no. 2 (2010).

Bibliography

Bravmann, René. *Open Frontiers: The Mobility of Art in Black Africa*. Seattle: Henry Art Gallery by the University of Washington Press, 1973.

Clifford, James. *The Predicament of Culture: Twentieth-Century Ethnography, Literature and Art*, Cambridge, MA: Harvard University Press, 1988.

Crowley, Daniel. "The Art Market in Cameroon and the Central African Empire." *African Arts* 12, no. 3 (1979): 74–75

———. "The Contemporary–Traditional Art Market in Africa." *African Arts* 4, no. 1 (1970): 43–49, 80.

Forni, Silvia. "Ambiguous Values and Incommensurable Claims: The Canon, the Market and Entangled Histories of Collections and Exhibits." *Critical Internventions: Journal of African Art History and Visual Culture* 4, no. 2 (2010): 150–59.

Fowler, Ian. "Tribal and Palatine Arts of the Cameroons Grassfields: Elements for a 'Traditional' Regional Identity." In *Contesting Art: Art, Politics and Identity in the Modern World*, edited by Jeremy MacClancey, 63–84. New York: Oxford, 1997.

Geary, Christraud M. *Bamum*. Milano: 5 Continents, 2011.

———.*Things of the Palace*. Wiesbaden: Franz Steiner Verlag, 1983.

Geary, Christraud M. and Stephanie Xatart. *Material Journeys: Collecting African and Oceanic Art, 1945–2000*. Boston: Museum of Fine Arts, 2007.

Gebauer, Paul. *Art of Cameroon*. Portland: Portland Museum of Art, 1979.

Jules-Rosette, Bennetta. *The Message of Tourist Art: An African Semiotic System in Comparative Perspective*. New York: Plenum Press, 1984.

Knöpfli, Hans. *Crafts and Technologies: Some Traditional Craftsmen of the Western Grasslands of Cameroon*. British Museum, 1997.

Latour, Bruno. "What Is Iconoclash? Or Is There a World Beyond the Image Wars?" In *Iconoclash: Beyond Image Wars in Science, Religion and Art*, edited by Bruno Latour and Peter Weibel, 13–28. Karlsruhe, Germany: Center for Art and Media, 2002.

Loumpet-Galitzine, Alexandra. *Njoya et le royaume bamoun: Les archives de la société des missions* évangéliques *de Paris, 1917–1937*. Paris: Karthala, 2006.

Mudimbe, V. Y. "African Art as a Question Mark." *African Studies Review* 29, no. 1 (1986): 3–4.

Nelson, Steven. "Collection and Context in a Cameroonian Village." *Museum International* 59, no. 3 (2007): 22–30.

Nemeth, Erik. "Art Sales as Cultural Intelligence: Analysis of the Auction Market for African Tribal Art." *African Security* 4, no. 2 (2011): 127–144.

Njoya, Sultan, and Pasteur Henri Martin. "Histoire et coutumes des Bamum. Rédigées sous la direction du Sultan Njoya." *Memoires de L'Institut Français d'Afrique Noire*, no. 5 (1952).

Northern, Tamara. *The Art of Cameroon*. Washington: Smithsonian, 1984.

Notué, Jean-Paul, and Bianca Triaca. *Babungo: Treasures of the Sculptor Kings in Cameroon: Memory, Arts and Techniques*. Catalogue of the Babungo Museum. Milano: 5 Continents, 2005.

———. *Baham: Arts, Mémoire et pouvoir dans le royaume de Baham (Cameroun)*. Catalogue du Musée de Baham. Milano, Barzio (Lecco): 5 Continents; COE, 2005.

———. *Bandjoun: Trésors royaux au Cameroun: Tradition dynamique, création et Vie, Musée de Babungo*. Milano: 5 Continents, 2005.

———. *Mankon: Catalogue of the Mankon Museum*. Milano: 5 Continents, 2005.

Oberhofer, Michaela. "Die Wiederentdeckung und Reinterpretation einer verloren geglaubten Afrika-Sammlung aus Bamum (Kamerun)." *Mitteilungen der Berliner Gesellschaft für Anthropologie, Ethnologie und Urgeschichte* Bd. 31 (2010): 73–88.

Perrois, Louis, and Jean-Paul Notué. *Rois et sculpteurs de l'Ouest Cameroun: La panthère et la mygale*. Paris: Karthala Editions, 1997.

Probst, Peter. "Inconclash in the Age of Heritage African Arts." *African Arts* 45, no. 3 (2012): 10–13.

Schildkrout, E., J. Hellman, and C. Keim. "Mangbetu Pottery: Tradition and Innovation in Northeast Zaire." *African Arts* 22, no. 2 (1989): 38–47, 102.

Schildkrout, Enid, Jill Hellman, and Curtis Keim. *African Reflections: Art from Northeastern Zaire*. Seattle: University of Washington Press, 1990.

——— *The Scramble for Art in Central Africa*. Cambridge, UK: Cambridge University Press, 1998.

Sotheby's."Philippe Guimot and Domitilla de Grunne Collection d'Art Premier." *Sotheby's*, Paris, June 17, 2009.

Steiner, Christopher B. *African Art in Transit*. Cambridge: Cambridge University Press, 1994.

———. "Can the Canon Burst?" *The Art Bulletin* 78, no. 2 (1996): 213–17.

———. "The Taste of Angels in the Art of Darkness: Fashioning the Canon of African Art" In *Art History and Its Institutions: Foundations of a Discipline*, edited by Elizabeth Mansfield, 132–45. London and New York: Routledge, 2002.

Strother, Z. S. "Iconoclash: From 'Tradition' to 'Heritage' in Global Africa." *African Arts* 45, no. 3 (2012): 1–6.

Tardits, Claude. *L'Histoire singulière de l'art bamoun: Cameroun*. Paris: Afredit; Maisonneuve & Larose, 2004.

———. *Le Royaume Bamoun*. Paris: A. Colins, 1980.

Warnier, Jean-Pierre. *Échanges, développement et hiérarchies dans le Bamenda pré-colonial (Cameroun)*. Studien zur Kulturkunde, 76. Stuttgart: Steiner-Verlag, 1985.

———. "The Grassfields of Cameroon: Ancient Center or Recent Periphery?" *Africa Today* 53, no. 3 (2012): 59–72.

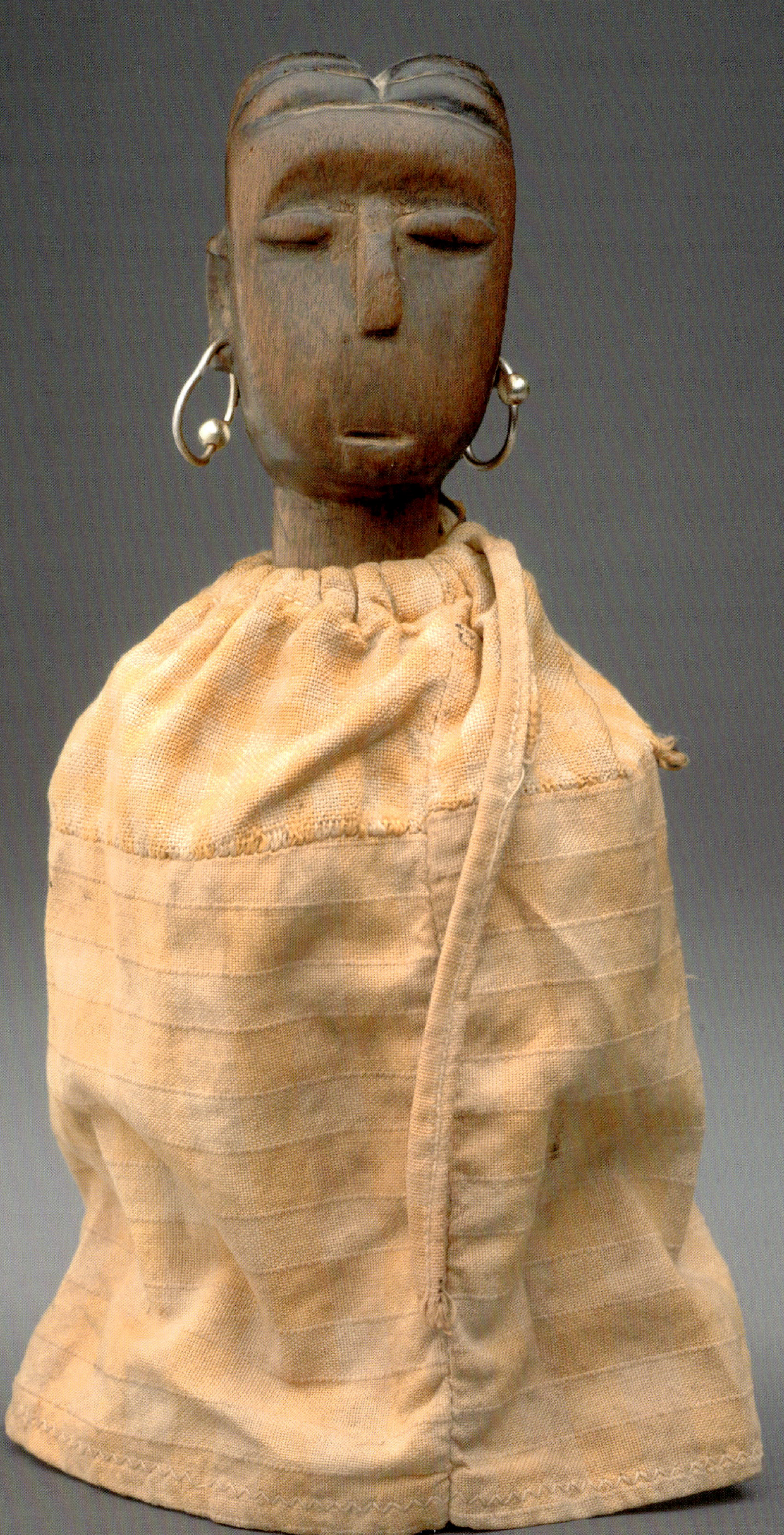

plate 11

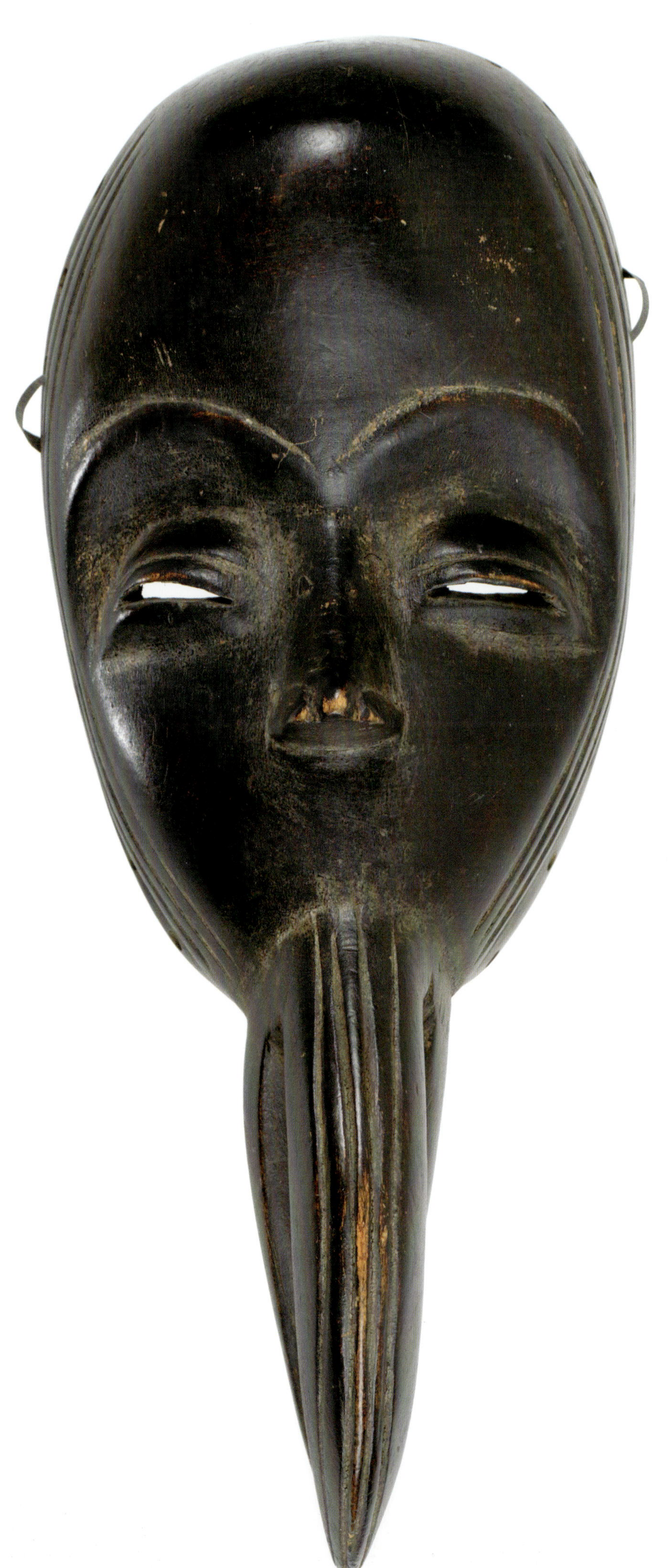

plate 12

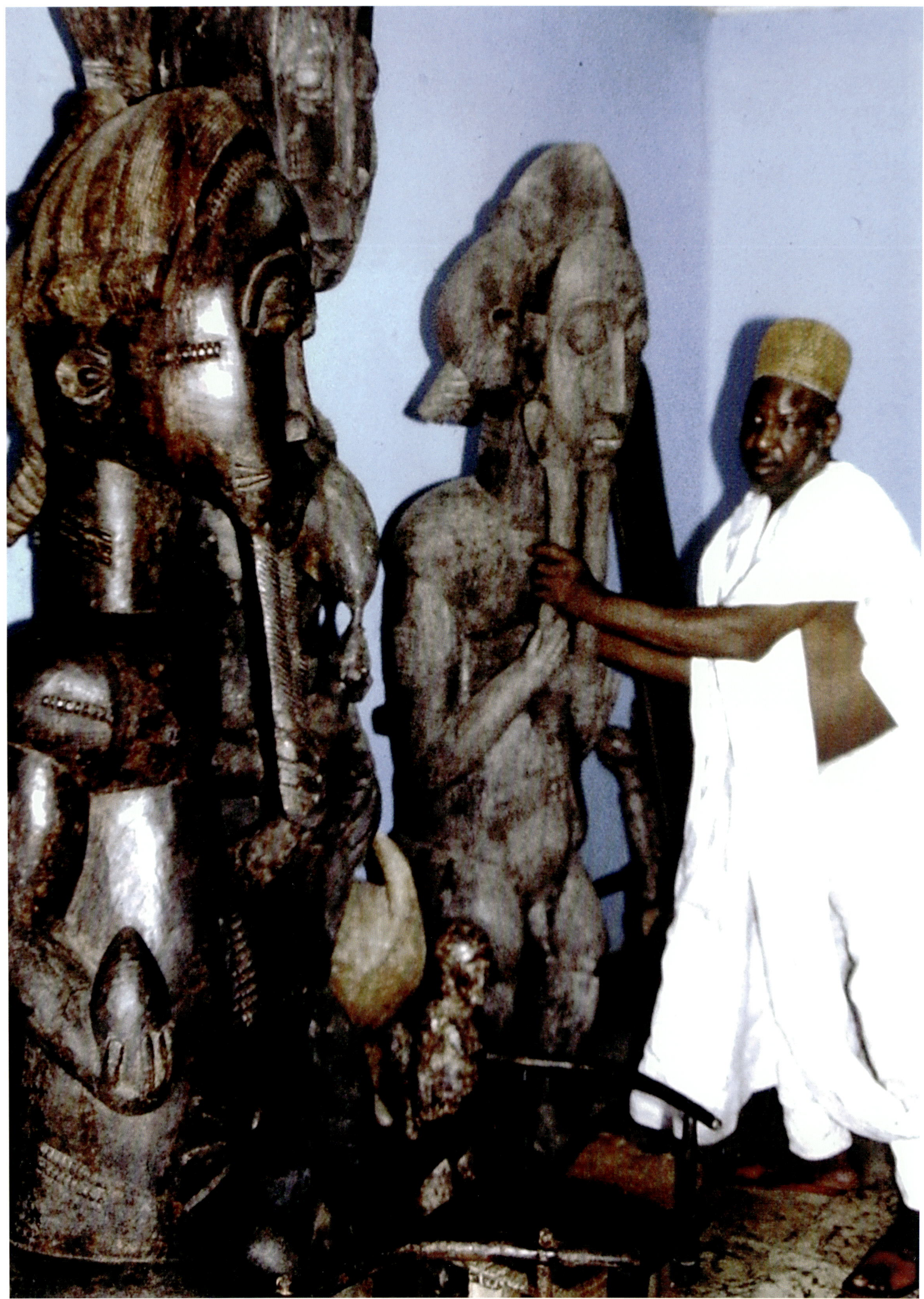

CHAPTER 7

THE SECRET OF THE MASKS: ON THE SOCIAL CONSTRUCTION OF POWER AND DESIRE IN THE AFRICAN ART MARKET

CHRISTOPHER B. STEINER

In many African societies masks and masking are shrouded behind a veil of secrecy. In some cultures the ritual functions and esoteric symbolism of masks are guarded from the uninitiated; in others, the details of their production and even existence are hidden from public view. While the specific function of secrecy may vary from one culture to the next, in general the "secret of the masks" serves to heighten their perceived power within the social, political or religious arena in which they function and perform. By concealing the identity of the wearer, the mask is imbued with an aura of mysterious authority that gives it an influence and value far greater than what might be possible if the masked identity were transparent and clear.

The literature on African art has produced some important analyses of how secrecy functions in the realm of African masks and masquerades. Beginning in the 1950s with the work of Dr. George W. Harley, author of *Masks as Agents of Social Control in Northeast Liberia* (1950), the anthropology of masks has concentrated on the political function of secrecy and secret societies. How does secrecy serve to enforce customary law? What is the role of the secret society in relation to the broader political system? Does the "secret of the masks" conceal an actual body of hidden knowledge and practices? Or is secrecy a more generalized metaphor for social interaction that structures particular relations according to rules of hierarchy and differential access to power?[1]

In this essay, I propose to explore the notion of "secrecy" in relation to African masks (and other objects) that circulate in the international art market. I will argue that the secrets, ambiguities and indeterminacies that imbue African masks with power in their culture of origin continue to function as a critical element of power even when an African object has been removed from its indigenous cultural milieu. When a mask is acquired by an itinerant African art trader, and enters the art market as a commodity and collectible, the "secret of the masks" remains as a powerful conceptual framework to instill the object with authority and value. However, the nature of the "secret" itself shifts dramatically from its original context of use to its new context of collection and display outside of Africa.

When acquired by outsiders for collection and consumption, masks are generally silent about their age, their true origin, their authenticity and their intrinsic economic value. Masks and other objects of African art travel through the international art market as mute objects harbouring deep mysteries about their genuineness, their financial worth, and their aesthetic meaning and import. These profound "unknowns" or silences may be interpreted, I would argue, as a new form of secrecy serving to endow an object with greater power and value (cultural capital). In many cases, all knowledge about a mask or other object once it has been removed from its site of creation and use can only be ascertained by projecting onto it Western conjecture about its source, and idiosyncratic assumptions about its value, age and authenticity. Just as in its original setting the mask gains prestige through mystery,

detail
Hausa trader in Treichville Quarter displaying a newly arrived shipment of massive Baule-style spirit figures. Abidjan, Côte d'Ivoire, 1987–88
Photo by Christopher B. Steiner

subterfuge and ambiguity, so too in the context of the market economy the mask may become elevated to "something it is not" through the fantasy and imagination of its interlocutors—merchants, collectors, speculators, viewers.

The discussion that follows is organized around four key areas in which I believe "mystery" or "secrecy" informs the transactions of market participants who negotiate economic and aesthetic values: monetary price, cultural or ethnographic meaning, discovery of the real thing and object authenticity.

The Secrecy of Economic Value

African objects that circulate in the international art market do not have fixed prices. In each transaction along its path from site of production to site of consumption, an object is continuously subjected to a rigorous examination by various market participants seeking to probe and uncover its fair market value. In *Capital*, Karl Marx described a similar process of commodity interrogation that he understood to be an inherent quality of late capitalism: "Value does not have its description branded on its forehead; it rather transforms every product of labour into a social hieroglyphic. Later on, men try to decipher the hieroglyphic, to get behind the secret of their own social product."[2] While Marx in this passage is talking about the alienation of labour, I would argue that his statement applies equally well to the international African art market, in which we might better speak of an alienation not of labour but of truth—the truth of an object's real identity, value and genuineness. At each moment of exchange, from African village to Western collection, market participants interrogate each other through the common medium of the object, trying to "decipher the hieroglyphic" hidden deep inside the object's past or social life.[3] Much of this negotiation of value takes place in the verbal exchange between seller and buyer, or in other words, through bargaining.

When bargaining to establish the price of an African artwork, there is almost always a bilateral asymmetry between the African art trader and the Western consumer. The negotiation that takes place at the point of sale is a transaction aimed at gauging the value of an object in terms of the "opponent's" value system—that is, how much can the seller get away with asking, and how little can the buyer pay. Indeed, one of the key functions of bargaining is to overcome indeterminacy in situations where only limited market information is available.

No trader wants other marketplace traders to know how much he has paid for any item in his stock, nor does he want anyone to know for how much he sold an item to either another trader or to a foreign buyer. When traders sell art objects to Western collectors or tourists in the marketplace, they often take the person aside so that other traders cannot overhear the prices that are being discussed and negotiated. If it is not possible to move away from a group of traders, the seller might whisper prices in the buyer's ear (especially as the price negotiation reaches its conclusion). There are at least three explanations for why a merchant would want to tell a client his price in confidence. First, it is a dramatic technique, calculated to let clients believe they are getting such a good price that the trader would be embarrassed to have his rivals know that he is selling something so inexpensively. In fact, traders will even tell the buyer not to repeat the price to anyone else for fear that others will want to buy a similar item for the same low price ("This price is *only for you*.").

A second motivation for stating the price in confidence is in point of fact to discourage the consumer from repeating the purchase price—not, however, out of fear of embarrassment for having underpriced an item, but in order for a trader to keep his financial affairs confidential. If the seller owed money to another marketplace trader, for example, he would not want that trader to find out that he had just earned enough cash to be able to repay his debt.

Finally, a third reason why a trader would want to conceal his prices is to prevent others from gaining "free" market information about the current rate on a certain type of item. Say, for example, that a trader sells a particular style of Senufo or Baule mask to a Western dealer for a considerable profit. The trader also knows that another stallholder in the marketplace has a very similar mask of the same type in his stock. The trader intends to get that object on credit from the stallholder and offer it for sale to the same dealer at his hotel later that day. If the other trader found out how much the foreign buyer had paid for the first mask, he would demand to receive that amount from the trader, or he would attempt to find the foreign buyer himself in order to sell the mask directly to him. If the stallholder is not aware of how much was paid, however, then the trader can try to get the mask for a lower credit price and make another worthwhile profit (from the same buyer) on the sale of the second mask.

Bargaining is a form of linguistic exchange. In some cases the seller may intentionally mask his language competency in order to gain an advantage in verbal negotiations. While conducting research in Côte d'Ivoire among African art traders in the late 1980s, I experienced a bargaining exchange that proved to be very instructive about language manipulation and concealment. In a remote farming village to the east of the capital, Korhogo, Abdurraham Madu was negotiating with an itinerant supplier over the purchase of a small, seated Senufo figure. The supplier was very insistent on getting a high price for what he considered to be a fine ("top") object. Madu was nervous about committing that much money to a single purchase, but he too thought it might be an exceptionally good piece that would sell well back in Abidjan.

Throughout the negotiations, which took place between Madu and the supplier in a combination of Hausa, Dioula and French, Madu repeatedly consulted with me about my opinion on the object's value and authenticity. We spoke in English, assuming the supplier could not understand our "back channel" chatter. After a very lengthy negotiation, lasting over a half hour, Madu finally reached an agreement to buy the Senufo statuette for a considerably higher price than he would have hoped. As we all shook hands to say goodbye, the supplier said, in perfect English, "it was a pleasure doing business with you." What we did not know while the bargaining was under way is that the supplier had just come from several years working in English-speaking Ghana. He understood every word Madu and I had been saying, and secretly garnered from our conversation that we both felt this was an extraordinarily good piece. By not revealing to us that he spoke English, the supplier was able to work to his advantage the knowledge he gained from our private exchanges—he could hold out for his higher price.

Language obfuscation may also be an advantage to the seller if he wants to stall the pace of the negotiations to better calculate "on the fly" his asking prices and profit margin. In the preface to a catalogue on African art collected by John Rohner from itinerant traders in Colorado, the collector describes just this situation: "A few [runners] pretend not to understand English," he writes, "which gives them an edge time-wise to internally calculate the deal in progress. Once the deal is set, their English improves remarkably."[4] Well-known African art dealer Lance Entwistle has suggested that the advantage of knowledge, which once lay on the side of the Western collector, has now shifted to the side of the African trader.

> The closer you get to the present, the more perilous it is to deal with runners.... You go back forty years, you may buy something very good from a runner. You might be more informed than he was, and better able to get the better end of the deal. But today, these runners—ninety-nine percent will get the better of the people they deal with.[5]

Once an African art object has left the continent of Africa, the value established through the series of market transactions that led to its extraction from the local economy generally becomes forgotten as the object forges a new path in the international art economy. The market negotiations that served to extract the object from its original milieu now become a distant memory in the social life of that object. What counts now is the establishment of value within the Western art-collection scale of economic value—a scale that has little or no relation to the scale of value that served to bring the object out of Africa.

Many of the objects acquired by Esther Dagan were purchased in African marketplaces through bargaining and verbal negotiation. When sold through her gallery in Montreal, it is likely the price she assigned to an object was not in direct relation to the amount she had paid in Africa. The gallery price is generally a reflection of the "Western value" assigned to different categories or qualities of African objects. Sometimes those values fall into line within the hierarchy of value established in the African marketplace, but sometimes they are unrelated and based on vastly different criteria.

The Secrecy of Meaning

Among collectors in Europe and North America, often one of the most appealing aspects of African art is the mystery and magic that surrounds certain types of objects. Masks, shrine figures, divination implements are all seen to carry particular meanings that are framed by collectors as puzzles or secrets that need to be understood or resolved. Just as it may be argued that secrecy functions in the object's original context to underscore political or religious power, so too secrecy in the realm of the collection serves to heighten the desire and appeal of a particular object or class of objects.

Collectors sometimes speak of being attracted to African art because they know so little about its history, function or creation. Knowing too much would spoil the mystery and secrecy that for them gives African art its power and attractiveness. "Part of my desire to collect magical, strange objects," said one American collector, "would be destroyed if I knew it was carved by Mr. X in such and such a village and [that] he spent so much time carving it. If I knew the whole process so exactly, it would take away some of the magic and mystery."[6]

Many catalogues of private African art collections contain statements by the collectors that indicate the initial attraction to African objects is the "mystery" and "secrecy" that such objects often hold. These statements sometimes read like confessionals, suggesting that despite their initial reluctance to collect African art, they eventually became inexplicably seduced by some "secret" or "magical" powers hidden within the objects themselves. Renowned African art collector Paul Tishman, for example, describes in the preface to one of the early catalogues of his private collection how his spouse came to appreciate the arts of Africa: "Although my interest in collecting African art was at first not fully shared by my wife...it was not long before the purity and force of the material *worked their spell on her* [emphasis added]."[7] Thelma Lehmann recounts a similar magical experience when her husband first introduced her to African art: "...when Hans returned [from Africa] a month later with three dominating works carved by those...'uncultivated' tribesmen, I took my first objective look—and *the spell was cast* [emphasis added]."[8]

Esther Dagan's own narrative of transformation and self-awareness is a bit more nuanced and complex than those of the Tishmans or Lehmanns. In her catalogue, *Man and His Vision*, Dagan suggests that the magical qualities of the African objects she first encountered initially caused her to resist their acquisition: These were sacred objects, not commodities. But eventually her narrative shifts as her desire to uncover the magic overcomes her reticence.

> The sense of the sacredness of these objects overwhelmed any immediate desire to purchase and thus to uproot them from the continuity of their existence in their natural environment. However, eight pieces were acquired from a private collection offered for sale by a French collector in Ouagadougou in 1960, and thus the seed was planted.

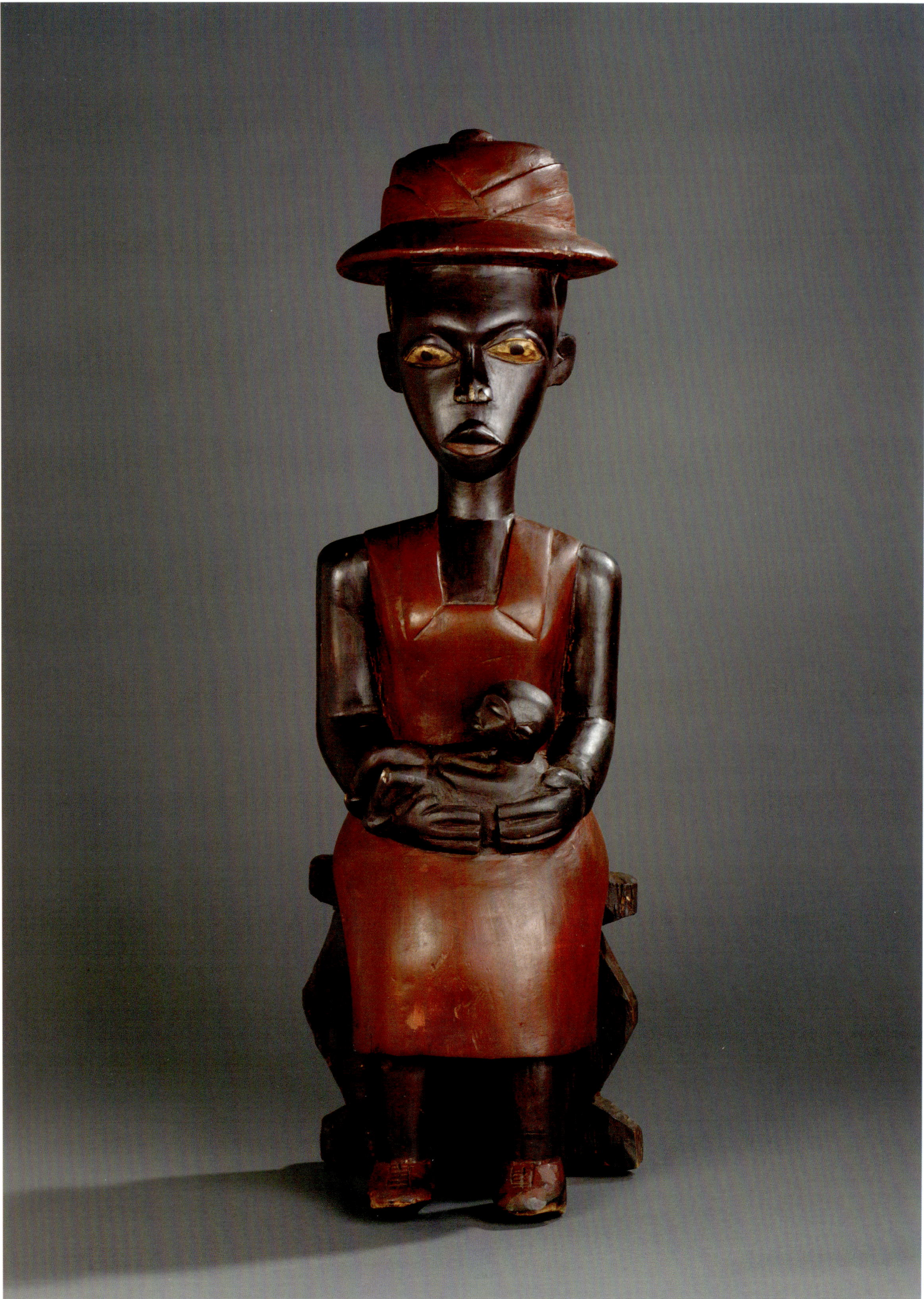

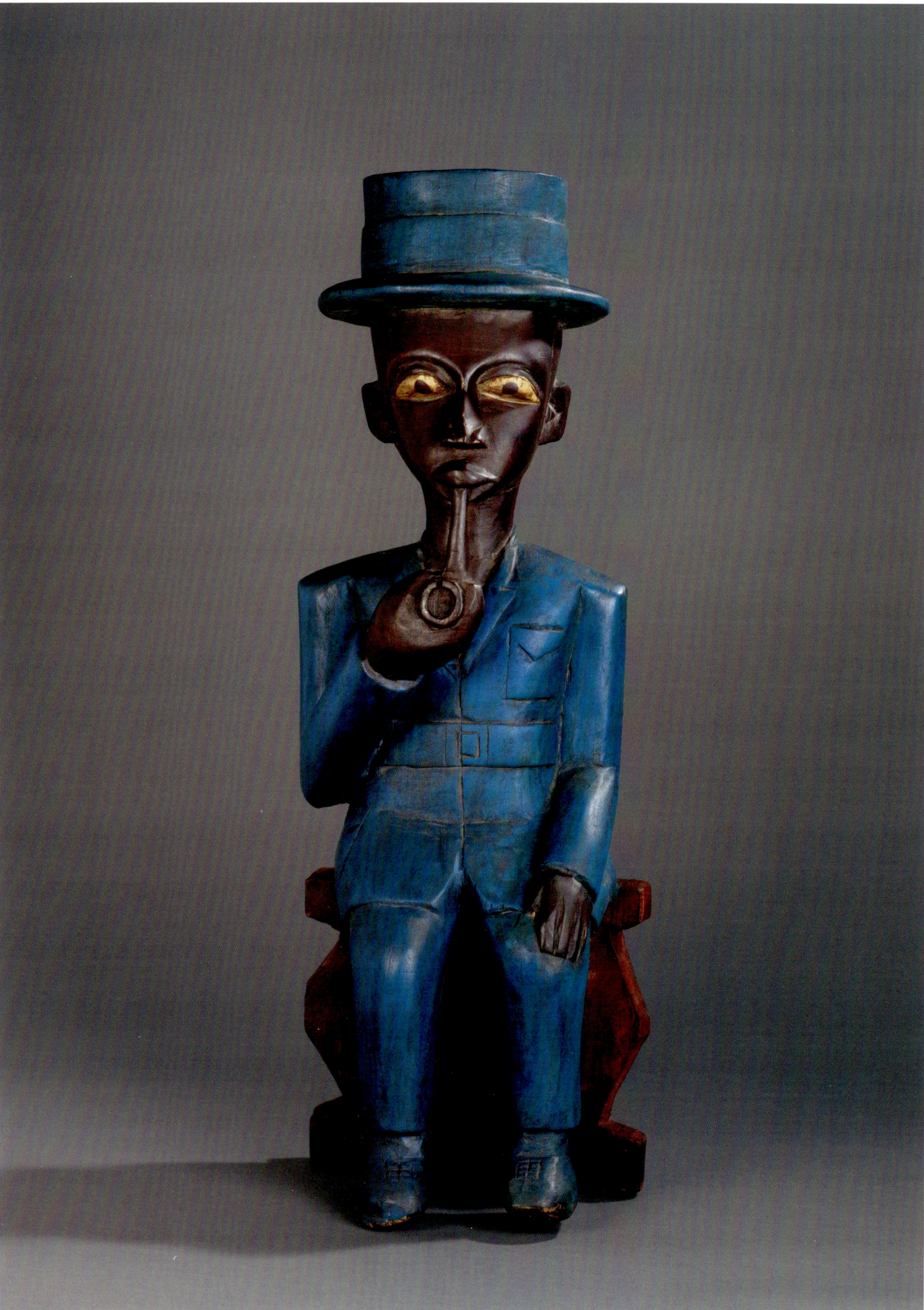

> The twenty-eight years that have passed have only served to reinforce and deepen my desire to penetrate the mysteries of these art forms.[9]

One can sense in this passage Dagan's ambivalence about whether or not it would be ethical to "uproot" objects from their indigenous context. Buying her first pieces from a private collection seems to sidestep the concern for her, because the objects have already been removed from their site of production and use. Moving forward in her career as a dealer, Dagan now equates collecting with uncovering "mysteries"—the act of acquisition becomes a form of personal research aimed at penetrating, as it were, the "secrets of the masks." Like other collectors, the ethical justification for removing objects from their original environment hinges on personal exploration and cross-cultural understanding. As Dagan says in another one of her publications: "This publication should not be considered as research-based. Rather, it is a purely personal point of view based on observations and experiences over an extended period of time."[10]

It is also important to note in this context the difference between African ritual objects that become commodified through the forces of the market economy and those that are produced solely as commodities to be sold for export. There is often a slippage or confusion in the way Dagan (and other collector–dealers) position objects along this continuum from sacred relic to commodity. Consider, for example, the male and female pair of Baule colonial-style figures from Côte d'Ivoire (Fig. 1 and 2). Objects such as these do have a traditional history in Baule culture, where they served as "spirit mates" or personal guardians that protected believers against misfortune and offered a line of communication between this world and the other world. During the colonial period, Baule carvers sometimes included Western elements into their carvings of the spirit mates: pith helmets, military caps, belts and other elements of Western attire. These additions not only made the spirit mates more contemporary and fashionable, they also infused the object's spiritual power with the material power associated with foreigners and their colonial military might.[11]

The figures acquired by Dagan in 1984–1985 are related stylistically to this tradition of carving Baule spirit mates in colonial garb, but this pair was carved for sale to the export market, not for use in indigenous religious practices. During the late 1950s, towards the end of French colonial rule in Côte d'Ivoire, foreign administrators, civil servants, soldiers and other colonial agents began commissioning portraits of themselves as souvenirs to take back home. A lively market in these market-driven *colon* figures flourished in the early 1980s in Côte d'Ivoire. French expatriates, still living and working in Abidjan and its vicinity, collected *colon* figures from the tourist marketplaces and from itinerant vendors who sold them door-to-door.

figures 1 & 2 (pages 150 & 151)
Colon couple
Unidentified artist or workshop
Baule style
Wood, pigment
Purchased from a dealer in Abidjan, Côte d'Ivoire, in 1984–1985
Height: 76 cm, Width: 22 cm, Depth: 21 cm (female)
Height: 69 cm, Width: 23 cm, Depth: 18 cm (male)
ROM 2009.126.52.1–2

figure 3 (opposite)
Colon figure
Unidentified artist or workshop
Baule style
Wood, pigment
Purchased from a dealer in Bouaké, Côte d'Ivoire, in 1987
Height: 41.1 cm, Width: 11.1 cm, Depth: 8 cm
ROM 2009.126.288

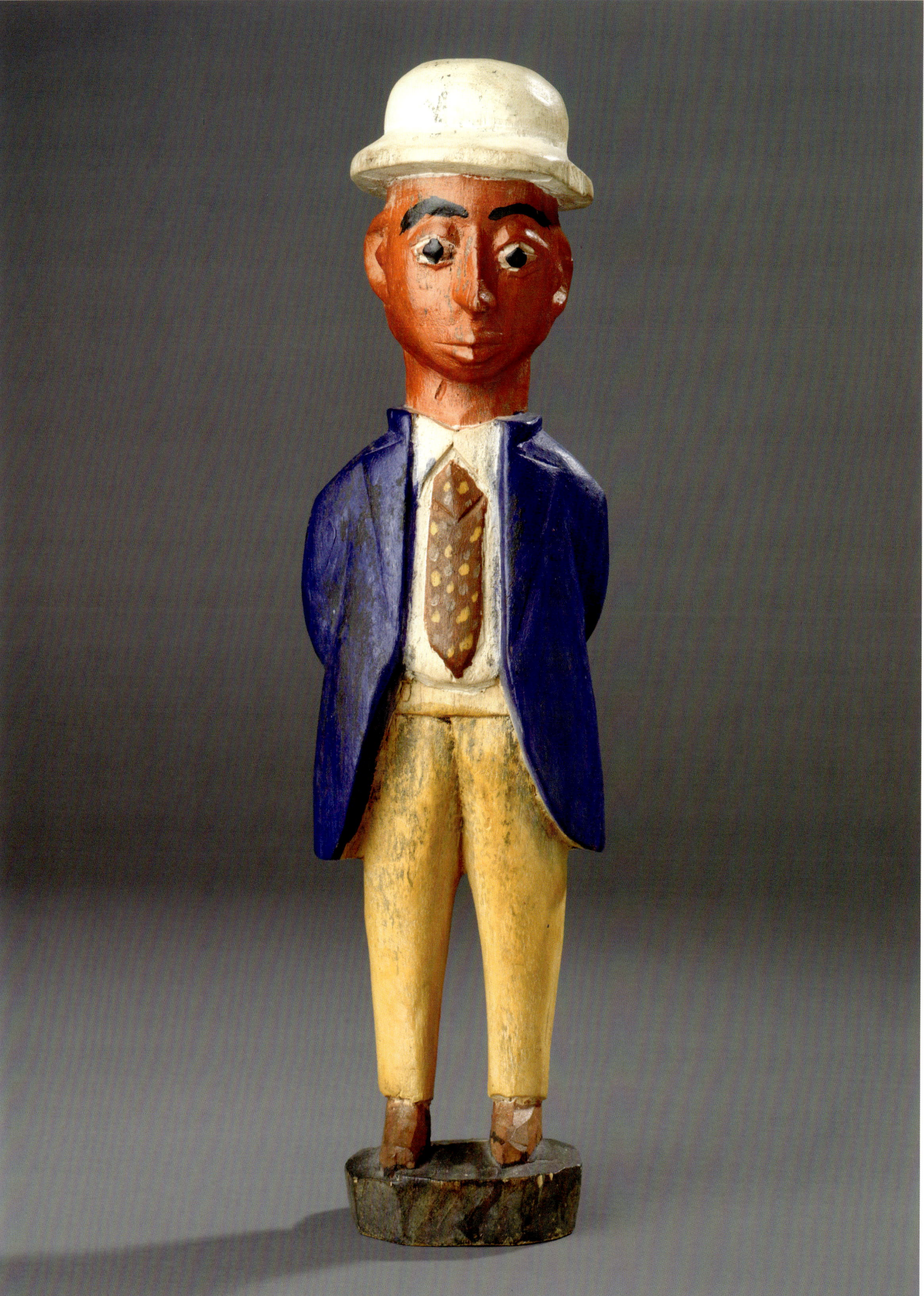

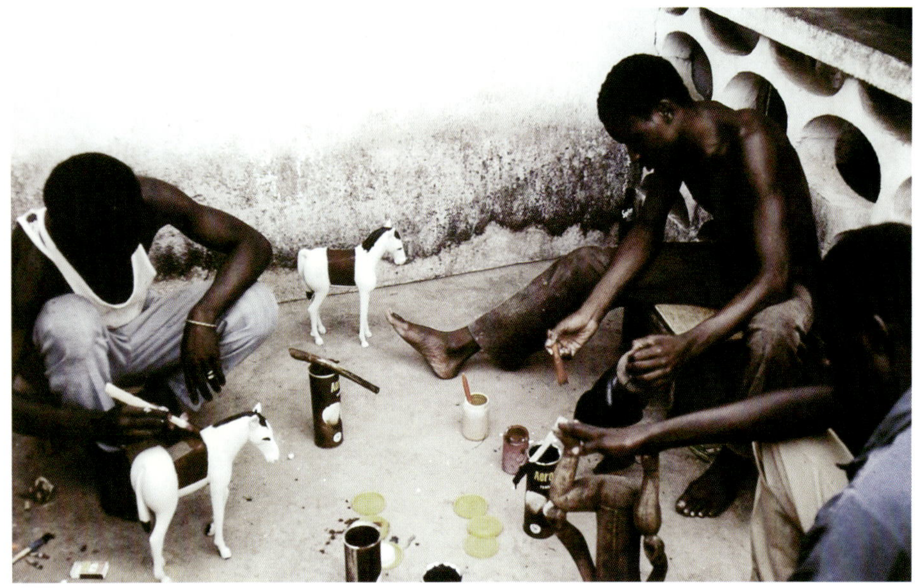

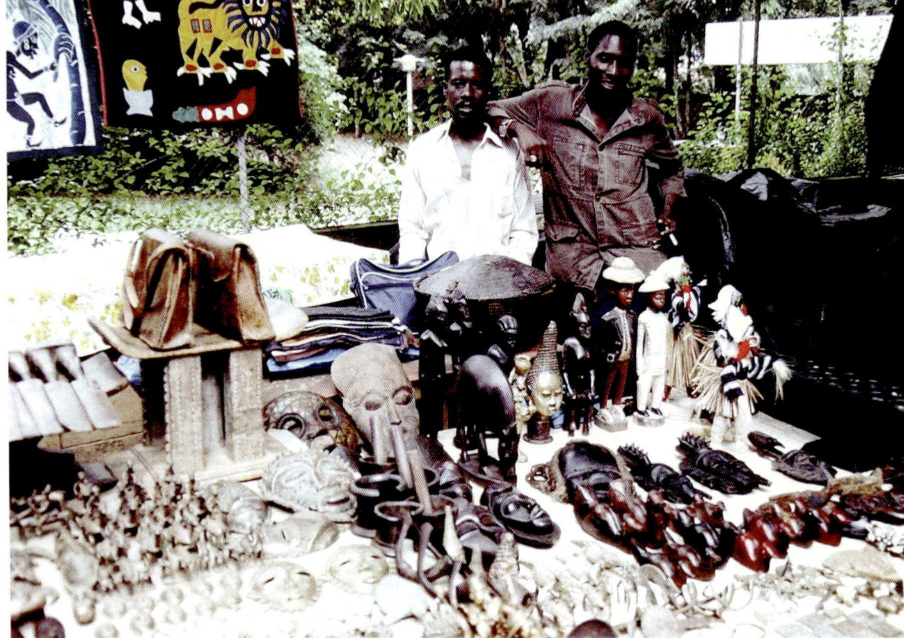

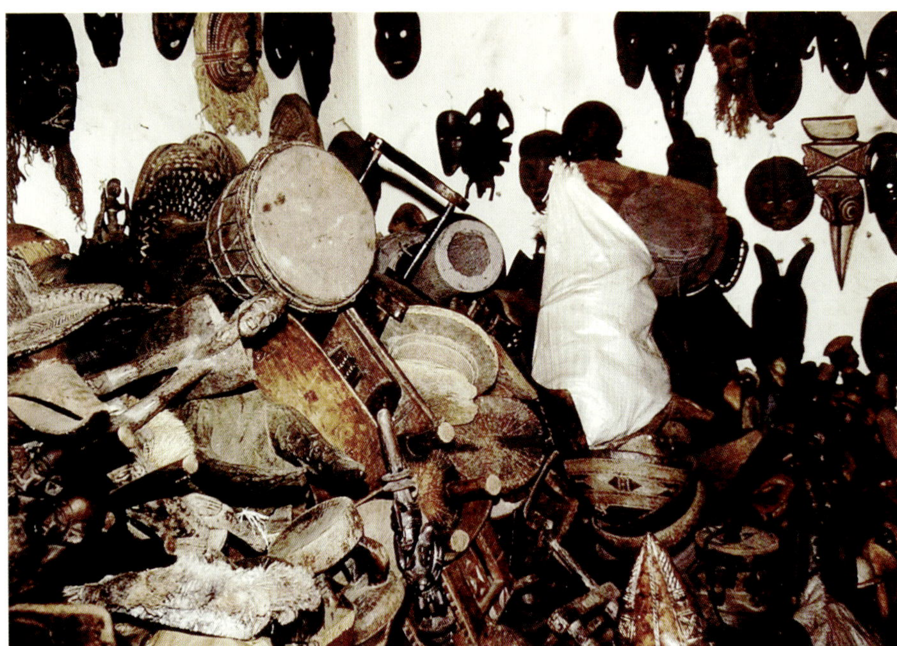

figure 4 (top)
Workshop apprentices paint "colonial" equestrian figures for the export or tourist trade
Bouaké, Côte d'Ivoire, 1987–1988
Photo by Christopher B. Steiner

figure 5 (middle)
Traders displaying art for sale outside the Hotel Mont Korhogo. Included in their display are two "colonial" figures, at the far right
Korhogo, Côte d'Ivoire, 1987–1988
Photo by Christopher B. Steiner

figure 6 (bottom)
A cluttered storage facility belonging to an African art dealer in Quartier Treichville, Abidjan, Côte d'Ivoire, 1987–1988
Photo by Christopher B. Steiner

figure 7 (opposite)
Colon figure
Unidentified artist or workshop
Baule style
Wood, pigment
Purchased from a dealer in Bouaké, Côte d'Ivoire, in 1987
Height: 33.6 cm, Width: 13.8 cm, Depth: 9.1 cm
ROM 2009.126.289

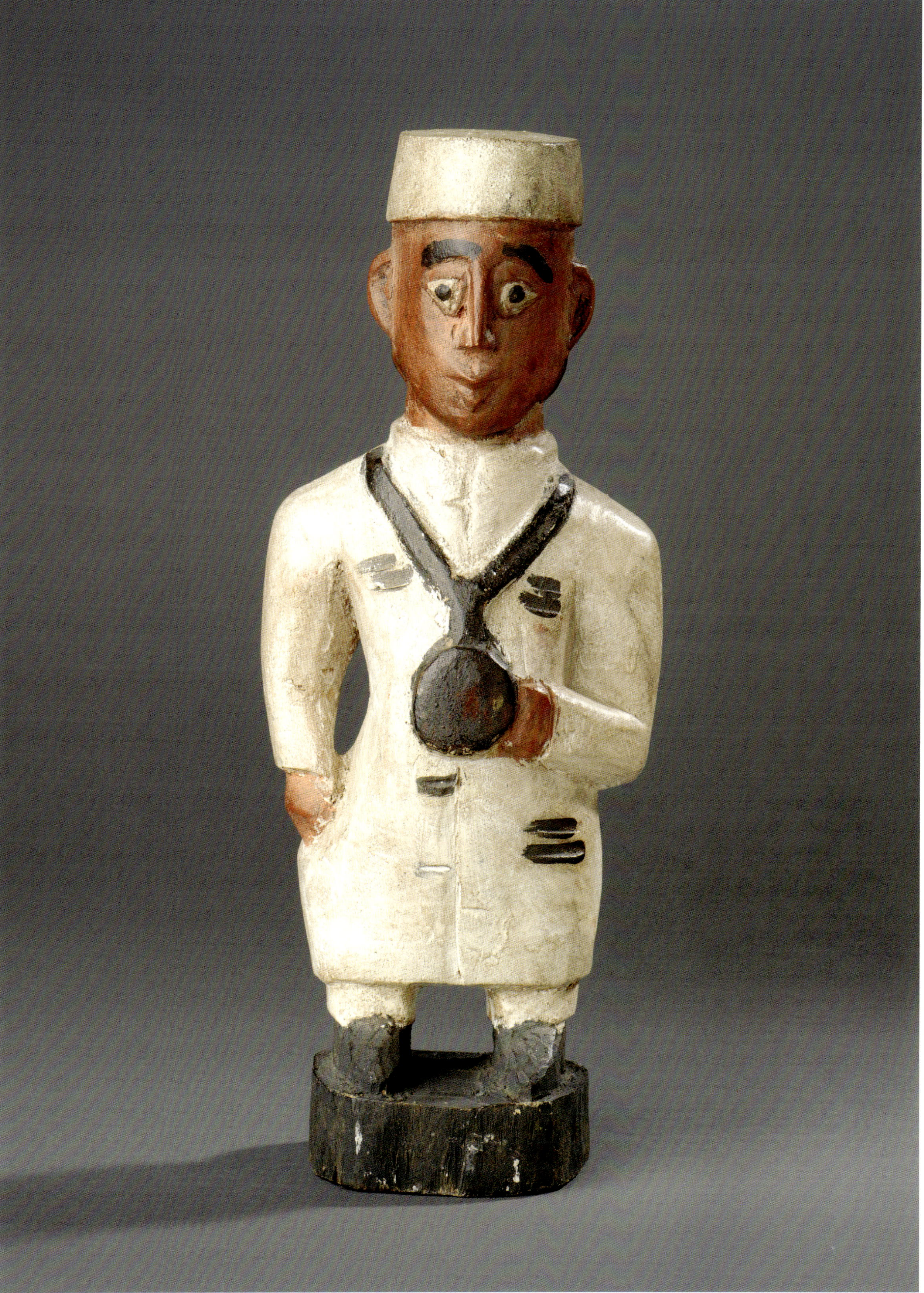

A wildly diverse range of object types was invented for this new export trade—figures dressed as doctors, tourists, golfers, tennis players, chefs, equestrians and so forth (Figs. 4 & 5). The Dagan collection includes some good examples of these object types (Figs. 3 & 7).

Today, the meaning of these objects has shifted radically. Originally conceived as objects that sought to appropriate Western power through the incorporation of modernity, these seemingly similar statues are now being sold back to the very agents of change whose power was once appropriated. Rather than achieve their value or authenticity by an emphatic denial of foreign contact, *colon* figures are interpreted by their buyers as a celebration of modern Western expansionism.[12] The male and female couple acquired by Dagan in the 1980s is rendered in a rather comical style, offering perhaps a tongue-in-cheek celebration of Western influence on this married couple. Their brightly colored attire (each one matching from head to toe), their stiff and awkward postures, and their highly gendered roles can be read as a kind of playful or self-ironizing comment on outsiders and the foreign market for Baule colonial figures.

Secret Desires of the Treasure Hunter

At a rational level, most collectors of African art will admit that it would be highly unlikely today to haphazardly uncover a genuine, monumental "masterpiece" in an African village, in the cargo truck of an itinerant African art trader, or even on eBay. Yet, many collectors of African art continue to hope (sometimes even in "secret") that they will be fortunate enough to stumble upon an undiscovered gem hidden in the normal "detritus" of the tourist or commercial art trade. "I had been assured by American dealers," writes one collector, "that we would no longer find [in Africa] art of consequence to bring home, and while I believed them, I had a *secret hope* [emphasis added] that we might...and we did."[13] The wife of a collector in New York told me once that her husband saw nearly every African "runner" that called him at his Manhattan office. "He keeps hoping to find that one masterpiece, like a real Fang reliquary figure or something, buried in the junk that the runners usually sell."[14]

Part of the reason collectors secretly hope to find buried treasures can be explained, at least in part, by the differential access to knowledge and expertise. There is always that chance that someone is selling inexpensively on eBay an object that they failed to recognize as valuable or authentic. There is always a possibility that an African trader mistakes a "real" object for a copy, or fails to grasp the importance of a particular piece. As Nicholas Lemann notes in an article about the African art trade in the 1980s: "[those who] patronize the runners [are] convinced that these people—usually illiterate and speaking only broken English—can't possibly know what stuff they're selling is really worth."[15]

In an industrial corner of Abidjan, there is a neighbourhood that was dominated in the 1980s by warehouses full of African art. These storerooms in Quartier Treichville served the Abidjan-based African art traders as a place to keep their cache of objects, either to supply the local marketplace stalls or in preparation for shipment overseas. Objects in these warehouses were generally dumped in huge piles on the floor, stuffed in cardboard boxes or wooden crates, or stacked fairly haphazardly along the top of makeshift tables and shelves (Fig. 6). In contrast to the upscale African art galleries in Abidjan (e.g., La Rose d'Ivoire or Galerie Pokou), these industrial lots made no effort to display, light or make accessible the objects that they contained.

Several American expatriate collectors of my acquaintance would regularly spend their Sunday afternoons visiting these warehouses in hopes of uncovering (literally) a masterpiece buried under piles of wooden masks, statues and stools. To my knowledge, collectors rarely found anything of real value in these piles of "wood," but they continued to hold out hope. One reason the collectors imagined they might find treasures in the storeroom chaos has to do, again, with differential access to knowledge and expertise. They believed that traders may be ignorant about the true value of certain objects, and would toss them mistakenly in their pile of art. For their part, the traders were fully aware that foreign collectors enjoyed rummaging through this mess of seemingly neglected objects; traders created an opportunity for the "diggers" to fantasize about making a great "discovery" or finding the occasional gem. If a collector did discover something great in the storehouse mayhem, the lore of the "find" would travel quickly among other expatriate collectors and stoke their desire to go on another treasure hunt.

Secrecy is at the heart of these exchanges. Not knowing whether or not a trader has the expertise to recognize what he is actually selling; having incomplete information about what is in a trader's stock of objects; not having any foolproof method of actually determining object value and authenticity—all contribute to a mode of social and economic transaction filled with indeterminacy and ambiguity.

figure 8
mblo mask
Unidentified artist or workshop
Baule style
Wood, pigment
Purchased from a New York gallery in the late 1980s
Height: 42 cm, Width: 29 cm, Depth: 19.5 cm
ROM 2009.126.182

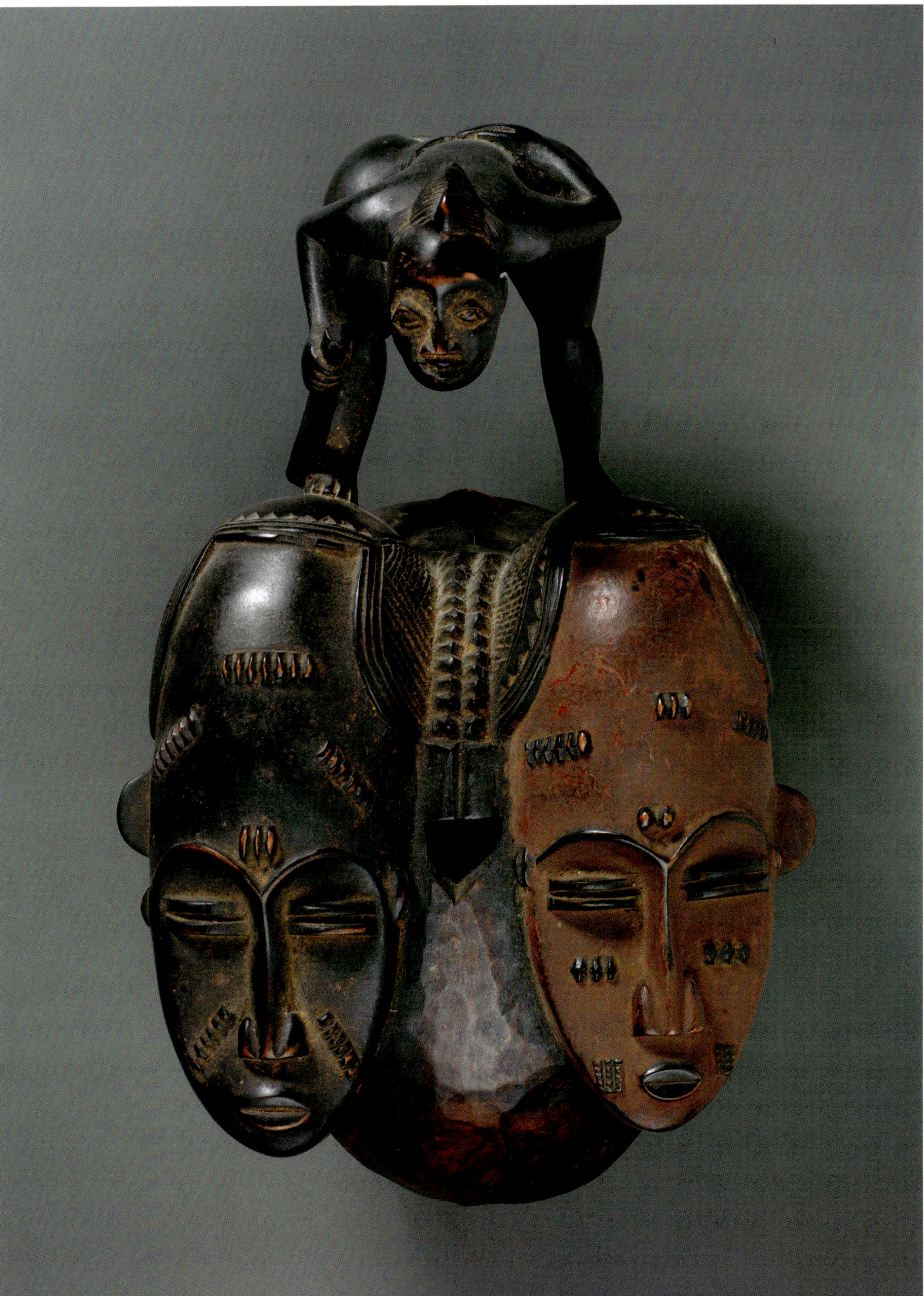

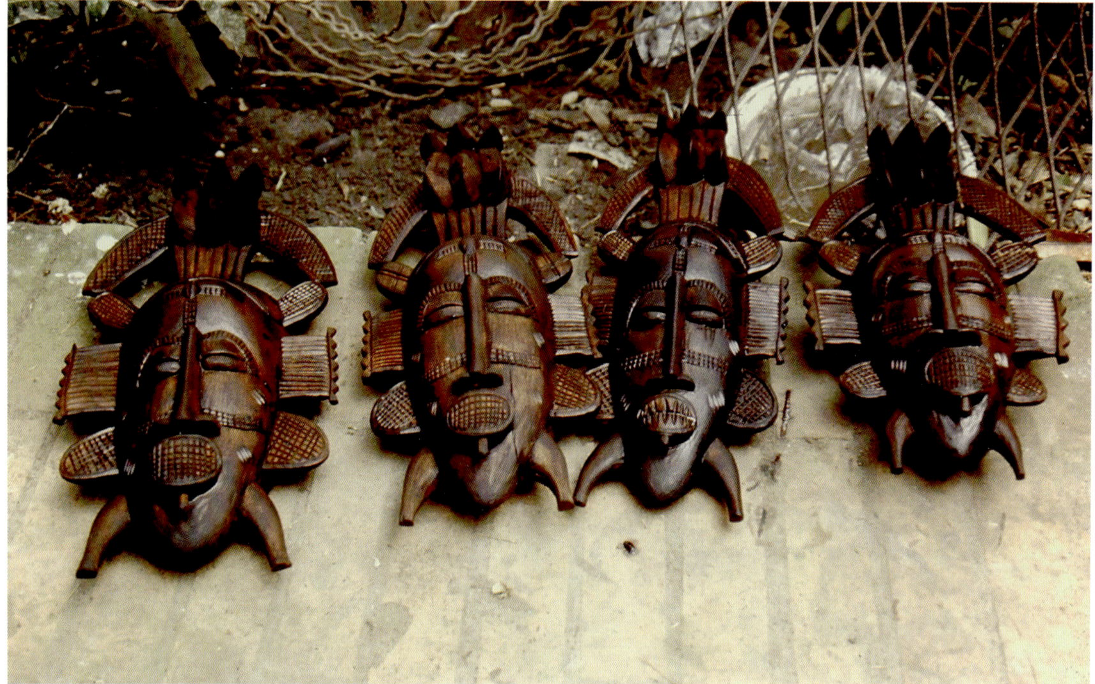

figure 9
Senufo *kpelie* style masks being stained with potassium permanganate
Plateau marketplace,
Abidjan, Côte d'Ivoire, 1987–1988
Photo by Christopher B. Steiner

figure 10 (opposite)
Anklet
Unidentified artist or workshop
Baule style
Brass
Purchased from a dealer in Abidjan, Côte d'Ivoire, in 1985
Height: 8.5 cm, Width: 12 cm, Depth: 12 cm
ROM 2009.126.350

The Secrecy of Authenticity

When an African art object is proffered for sale in Europe or North America, one of the key indeterminacies of the transaction has to do with the object's authenticity. Was the object created for indigenous use? Was it created for export or trade? Was it created for the tourist market? Or was it created as a fake intended to deceive the buyer about its truth and genuineness? Most collectors, whether serious or casual, expect an object of African art to be culturally genuine rather than made for commerce or as a deliberate fake. Within the complex category of fake African art is sometimes included so-called "tourist art" or art made expressly for trade and export rather than indigenous use.

There is, of course, enormous room for slippage between these various ill-defined categories. Sometimes an object can even move from one category to another depending on how it is interpreted or the specific circumstances of its life history. In their quest to identity objects as "authentic," collectors will sometimes perform extraordinary mental gymnastics of rationalization aimed at ascribing authenticity to an object. One strategy is to locate authenticity not within the qualities of the object itself, but rather in the narratives and tales that surround the collection of the object.

So while the object may appear inauthentic to others, from the collector's point of view it is a memento of an authentic cultural exchange. In the preface to their collection catalogue, Hans and Thelma Lehmann write: "Many of our pieces are associated with...memories, the ones from Africa often being more vivid than those from such places as Christie's or Sotheby's in London or dealers in Europe or America."[16]

Traders and artists in Africa are acutely aware of Western desire for authentic objects. In some cases artists have been known to copy artworks from African art publications—exhibition catalogues, magazines or auction sales catalogues. In general, the decision to reproduce a particular object or style of object is based on the perceived potential for that kind of piece in the international market.

Esther Dagan documented this process of (re)production in her catalogue *The Spirit's Image: The African Masking Tradition—Evolving Continuity*.

> In 1985, I published a book on African stools *Man at Rest*. In 1986 I gave copies of this book to all the African art dealers who had sold me stools. A year later I returned to the same dealers, to find them offering me large numbers of African stools similar to those they had sold me years earlier, but because they had been published in my book, the prices were almost triple those I had previously paid. To justify the higher prices, the traders told me that the value had increased simply because similar pieces had been published in my book.[17]

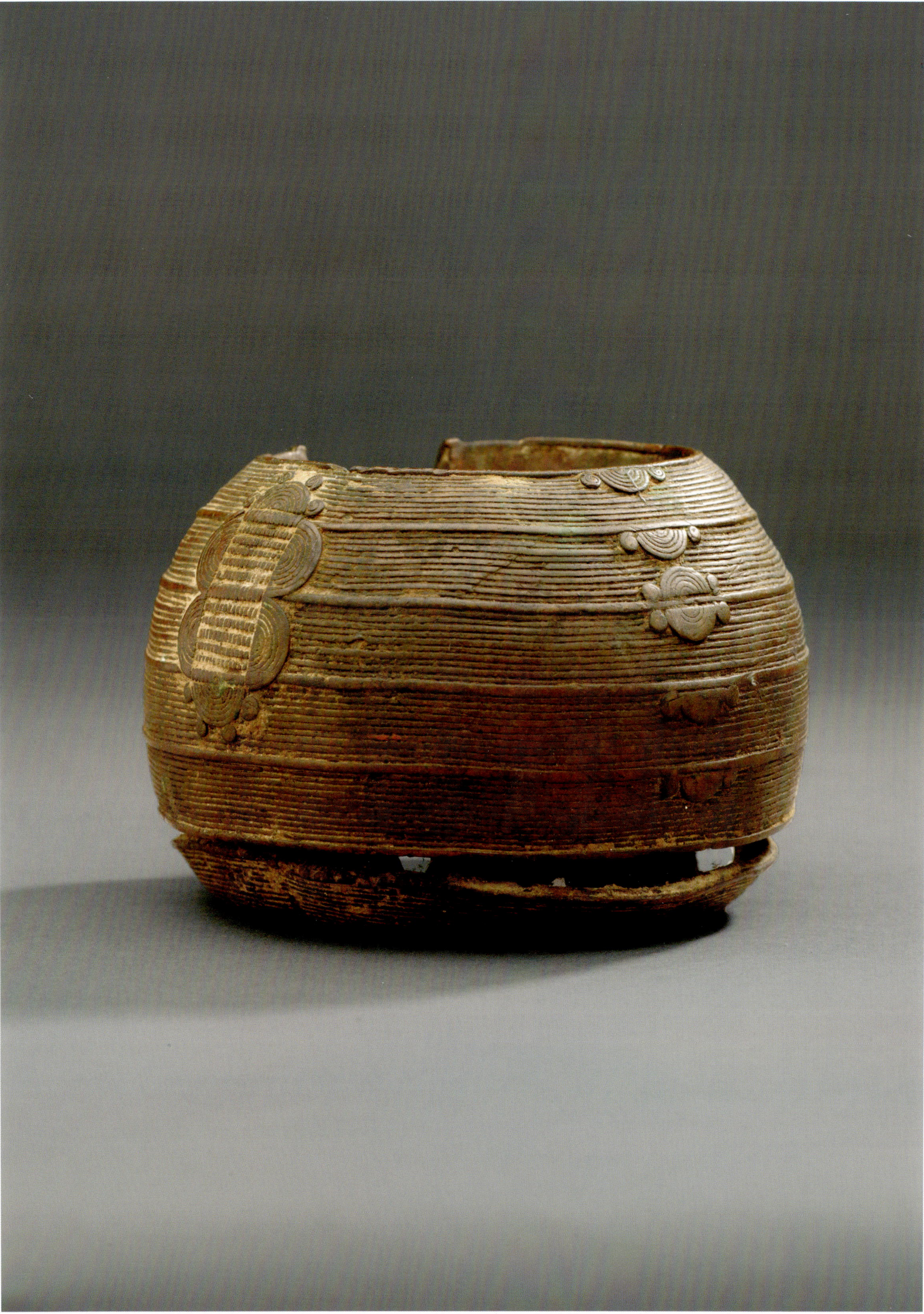

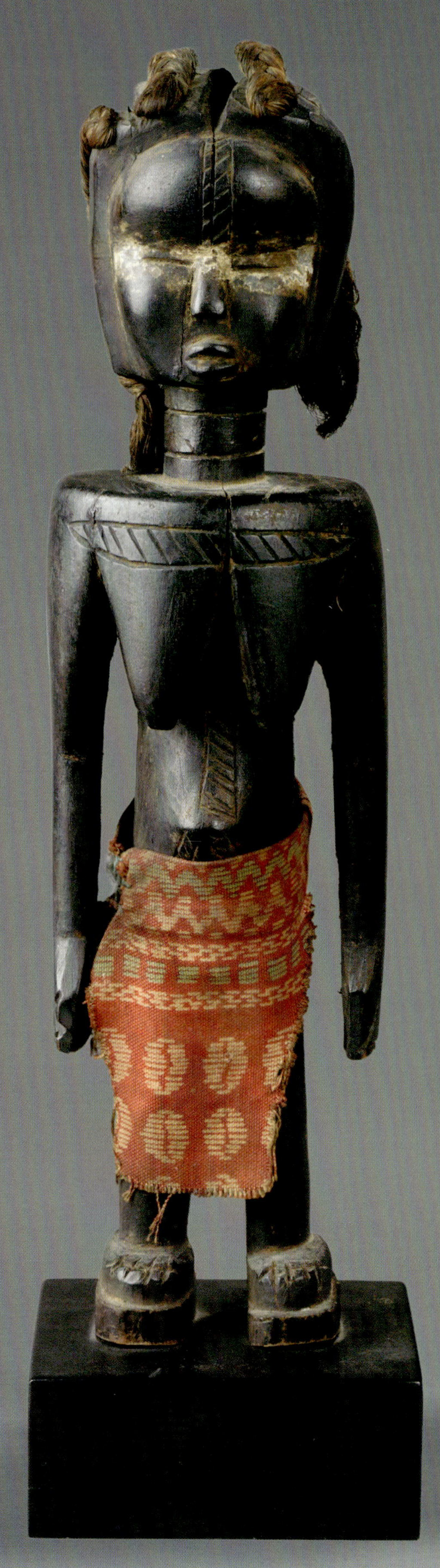

figure 11
Figure
Unidentified artist or workshop
Dan or Bassa style
Wood, cloth
Purchased from an African dealer
in Montreal in 1988
Height: 41 cm, Width: 11.8 cm, Depth: 10.5 cm
ROM 2009.126.257

Reproducing objects copied from books or sales catalogues has several potential outcomes. First, objects with high auction records or objects included in major museum exhibitions are reproduced more frequently because it is assumed that they will find eager buyers. A well-known and often reproduced *kpelie* mask from the Senufo region in northern Côte d'Ivoire was a standard model for export copies made during the 1980s.[18] This distinctive mask, acquired by Nelson A. Rockefeller in 1964, features a row of three birds carved atop the crest of the mask's face. The image of the mask has been published in numerous books on African art, and is featured in the widely distributed catalogue of the Rockefeller collection at the Metropolitan Museum of Art.[19] The result of copying objects from well-known collections, of course, is that the consumer is presented with a copy of a "famous" object, thought the authenticity of that copy is even more dubious than of the average market copy. Yet these reproductions of "famous" pieces do find buyers and a place in the international African art market.

A good example may be found in the cover illustration of Esther Dagan's catalog *The Spirit's Image* (1992). The Baule-style *mblo* mask (Fig. 8) representing twins is a fairly typical market copy based on a frequently reproduced Baule mask from the collection of the Barbier-Mueller Museum in Geneva. The Barbier-Mueller mask was acquired by Henri Kamer in 1955 from Roger Bédiat, a West Indian dealer settled in Côte d'Ivoire, who likely acquired the mask in the mid-1930s.[20] The mask represents twins, with the female in red (on the left) and the male in black (on the right). The mask was first exhibited in 1958 in the exhibition *L'Art de l'Afrique Noire*, organized by Jacqueline Delange at the Palais Granvelle in Besançon, France. It has subsequently been widely published in exhibition catalogues and in at least a half dozen popular picture books on African art, including *The Arts of Black Africa* by Jean Laude (1973) and *Les Arts d'Afrique* by Alain-Michel Boyer (2006). The wide circulation of this mask's image in both colour and black-and-white photographs not only helps establish it as a (valuable) canonical form, but also makes it easily available to artists in Africa looking for models to copy and reproduce for the marketplace. While there exist very few examples of this style of mask that are known to have been produced and collected early in the twentieth century (a second Baule twin, though slightly different in style, was acquired by Paul Guillaume prior to 1920; it is currently in the collection of the Metropolitan Museum of Art), there are scores of contemporary reproductions on the market. In addition to the one on the cover of Dagan's book, a quick search on eBay uncovers nearly twenty examples for sale, ranging in asking price from $90 to $590.

What makes the Baule mask on the cover of Dagan's book even more interesting is the added superstructure depicting a male figure leaning forward towards the front of the mask. Neither of the Baule twin masks collected in the early twentieth century includes a superstructure of any kind. The male figure appears to be an invention on the part of the artist, who copied the basic form of the twin mask but then added a unique embellishment. Carving a figure on top of the twin mask is a good example of "creativity" within the framework of artistic (re)production for the export market. The artist knows that the Baule twin mask is a popular genre that is likely to sell; yet the artist also wants a vehicle for self-expression, creativity and innovation. So, the superstructure becomes a kind of aesthetic "add on" that not only enables the artist to demonstrate virtuosity in his craft, but also potentially distinguishes the twin mask from other more-literal copies of the early prototype models.

Some collectors of African art focus their attention largely on utilitarian objects, where the possibility of mistakenly acquiring a fake is greatly reduced in contrast to the market for masks and statues that is "infested" with replicas and forgeries (Fig. 9). The Baule anklet (Fig. 10) acquired by Dagan is a good example of an object for which there is no market for replicas or forgeries. Worn by Baule women of all ages during the nineteenth century, hollow-cast brass anklets such as this fell out of fashion by the 1930s. Built up from dozens of rows of wax threads laid over a charcoal core before casting, these anklets are among the most sophisticated and elaborate in all of West Africa. Because they are all "old" and "used," their authenticity is not in question. Their economic value thus depends on other qualities, such as the detail and sophistication of the design, the condition they are in (many are cracked and battered because they were generally removed from the wearer's leg with the aid of mallets), and whether they have survived as a matching pair or, as in this case, have been separated over time from their mate.[21]

The challenge of determining "authenticity" is often far more difficult within the category of masks and statues than within the category of utilitarian or functional objects for which there is little or no market in fakes. An example of an object whose age and authenticity is difficult to establish is the Dan/Bassa carving of a standing female figure in the Dagan collection (Fig. 10). The statue is elegantly carved and, as they say, "shows its age." But it is difficult, perhaps even impossible, to know whether it was carved for export or for indigenous use. Beginning in the 1930s, carvers in northern Liberia were already making figures for sale to missionaries, travellers and other foreign buyers. The trade objects were often made in the same villages (and in some cases likely by the same artists) where objects were being made for local patrons and local use.

American medical missionary Dr. George W. Harley collected in the mid-1930s about a half dozen carved female figures from among the Dan people in Liberia. One of these figures, now at the Peabody Museum at Harvard University, is generally regarded as among the best examples of the style and is routinely exhibited in museums and published in catalogues. Yet, it is interesting to note that in the same year that Harley sold this carving to the Peabody Museum, he also sold two others that he himself describes as tourist copies, or "made on request" for the collector.[22] Because objects such as these were prized by local patrons as status symbols and not religious icons, they did not receive any ritual use or sacrificial patina. Therefore, it is nearly impossible to differentiate "authentic" from "inauthentic" in the case of the Harley-collected objects because they all date to the 1930s.

Conclusion

The international market for African art creates a curious set of visual "dialogues" across time and across boundaries of value and authenticity. Canonical prototypes get reproduced and sell because they are assumed to retain some of the desirable qualities recognized by major collectors of African art: it looks like the one in the book, so it must be "real." And then in its secondary market circulation, the reproduction gets published in its own book (e.g., the Baule mask on the cover of Dagan's *The Spirit's Image*), which then revitalizes the "authenticity" of the form. The copy, now validated by its own publication, becomes its own measure of authenticity.

Looking at African art offered for sale on eBay, it is interesting to note that Esther Dagan's exhibition catalogues are now cited as sources of authenticity for the export copies that are being sold. Africa Direct, one of the most prominent eBay merchants of African art since 1997, frequently cites Dagan's books for comparative examples of similar object types. For example, a recent listing for an "Omdurman Baggara Doll Beaded with With Bark Cloth African" references in its object description Dagan's catalogue *African Dolls* (1990): "The figure shows similarities with the one published in Esther A. Dagan, AFRICAN DOLLS, fig.74 p.141 attributed to the Omdurman people of South Sudan."

I have argued in this essay that the mystery and secrecy that empowers certain works of African art in their indigenous context continues to instill objects with power and value in the context of the market economy. The nature of what is being kept secret changes dramatically from the world of ritual and religion to the world of collection and trade, but the general practice of guarding proprietary knowledge extends across these two domains. When objects of African art appear in a Western collection or museum exhibition, as if by magic, with no record of their trajectory from Africa to the West (see the Introduction), the reason for such silences may not simply be the loss of information over time but rather a conscious effort to obfuscate certain knowledge and information in order to heighten the "power" of an object. Knowing the "secret of the masks" in traditional African religious practices may undermine the power of the cult through debunking magical authority; knowing the "secret of the masks" in the context of the art market and international trade may demystify the perceived value and authority of an object by revealing the logic of mercantile capitalism and rational economic exchange that underlies the production and circulation of African art in the market today.

---

1 Beryl L. Bellman, *The Language of Secrecy: Symbols and Metaphors in Poro Ritual* (New Brunswick, NJ: Rutgers University Press, 1984).

2 Karl Marx, *Capital* (New York: Modern Library, 1906), XX.

3 Igor Kopytoff, "The Cultural Biography of Things," in *The Social Life of Things: Commodities in Cultural Perspective*, ed. Arjun Appadurai (Cambridge: Cambridge University Press, 1986).

4 John R. Rohner, *Art Treasures from African Runners* (Niwot, CO: University Press of Colorado, 2000), 2.

5 Quoted in Frederick John Lamp, Amanda M. Maples, and Laura M. Smalligan, *Accumulating Histories: African Art from the Charles B. Benenson Collection at the Yale University Art Gallery* (New Haven: Yale University Press, 2012), 27.

6 Quoted in Christopher B. Steiner, *African Art in Transit* (Cambridge: Cambridge University Press, 1994), 163.

7 Roy Sieber and Arnold Rubin, *Sculptures of Black Africa: The Paul Tishman Collection* (Los Angeles: Los Angeles County Museum of Art, 1968).

8 René A. Bravmann, *The Poetry of Form: The Hans and Thelma Lehmann Collection of African Art* (Seattle: Henry Art Gallery, University of Washington, 1982), 8.

9 Esther A. Dagan, *Man and His Vision: The Traditional Wood Sculpture of Burkina Faso* (Montreal: Galerie Amrad African Arts, 1987), 7.

10 Esther A. Dagan, *Tradition in Transition: Mother and Child in African Sculpture—Past and Present* (Montreal: Galerie Amrad African Arts, 1989), 11.

11 Phillip L. Ravenhill, *Dreams and Reverie: Images of Otherworld Mates Among the Baule, West Africa* (Washington, DC: Smithsonian Institution Press, 1996).

12 Steiner, *African Art in Transit*, 148–54.

13 Bravmann, *The Poetry of Form*, 8.

14 Steiner, *African Art in Transit*, 9–10.

15 Nicholas Lemann, "Fake Masks," *The Atlantic* 260, no. 5 (1987): 28.

16 Bravmann, *The Poetry of Form*, 9.

17 Esther A. Dagan, *The Spirit's Image: The African Masking Tradition—Evolving Continuity* (Montreal: Galerie Amrad African Arts, 1992), 177.

18 Ibid.

19 Douglas Newton, *Masterpieces of Primitive Art: The Nelson A. Rockefeller Collection* (New York: Alfred A. Knopf, 1978); see

also Roy Sieber and Roslyn Adele Walker, *African Art in the Cycle of Life* (Washington, DC: National Museum of African Art, Smithsonian Institution, 1987), 135.

20 Jean Paul Barbier, ed., *Art of Côte d'Ivoire from the Collections of the Barbier-Mueller Museum*. vol 2. (Geneva: Barbier-Mueller Museum, 1993), 118.

21 Ibid., 166–67.

22 See George Schwab, *Tribes of the Liberian Hinterland*, ed. George Schwab with additional material by George W. Harley, Papers of the Peabody Museum of American Archaeology and Ethnology, Harvard University, vol. 31 (Cambridge, MA: Peabody Museum Press, 1947): figures 72b and 72e-f.

Bibliography

Barbier, Jean Paul. ed. *Art of Côte d'Ivoire from the Collections of the Barbier-Mueller Museum*. Vol 2. Geneva: Barbier-Mueller Museum, 1993.

Bellman, Beryl L. *The Language of Secrecy: Symbols and Metaphors in Poro Ritual*. New Brunswick, NJ: Rutgers University Press, 1984.

Boyer, Alain-Michel. *Les Arts d'Afrique*. Paris: Hazan, 2006.

Bravmann, René A. *The Poetry of Form: The Hans and Thelma Lehmann Collection of African Art*. Seattle: Henry Art Gallery, University of Washington, 1982.

Dagan, Esther A. *African Dolls: For Play and For Magic*. Montreal: Galerie Amrad African Arts, 1990.

———. *Man and His Vision: The Traditional Wood Sculpture of Burkina Faso*. Montreal: Galerie Amrad African Arts, 1987.

———. *The Spirit's Image: The African Masking Tradition—Evolving Continuity*. Montreal: Galerie Amrad African Arts, 1992.

———. *Tradition in Transition: Mother and Child in African Sculpture—Past and Present*. Montreal: Galerie Amrad African Arts, 1989.

Harley, George W. *Masks as Agents of Social Control in Northeast Liberia*. Papers of the Peabody Museum of American Archaeology and Ethnology. Cambridge, MA: Harvard University Press, 1950.

Kopytoff, Igor. "The Cultural Biography of Things." In *The Social Life of Things: Commodities in Cultural Perspective*, edited by Arjun Appadurai, 64–91. Cambridge: Cambridge University Press, 1986.

Lamp, Frederick John, Amanda M. Maples and Laura M. Smalligan. *Accumulating Histories: African Art from the Charles B. Benenson Collection at the Yale University Art Gallery*. New Haven: Yale University Press, 2012.

Laude, Jean. *The Arts of Black Africa*. Los Angeles: University of California Press, 1973.

Lemann, Nicholas. "Fake Masks," *The Atlantic* 260, no. 5 (1987): 24–38.

Marx, Karl. *Capital*. Vol. 1. New York: Modern Library, 1906.

Newton, Douglas. *Masterpieces of Primitive Art: The Nelson A. Rockefeller Collection*. New York: Alfred A. Knopf, 1978.

Ravenhill, Phillip L. *Dreams and Reverie: Images of Otherworld Mates Among the Baule, West Africa*. Washington, DC: Smithsonian Institution Press, 1996.

Rohner, John R. *Art Treasures from African Runners*. Niwot, CO: University Press of Colorado, 2000.

Schwab, George. *Tribes of the Liberian Hinterland*. Edited by George Schwab with additional material by George W. Harley. Papers of the Peabody Museum of American Archaeology and Ethnology, Harvard University, volume 31. Cambridge, MA: Peabody Museum Press, 1947.

Sieber, Roy and Roslyn Adele Walker. *African Art in the Cycle of Life*. Washington, DC: National Museum of African Art, Smithsonian Institution, 1987.

Sieber, Roy and Arnold Rubin. *Sculptures of Black Africa: The Paul Tishman Collection*. Los Angeles: Los Angeles County Museum of Art, 1968.

Steiner, Christopher B. *African Art in Transit*. Cambridge: Cambridge University Press, 1994.

MAP OF AFRICA

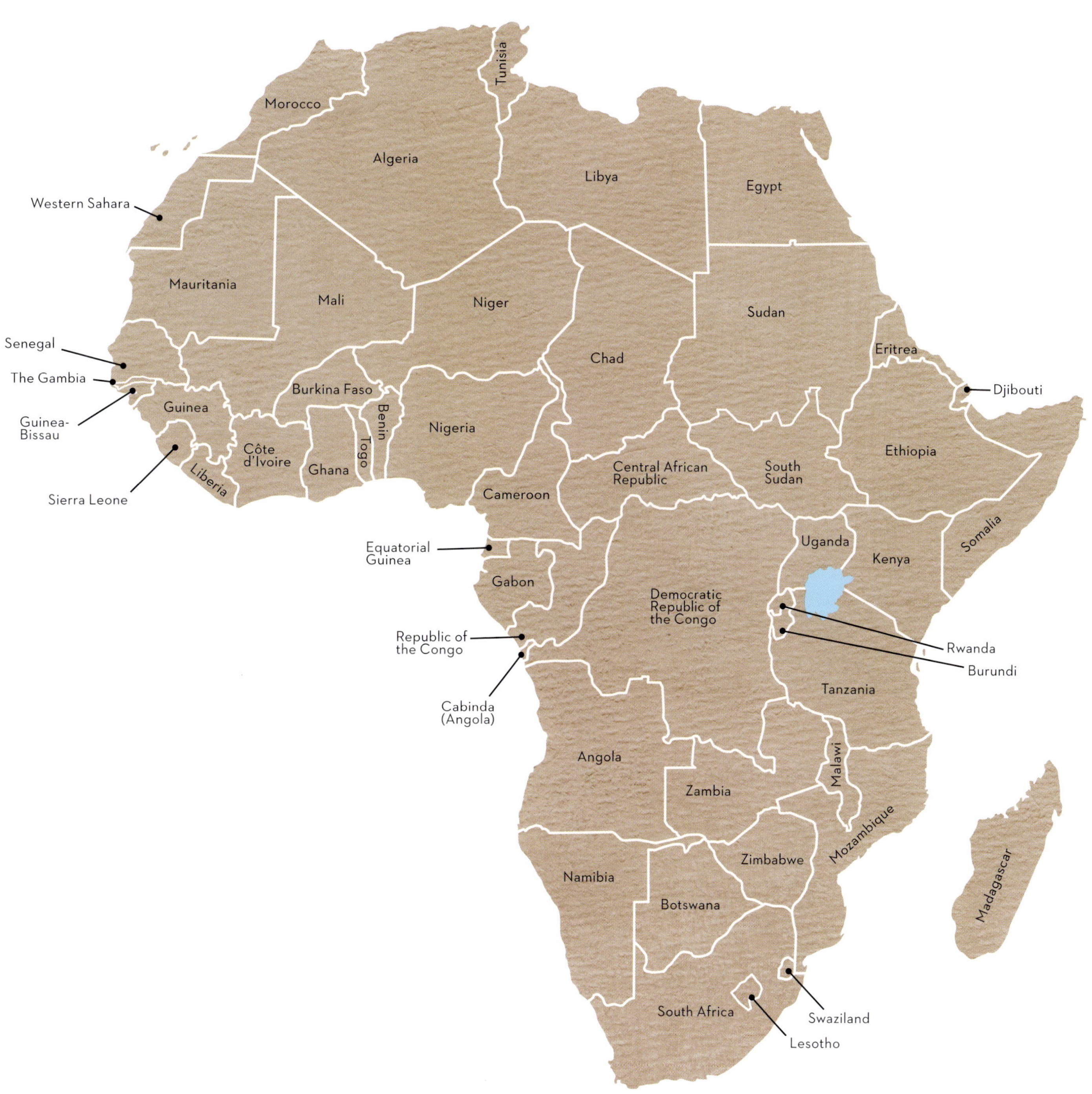

The majority of the objects illustrated in this volume were acquired by Esther Amrad Dagan during her travels in Africa. From 1959 to 2001, Ms. Dagan visited some of the largest markets for African art on the African continent. The object labels and the catalogue at the end of the volume highlight the place where object were acquired by the collector.

AMRAD AFRICAN ART COLLECTION CATALOGUE

The following catalogue is a listing of the artworks in the Amrad African Art Collection by place of acquisition. This list provides an interesting snapshot of objects circulating in markets during the second half of the twentieth century, as well as a glimpse into the activity of various art-producing workshops throughout the continent.

Esther Amrad Dagan has dedicated her gift to the Royal Ontario Museum "in memory of her daughter Halit and in homage to the anonymous African artists."

168 Senegal (1984–1989)

169 Côte d'Ivoire (1961–1988)

172 Burkina Faso (1961–1987)

176 Ghana (1973–1988)

176 Togo (1973–1988)

178 Republic of Benin (1973–1988)

178 Cameroon (1986–1989)

180 Gabon (1966–1986)

181 Democratic Republic of the Congo (1961–1987)

182 Zimbabwe (1994)

182 Kenya (1964–1983)

183 Ethiopia (1964–1966)

183 Europe and North America (1959–2004)

188 Unrecorded Place and Date of Acquisition

Senegal (1984–1989)

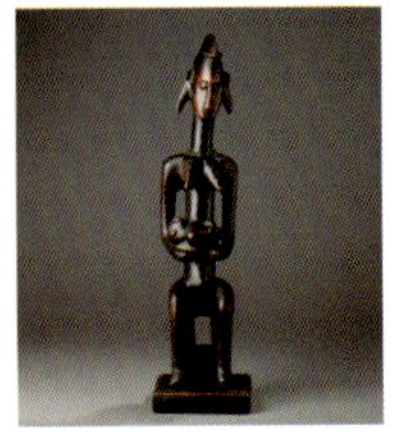
Figure
Wood, iron, brass
Bamana style
Purchased from a private collector in Dakar in 1984
H. 56 cm, W. 13 cm, D. 10 cm
ROM 2009.126.41

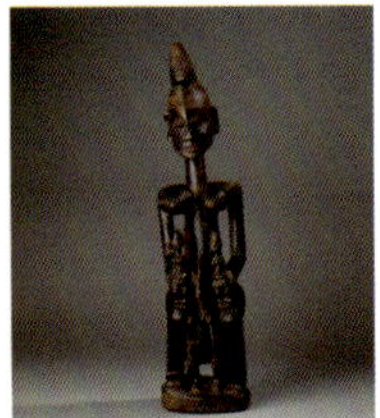
Figure
Wood
Dogon style
Purchased in Dakar in 1984
H. 64 cm, W. 16 cm, D. 17 cm
ROM 2009.126.44

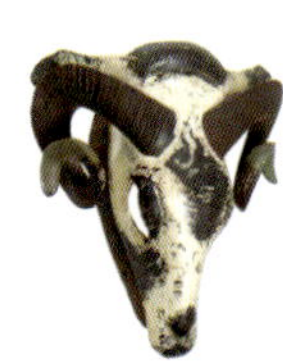
Mask
Wood, pigment
Baule style
Purchased from a private collector in Dakar in 1985
H. 28 cm, W. 22.8 cm, D. 11.5 cm
ROM 2009.126.158

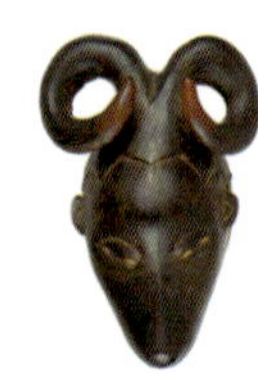
Mask
Wood, pigment
Baule style
Purchased from a private collector in Dakar in 1985
H. 36 cm, W. 23.5 cm, D. 13 cm
ROM 2009.126.159

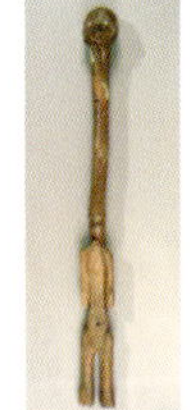
Figure
Wood, shell
Mossi style
Purchased from a private collector in Dakar in 1985
H. 110.5 cm, W. 11 cm, D. 11.5 cm
ROM 2009.126.249

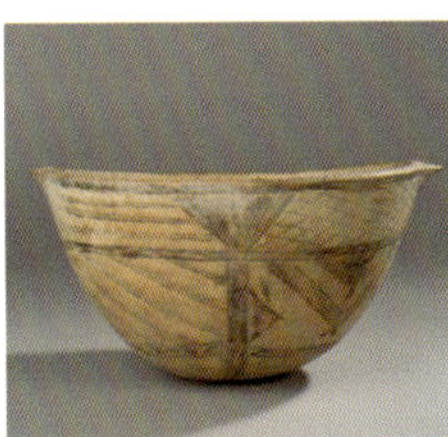
Bowl
Wood
Tuareg style
Purchased in Dakar in 1986
H. 13.5 cm, Diam. 28 cm
ROM 2009.126.276

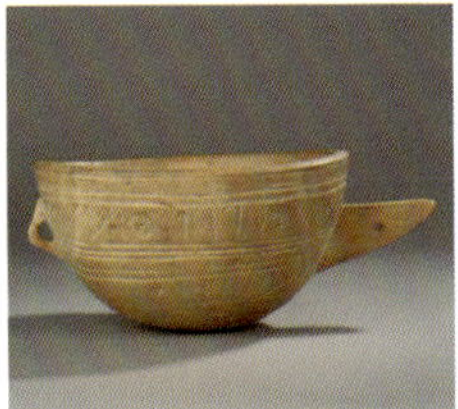
Bowl
Wood
Tuareg style
Purchased in Dakar in 1986
H. 12 cm, Diam. 23.5 cm
ROM 2009.126.277

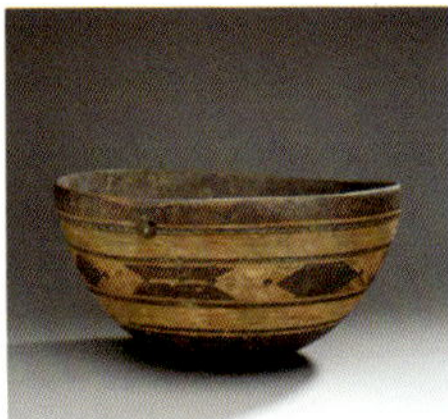
Bowl
Wood
Tuareg style
Purchased in Dakar in 1986
H. 21.7 cm, Diam. 37.5 cm
ROM 2009.126.278

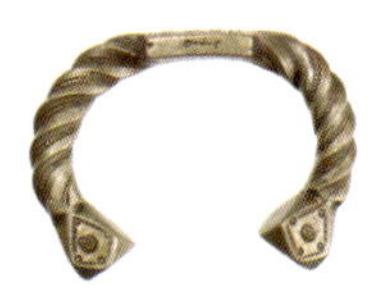
Bracelet
Silver alloy
Tuareg style
Purchased in Dakar in 1987
H. 2 cm, W. 7 cm, D. 5.2 cm
ROM 2009.126.357

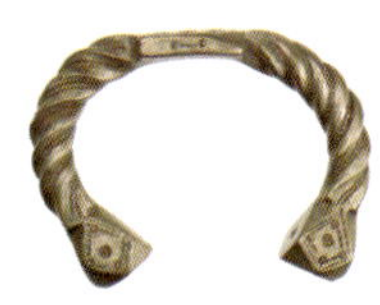
Bracelet
Silver alloy
Tuareg style
Purchased in Dakar in 1987
H. 2.1 cm, W. 7 cm, D. 5.3 cm
ROM 2009.126.358

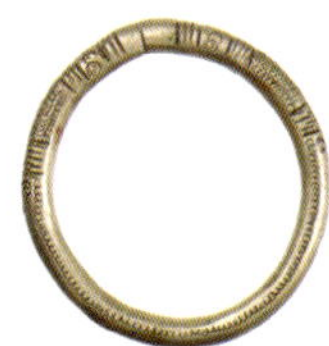
Bracelet
Silver alloy
Tuareg style
Purchased in Dakar in 1987
H. 0.8 cm, Diam. 7.7 cm
ROM 2009.126.359

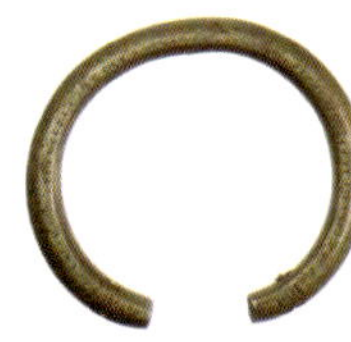
Bracelet
Silver alloy
Tuareg style
Purchased in Dakar in 1987
H. 0.7 cm, Diam. 5.8 cm
ROM 2009.126.360

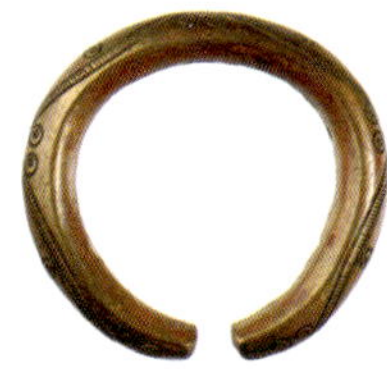
Bracelet
Copper alloy
Purchased in Dakar in 1987
H. 2 cm, Diam. 9.8 cm
ROM 2009.126.361

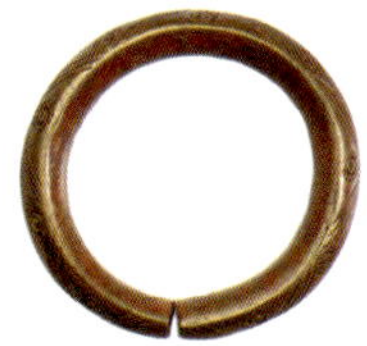
Bracelet
Copper alloy
Purchased in Dakar in 1987
H. 2 cm, Diam. 9.2 cm
ROM 2009.126.362

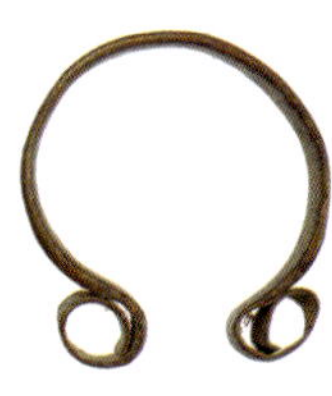
Bracelet
Brass
Purchased in Dakar in 1987
H. 1.8 cm, W. 5.5 cm, D. 6 cm
ROM 2009.126.369

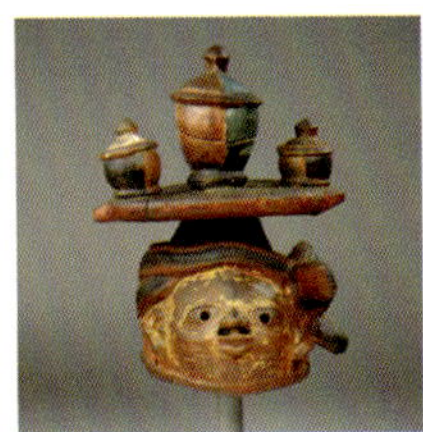
Gelede mask
Wood, pigment
Yoruba style
Purchased from a private collector in Dakar in 1988
H. 40 cm, W. 31.7 cm, D. 30.3 cm
ROM 2009.126.201

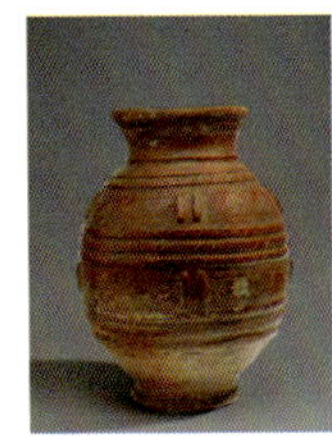
Pot
Terracotta
Bamana style
Purchased in Dakar in 1988
H. 56 cm, Diam. 33 cm
ROM 2009.126.234

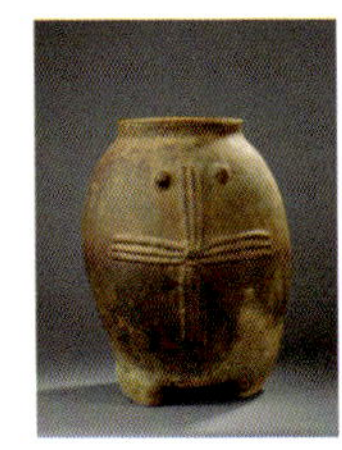
Pot
Terracotta
Lobi style
Purchased in Dakar in 1988
H. 55 cm, Diam. 33 cm
ROM 2009.126.235

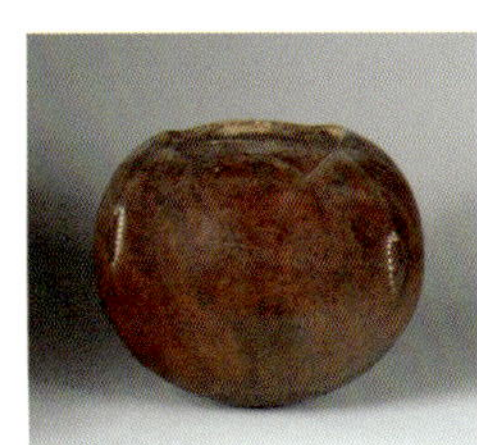
Pot
Terracotta
Lobi style
Purchased in Dakar in 1988
H. 28 cm, Diam. 34 cm
ROM 2009.126.236

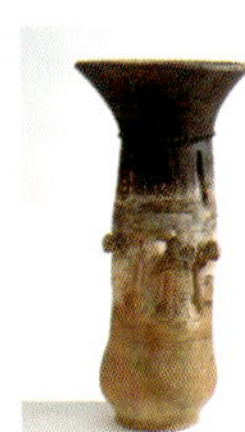
Pot
Terracotta
Nupe style
Purchased in Dakar in 1988
H. 63 cm, Diam. 30 cm
ROM 2009.126.237

Senegal (1984–1989)

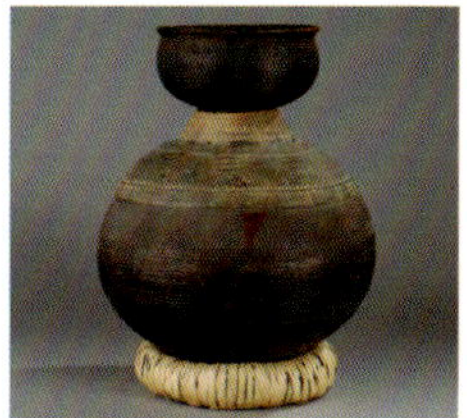
Water or palm wine container
Terracotta
Nupe style
Purchased in Dakar in 1988
H. 41.5 cm, Diam. 30 cm
ROM 2009.126.238

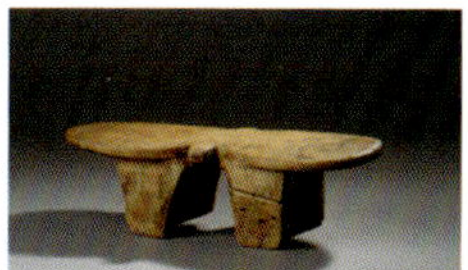
Stool
Wood
Purchased in Dakar in 1989
H. 12.7 cm, W. 43 cm, D. 19.1 cm
ROM 2009.126.32

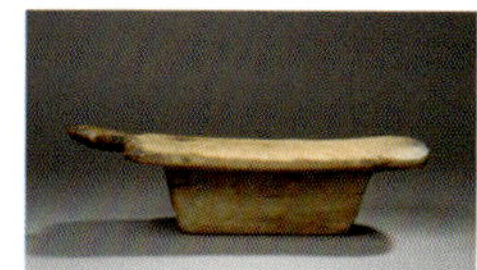
Stool
Wood
Purchased in Dakar in 1989
H. 15.9 cm, W. 56.7 cm, D. 22.2 cm
ROM 2009.126.33

Côte d'Ivoire (1961–1988)

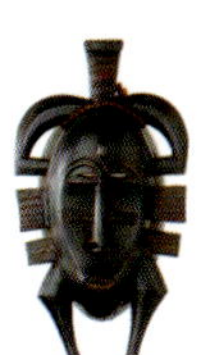
Mask
Wood and fiber
Senufo style
Received as a gift in the village of Djigo-dougou in 1961
H. 28 cm, W. 15.5 cm, D. 9 cm
ROM 2009.126.183

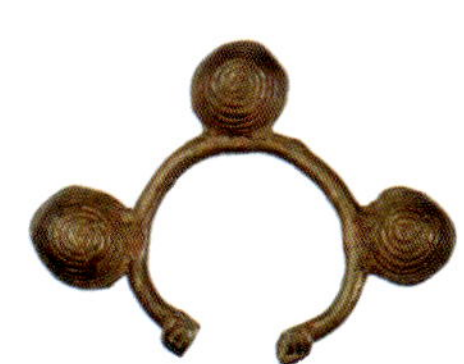
Bracelet with bells
Brass
Dan style
Purchased in Abidjan in 1981
H. 2.5 cm, W. 10 cm, D. 7.5 cm
ROM 2009.126.368

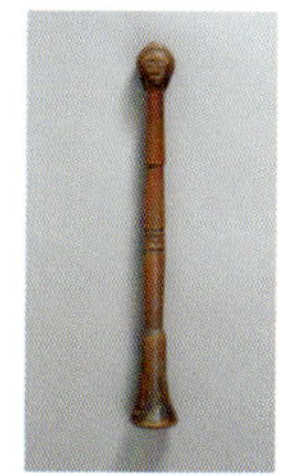
Pestle
Wood
Baule or Senufo style
Purchased from a private collector in Abidjan in 1983
H. 44 cm, W. 6 cm, D. 6 cm
ROM 2009.126.295

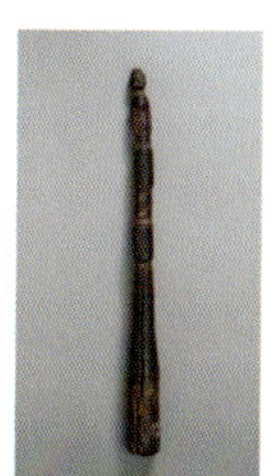
Pestle
Wood
Baule or Senufo style
Purchased from a private collector in Abidjan in 1983
H. 57 cm, W. 5.3 cm, D. 5.5 cm
ROM 2009.126.296

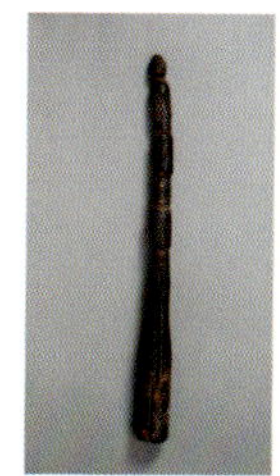
Pestle
Wood
Baule or Senufo style
Purchased from a private collector in Abidjan in 1983
H. 59.5 cm, W. 5.5 cm, D. 6 cm
ROM 2009.126.297

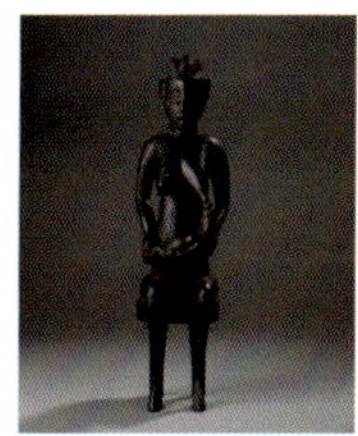
Mother and child figure
Wood
Senufo style
Purchased in Abidjan in 1983
H. 45 cm, W. 10 cm, D. 12 cm
ROM 2009.126.49

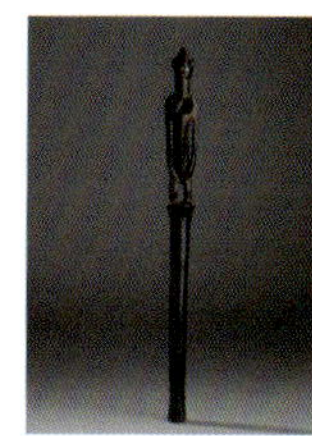
Staff
Wood, metal
Bamana style
Purchased in Abidjan in 1985
H. 58 cm, W. 5.5 cm, D. 5 cm
ROM 2009.126.126

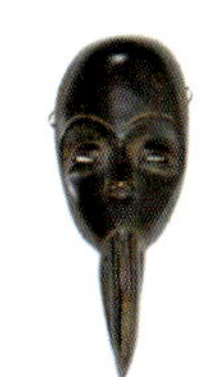
Mask
Wood
Dan style
Purchased in Abidjan in 1985
H. 37 cm, W. 15.1 cm, D. 11 cm
ROM 2009.126.149

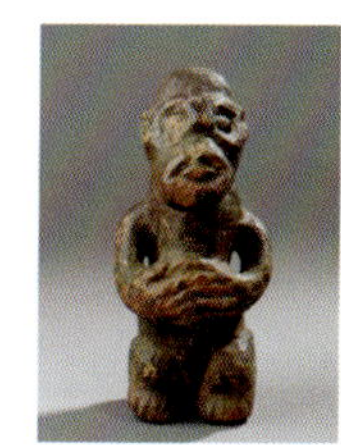
Figure
Stone
Kissi or Mende style
Purchased in Abidjan in 1985
H. 24 cm, W. 11.5 cm, D. 10 cm
ROM 2009.126.152

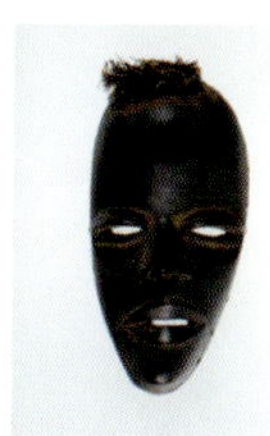
Mask
Wood, feathers
Dan style
Purchased in Abidjan in 1985
H. 27 cm, W. 13.8 cm, D. 8.3 cm
ROM 2009.126.162

Côte d'Ivoire (1961–1988)

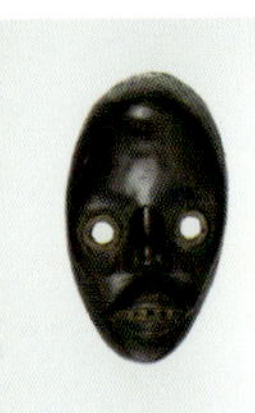

Mask
Wood, metal
Dan style
Purchased in Abidjan in 1985
H. 25 cm, W. 14.7 cm, D. 7.7 cm
ROM 2009.126.163

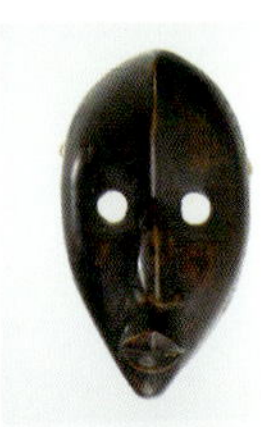

Mask
Wood, feathers
Dan style
Purchased in Abidjan in 1985
H. 24.2 cm, W. 14 cm, D. 8 cm
ROM 2009.126.165

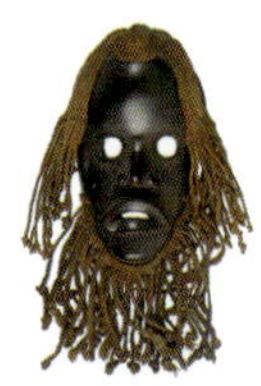

Mask
Wood, fiber
Dan style
Purchased in Abidjan in 1985
H. 38.9 cm, W. 22 cm, D. 7.9 cm
ROM 2009.126.166

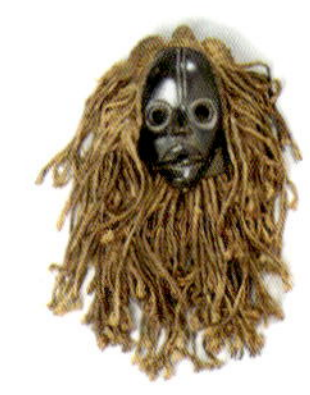

Mask
Wood, metal, fiber
Dan style
Purchased in Abidjan in 1985
H. 58 cm, W. 37.4 cm, D. 11 cm
ROM 2009.126.167

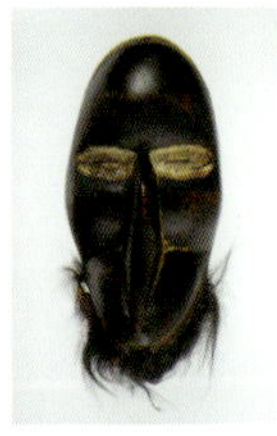

Mask
Wood, hide
Dan style
Purchased in Abidjan in 1985
H. 42.2cm, W. 17.8 cm, D. 14 cm
ROM 2009.126.168

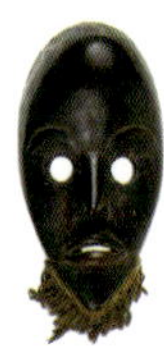

Mask
Wood, fiber
Dan style
Purchased in Abidjan in 1985
H. 31 cm, W. 14.3 cm, D. 8 cm
ROM 2009.126.173

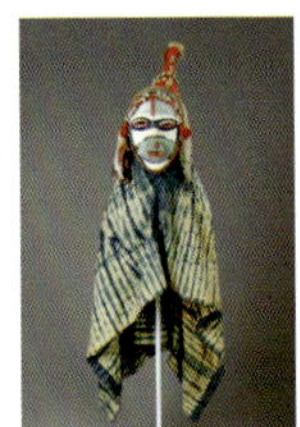

Mask
Wood, cloth, cowrie shells, pigment
Wè style
Purchased in Abidjan in 1985
H. 150 cm, W. 21 cm, D. 47.2 cm
ROM 2009.126.174

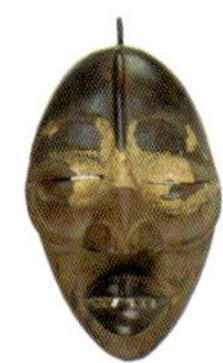

Mask
Wood, metal, pigment
Wè style
Purchased in Abidjan in 1985
H. 30.5 cm, W. 17.5 cm, D. 13.1 cm
ROM 2009.126.175

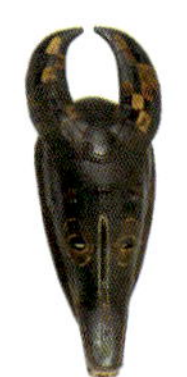

Mask
Wood
Guro style
Purchased in Abidjan in 1985
H. 37.6 cm, W. 14.7 cm, D. 10.1 cm
ROM 2009.126.176

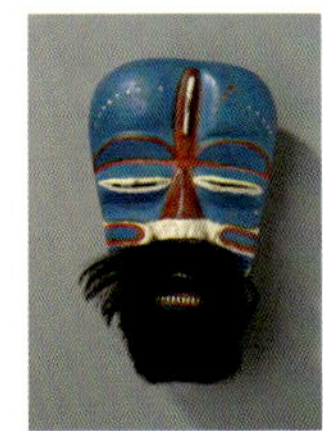

Mask
Wood, hair, pigment
Wè style
Purchased in Abidjan in 1985
H. 32.5 cm, W. 19.9 cm, D. 11.2 cm
ROM 2009.126.190

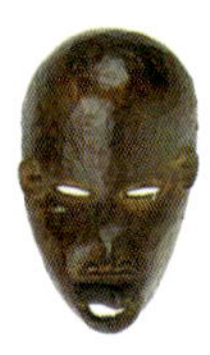

Mask
Wood
Dan style
Purchased in Abidjan in 1985
H. 26.8 cm, W. 16.8 cm, D. 10 cm
ROM 2009.126.191

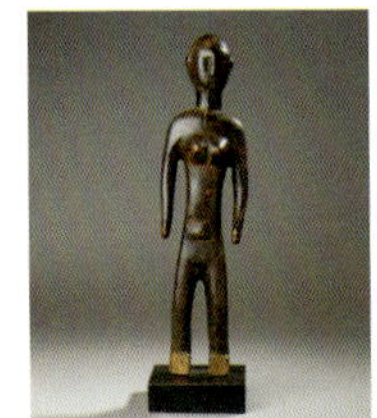

Figure
Wood
Mossi style
Purchased from a private collector in Abidjan in 1985
H. 46.5 cm, W. 12 cm, D. 8 cm
ROM 2009.126.250

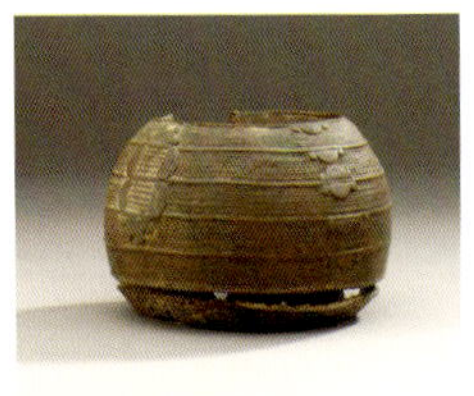

Anklet
Brass
Baule style
Purchased in Abidjan in 1985
H. 8.5 cm, W. 12 cm, D. 12 cm
ROM 2009.126.350

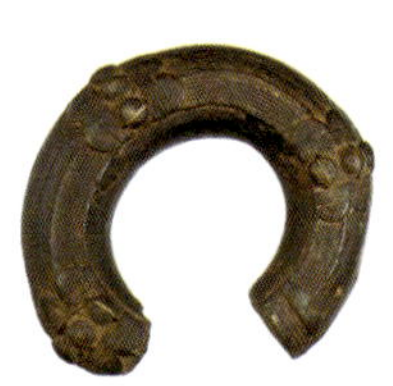

Bracelet
Brass
Baule style
Purchased in Abidjan in 1985
H. 4 cm, W. 13 cm, D. 12 cm
ROM 2009.126.351

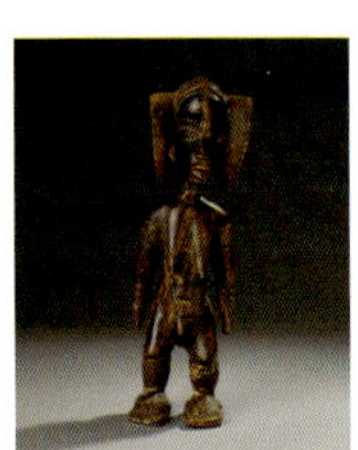

Mother and child figure
Wood
Dan style
Purchased in Abidjan in 1985
H. 36.5 cm, W. 11 cm, D. 9 cm
ROM 2009.126.48

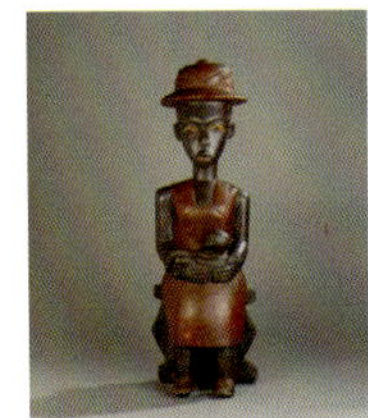

Figure
Wood, pigment
Baule style
Purchased in Abidjan in 1984-5
H. 76 cm, W. 22 cm, D. 21 cm
ROM 2009.126.52.1

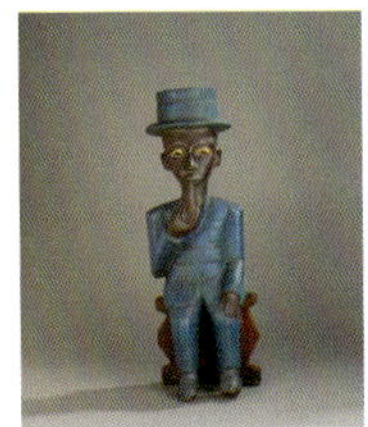

Figure
Wood, pigment
Baule style
Purchased in Abidjan in 1984-5
H. 69 cm, W. 23 cm, D. 18 cm
ROM 2009.126.52.2

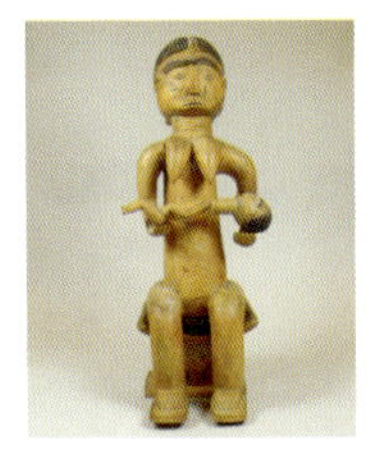

Mother and child figure
Wood, pigment
Fante style
Purchased in Abidjan in 1985
H. 52 cm, W. 14 cm, D. 14 cm
ROM 2009.126.56.1–3

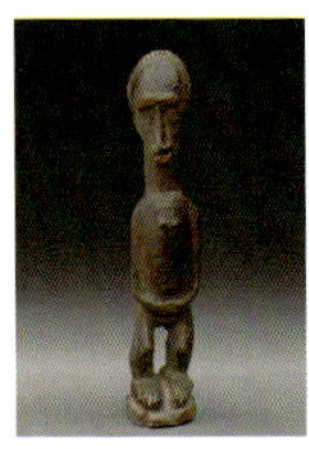

Figure
Wood
Baule style
Purchased in Abidjan in 1985
H. 20 cm, W. 4 cm, D. 5 cm
ROM 2009.126.93

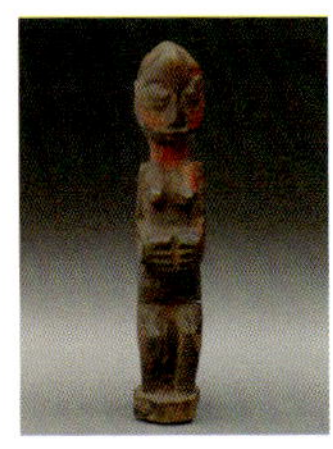

Figure
Wood
Purchased in Abidjan in 1985
H. 15 cm, W. 3 cm, D. 4 cm
ROM 2009.126.94

Côte d'Ivoire (1961–1988)

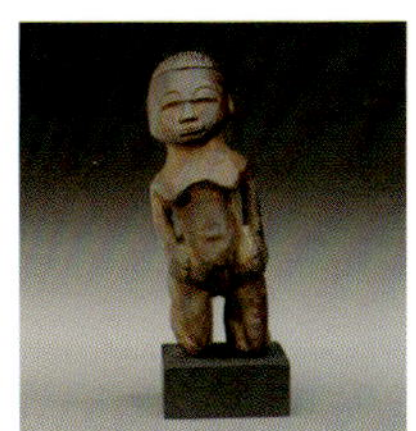
Figure
Wood
Purchased in Abidjan in 1985
H. 13.5 cm, W. 4 cm, D. 4 cm
ROM 2009.126.95

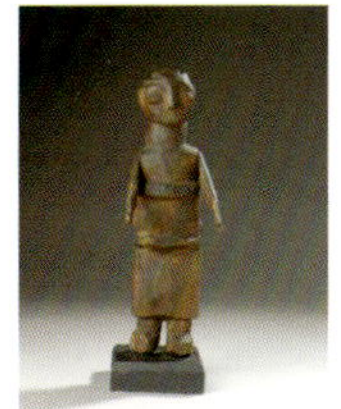
Figure
Wood
Purchased in Abidjan in 1986
H. 31.3 cm, W. 10.5 cm, D. 11.8 cm
ROM 2009.126.42

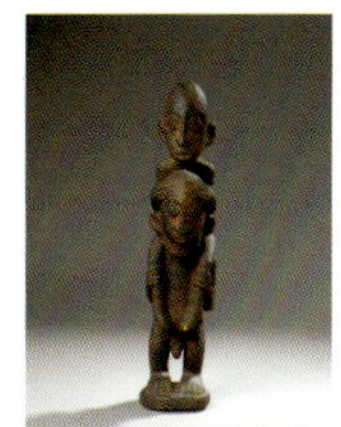
Figure
Wood
Dogon style
Purchased in Abidjan in 1986
H. 43 cm, W. 9 cm, D. 9 cm
ROM 2009.126.43

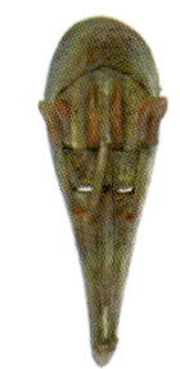
Mask
Wood, metal
Marka or Sorogo style
Purchased from a private collector in Abidjan in 1987
H. 37 cm, W. 12.5 cm, D. 10 cm
ROM 2009.126.144

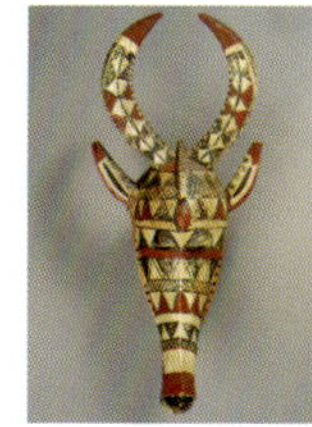
Mask
Wood, pigment
Bobo style
Purchased in Abidjan in 1987
H. 71.7 cm, W. 34.5 cm, D. 38.3 cm
ROM 2009.126.151

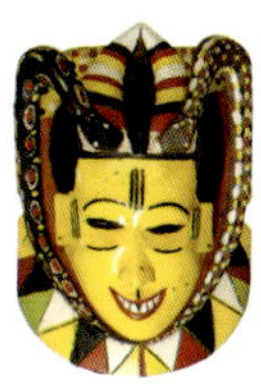
Mask
Wood, pigment
Guro style
Purchased in Abidjan in 1987
H. 31.5 cm, W. 22 cm, D. 12.2 cm
ROM 2009.126.178

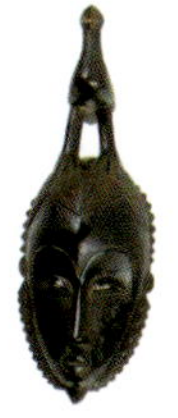
Mask
Wood, pigment
Guro style
Purchased in Abidjan in 1987
H. 31.5 cm, W. 22 cm, D. 12.2 cm
ROM 2009.126.179

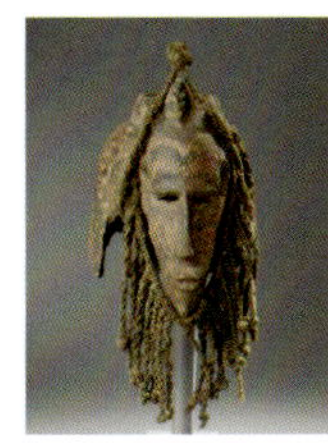
Mask
Wood, cloth
Marka style
Purchased in Abidjan in 1987
H. 50.9 cm, W. 24.1 cm, D. 27.3 cm
ROM 2009.126.196

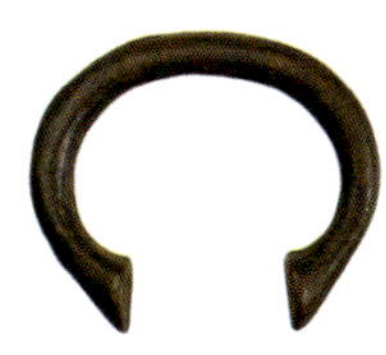
Manilla
Brass
Purchased in Abidjan in 1987
H. 1.8 cm, W. 8.5 cm, D. 7 cm
ROM 2009.126.370

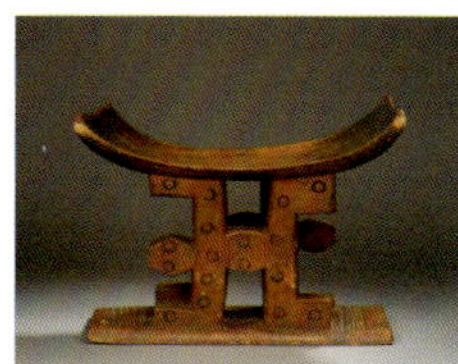
Stool
Wood
Asante style
Purchased in Abidjan in 1988
H. 39.8 cm, W. 54.5 cm, D. 29.5 cm
ROM 2009.126.23

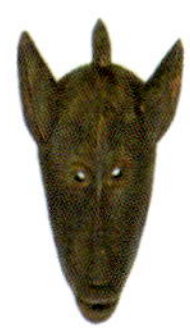
Mask
Wood
Guro style
Purchased in Bouaké in 1981
H. 31.5 cm, W. 17.8 cm, D. 9 cm
ROM 2009.126.177

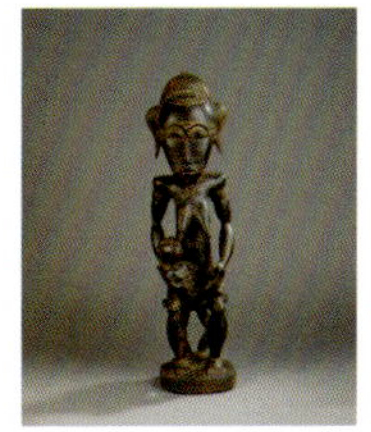
Figure
Wood
Baule style
Purchased in Bouaké in 1985
H. 66 cm, W. 18 cm, D. 17 cm
ROM 2009.126.50

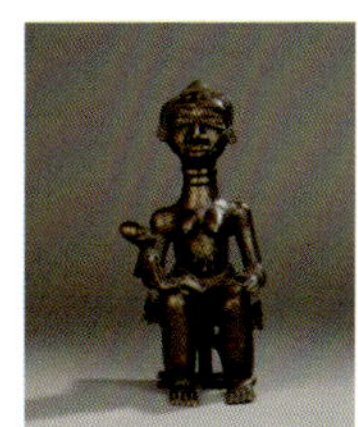
Mother and child figure
Brass
Baule style
Purchased in Bouaké in 1985
H. 31.5 cm, W. 15 cm, D. 16 cm
ROM 2009.126.53.1–2

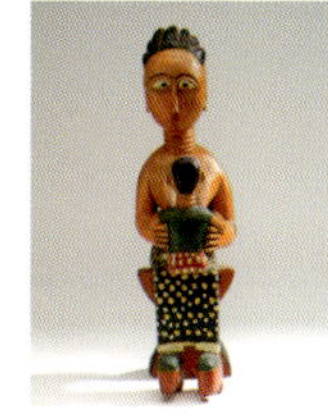
Figure
Wood, pigment
Baule style
Purchased in Bouaké in 1986
H. 47.5 cm, W. 16 cm, D. 20 cm
ROM 2009.126.51

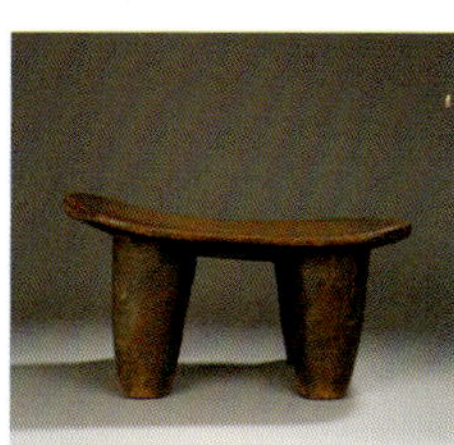
Stool
Wood
Senufo style
Purchased in Korhogo in 1981
H. 23.5 cm, W. 48 cm, D. 31.5 cm
ROM 2009.126.15

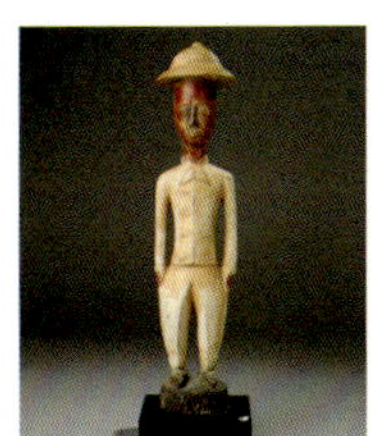
Figure
Wood, pigment
Baule style
Purchased in Bouaké in 1987
H. 42 cm, W. 9.6 cm, D. 9.2 cm
ROM 2009.126.287

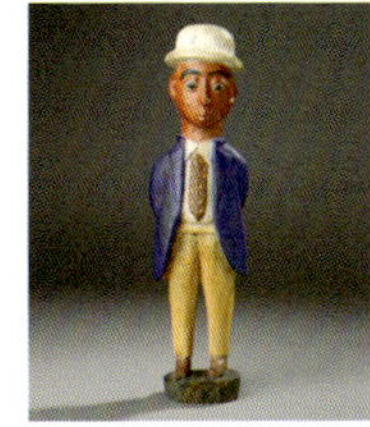
Figure
Wood, pigment
Baule style
Purchased in Bouaké in 1987
H. 41.1 cm, W. 11.1 cm, D. 8 cm
ROM 2009.126.288

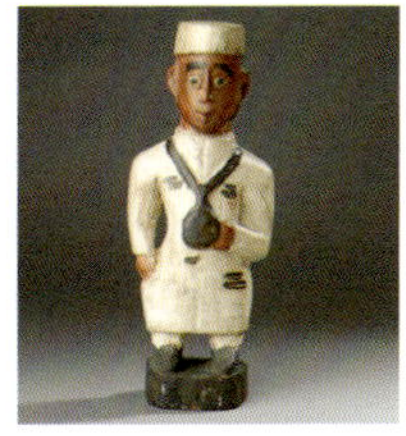
Figure
Wood, pigment
Baule style
Purchased in Bouaké in 1987
H. 33.6 cm, W. 13.8 cm, D. 9.1 cm
ROM 2009.126.289

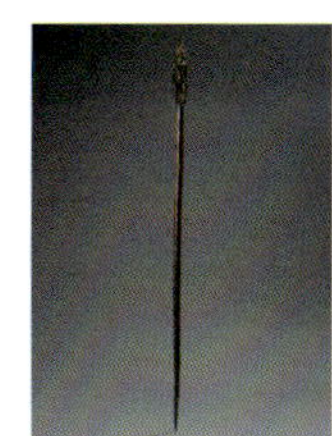
Staff
Wood, iron
Senufo style
Purchased in Korhogo in 1981
H. 141 cm, Diam. 6 cm
ROM 2009.126.127

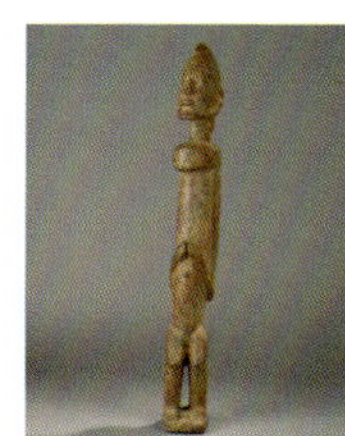
Figure
Wood
Dogon style
Purchased in Korhogo in 1981
H. 79 cm, W. 9.5 cm, D. 19 cm
ROM 2009.126.239

Côte d'Ivoire (1961–1988)

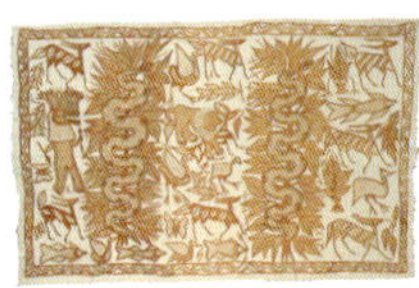

Painted cloth
Cotton
Senufo style
Purchased in Korhogo in 1981
L. 287 cm, H. 176.5 cm
ROM 2009.126.231

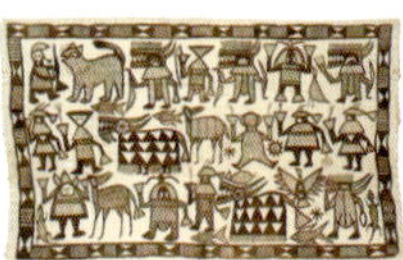

Painted cloth
Cotton
Senufo style
Purchased in Korhogo in 1981
L. 282 cm, H. 169 cm
ROM 2009.126.232

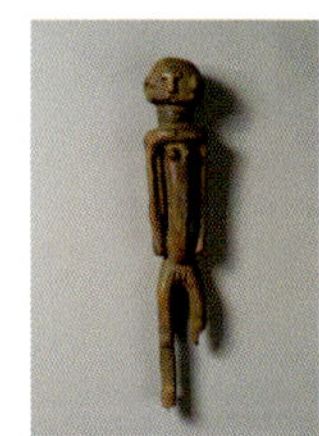

Figure
Wood
Purchased in Korhogo in 1981
H. 41.5 cm, W. 8 cm, D. 7 cm
ROM 2009.126.240

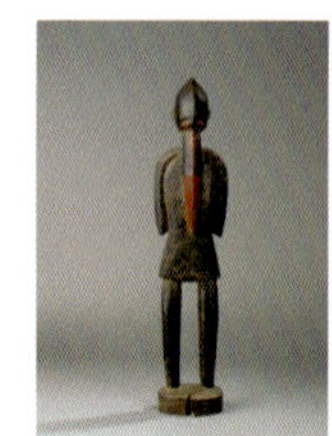

Figure
Wood
Senufo style
Purchased in Korhogo in 1981
H. 65 cm, W. 15 cm, D. 11.5 cm
ROM 2009.126.252

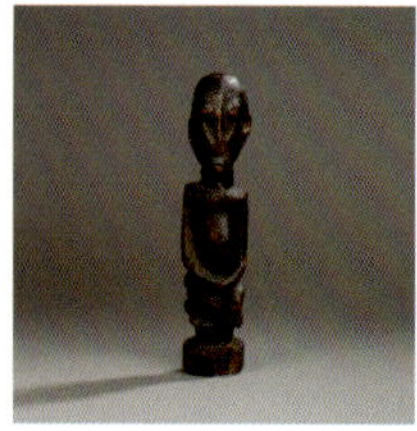

Figure
Wood
Dogon style
Purchased in Korhogo in 1981
H. 25.8 cm, W. 6.5 cm, D. 6.3 cm
ROM 2009.126.69

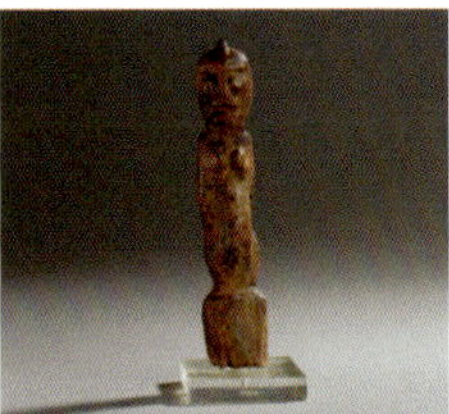

Figure
Wood
Purchased in Korhogo in 1981
H. 18 cm, W. 4.4 cm, D. 3.5 cm
ROM 2009.126.71

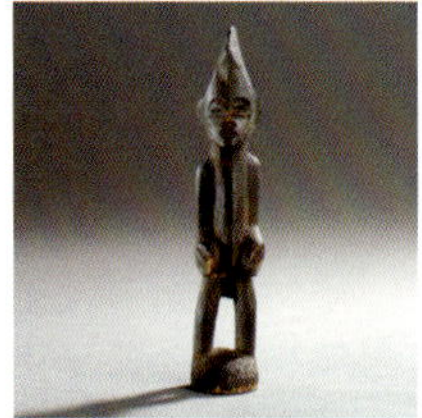

Figure
Wood
Senufo style
Purchased in Korhogo in 1981
H. 15 cm, W. 3 cm, D. 3 cm
ROM 2009.126.90

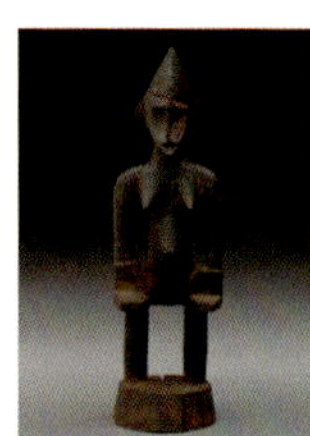

Figure
Wood
Senufo style
Purchased in Korhogo in 1981
H. 16.5 cm, W. 5 cm, D. 4.5 cm
ROM 2009.126.91

Burkina Faso (1961–1987)

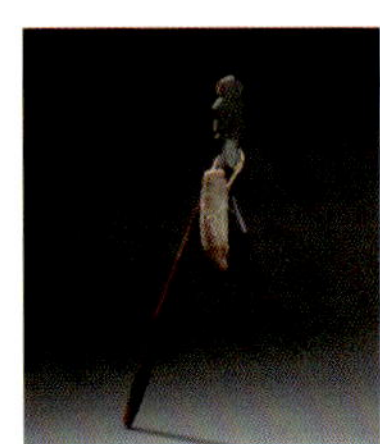

Staff
Wood, fiber, seed pod, corn cob
Mossi style
Purchased in Ouagadougou in 1961
H. 61.5 cm, W. 18.5 cm, D. 4 cm
ROM 2009.126.131

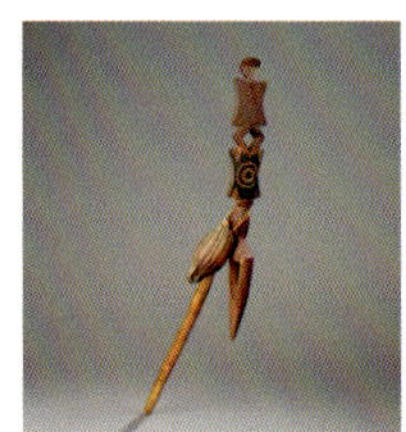

Staff
Wood, fiber, seed pod, bamboo
Mossi style
Purchased in Ouagadougou in 1961
H. 68 cm, W. 30 cm, D. 6 cm
ROM 2009.126.132

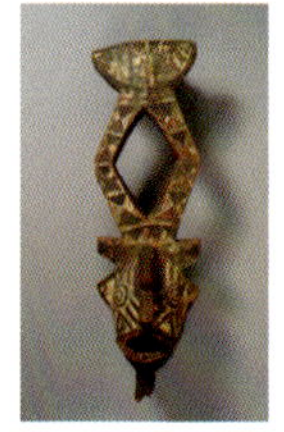

Mask
Wood
Gurunsi style
Purchased in Ouagadougou in 1961
H. 85 cm, W. 26 cm, D. 26 cm
ROM 2009.126.192

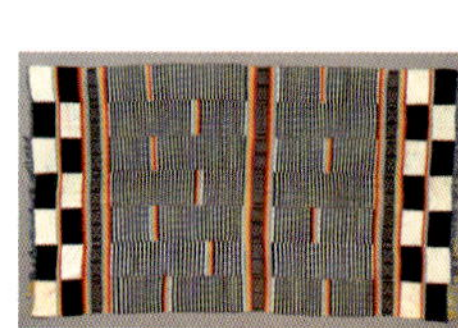

Blanket
Cotton
Purchased in Ouagadougou in 1961
L. 232 cm, W. 131 cm
ROM 2009.126.225

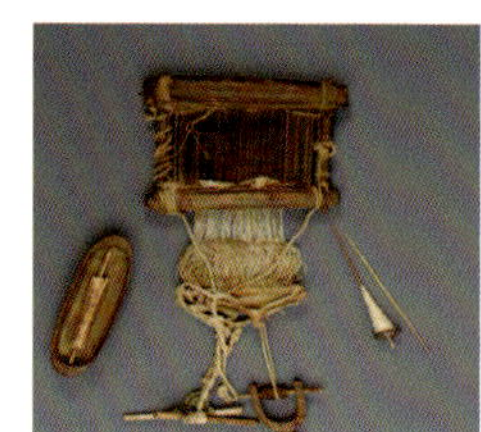

Loom with spindle, weft and pulley
Wood, rope, thread
Purchased in Ouagadougou in 1961
L. 67 cm, W. 25 cm, D. 4.5 cm
ROM 2009.126.282.1–4

Burkina Faso (1961–1987)

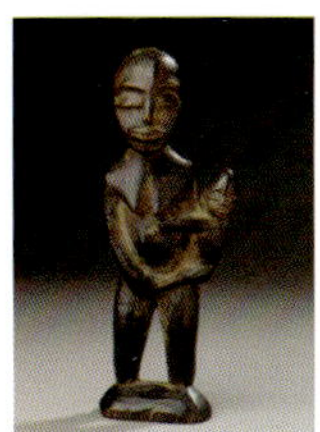
Mother and child figure
Wood
Lobi style
Purchased in
Ouagadougou in 1961
H. 17.5 cm, W. 7 cm,
D. 4.5 cm
ROM 2009.126.46

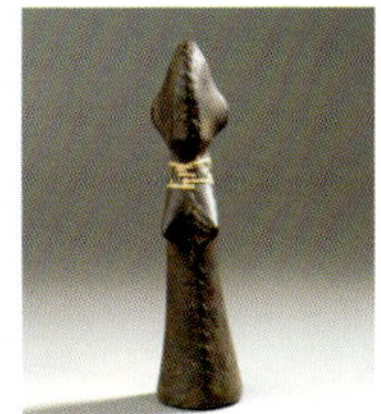
Doll
Wood, leather
Mossi style
Purchased in
Ouagadougou in 1961
H. 21 cm, W. 5 cm, D. 6 cm
ROM 2009.126.73

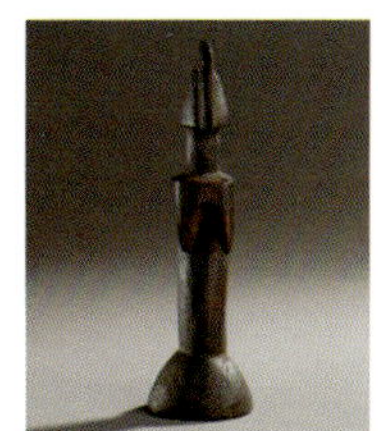
Doll
Wood, leather
Mossi style
Purchased in
Ouagadougou in 1961
H. 21cm, W. 5 cm, D. 6 cm
ROM 2009.126.74

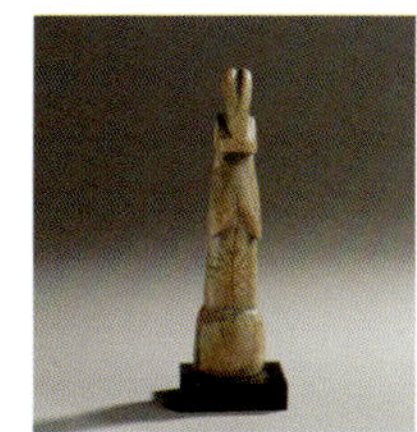
Doll
Wood
Mossi style
Purchased in
Ouagadougou in 1961
H. 14.3 cm, W. 3.6 cm,
D. 5 cm
ROM 2009.126.75

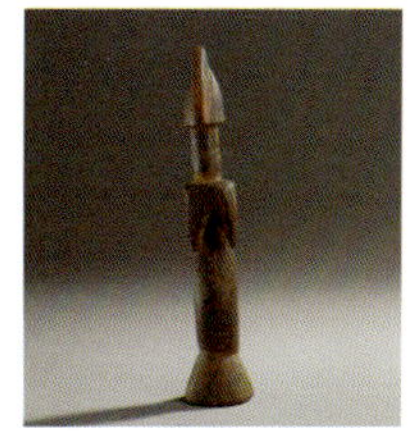
Doll
Wood
Mossi style
Purchased in
Ouagadougou in 1961
H. 21 cm, W. 4.2 cm,
D. 6 cm
ROM 2009.126.76

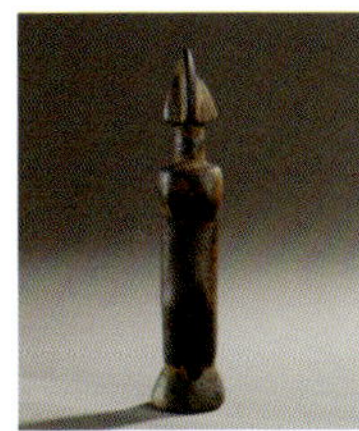
Doll
Wood
Mossi style
Purchased in
Ouagadougou in 1961
H. 16.5 cm, W. 3.5 cm,
D. 4 cm
ROM 2009.126.77

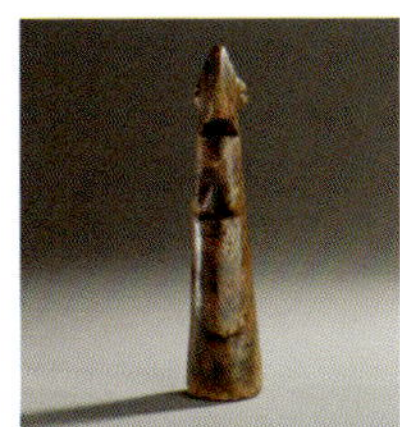
Doll
Wood
Mossi style
Purchased in
Ouagadougou in 1961
H. 20.7 cm, W. 4.5 cm,
D. 5 cm
ROM 2009.126.78

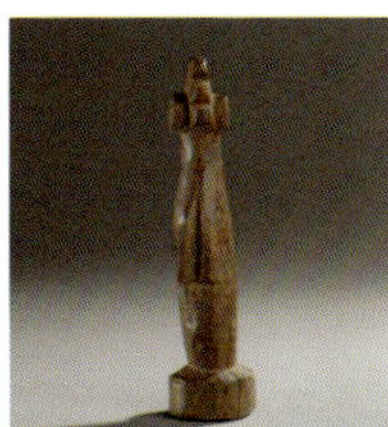
Doll
Wood
Mossi style
Purchased in
Ouagadougou in 1961
H. 18 cm, W. 4 cm, D. 4 cm
ROM 2009.126.79

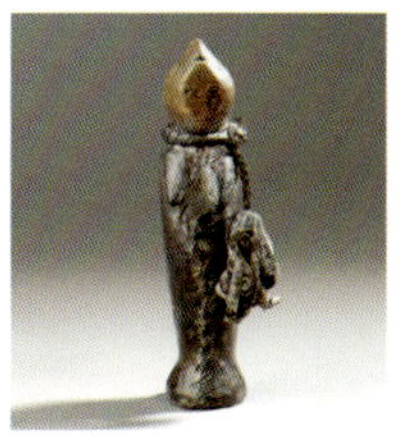
Doll
Wood, leather
Mossi style
Purchased in
Ouagadougou in 1961
H. 18.4 cm, W. 4.5 cm,
D. 6 cm
ROM 2009.126.80

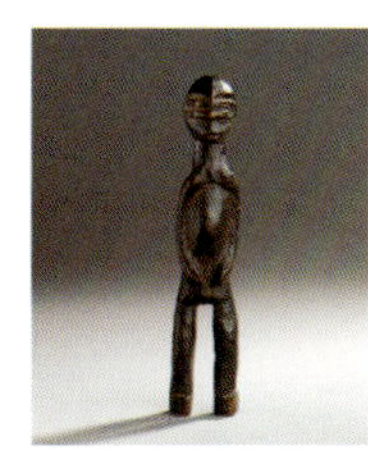
Figure
Wood
Lobi style
Purchased in
Ouagadougou in 1961
H. 22 cm, W. 4.5 cm,
D. 3 cm
ROM 2009.126.86

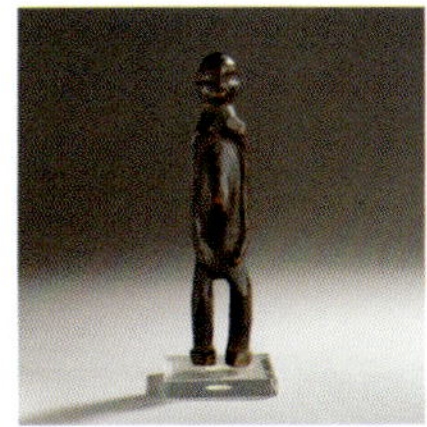
Figure
Wood
Lobi style
Purchased in
Ouagadougou in 1961
H. 21.4 cm, W. 4.5 cm,
D. 4.1 cm
ROM 2009.126.87

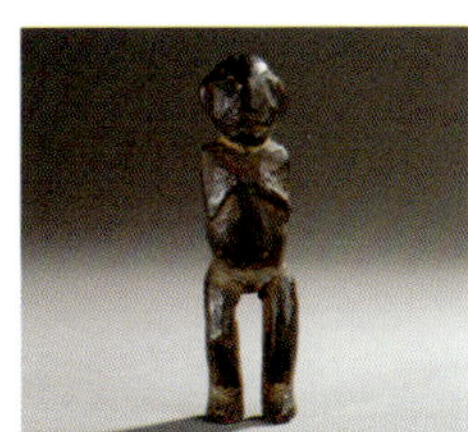
Figure
Wood
Lobi style
Purchased in
Ouagadougou in 1961
H. 11.2 cm, W. 3.4 cm,
D. 3 cm
ROM 2009.126.88

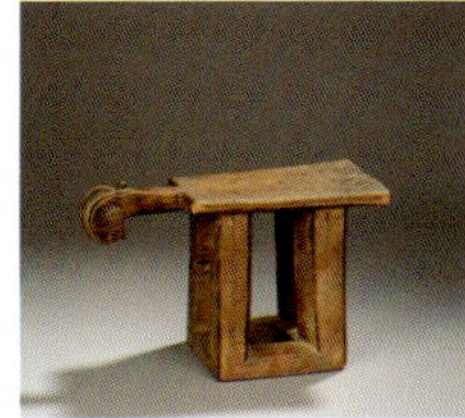
Stool
Wood
Bwa style
Purchased in
Ouagadougou in 1981
H. 21.6 cm, W. 35 cm,
D. 17 cm
ROM 2009.126.10

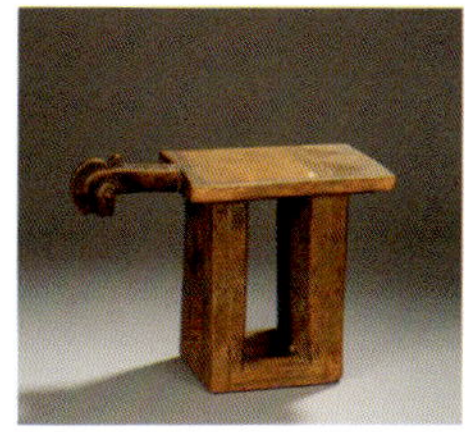
Stool
Wood
Bwa style
Purchased in
Ouagadougou in 1981
H. 23 cm, W. 34 cm,
D. 14.5 cm
ROM 2009.126.11

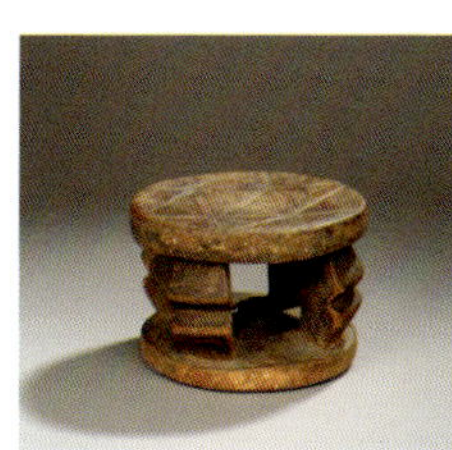
Stool
Wood
Mossi style
Purchased in
Ouagadougou in 1981
H. 16 cm, W. 23 cm,
D. 21 cm
ROM 2009.126.12

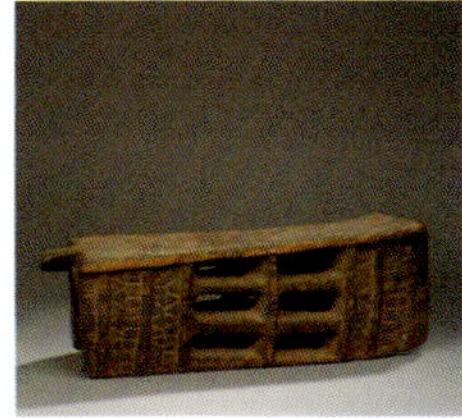
Stool
Wood
Dogon style
Purchased in
Ouagadougou in 1981
H. 22 cm, W. 69.5 cm,
D. 17.7 cm
ROM 2009.126.9

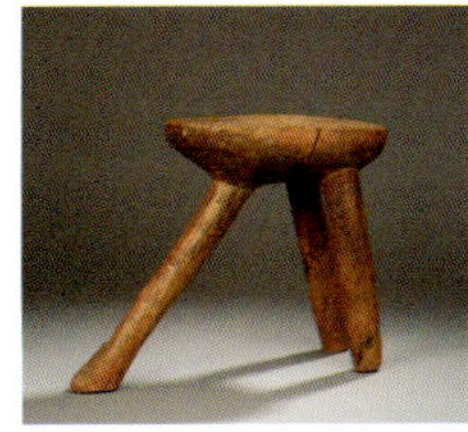
Stool
Wood
Lobi style
Purchased in
Ouagadougou in 1981
H. 33 cm, W. 19.5 cm,
D. 43 cm
ROM 2009.126.13

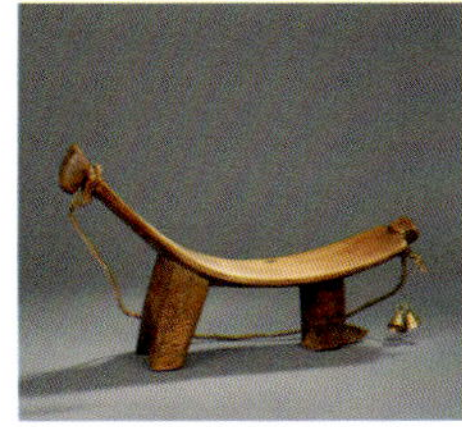
Stool
Wood, fiber, brass, wire
Lobi style
Purchased in
Ouagadougou in 1981
H. 31 cm, W. 13 cm,
D. 52 cm
ROM 2009.126.14

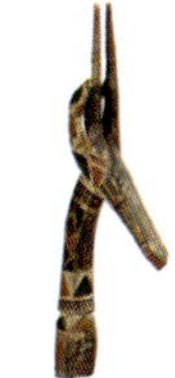
Antelope headcrest
Wood, pigment
Kurumba style
Purchased in
Ouagadougou in 1981
H. 83 cm, W. 9.5 cm,
D. 31 cm
ROM 2009.126.147

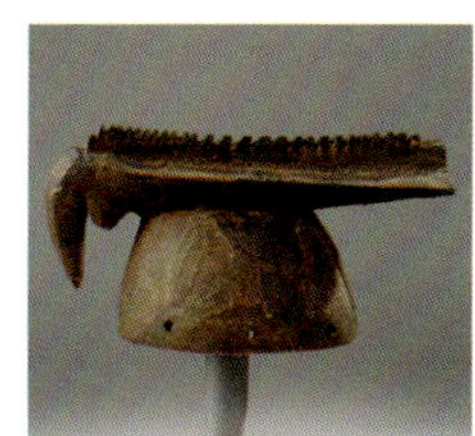
Bird helmet mask
Wood
Mossi style
Purchased in
Ouagadougou in 1981
H. 29.5 cm, W. 17.5 cm,
D. 14.5 cm
ROM 2009.126.148

Burkina Faso (1961–1987)

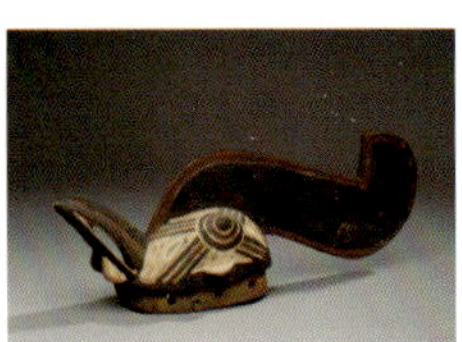
Bird mask
Wood, pigment
Nuna style
Purchased in
Ouagadougou in 1981
H. 20.4 cm, W. 16.4 cm,
D. 54.6 cm
ROM 2009.126.154

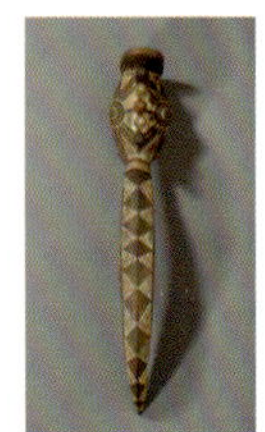
Bird mask
Wood, pigment
Gurunsi style
Purchased in
Ouagadougou in 1981
H. 23.4 cm, L. 117.3 cm,
W. 19.8 cm
ROM 2009.126.155

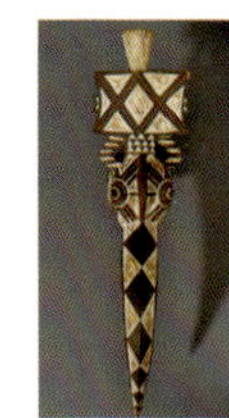
Bird mask
Wood, pigment
Nuna style
Purchased in
Ouagadougou in 1981
H. 22.7 cm, L. 99 cm,
W. 25 cm
ROM 2009.126.156

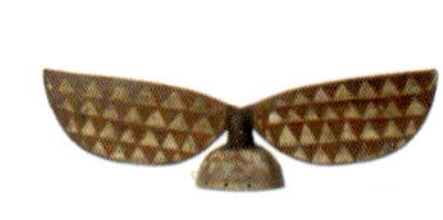
Butterfly headcrest
Wood, pigment
Gurunsi style
Purchased in
Ouagadougou in 1981
H. 24.1 cm, W. 81.5 cm,
D. 18.5 cm
ROM 2009.126.157

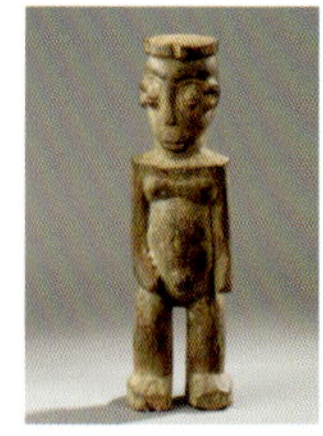
Figure
Wood
Lobi style
Purchased in
Ouagadougou in 1981
H. 40.5 cm, W. 12 cm,
D. 11 cm
ROM 2009.126.164

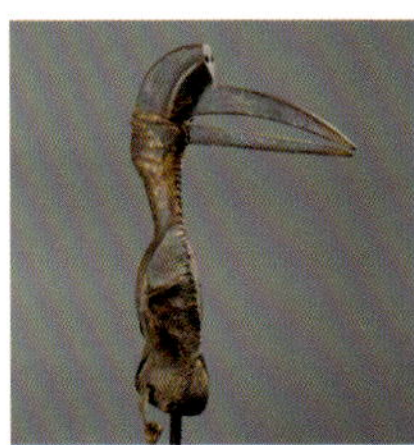
Hunting decoy in the
shape of a bird
Wood, leather, bird beak
Hausa style
Purchased in
Ouagadougou in 1981
H. 38 cm, W. 10.7 cm,
D. 26 cm
ROM 2009.126.241

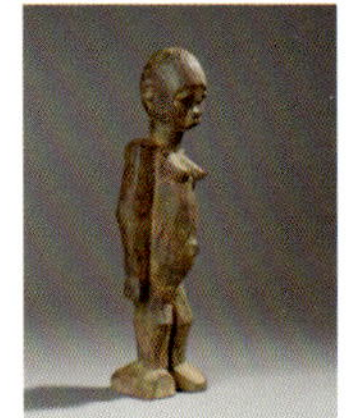
Figure
Wood
Lobi style
Purchased in
Ouagadougou in 1981
H. 39.5 cm, W. 10 cm,
D. 11 cm
ROM 2009.126.244

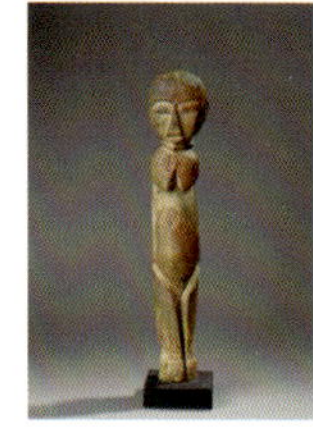
Figure
Wood
Lobi style
Purchased in
Ouagadougou in 1981
H. 54.5 cm, W. 11 cm,
D. 9.5 cm
ROM 2009.126.245

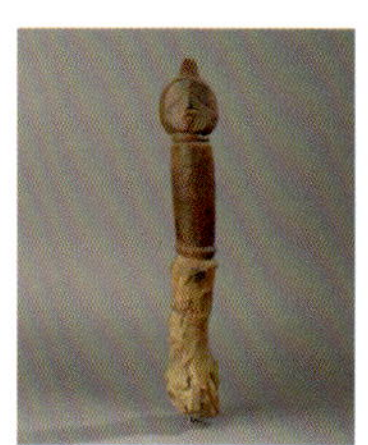
Figure
Wood
Mossi style
Purchased in
Ouagadougou in 1981
H. 57 cm, W. 9 cm, D. 11 cm
ROM 2009.126.251

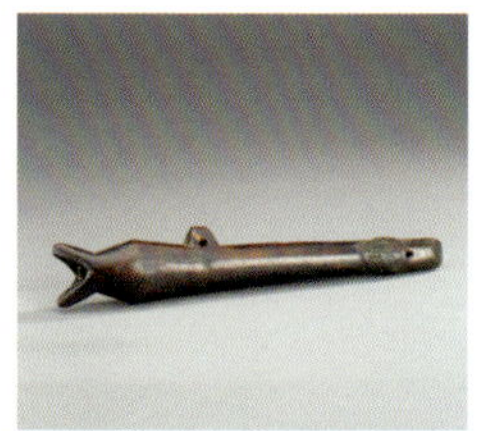
Flute
Wood
Mossi style
Purchased in
Ouagadougou in 1981
L. 24.8 cm, W. 4.6 cm,
D. 2.6 cm
ROM 2009.126.280

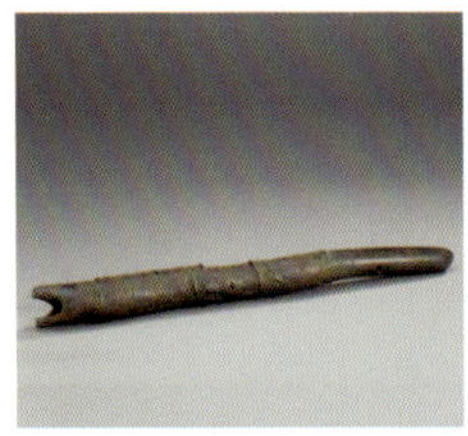
Flute
Wood
Mossi style
Purchased in Ouagadou-
gou in 1981
L. 38.5 cm, Diam. 3.5 cm
ROM 2009.126.281

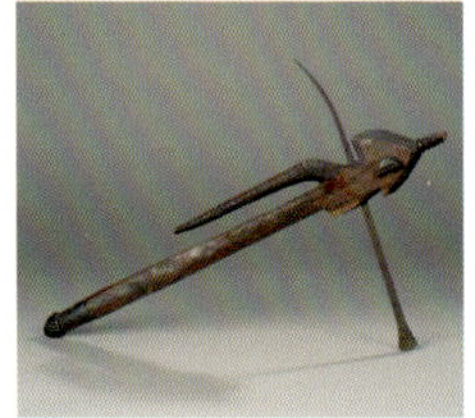
Axe
Wood, iron
Mossi style
Purchased in
Ouagadougou in 1981
H. 38 cm, L. 57.5 cm,
W. 3.5 cm
ROM 2009.126.283

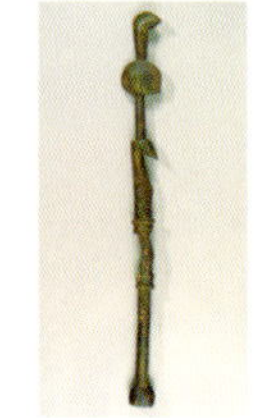
Walking stick
Wood
Mossi style
Purchased in
Ouagadougou in 1981
H. 93 cm, W. 6 cm,
D. 10.7 cm
ROM 2009.126.308

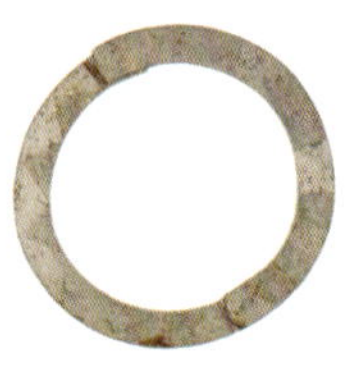
Choker
Aluminum
Lobi or Frafra style
Purchased in
Ouagadougou in 1981
Diam. 16.5 cm
ROM 2009.126.341

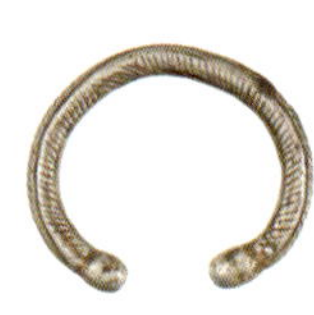
Bracelet
Aluminum
Lobi style
Purchased in
Ouagadougou in 1981
H. 0.8 cm, Diam. 7.4 cm
ROM 2009.126.342

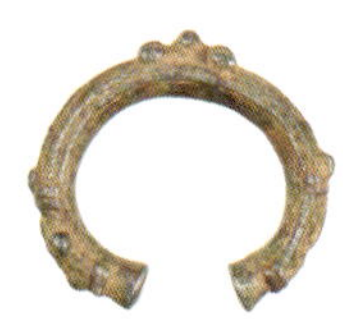
Bracelet
Aluminum
Lobi style
Purchased in
Ouagadougou in 1981
H. 1.3 cm, Diam. 8 cm
ROM 2009.126.343

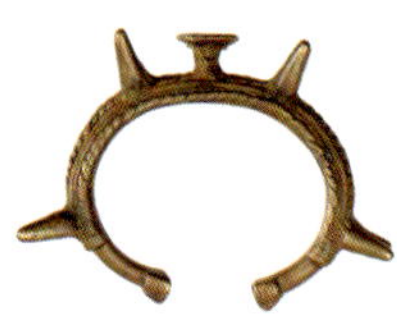
Bracelet
Brass
Lobi or Gurunsi style
Purchased in
Ouagadougou in 1981
H. 1.5 cm, W. 8.8 cm,
D. 6.3 cm
ROM 2009.126.355

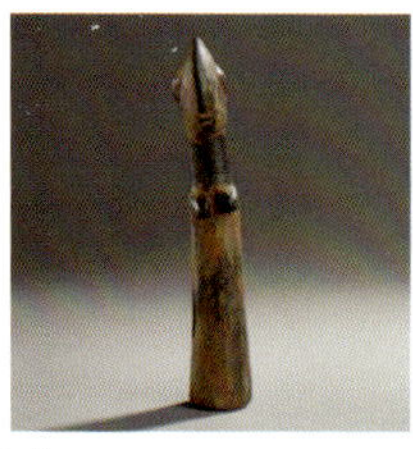
Doll
Wood
Mossi style
Purchased in
Ouagadougou in 1981
H. 23 cm, W. 4 cm, D. 6 cm
ROM 2009.126.81

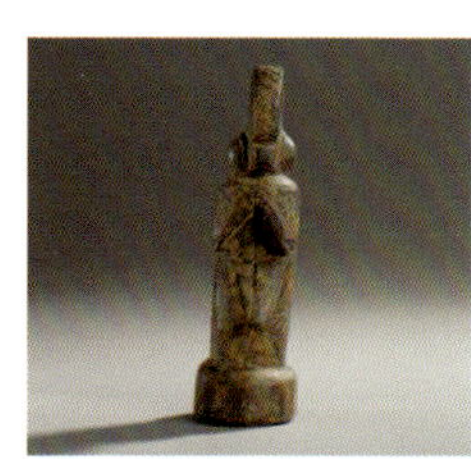
Doll
Wood
Mossi style
Purchased in
Ouagadougou in 1981
H. 17 cm, W. 4 cm,
D. 5.2 cm
ROM 2009.126.82

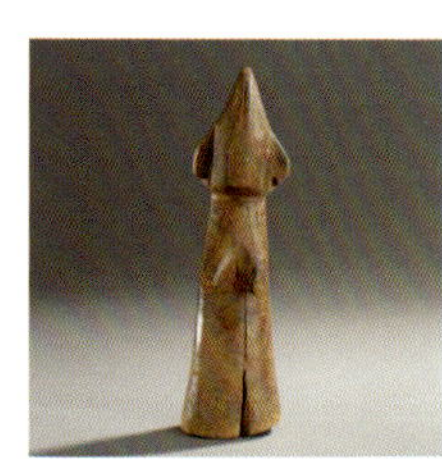
Doll
Wood
Mossi style
Purchased in
Ouagadougou in 1981
H. 21.1 cm, W. 7 cm,
D. 7.5 cm
ROM 2009.126.83

Burkina Faso (1961–1987)

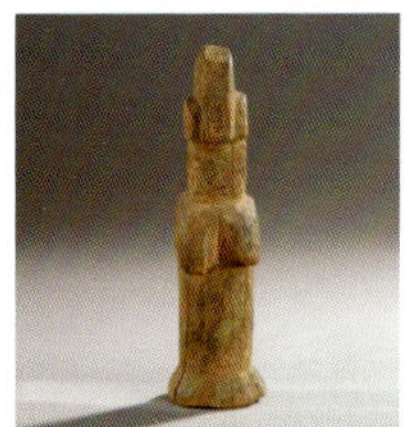
Doll
Wood
Mossi style
Purchased in Ouagadougou in 1981
H. 17 cm, W. 5 cm, D. 4.5 cm
ROM 2009.126.84

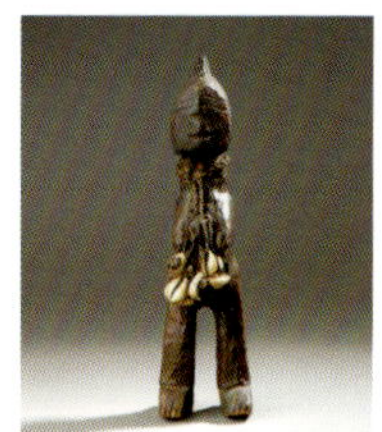
Doll
Wood, leather, cowrie shells
Mossi style
Purchased in Ouagadougou in 1981
H. 32.4 cm, W. 8.5 cm, D. 10.7 cm
ROM 2009.126.85

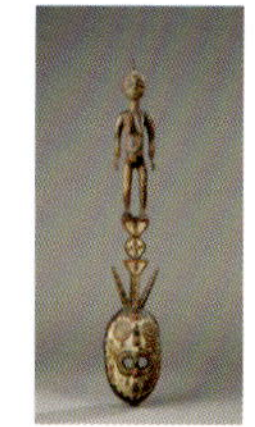
Face mask surmounted by figure
Wood
Mossi style
Purchased in Ouagadougou in 1985
H. 82.6 cm, W. 14.2 cm, D. 10 cm
ROM 2009.126.150

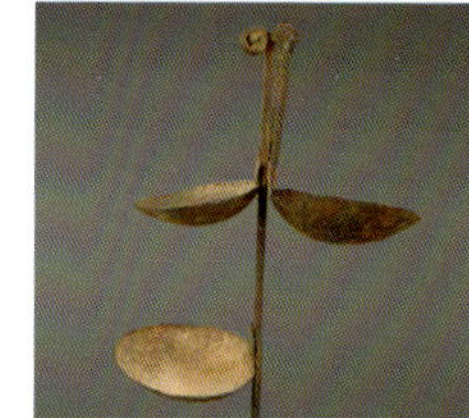
Lamp
Iron
Bamana style
Purchased in Ouagadougou in 1985
H. 101 cm, L. 23.5 cm, W. 14 cm
ROM 2009.126.301

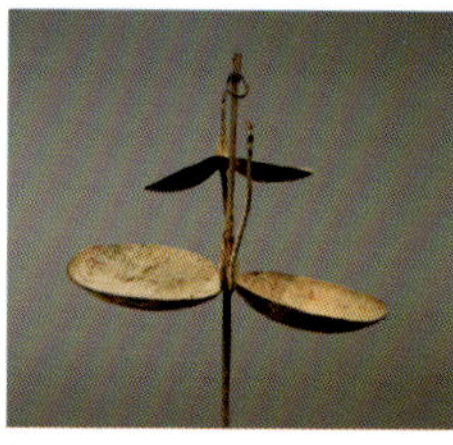
Lamp
Iron
Bamana style
Purchased in Ouagadougou in 1985
H. 68 cm, L. 23 cm, W. 17 cm
ROM 2009.126.302

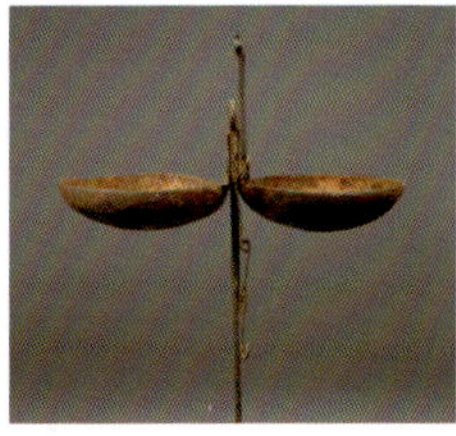
Lamp
Iron
Bamana style
Purchased in Ouagadougou in 1985
H. 57 cm, L. 24 cm, W. 12.5 cm
ROM 2009.126.303

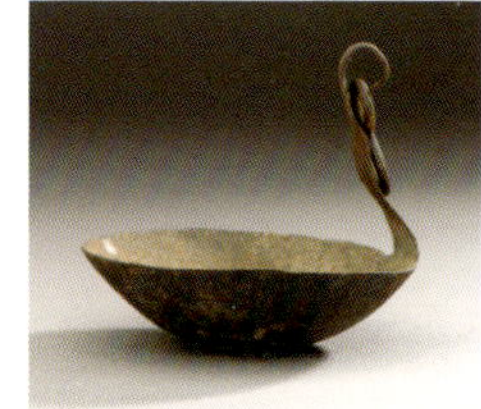
Lamp
Iron
Bamana style
Purchased in Ouagadougou in 1985
H. 8 cm, Diam. 8.7 cm
ROM 2009.126.304

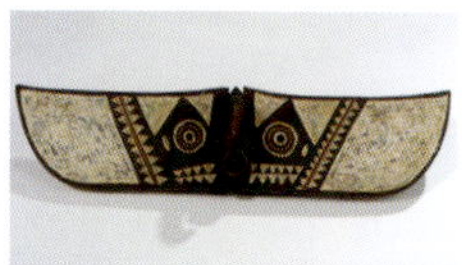
Butterfly mask
Wood, pigment
Bwa style
Purchased in Ouagadougou in 1986
H. 30.8 cm, W. 117.9 cm, D. 22.2 cm
ROM 2009.126.172

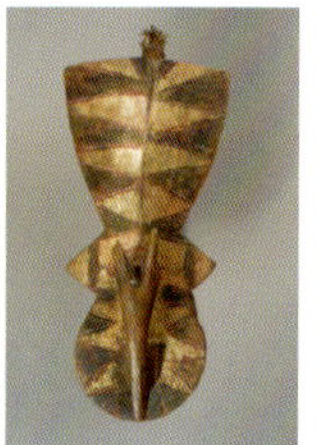
Antelope mask
Wood, pigment
Mossi style
Purchased in Ouagadougou in 1986
H. 32 cm, W. 23.5 cm, D. 17.7 cm
ROM 2009.126.193

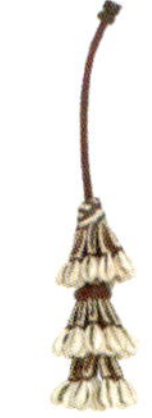
Kohl container
Leather, cowrie shells
Lobi style
Purchased in Ouagadougou in 1986
L. 24.5 cm, D. 4.8 cm
ROM 2009.126.340

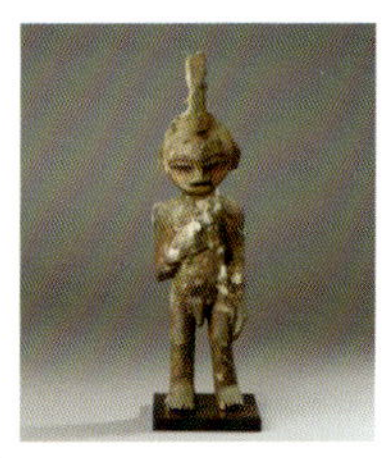
Figure
Wood
Lobi style
Purchased in Ouagadougou in 1989
H. 33 cm, W. 9.5 cm, D. 10 cm
ROM 2009.126.246

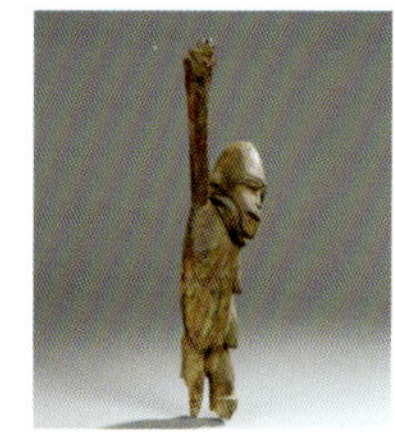
Figure with outstretched arm
Wood
Lobi style
Purchased in Ouagadougou in 1989
H. 31 cm, W. 14 cm, D. 5 cm
ROM 2009.126.247

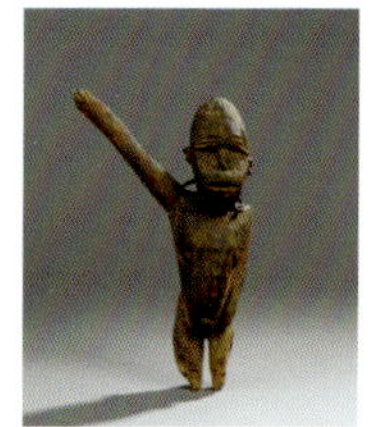
Figure with outstretched arm
Wood
Lobi style
Purchased in Ouagadougou in 1989
H. 26.5 cm, W. 16 cm, D. 7.5 cm
ROM 2009.126.248

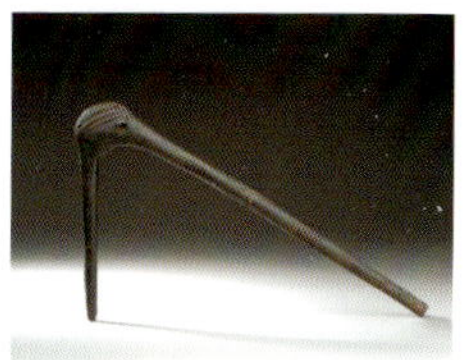
Staff
Wood
Lobi style
Purchased in Bobo-Dioulasso in 1981
H. 44 cm, W. 21.5 cm, D. 4 cm
ROM 2009.126.128

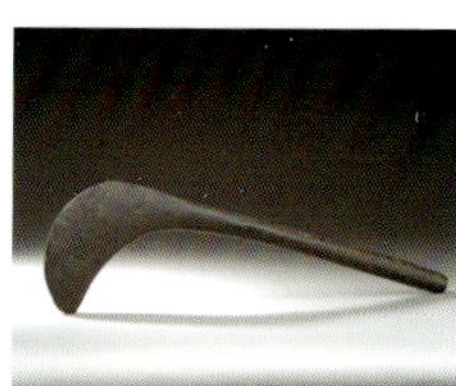
Staff
Wood
Lobi style
Purchased in Bobo-Dioulasso in 1981
H. 48 cm, W. 15 cm, D. 2.5 cm
ROM 2009.126.129

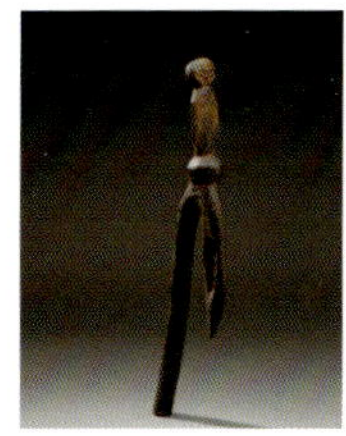
Staff
Wood
Mossi style
Purchased in Bobo-Dioulasso in 1981
H. 49 cm, W. 11.5 cm, D. 4 cm
ROM 2009.126.130

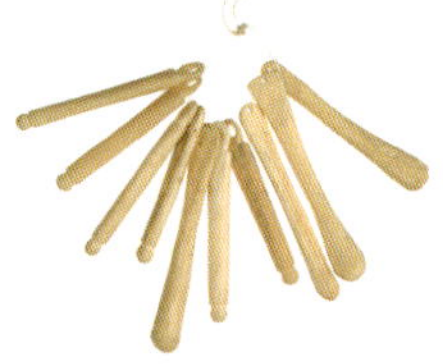
Charm
Bone
Purchased in a market in 1981
L. 9.5 cm, W. 10.5 cm, D. 0.5 cm
ROM 2009.126.309

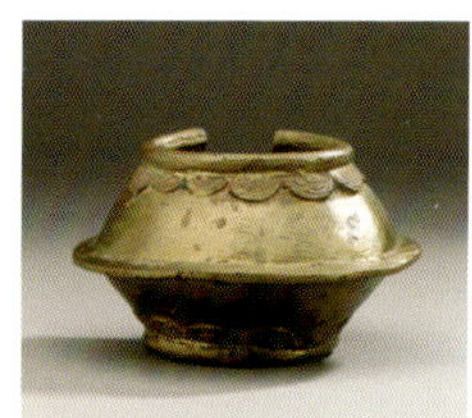
Bracelet *kobré*
Brass
Mossi style
Purchased in a market in 1981
H. 6.5 cm, Diam. 11.5 cm
ROM 2009.126.349

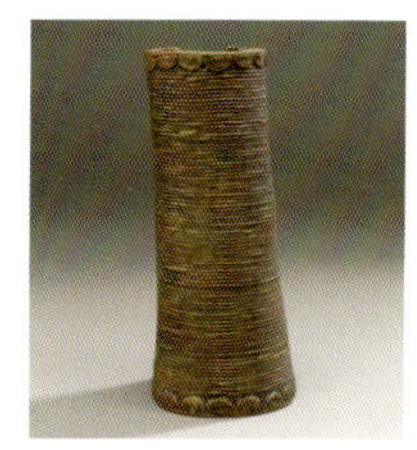
Bracelet
Brass
Gurunsi style
Purchased in a market in 1981
H. 19.5 cm, Diam. 8.8 cm
ROM 2009.126.352

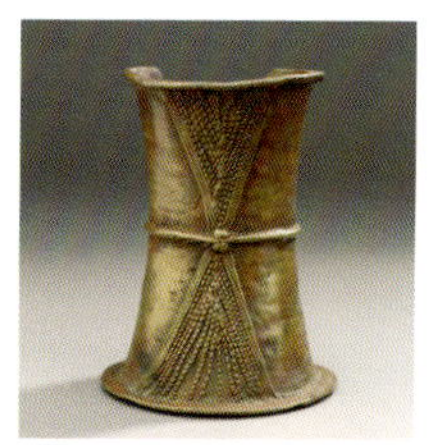
Bracelet
Brass
Gurunsi or Frafra style
Purchased in a market in 1981
H. 16 cm, Diam. 12.3 cm
ROM 2009.126.353

Ghana (1973–1988)

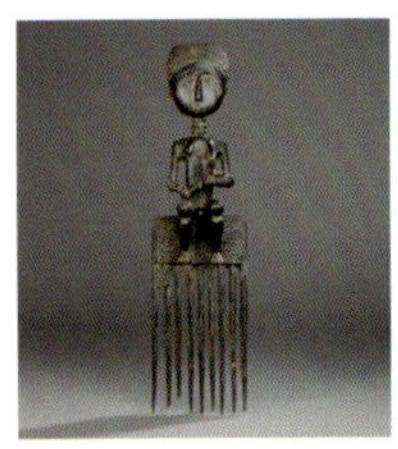
Comb
Wood
Asante style
Purchased in Accra in 1973
H. 46 cm, W. 11 cm, D. 7 cm
ROM 2009.126.54

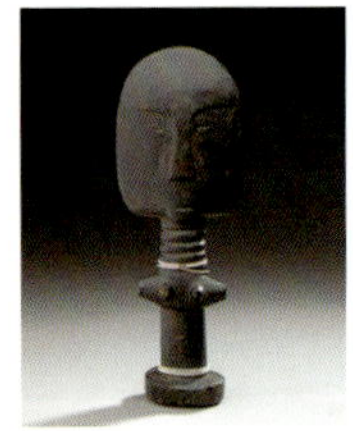
Doll
Wood, glass beads, fiber
Asante style
Purchased in Accra in 1973
H. 28.5 cm, W. 10.5 cm, D. 5 cm
ROM 2009.126.96

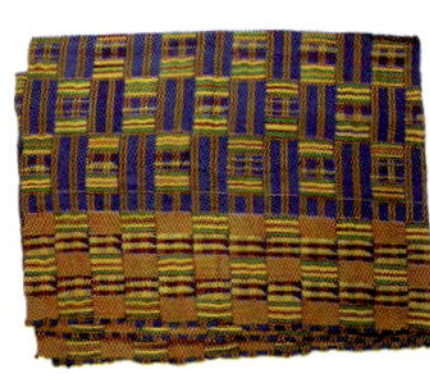
Kente cloth (detail)
Rayon
Asante style
Purchased in Accra 1988
L. 302 cm, W. 216 cm
ROM 2009.126.226

Togo (1973–1988)

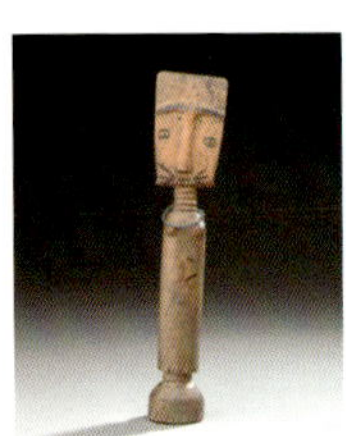
Doll
Wood
Fante style
Purchased in Lomé in 1973
H. 29 cm, W. 6.5 cm, D. 4 cm
ROM 2009.126.100

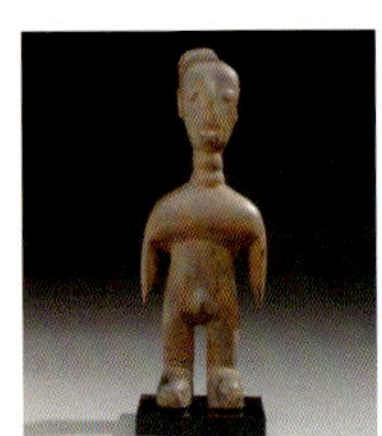
Doll
Wood
Ewe style
Purchased in Lomé in 1973
H. 21.3 cm, W. 7.9 cm, D. 5.8 cm
ROM 2009.126.101

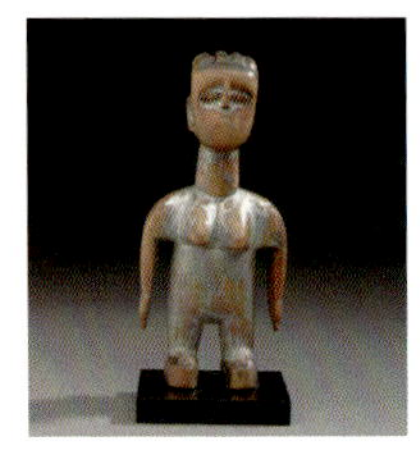
Doll
Wood
Ewe style
Purchased in Lomé in 1973
H. 16.7 cm, W. 8.7 cm, D. 5 cm
ROM 2009.126.102

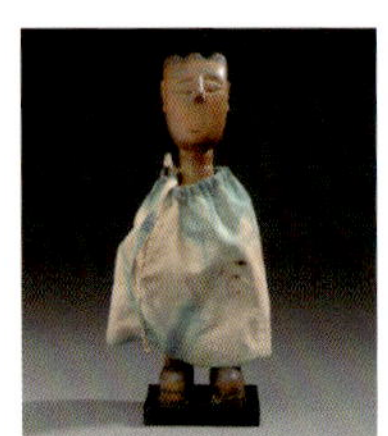
Doll
Wood, cotton cloth
Ewe style
Purchased in Lomé in 1973
H. 22.7 cm, W. 9 cm, D. 6 cm
ROM 2009.126.103

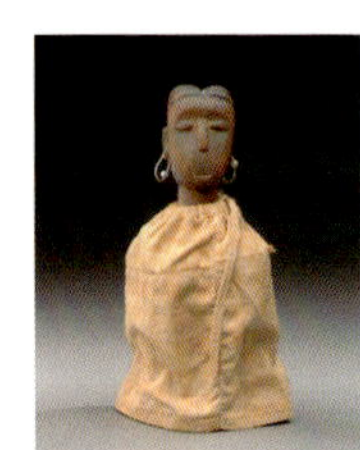
Doll
Wood, cloth, metal
Ewe style
Purchased in Lomé in 1973
H. 18.5 cm, W. 10 cm, D. 8 cm
ROM 2009.126.104

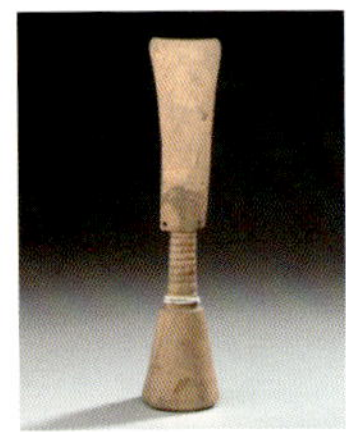
Doll
Wood
Fante style
Purchased in Lomé in 1973
H. 26 cm, W. 6 cm, D. 6 cm
ROM 2009.126.98

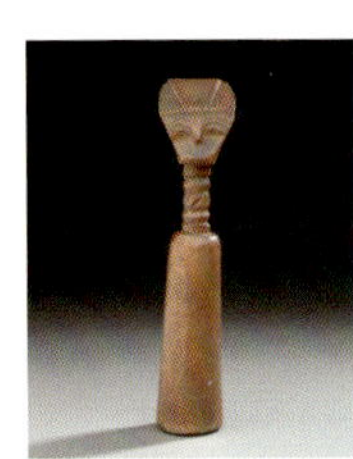
Doll
Wood, beads
Fante style
Purchased in Lomé in 1973
H. 27.5 cm, W. 6.3 cm, D. 6 cm
ROM 2009.126.99

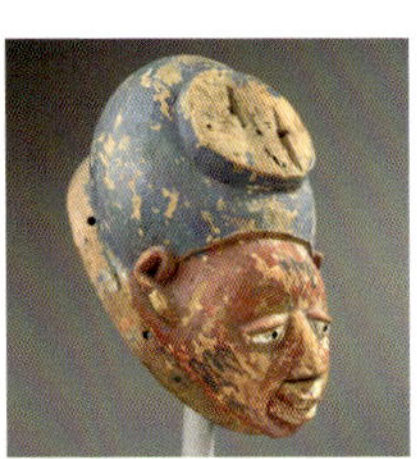
Gelede mask
Wood, pigment
Yoruba style
Purchased in Lomé in the early 1980s
H. 32.5 cm, W. 21.7 cm, D. 14.4 cm
ROM 2009.126.199

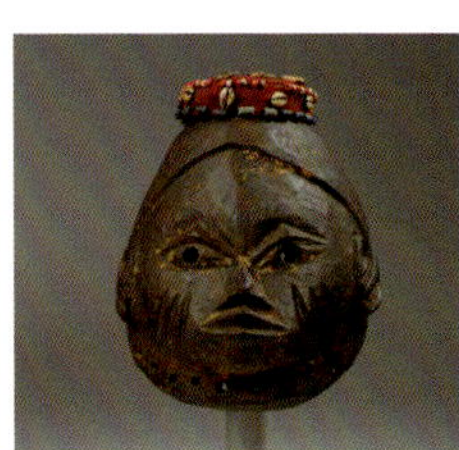
Gelede mask
Wood, pigment, cloth, cowrie shells
Yoruba style
Purchased in Lomé in the early 1980s
H. 26.5 cm, W. 19.4 cm, D. 18 cm
ROM 2009.126.200

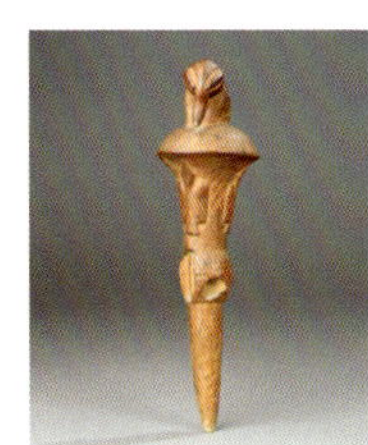
Fly whisk handle
Wood, metal
Baule style
Purchased in Lomé in 1983
H. 34 cm, W. 10 cm, D. 11 cm
ROM 2009.126.133

Togo (1973–1988)

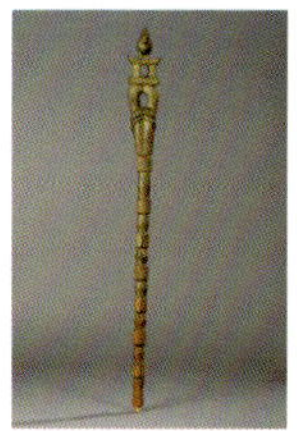
Staff
Wood
Purchased in Lomé in 1983
H. 113 cm, W. 9 cm,
D. 15 cm
ROM 2009.126.134

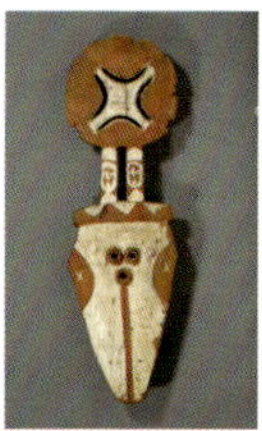
Mask
Wood, pigment
Nafana style
Purchased in Lomé in 1983
H. 136.5 cm, W. 43.5 cm,
D. 11.2 cm
ROM 2009.126.197

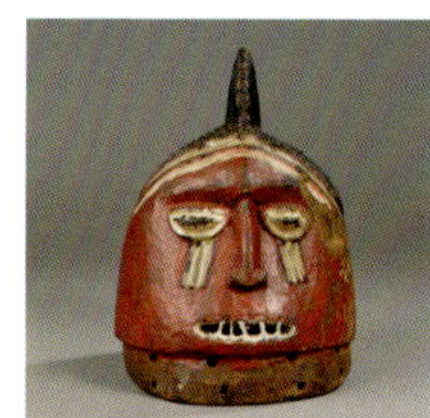
Mask
Wood, pigment
Ana or Yoruba style
Purchased in Lomé in 1983
H. 30 cm, W. 22.8 cm,
D. 28.2 cm
ROM 2009.126.198

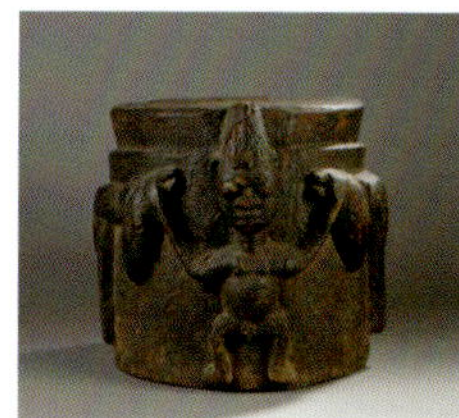
Stool
Wood
Yoruba style
Purchased in Lomé in 1983
H. 36 cm, Diam. 39 cm
ROM 2009.126.24

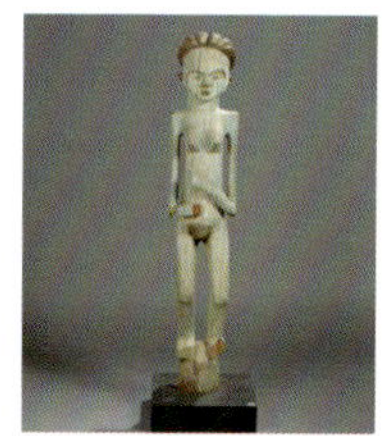
Figure
Wood, pigment
Tsogo(?) style
Purchased in Lomé in 1983
H. 128.5 cm, W. 25.5 cm,
D. 24 cm
ROM 2009.126.312

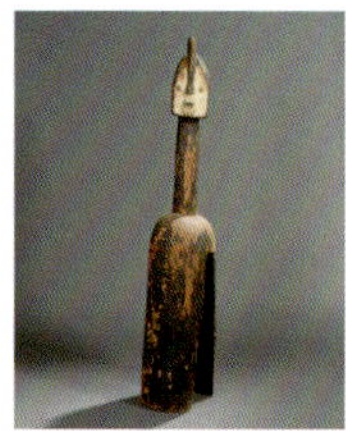
Shoulder mask
Wood, pigment
Purchased in Lomé in 1983
H. 157 cm, W. 29.5 cm,
D. 35.7 cm
ROM 2009.126.313

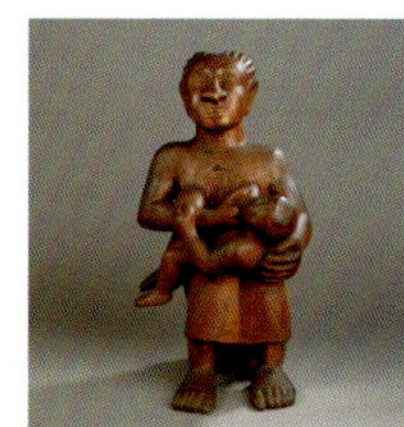
Figure
Wood
Ewe style
Purchased in Lomé in 1983
H. 50 cm, W. 28 cm,
D. 28 cm
ROM 2009.126.58

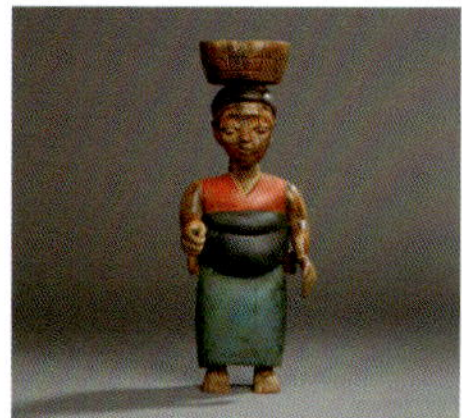
Figure
Wood, pigment
Ewe style
Purchased in Lomé in 1983
H. 53 cm, W. 14 cm,
D. 15 cm
ROM 2009.126.59

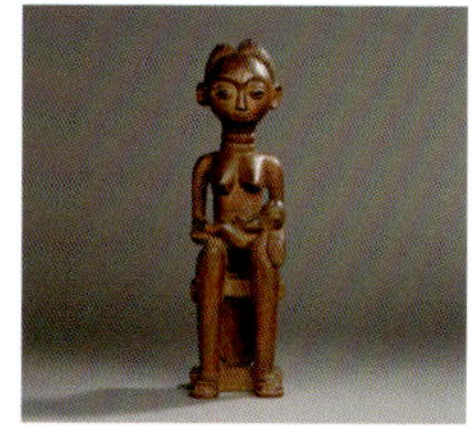
Figure
Wood
Akan style
Purchased in Lomé in 1983
H. 35 cm, W. 10 cm,
D. 10 cm
ROM 2009.126.60

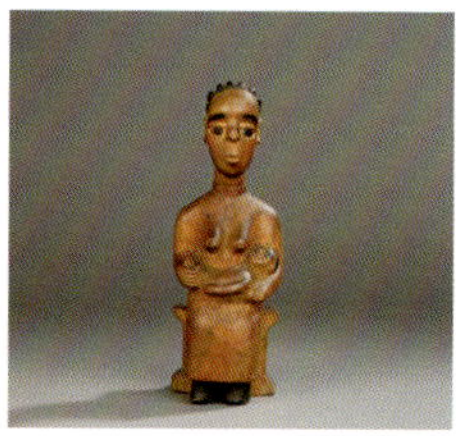
Figure
Wood, pigment
Ewe style
Purchased in Lomé in 1983
H. 25 cm, W. 9 cm, D. 9 cm
ROM 2009.126.61

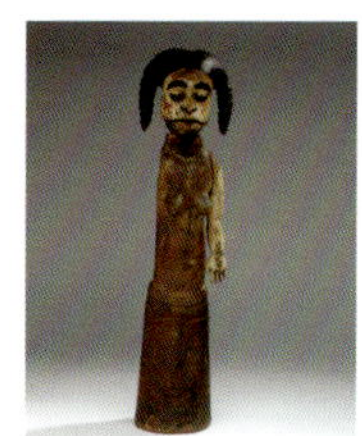
Puppet
Wood, metal, pigment
Ibibio style
Purchased from a private
collector in Lomé in the
mid-1980s
H. 61.9 cm, W. 15.5 cm,
D. 14.2 cm
ROM 2009.126.8.1–2

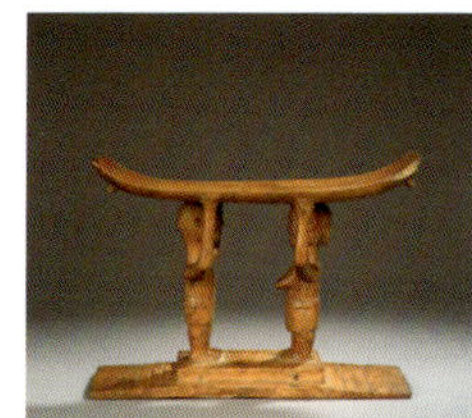
Stool
Wood
Asante or Ewe style
Purchased in Lomé in 1986
H. 27 cm, W. 38.5 cm,
D. 16 cm
ROM 2009.126.18

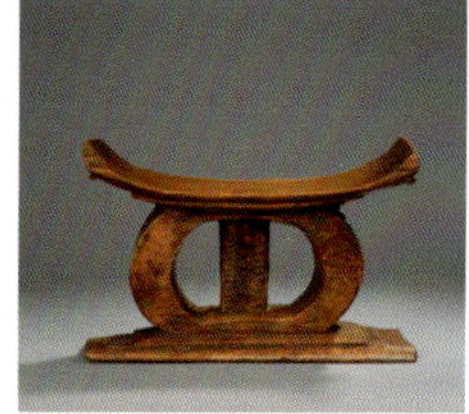
Stool
Wood
Asante style
Purchased in Lomé in 1986
H. 26.5 cm, W. 40.5 cm,
D. 17 cm
ROM 2009.126.19

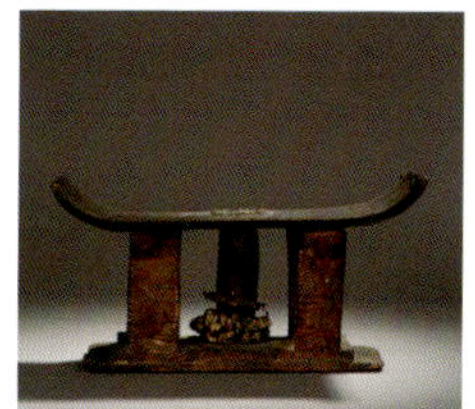
Stool
Wood, fiber, cowrie shells,
leather, metal
Asante style
Purchased in Lomé in 1986
H. 24.3 cm, W. 48.7 cm,
D. 18.3 cm
ROM 2009.126.20

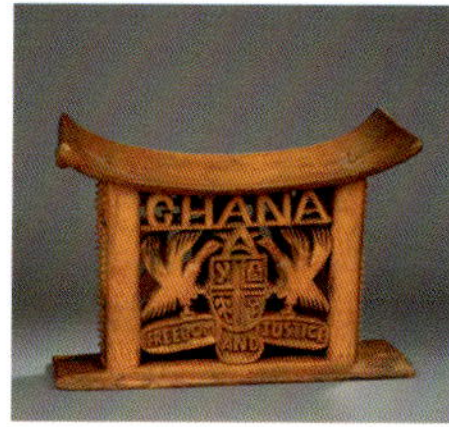

Stool
Wood
Asante style
Purchased in Lomé in 1986
H. 40 cm, W. 57 cm,
D. 25 cm
ROM 2009.126.21

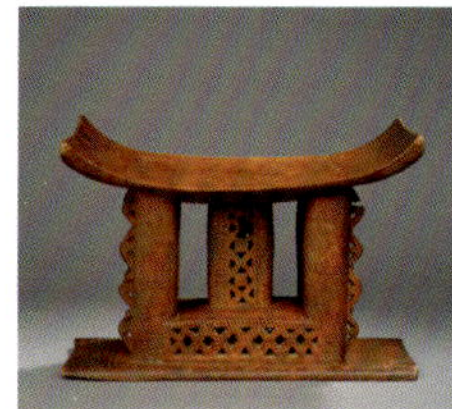
Stool
Wood
Asante style
Purchased in Lomé in 1986
H. 34 cm, W. 50 cm,
D. 23 cm
ROM 2009.126.22

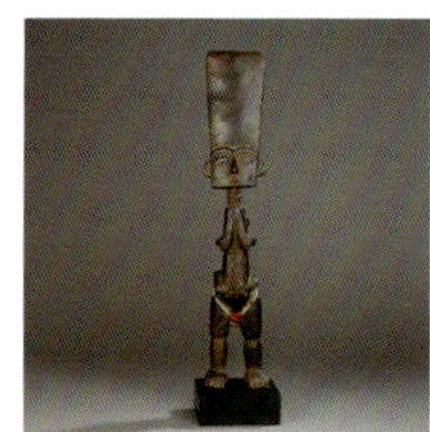
Figure
Wood
Fante style
Purchased in Lomé in 1987
H. 41.9 cm, W. 9.2 cm,
D. 6 cm
ROM 2009.126.55

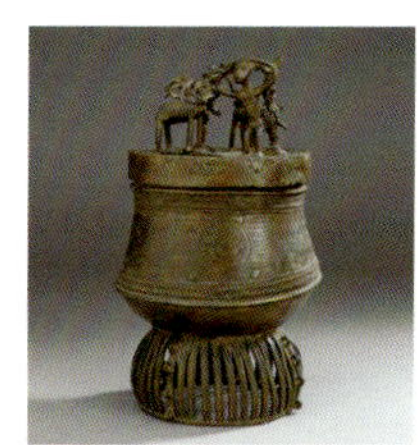
Container
Brass
Asante style
Purchased in Lomé in 1988
H. 27.5 cm, Diam. 15.5 cm
ROM 2009.126.290.1–2

Republic of Benin (1973–1988)

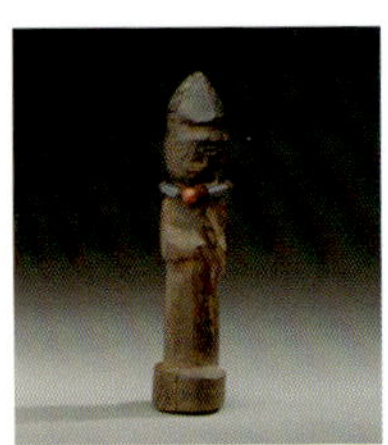

Female figurine
Wood, glass beads, fiber
Fon style
Purchased in Cotonou in 1973
H. 19.3 cm, W. 4.2 cm, D. 4.5 cm
ROM 2009.126.105

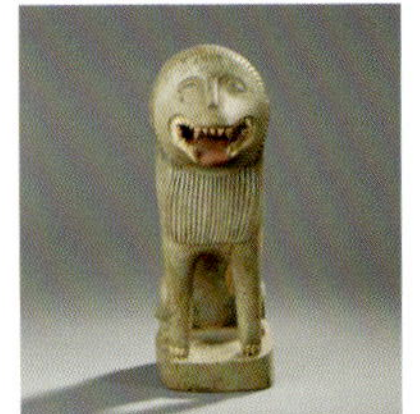

Lion figurine
Wood, pigment
Fon style
Purchased from a private collector in Cotonou in 1988
H. 30.3 cm, W. 11 cm, D. 19.5 cm
ROM 2009.126.291

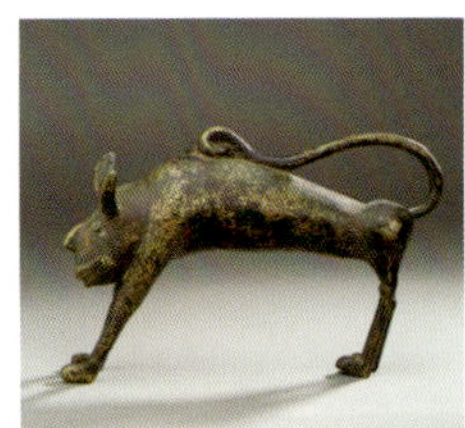

Lion figurine
Brass
Fon style
Purchased from a private collector in Cotonou in 1988
H. 17 cm, L. 27 cm, W. 7.8 cm
ROM 2009.126.300

Cameroon (1986–1989)

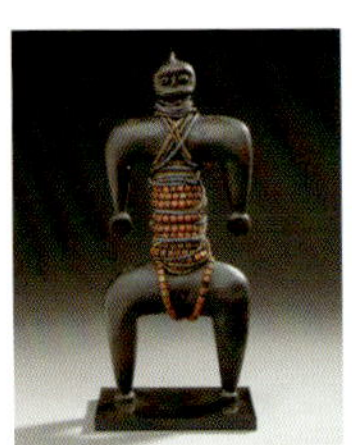

Doll
Wood, glass beads, fiber
Namji style
Purchased in Douala in 1986
H. 33.3 cm, W. 14.2 cm, D. 5.4 cm
ROM 2009.126.109

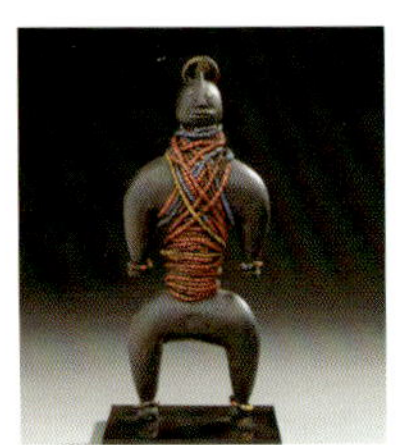

Doll
Wood, glass beads, fiber, metal
Namji style
Purchased in Douala in 1986
H. 26.2 cm, W. 11.4 cm, D. 4.9 cm
ROM 2009.126.110

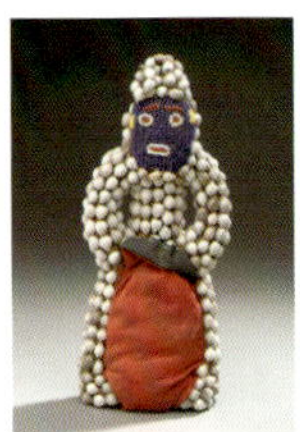

Figure
Cloth, fiber, seeds
Bamiléké style
Purchased in Douala in 1986
H. 29.2 cm, W. 11.2 cm, D. 6.4 cm
ROM 2009.126.112

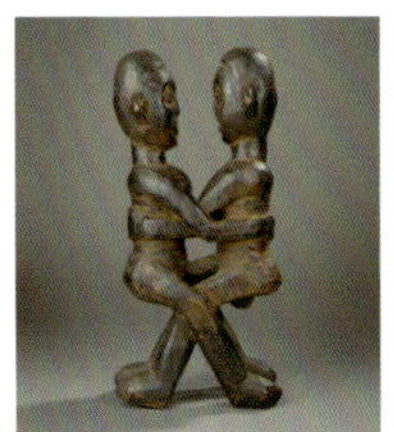

Embracing couple
Wood
Northern Grassfields, Babungo style
Purchased in Douala in 1986
H. 49 cm, W. 24 cm, D. 14 cm
ROM 2009.126.261

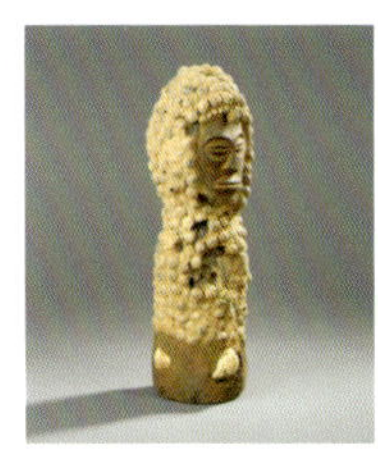

Figure
Wood, seeds
Songye style
Purchased in Douala in 1986
H. 33 cm, W. 11.5 cm, D. 9.5 cm
ROM 2009.126.270

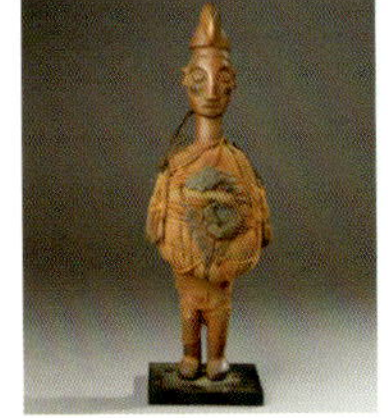

Figure
Wood, cloth, fiber, feathers
Yaka style
Purchased in Douala in 1986
H. 32.7 cm, W. 10.5 cm, D. 10 cm
ROM 2009.126.271

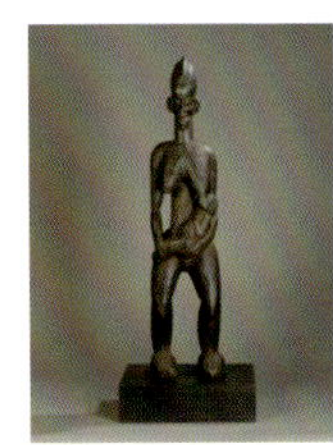

Mother and child figure
Wood
Bamiléké style
Purchased in Douala in 1986 or 1987
H. 88 cm, W. 22 cm, D. 19 cm
ROM 2009.126.62

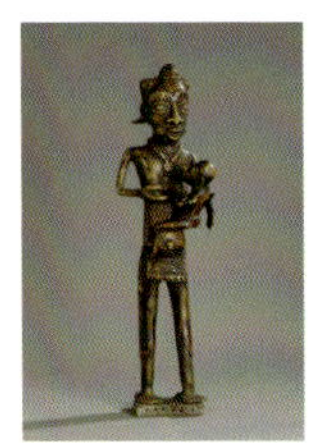

Mother and child figure
Brass
Bamum style
Purchased in Douala in 1986 or 1987
H. 64 cm, W. 20 cm, D. 15 cm
ROM 2009.126.64.1–2

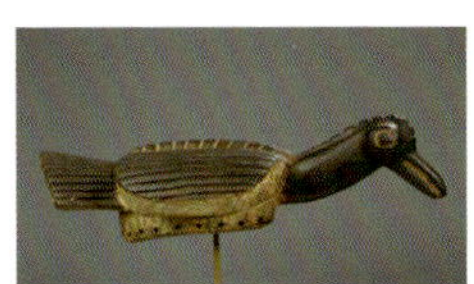

Bird helmet mask
Wood
Northern Grassfields style
Purchased in Douala in 1989
H. 15.3 cm, W. 27.5 cm, D. 61.1 cm
ROM 2009.126.213

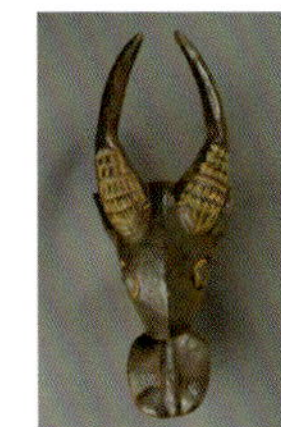

Buffalo helmet mask
Wood
Northern Grassfields style
Purchased in Douala in 1989
H. 16.2 cm, W. 30.4 cm, D. 82.1 cm
ROM 2009.126.214

Cameroon (1986–1989)

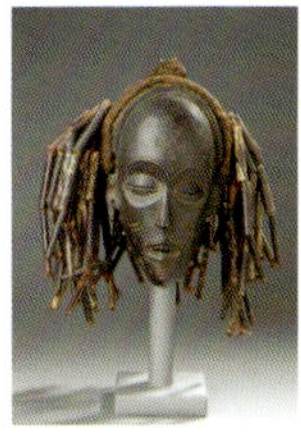

Mask
Wood, fiber, bamboo, metal
Chokwe style
Purchased in Douala in 1989
H. 35 cm, W. 31 cm, D. 31 cm
ROM 2009.126.221

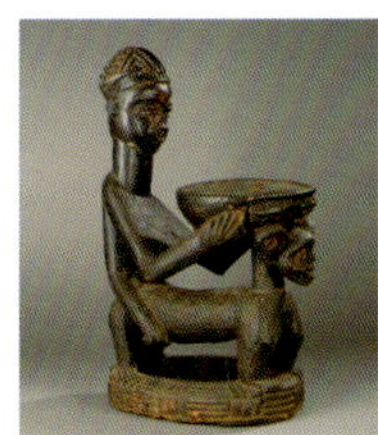

Royal stool
Wood
Northern Grassfields, Babungo style
Purchased in Foumban in 1986
H. 61 cm, W. 27 cm, D. 39 cm
ROM 2009.126.293

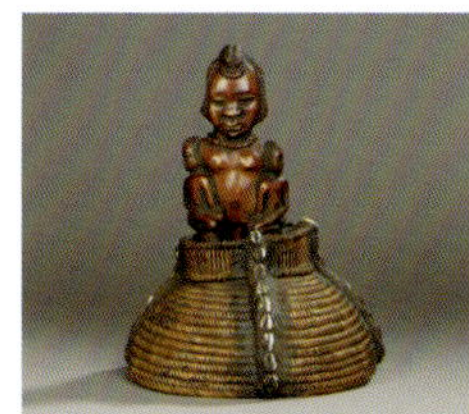

Pot lid surmounted by figure
Fiber, bone, cowrie shells
Purchased in Foumban in 1986
H. 30 cm, W. 25 cm, D. 23 cm
ROM 2009.126.63

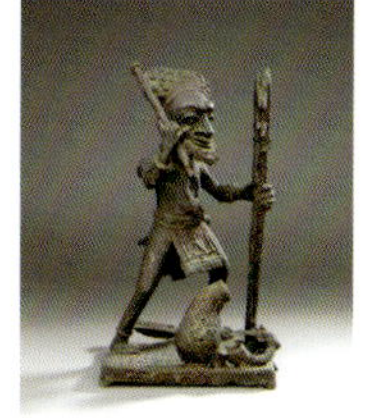

Warrior figure
Aluminum
Bamum style—made by El Hadji Ali
Purchased in Foumban in 1986
H. 35.5 cm, W. 27 cm, D. 27.5 cm
ROM 2009.126.345

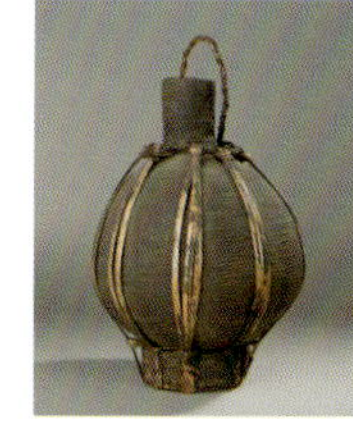

Palm wine container
Fiber, leather, resin
Bamum style
Purchased in Foumban in 1987
H. 49 cm, Diam. 24 cm
ROM 2009.126.294

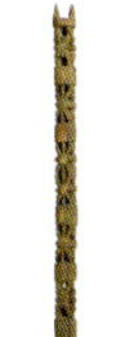

Architectural post
Wood
Northern Grassfields style
Purchased in Foumban in 1987
H. 270 cm, Diam. 22 cm
ROM 2009.126.314

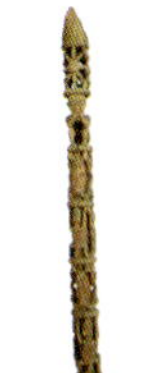

Architectural post
Wood
Northern Grassfields style
Purchased in Foumban in 1987
H. 269 cm, Diam. 17.7 cm
ROM 2009.126.315

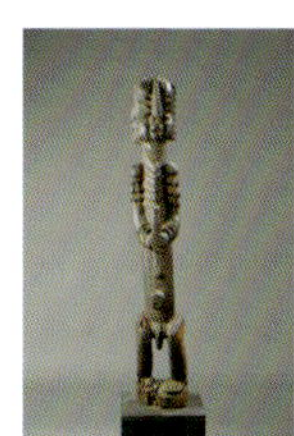

Figure
Wood
Purchased in Foumban in 1987
H. 140.5 cm, W. 22 cm, D. 24.5 cm
ROM 2009.126.316

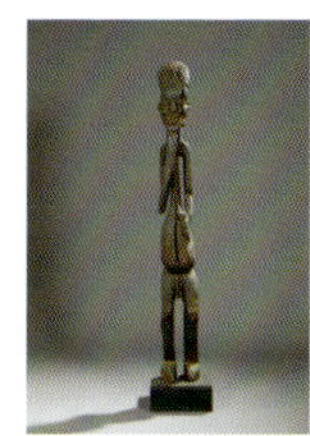

Figure
Wood
Kom style
Purchased in Foumban in 1987
H. 175 cm, W. 20 cm, D. 21 cm
ROM 2009.126.317

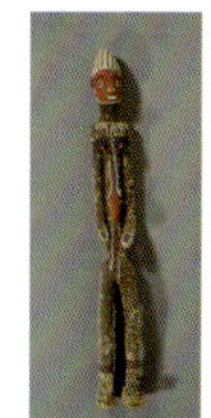

Figure
Wood, glass beads, seed, cowrie shells
Bamiléké style
Purchased in Foumban in 1987
H. 197 cm, W. 25 cm, D. 19 cm
ROM 2009.126.318

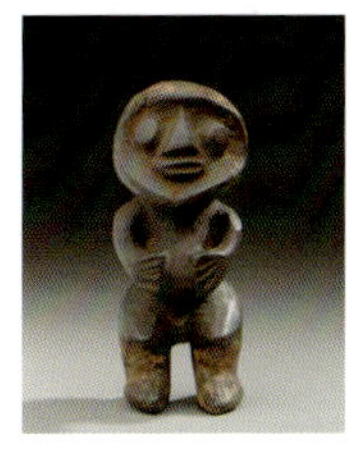

Figurine
Wood
Mambila style
Purchased in Yaoundé in 1986
H. 15.5 cm, W. 6 cm, D. 6 cm
ROM 2009.126.113

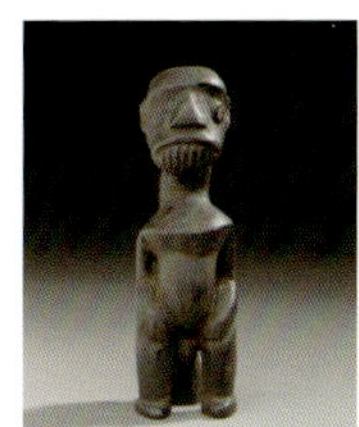

Figurine
Wood
Bamiléké style
Purchased in Yaoundé in 1986
H. 19 cm, W. 5.7 cm, D. 5 cm
ROM 2009.126.114

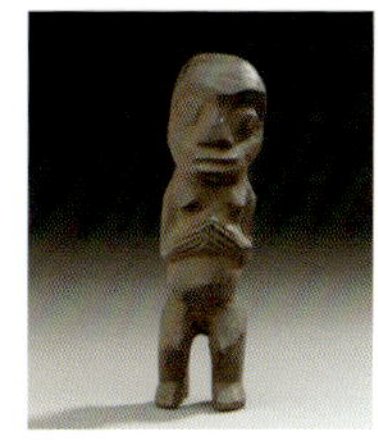

Figurine
Wood
Bamiléké style
Purchased in Yaoundé in 1986
H. 16 cm, W. 4.2 cm, D. 4 cm
ROM 2009.126.115

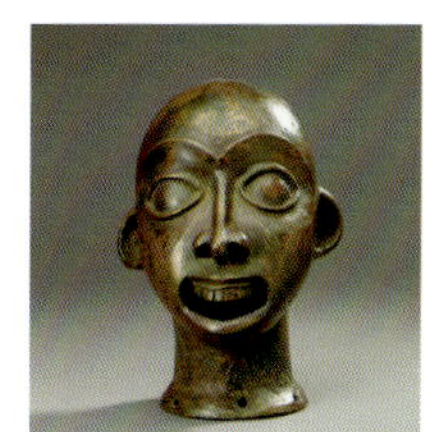

Headcrest
Brass
Bamum style
Purchased from a private collector in Yaoundé in 1986
H. 27.8 cm, W. 20.7 cm, D. 21 cm
ROM 2009.126.298

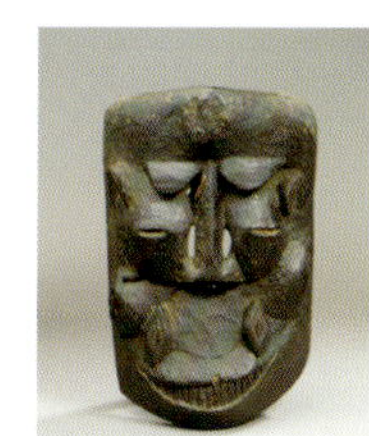

Mask
Wood
Meta? style
Purchased from a private collector in Yaoundé in 1989
H. 44.7 cm, W. 30.7 cm, D. 16.3 cm
ROM 2009.126.215

Gabon (1966–1986)

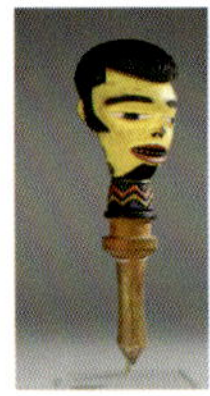

Kebe-kebe puppet head
Wood, pigment
Kuyu style
Purchased from a theatre troupe in a village in 1966
H. 39.8 cm, W. 14.4 cm, D. 13.7 cm
ROM 2009.126.2

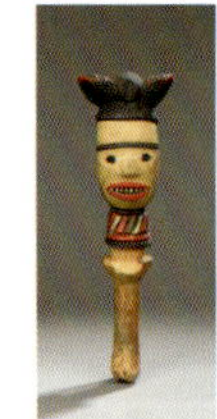

Kebe-kebe puppet head
Wood, pigment
Kuyu style
Purchased from a theatre troupe in a village in 1966
H. 43.3 cm, W. 13.6 cm, D. 13.2 cm
ROM 2009.126.3

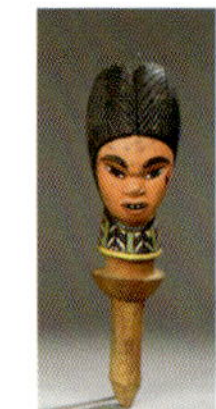

Kebe-kebe puppet head
Wood, pigment
Kuyu style
Purchased from a theatre troupe in a village in 1966
H. 41.5 cm, W. 10.8 cm, D. 13 cm
ROM 2009.126.4

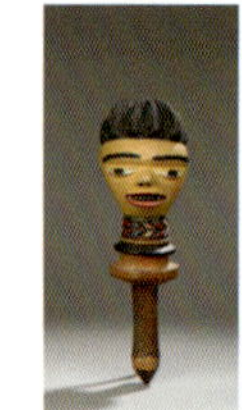

Kebe-kebe puppet head
Wood, pigment
Kuyu style
Purchased from a theatre troupe in a village in 1966
H. 41.5 cm, W. 12 cm, D. 13.1 cm
ROM 2009.126.5

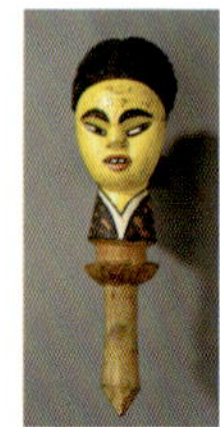

Kebe-kebe puppet head
Wood, pigment
Kuyu style
Purchased from a theatre troupe in a village in 1966
H. 40.1 cm, W. 10 cm, D. 14 cm
ROM 2009.126.6

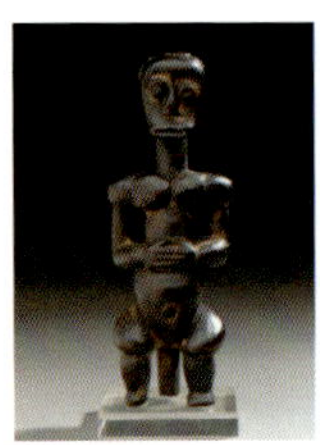

Figure
Wood
Fang style
Purchased in Libreville in 1966
H. 17.4 cm, W. 6.4 cm, D. 4.4 cm
ROM 2009.126.116

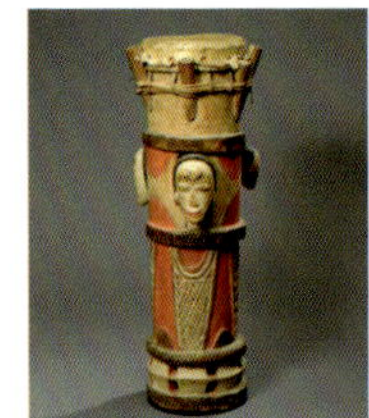

Drum
Wood, hide, fiber, pigment
Fang style
Bartered for a car in a village outside Libreville in 1966
H. 71 cm, Diam. 29 cm
ROM 2009.126.222

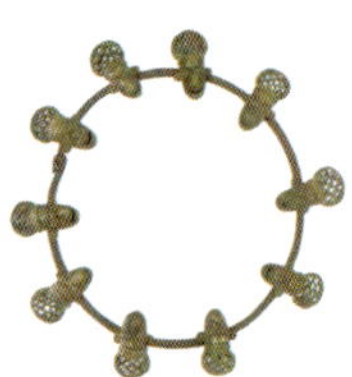

Neck ring
Brass
Bamum style
Purchased from a private collector in Libreville in 1966
H. 3.5 cm, Diam. 36 cm
ROM 2009.126.299

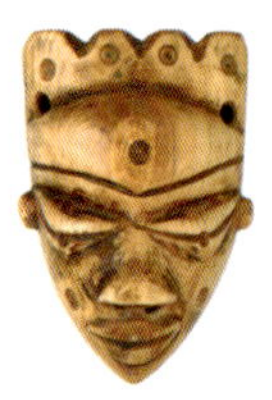

Pendant
Bone
Pende style
Purchased in Libreville in 1986
H. 6 cm, W. 4.2 cm, D. 2.4 cm
ROM 2009.126.346

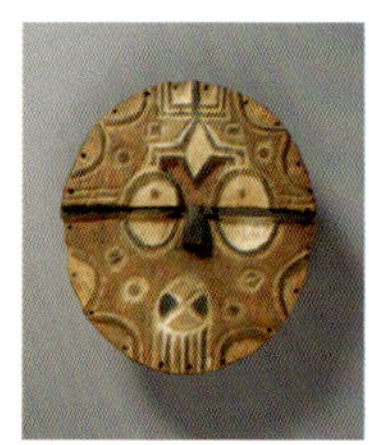

Mask
Wood, pigment
Teke style
Purchased in Libreville in 1986
H. 41 cm, W. 35.8 cm, D. 9 cm
ROM 2009.126.243

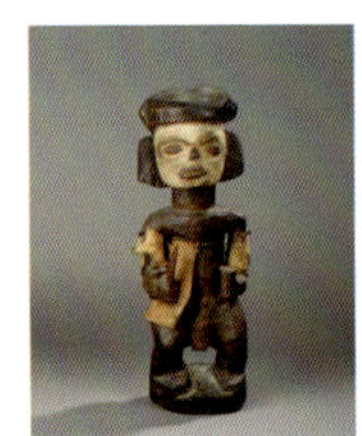

Figure
Wood, leather, pigment
Tsogo(?) style
Purchased in Libreville in 1986
H. 51.2 cm, W. 21.4 cm, D. 17.8 cm
ROM 2009.126.262

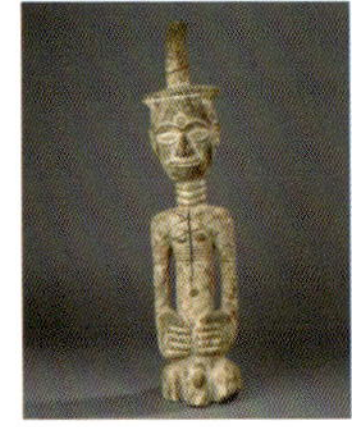

Figure
Wood, pigment
Ndengesh style
Purchased in Libreville in 1986
H. 68 cm, W. 16 cm, D. 17.4 cm
ROM 2009.126.263

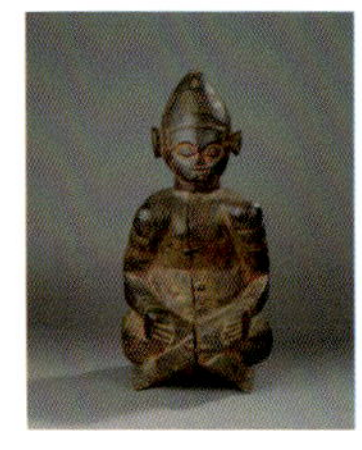

Figure
Wood, iron
Purchased in Libreville in 1986
H. 51.7 cm, W. 25.5 cm, D. 24 cm
ROM 2009.126.264

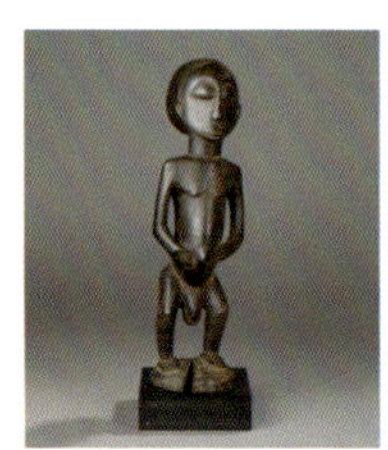

Figure
Wood
Tabwa style
Purchased in Libreville in 1986
H. 36.8 cm, W. 11 cm, D. 10.8 cm
ROM 2009.126.265

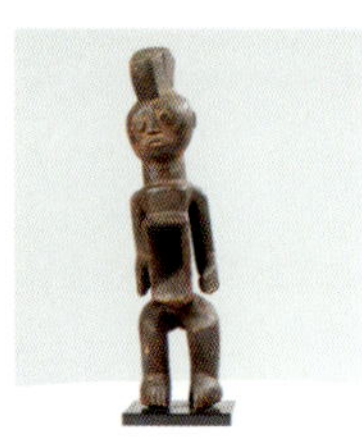

Figure
Wood
Purchased in Libreville in 1986
H. 38 cm, W. 10 cm, D. 10.7 cm
ROM 2009.126.272

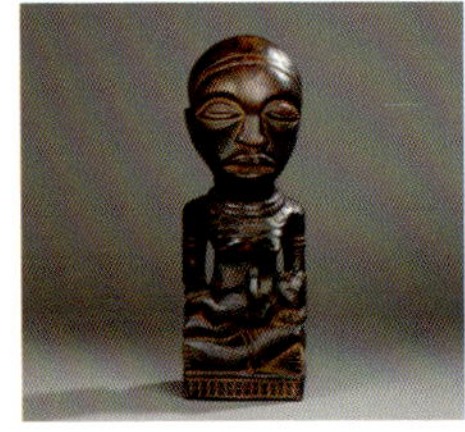

Figure
Wood
Yombe style
Purchased from a private collector in Libreville in 1986
H. 33 cm, W. 11 cm, D. 10 cm
ROM 2009.126.65

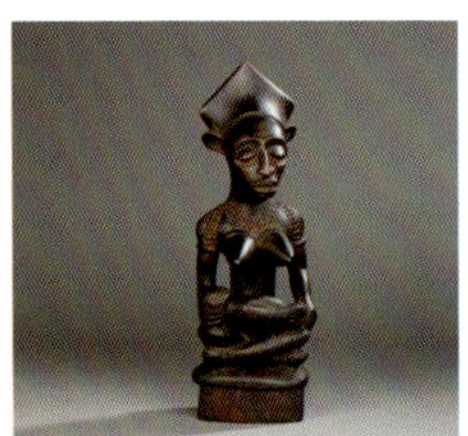

Figure
Wood
Yombe style
Purchased from a private collector in Libreville in 1986
H. 38.5 cm, W. 14 cm, D. 12 cm
ROM 2009.126.66

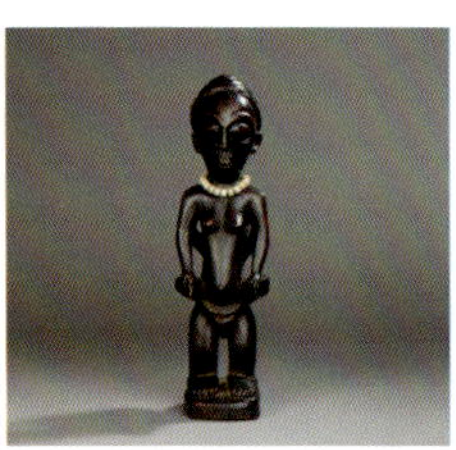

Figure
Wood, fiber, glass
Chokwe style
Purchased from a private collector in Libreville in 1986
H. 34 cm, W. 11 cm, D. 11 cm
ROM 2009.126.67

Democratic Republic of the Congo (1961–1987)

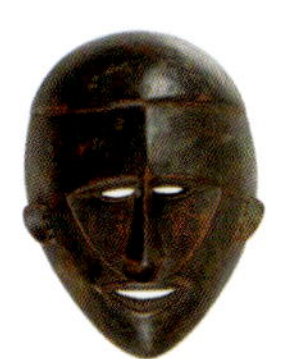
Mask
Wood
Bartered with a bull and 21 chickens in 1961
H. 18.7 cm, W. 14.3 cm, D. 7 cm
ROM 2009.126.138

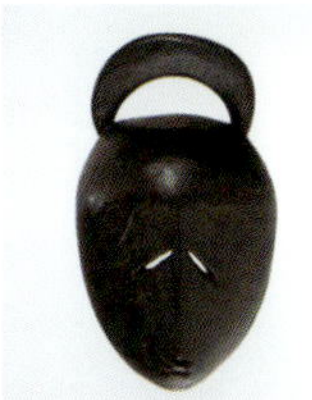
Mask
Wood
Purchased from a private collector in Kinshasa in 1966
H. 23.7 cm, W. 14 cm, D. 6.8 cm
ROM 2009.126.136

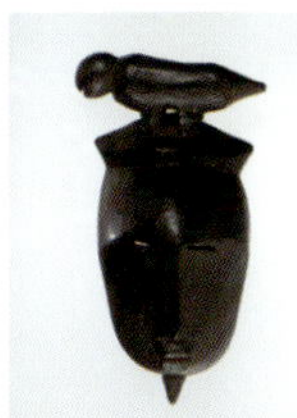
Mask
Wood
Purchased from private collector in Kinshasa in 1966
H. 28 cm, W. 16 cm, D. 7 cm
ROM 2009.126.137

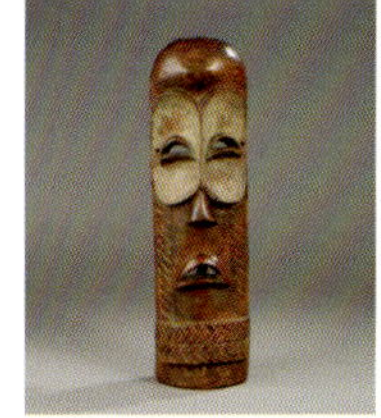
Mask
Wood, pigment
Bembe style
Purchased in Kinshasa in 1982
H. 50.1 cm, W. 14.2 cm, D. 5.6 cm
ROM 2009.126.211

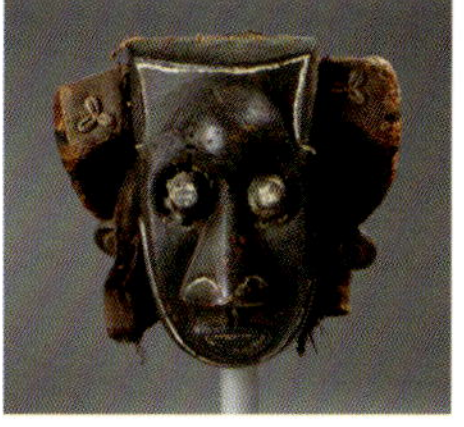
Mask
Wood, raffia, cowrie shells
Kuba style
Purchased in Kinshasa in 1982
H. 28 cm, W. 36 cm, D. 32 cm
ROM 2009.126.212

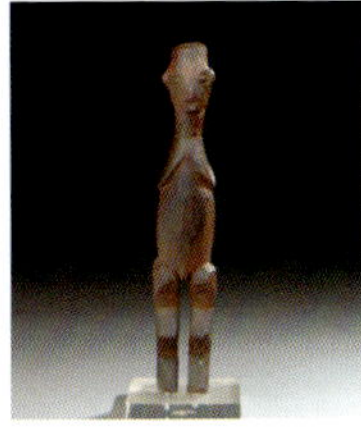
Figure
Wood
Suku style
Purchased in Kinshasa in 1985–6
H. 24.3 cm, W. 4.8 cm, D. 5.2 cm
ROM 2009.126.117

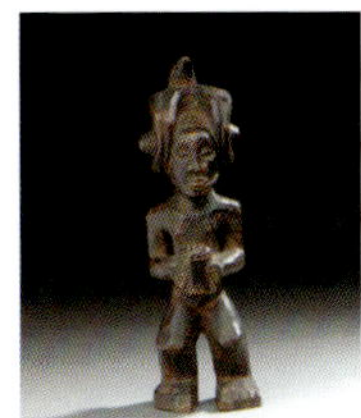
Figure
Wood
Chokwe style
Purchased in Kinshasa in 1986
H. 24 cm, W. 7.5 cm, D. 5.5 cm
ROM 2009.126.118

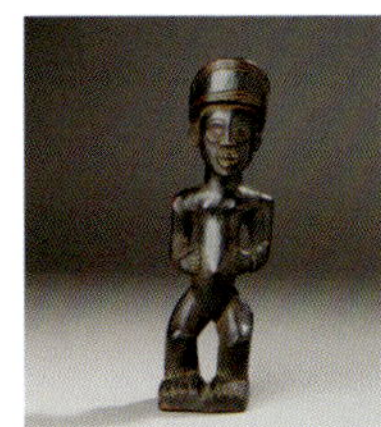
Figure
Wood
Chokwe style
Purchased in Kinshasa in 1986
H. 26.5 cm, W. 8.6 cm, D. 9 cm
ROM 2009.126.266

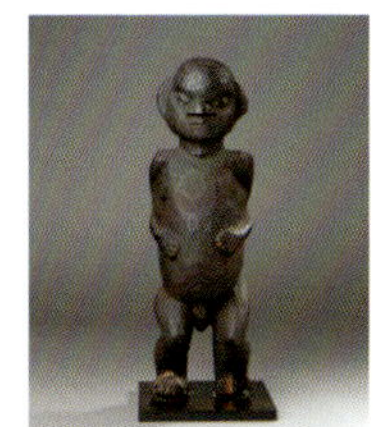
Figurine
Wood
Purchased from a private collector in Kinshasa in 1986
H. 36.9 cm, W. 13 cm, D. 12.9 cm
ROM 2009.126.268

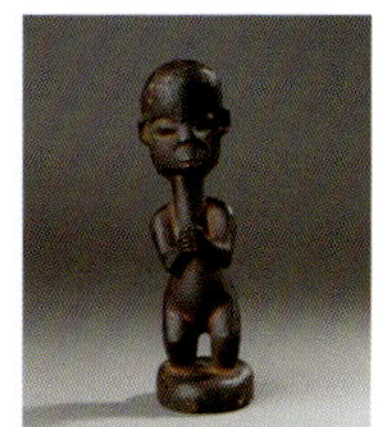
Figurine
Wood
Purchased from a private collector in Kinshasa in 1986
H. 23.5 cm, W. 7 cm, D. 7.8 cm
ROM 2009.126.269

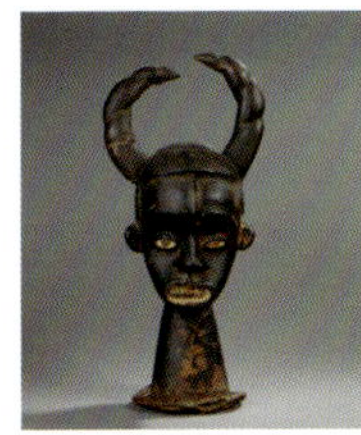
Headcrest
Wood, leather, fiber
Ejagham style
Purchased from a private collector in Kinshasa in 1987
H. 51.2 cm, W. 24 cm, D. 17 cm
ROM 2009.126.210

Zimbabwe (1994)

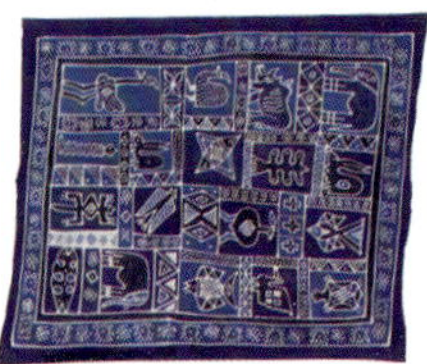

Textile
Cotton
Purchased in Zimbabwe in 1994
L. 189.4 cm, W. 156 cm
ROM 2009.126.233

Kenya (1964–1983)

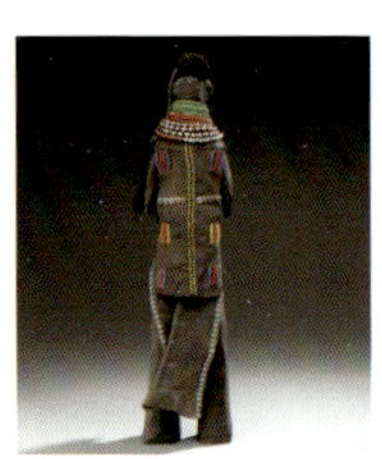

Doll
Wood, glass beads, leather, metal, hair
Maasai style
Purchased in Nairobi in 1964
H. 44 cm, W. 11 cm, D. 6.2 cm
ROM 2009.126.119

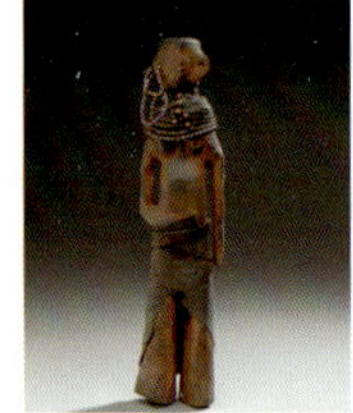

Doll
Wood, glass beads, leather, metal, hair
Turkana style
Purchased in Nairobi in 1964
H. 34.7 cm, W. 9 cm, D. 6 cm
ROM 2009.126.120

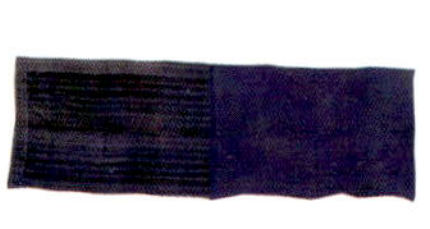

Cloth
Cotton
Turkana style
Purchased in Nairobi in 1964
L. 214 cm, W. 79 cm
ROM 2009.126.228

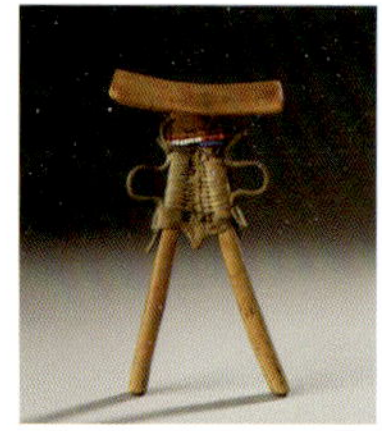

Headrest
Wood, leather, glass beads
Pokot or Turkana style
Purchased from a gallery in Nairobi in 1964
H. 19.5 cm, W. 10.4 cm, D. 5.7 cm
ROM 2009.126.39

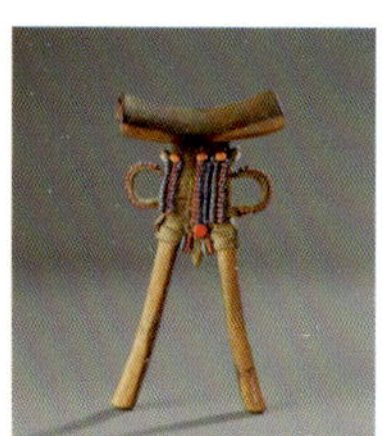

Headrest
Wood, leather, glass beads
Pokot or Turkana style
Purchased from a gallery in Nairobi in 1964
H. 20.3 cm, W. 10.5 cm, D. 5.4 cm
ROM 2009.126.40

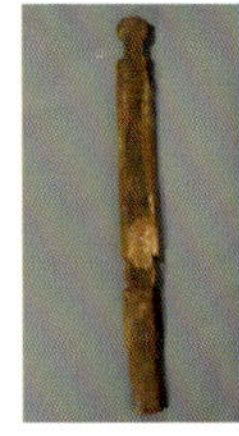

Grave post
Wood
Giriama style
Purchased in Nairobi in 1983
H. 199 cm, W. 20 cm, D. 6 cm
ROM 2009.126.319

Ethiopia (1964–1966)

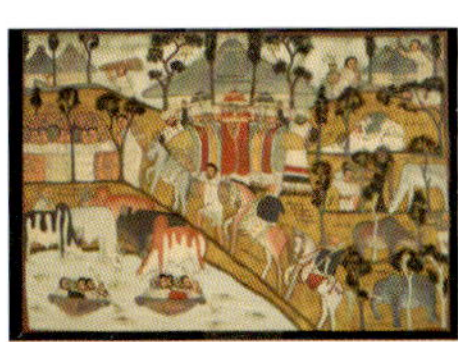

Painting
Oil on canvas
Marqos Jembere (b. 1958)
Received as a gift, date unrecorded
H. 81.9 cm, W. 118.7 cm
ROM 2009.126.306

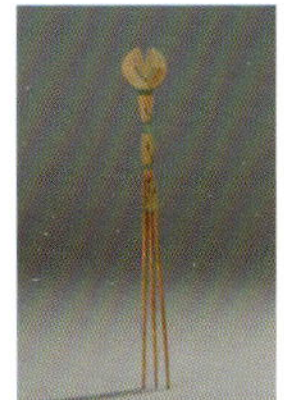

Comb
Wood
Galla style
Received as a gift in 1964
H. 24 cm, W. 3.2 cm, D. 0.8 cm
ROM 2009.126.273

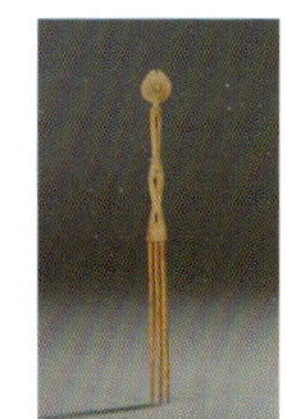

Comb
Wood
Galla style
Received as a gift in 1964
H. 23 cm, W. 2.1 cm, D. 0.4 cm
ROM 2009.126.274

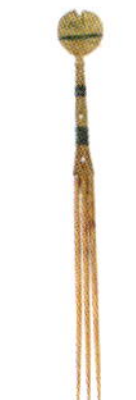

Comb
Wood
Galla style
Received as a gift in 1964
H. 23 cm, W. 2.9 cm, D. 0.5 cm
ROM 2009.126.275

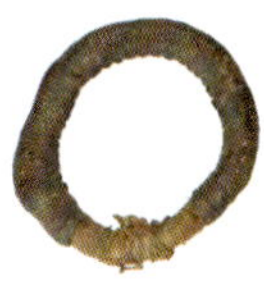

Bracelet
Fiber, snakeskin, cloth
Received as a gift in 1964
H. 3.7 cm, Diam. 12.5 cm
ROM 2009.126.284

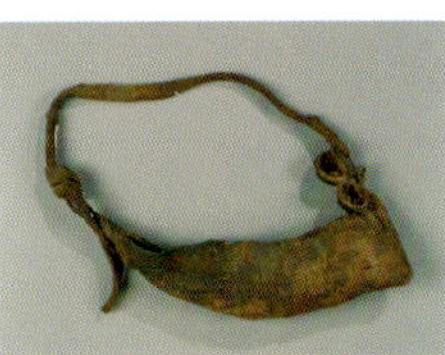

Pouch
Leather, metal
Received as a gift in 1964
H. 6.3 cm, W. 24 cm, L. 39.6 cm
ROM 2009.126.285

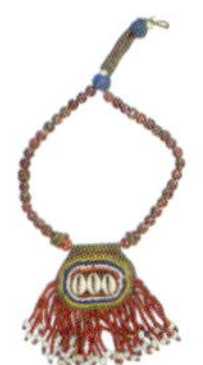

Necklace
Fiber, glass beads, leather, metal
Sidama style
Received as a gift in 1964
H. 44 cm, W. 15.5 cm, D. 2 cm
ROM 2009.126.371

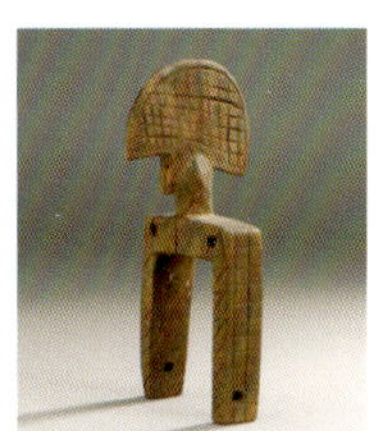

Heddle pulley
Wood
Morai style
Purchased in Addis Ababa in 1966
H. 19 cm, W. 7.7 cm, D. 8.5 cm
ROM 2009.126.305

Europe and North America (1959–2004)

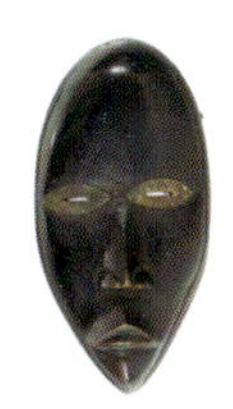

Mask
Wood, metal
Dan style
Purchased from a gallery in Paris in 1959
H. 21.7 cm, W. 11.2 cm, D. 7 cm
ROM 2009.126.169

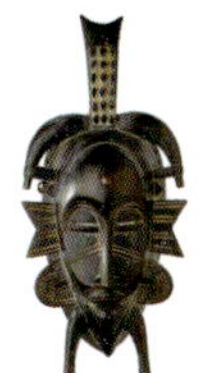

Mask
Wood
Senufo style
Purchased from a gallery in Paris in 1970
H. 32.5 cm, W. 14.7 cm, D. 7.2 cm
ROM 2009.126.184

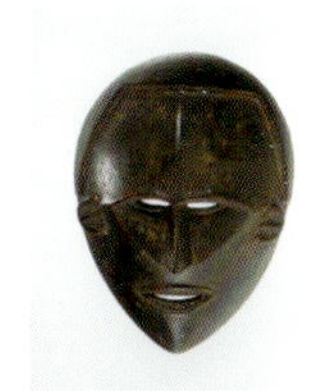

Mask
Wood
Purchased from a gallery in Paris in 1978
H. 21.5 cm, W. 16.4 cm, D. 8.5 cm
ROM 2009.126.139

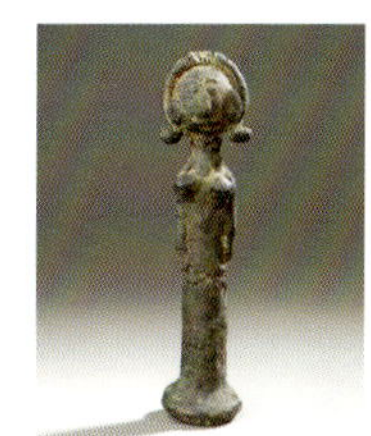

Doll
Clay, wood
Bamana style
Purchased from a gallery in Paris in 1988
H. 25.6 cm, W. 6.8 cm, D. 7 cm
ROM 2009.126.72

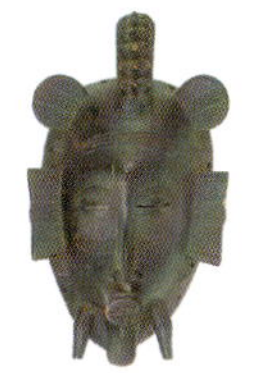

Mask
Wood
Senufo style
Purchased from a gallery in Amsterdam in 1975
H. 25.6 cm, W. 15.2 cm, D. 7 cm
ROM 2009.126.185

Europe and North America (1959–2004)

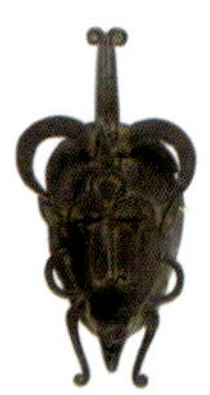
Mask
Brass
Senufo style
Purchased from a gallery in Amsterdam in 1975
H. 30.4 cm, W. 15.7 cm, D. 7.6 cm
ROM 2009.126.188

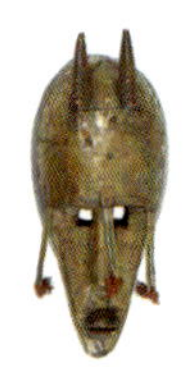
Mask
Wood, metal, cloth
Marka or Sorogo style
Purchased from an African dealer in Montreal in 1982
H 32.5 cm, W. 15.3 cm, D. 14.3 cm
ROM 2009.126.145

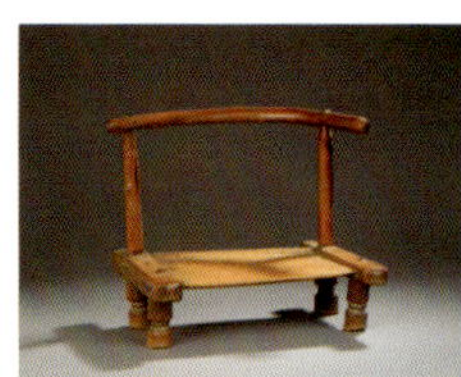
Chair
Wood
Dan or Bété style
Purchased from an African dealer in Montreal in 1982
H. 32 cm, W. 37 cm, D. 27 cm
ROM 2009.126.17

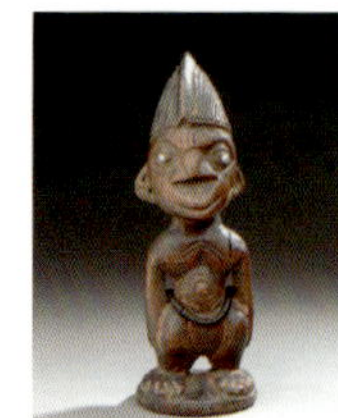
Twin figure
Wood, glass beads, metal
Yoruba style
Purchased from an African dealer in Montreal in the mid-1980s
H. 26.3 cm, W. 9.3 cm, D. 9 cm
ROM 2009.126.107

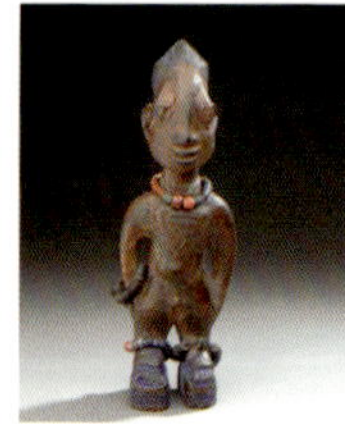
Twin figure
Wood, glass beads, coconut shell
Yoruba style
Purchased from an African dealer in Montreal in the mid-1980s
H. 26.3 cm, W. 8.5 cm, D. 7.5 cm
ROM 2009.126.108

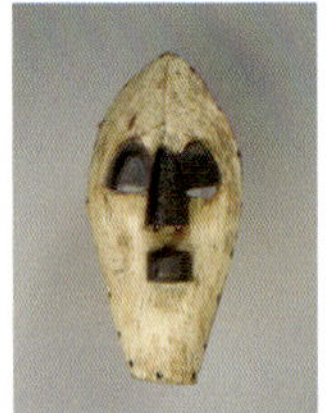
Mask
Wood, pigment
Songye style
Purchased from an African dealer in Montreal in the mid-1980s
H. 39.1 cm, W. 19.5 cm, D. 9.9 cm
ROM 2009.126.217

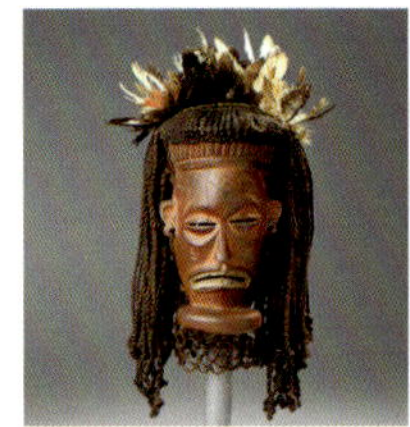
Mask
Wood, fiber, raffia, feathers, metal
Chokwe style
Purchased from an African dealer in Montreal in the mid-1980s
H. 42 cm, W. 29 cm, D. 23 cm
ROM 2009.126.220

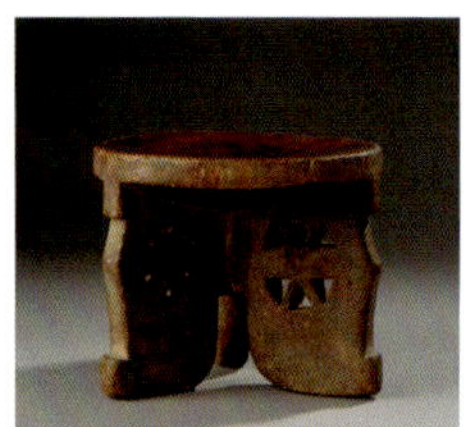
Stool
Wood
Kamba style
Purchased from an African dealer in Montreal in the mid-1980s
H. 16.3 cm, Diam. 20 cm
ROM 2009.126.29

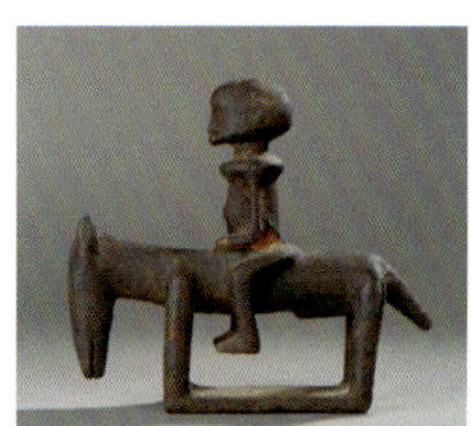
Rider figure
Wood
Dogon style
Purchased from an African dealer in Montreal in 1987
H. 22 cm, W. 5 cm, D. 25.5 cm
ROM 2009.126.279

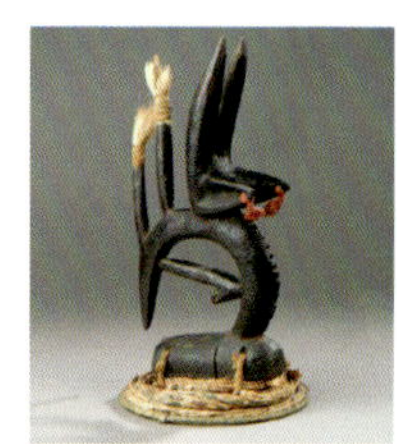
Headcrest
Wood, fiber
Bamana style
Purchased from an African dealer in Montreal in 1988
H 32.5 cm, Diam. 17.5 cm
ROM 2009.126.140

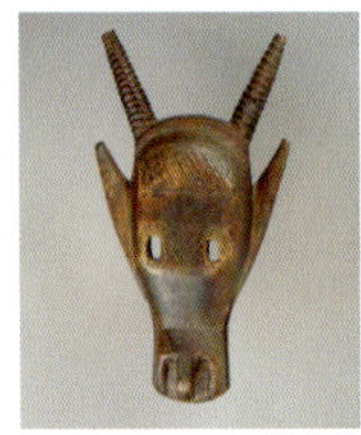
Mask
Wood
Purchased from an African dealer in Montreal in 1988
H. 43 cm, W. 24.5 cm, D. 9 cm
ROM 2009.126.194

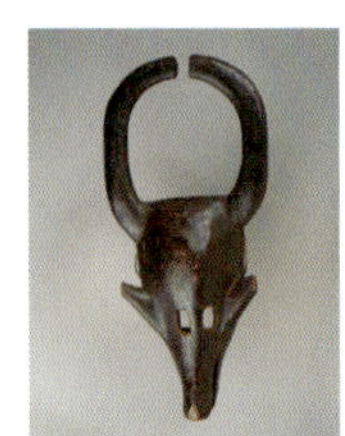
Mask
Wood
Purchased from an African dealer in Montreal in 1988
H. 61 cm, W. 30 cm, D. 11.5 cm
ROM 2009.126.195

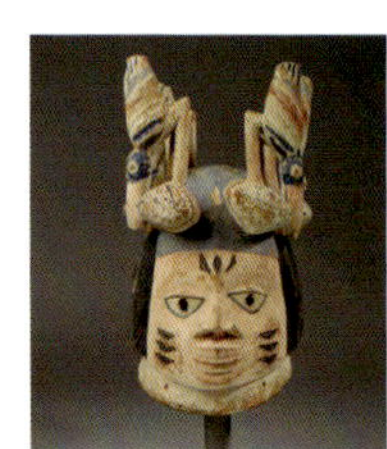
Gelede Mask
Wood, pigment
Yoruba style
Purchased from an African dealer in Montreal in 1988
H. 38.8 cm, W. 23.9 cm, D. 35.2 cm
ROM 2009.126.202

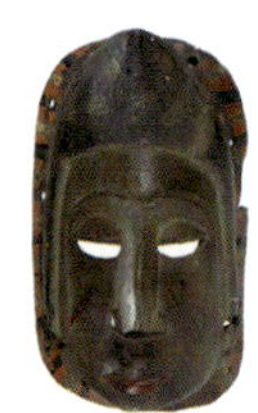
Mask
Wood
Ibibio style
Purchased from an African dealer in Montreal in 1988
H. 21.6 cm, W. 13.3 cm, D. 7 cm
ROM 2009.126.203

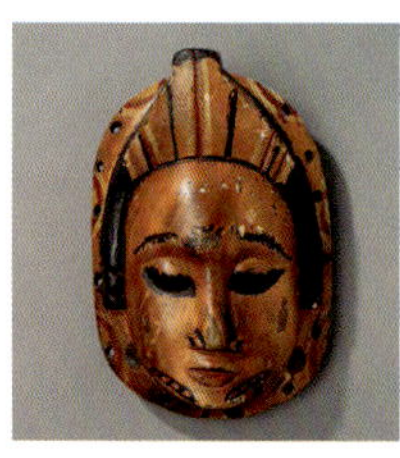
Mask
Wood, pigment
Ibibio style
Purchased from an African dealer in Montreal in 1988
H. 22.7 cm, W. 15.6 cm, D. 6.4 cm
ROM 2009.126.204

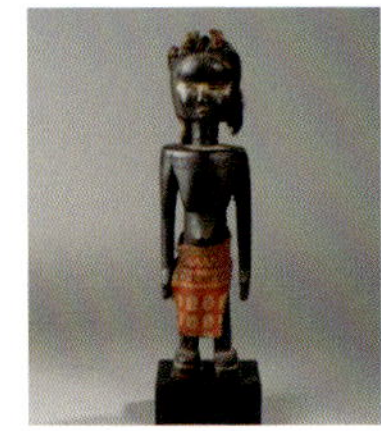
Figure
Wood, cloth
Dan or Bassa style
Purchased from an African dealer in Montreal in 1988
H. 41 cm, W. 11.8 cm, D. 10.5 cm
ROM 2009.126.257

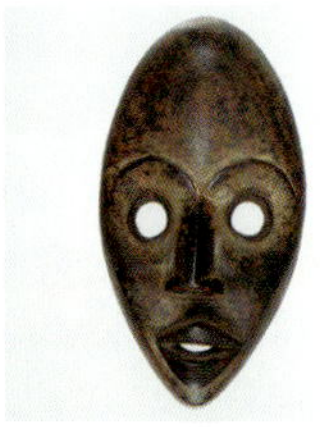
Mask
Wood
Dan style
Purchased from an African dealer in Montreal in 1989
H. 24.7 cm, W. 13.8 cm, D. 7.9 cm
ROM 2009.126.171

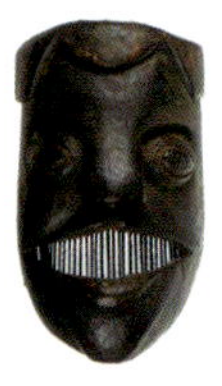
Mask
Wood
Ogoni style
Purchased from an African dealer in Montreal in 1989
H 32.2 cm, W. 19.5 cm, D. 12.5 cm
ROM 2009.126.208

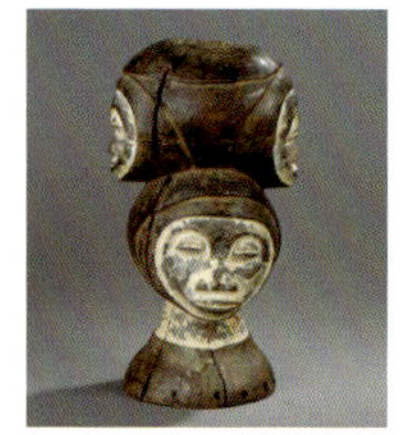
Mask
Wood, pigment
Idoma style
Purchased from an African dealer in Montreal in 1989
H. 37.8 cm, W. 17.5 cm, D. 20.5 cm
ROM 2009.126.209

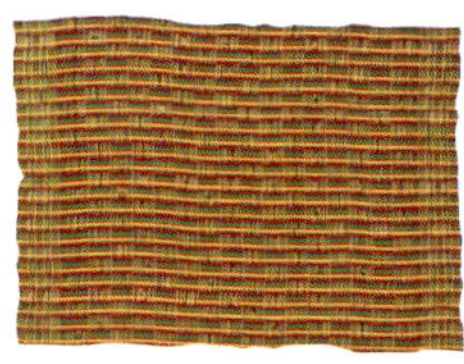
Kente cloth
Silk
Asante style
Purchased from an African dealer in Montreal in 1989
L. 302 cm, W. 216 cm
ROM 2009.126.227

Europe and North America (1959–2004)

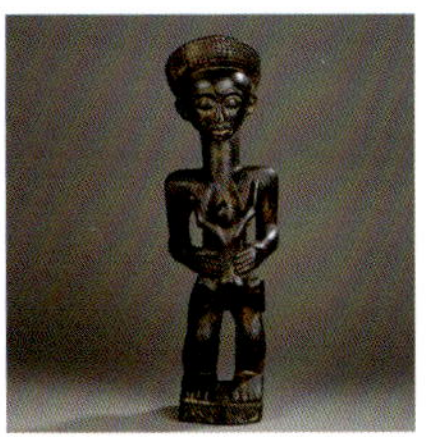
Figure
Wood
Chokwe style
Purchased from an African dealer in Montreal in 1991
H. 53 cm, W. 17 cm, D. 14 cm
ROM 2009.126.68

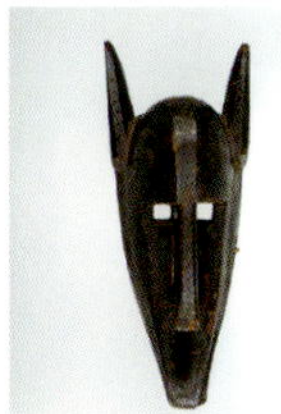
Mask
Wood, fiber
Bamana style
Purchased from an African dealer in Montreal in 1993
H. 38 cm, W. 14.6 cm, D. 15 cm
ROM 2009.126.142

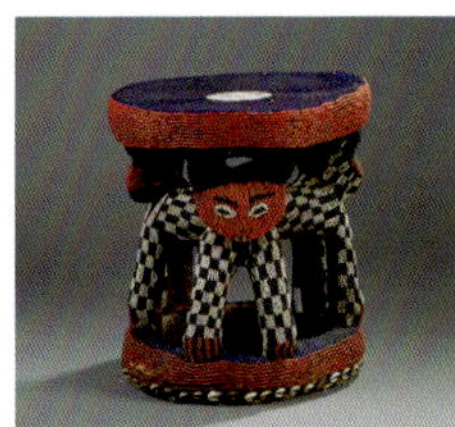
Stool
Wood, glass beads, cowrie shells, burlap
Bamiléké style
Purchased from a private collector in Montreal in 1983
H. 36 cm, Diam. 33 cm
ROM 2009.126.25

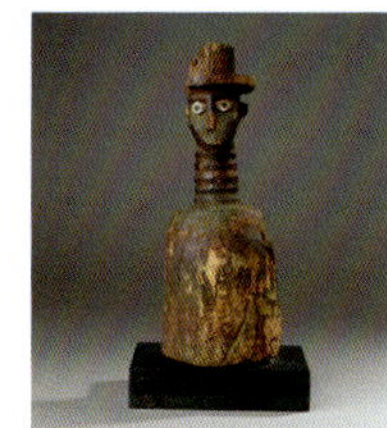
Figure
Wood, metal
Bijago style
Purchased from a private collector in Montreal in 1988
H. 31 cm, W. 12 cm, D. 11 cm
ROM 2009.126.256

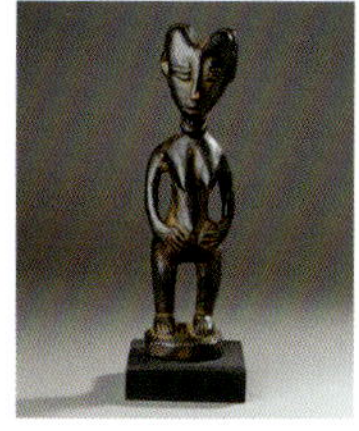
Figure
Wood
Fante style
Purchased from an auction house in Montreal in the mid-1980s
H. 27.5 cm, W. 8 cm, D. 6.5 cm
ROM 2009.126.258

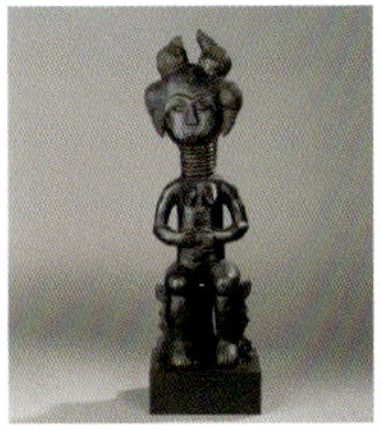
Figure
Wood
Asante style
Purchased from an auction house in Montreal in 1983
H. 48 cm, W. 14.5 cm, D. 11 cm
ROM 2009.126.259

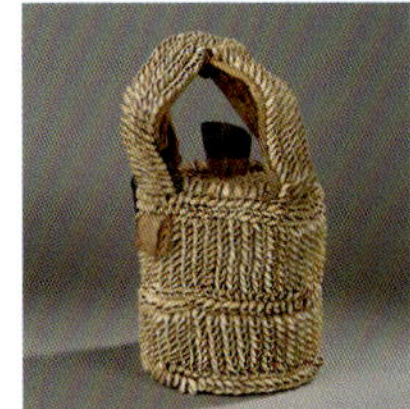
House of the head
Leather, cowrie shells, fiber
Yoruba style
Purchased from an auction house in Montreal in 1986
H. 37.5 cm, Diam. 23.3 cm
ROM 2009.126.292

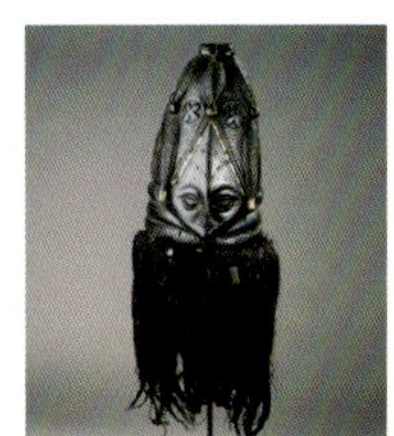
Mask
Wood, fiber, metal
Mende style
Purchased from an auction house in Montreal in 1988
H. 71.4 cm, Diam. 33.4 cm
ROM 2009.126.160

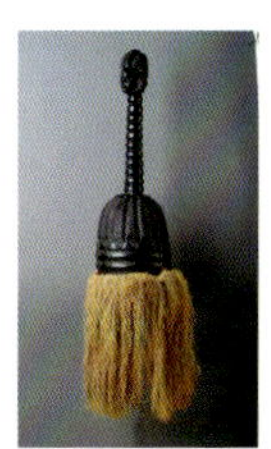
Helmet mask
Wood, raffia
Mende or Gola style
Purchased from an auction house in Montreal in 1988
H. 110 cm, Diam. 35 cm
ROM 2009.126.161

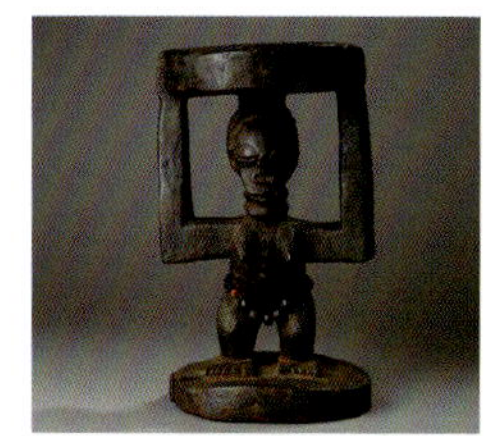
Caryatid stool
Wood, glass beads, fiber
Songye style
Purchased from an auction house in Montreal in 1988
H. 42.5 cm, W. 26 cm, D. 24 cm
ROM 2009.126.30

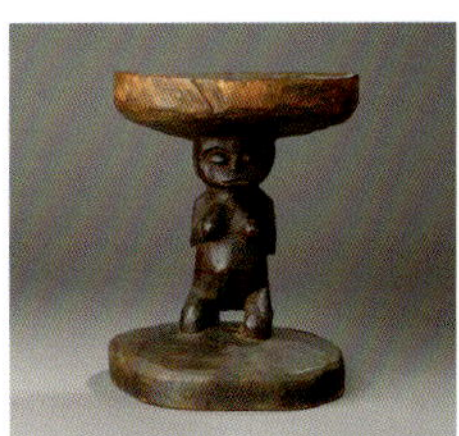
Caryatid stool
Wood
Purchased from an auction house in Montreal in 1990
H. 31.5 cm, W. 25 cm, D. 26 cm
ROM 2009.126.31

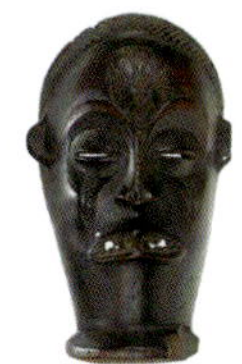
Mask
Wood
Chokwe style
Purchased from Galerie des 5 Continents, Montreal, in the mid-1980s
H. 24 cm, W. 15 cm, D. 9 cm
ROM 2009.126.218

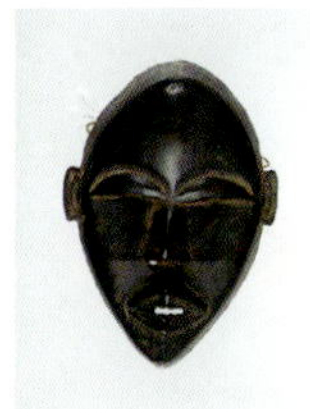
Mask
Wood
Dan style
Purchased from Galerie des 5 Continents, Montreal, in 1987
H. 24 cm, W. 17.1 cm, D. 7.9 cm
ROM 2009.126.170

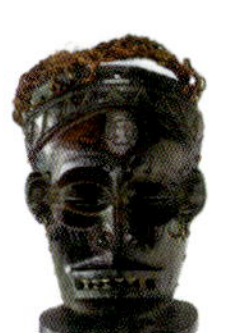
Mask
Wood, fiber, metal
Chokwe style
Purchased from Galerie des 5 Continents, Montreal, in the late 1980s
H. 30.5 cm, W. 17 cm, D. 17 cm
ROM 2009.126.219

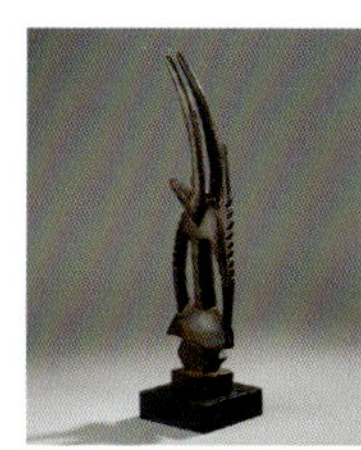
Headcrest
Wood
Bamana style
Purchased from Lippel Gallery, Montreal, in the mid-1980s
H. 48.5 cm, W. 5.7 cm, D. 13.8 cm
ROM 2009.126.141

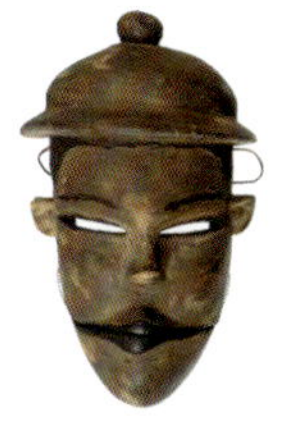
Mask
Wood, fiber, pigment
Ogoni style
Purchased from Lippel Gallery, Montreal, in 1988
H. 22 cm, W. 13.3 cm, D. 10.5 cm
ROM 2009.126.207

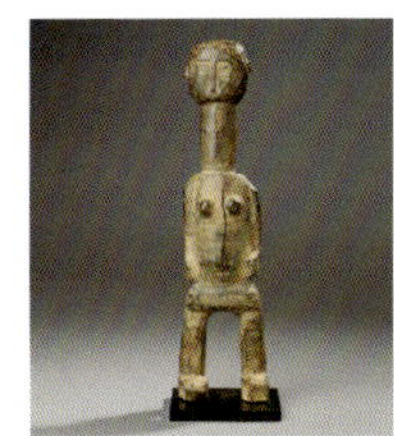
Figure
Wood
Purchased from Lippel Gallery, Montreal, in 1988
H. 41.5 cm, W. 10.7 cm, D. 8.6 cm
ROM 2009.126.253

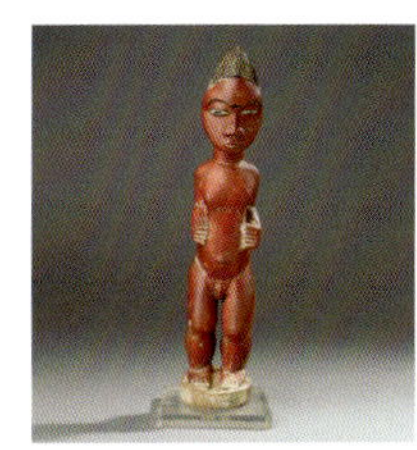
Figure
Wood
Baule style
Purchased from Lippel Gallery, Montreal, in 1988
H. 33.2 cm, W. 7 cm, D. 9.7 cm
ROM 2009.126.254

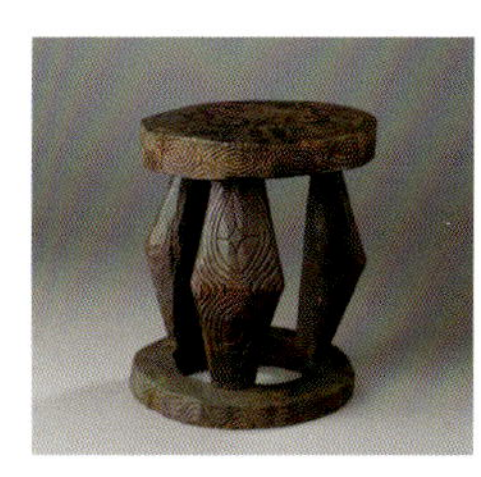
Stool
Wood
Bamum style
Purchased from Giraffe Gallery, Montreal, in 1988
H. 29.1 cm, Diam. 26.2 cm
ROM 009.126.26

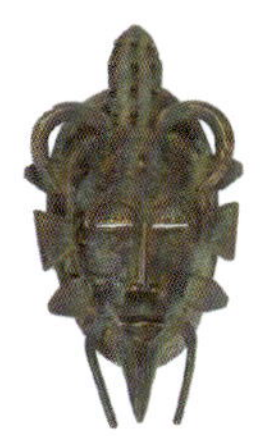
Mask
Brass
Senufo style
Purchased from Giraffe Gallery, Montreal, in 1990
H. 29 cm, W. 16.6 cm, D. 7.2 cm
ROM 2009.126.189

Europe and North America (1959–2004)

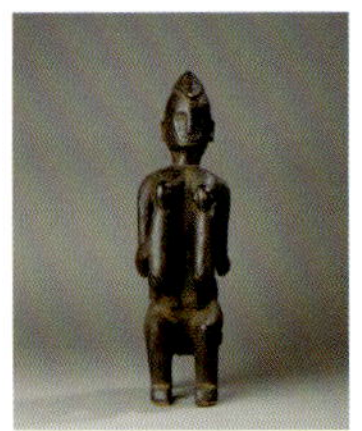
Mother and children figure
Wood
Dogon style
Purchased from Giraffe Gallery, Montreal, in 1990
H. 53 cm, W. 15 cm, D. 14.5 cm
ROM 2009.126.45

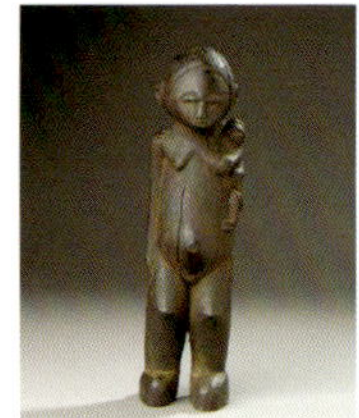
Mother and child figure
Wood
Lobi style
Purchased from Giraffe Gallery, Montreal, in the early 1990s
H. 28 cm, W. 8 cm, D. 8 cm
ROM 2009.126.47

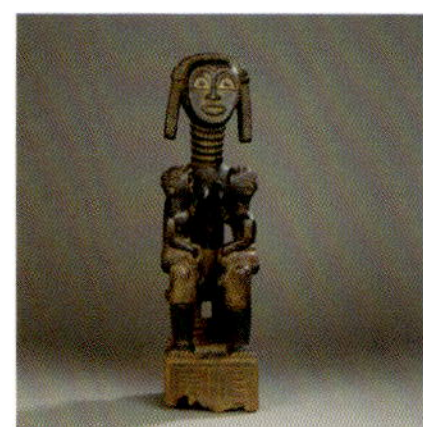
Mother and children figure
Wood
Anyi style
Purchased from Giraffe Gallery, Montreal, in 1996
H. 43 cm, W. 12 cm, D. 12.5 cm
ROM 2009.126.57

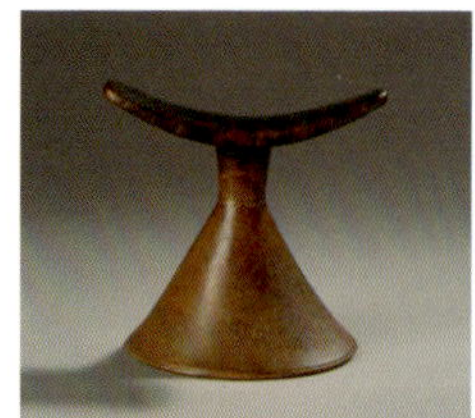
Headrest
Wood
Kaffa(?) style
Purchased from Giraffe Gallery, Montreal, in 2001
H. 15.3 cm, W. 16 cm, D. 13.5 cm
ROM 2009.126.34

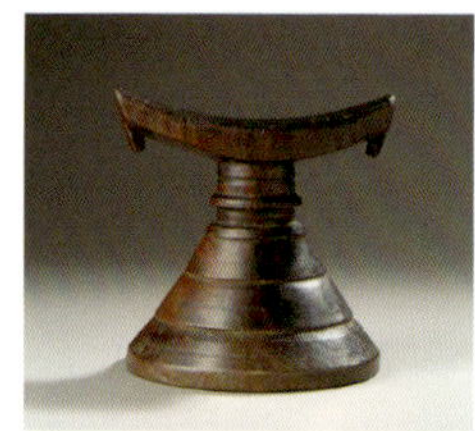
Headrest
Wood
Kaffa(?) style
Purchased from Giraffe Gallery, Montreal, in 2001
H. 17 cm, W. 17.2 cm, D. 16 cm
ROM 2009.126.35

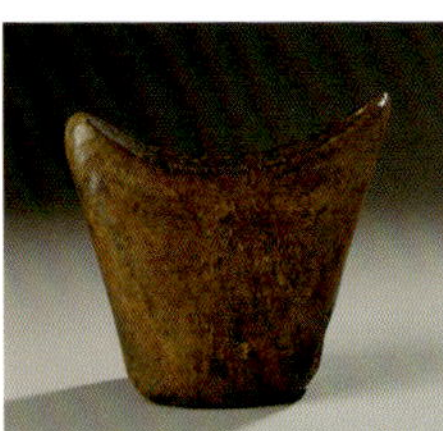
Headrest
Wood
Sidamo(?) style
Purchased from Giraffe Gallery, Montreal, in 2001
H. 15 cm, W. 17.2 cm, D. 8.7 cm
ROM 2009.126.36

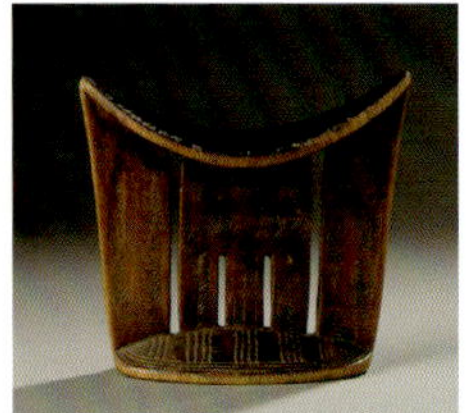
Headrest
Wood
Kambatta style
Purchased from Giraffe Gallery, Montreal, in 2001
H. 18.3 cm, W. 20.3 cm, D. 7.6 cm
ROM 2009.126.37

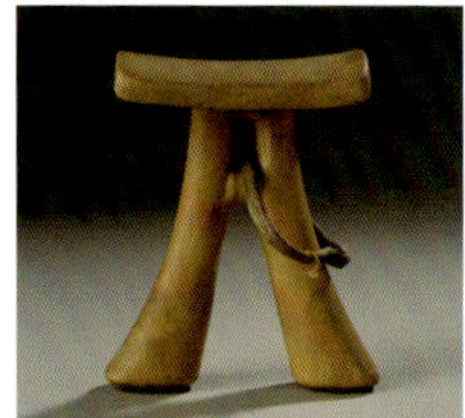
Headrest
Wood, leather
Pokot style
Purchased from Giraffe Gallery, Montreal, in 2001
H. 15.5 cm, W. 13.3 cm, D. 6.3 cm
ROM 2009.126.38

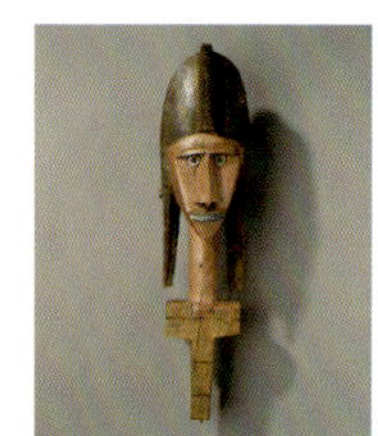
Puppet head
Wood, pigment
Bamana style
Purchased from a New York gallery in 1983
H. 49 cm, W. 11.2 cm, D. 10 cm
ROM 2009.126.1

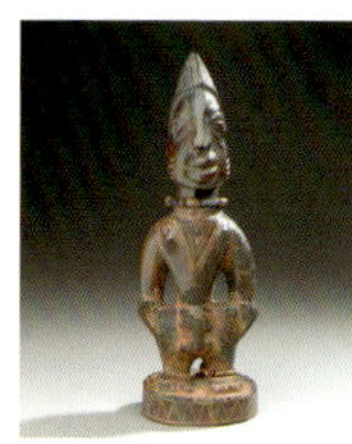
Twin figure
Wood, glass beads
Yoruba style
Purchased from a New York gallery in the mid-1980s
H. 27 cm, W. 9 cm, D. 9 cm
ROM 2009.126.106.1

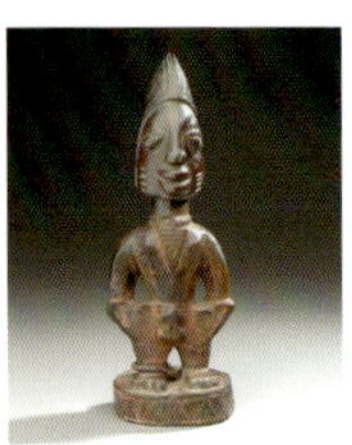
Twin figure
Wood, glass beads
Yoruba style
Purchased from a New York gallery in the mid-1980s
H. 26.5 cm, W. 9.3 cm, D. 9 cm
ROM 2009.126.106.2

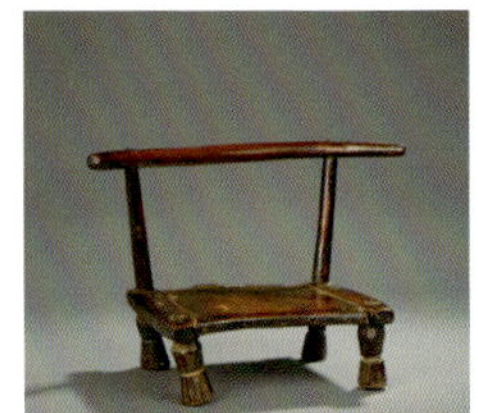
Chair
Wood
Dan style
Purchased from a New York gallery in the mid-1980s
H. 28 cm, W. 44 cm, D. 25.5 cm
ROM 2009.126.16

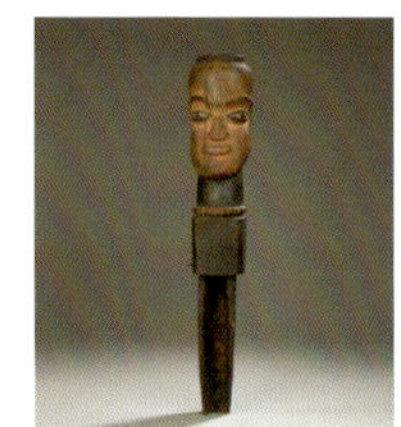
Puppet head
Wood, pigment
Ibibio style
Purchased from a New York gallery in the mid-1980s
H. 56.3 cm, W. 11 cm, D. 10.9 cm
ROM 2009.126.7

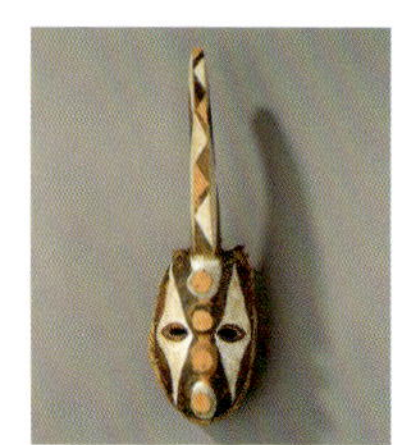
Mask
Wood, raffia, pigment
Afikpo style
Purchased from a New York gallery in 1985
H. 38.2 cm, W. 10.6 cm, D. 12 cm
ROM 2009.126.205

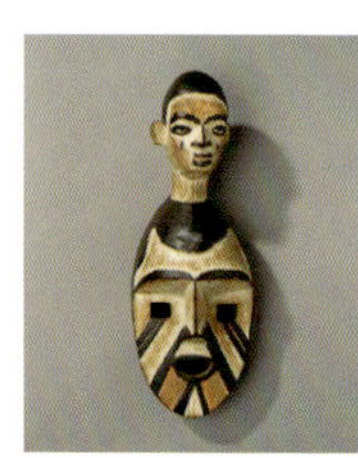
Mask
Wood, raffia, pigment
Afikpo style
Purchased from a New York gallery in 1985
H. 30.8 cm, W. 11.7 cm, D. 7.3 cm
ROM 2009.126.206

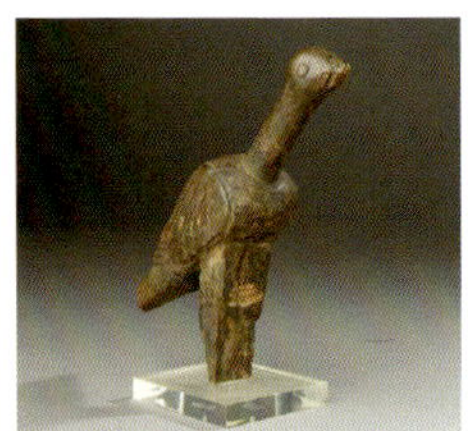
Bird figure
Wood
Lobi style
Purchased from a New York gallery in 1985
H. 17.9 cm, W. 5.1 cm, D. 16.5 cm
ROM 2009.126.307

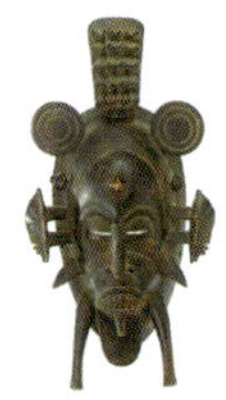
Mask
Wood
Senufo style
Purchased from a gallery in Amsterdam in 1975
H. 33.5 cm, W. 18 cm, D. 9 cm
ROM 2009.126.186

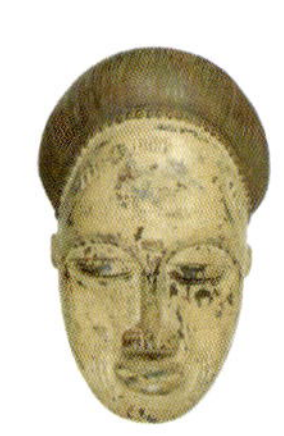
Mask
Wood, pigment
Baule style
Purchased from a New York gallery in the late 1980s
H. 33.3 cm, W. 21.3 cm, D. 12 cm
ROM 2009.126.181

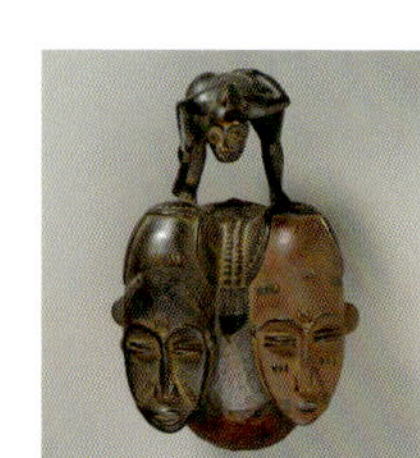
Mask surmounted by figure
Wood, pigment
Baule style
Purchased from a New York gallery in the late 1980s
H. 45 cm, W. 29 cm, D. 22 cm
ROM 2009.126.182

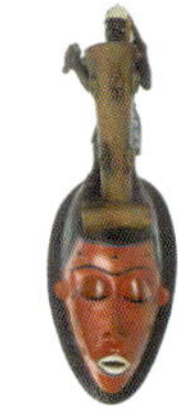
Mask surmounted by figure
Wood, pigment
Yaure or Baule style
Purchased from a New York gallery in 1990
H. 50 cm, W. 15.5 cm, D. 12.5 cm
ROM 2009.126.180

Europe and North America (1959–2004)

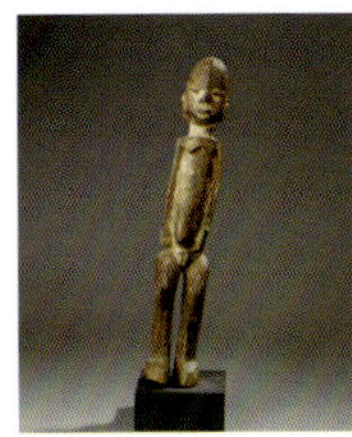
Figure
Wood
Lobi style
Purchased from Craft Caravan Gallery, New York, in 1983
H. 53 cm, W. 9 cm, D. 8.5 cm
ROM 2009.126.242.1

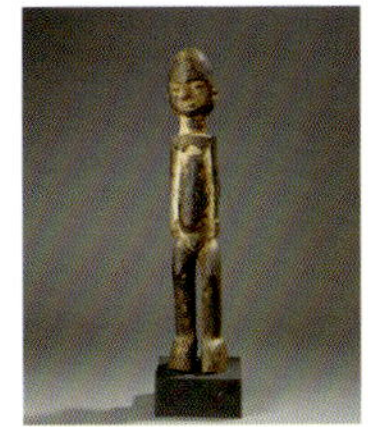
Figure
Wood
Lobi style
Purchased from Craft Caravan Gallery, New York, in 1983
H. 54 cm, W. 10 cm, D. 10.5 cm
ROM 2009.126.242.2

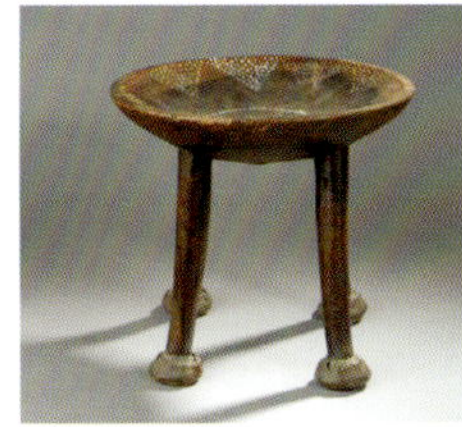
Stool
Wood, glass beads, leather
Luo style
Purchased from Craft Caravan Gallery, New York, in 1983
H. 34.2 cm, Diam. 39.4 cm
ROM 2009.126.27

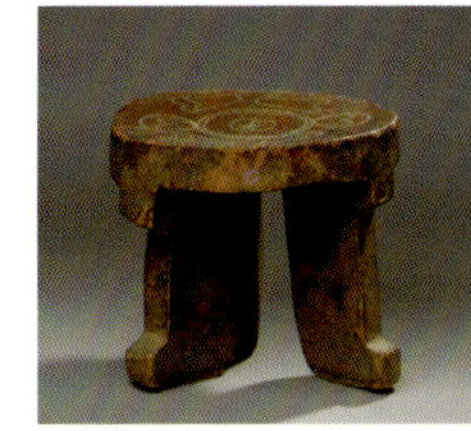
Stool
Wood, brass
Kamba style
Purchased from Craft Caravan Gallery, New York, in 1983
H. 31 cm, W. 34.5 cm, D. 28 cm
ROM 2009.126.28

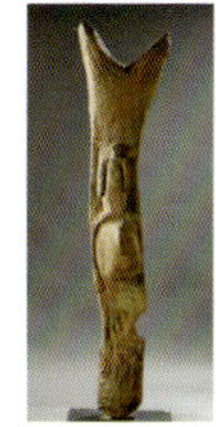
Architectural post
Wood
Dogon style
Purchased from Craft Caravan Gallery, New York, in 1983
H. 187 cm, W. 46 cm, D. 37 cm
ROM 2009.126.310

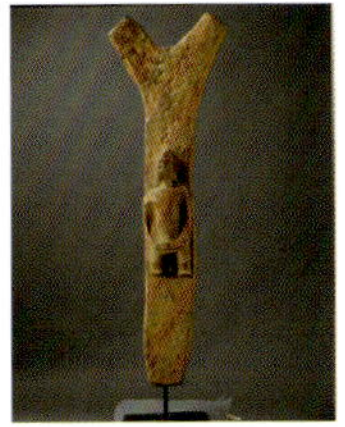
Architectural post
Wood
Dogon style
Purchased from Craft Caravan Gallery, New York, in 1983
H. 182 cm, W. 59 cm, D. 25.5 cm
ROM 2009.126.311

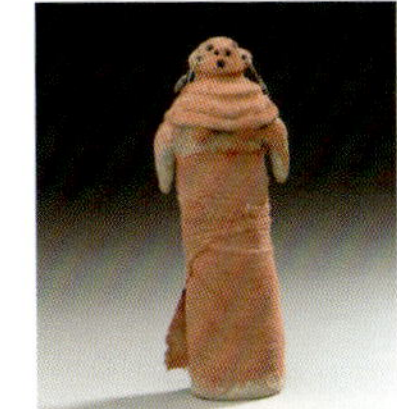
Doll
Clay, cloth, glass beads, metal, pigment
Turkana style
Purchased from Craft Caravan Gallery, New York, in 1984–5
H. 15.5 cm, W. 6 cm, D. 4 cm
ROM 2009.126.121

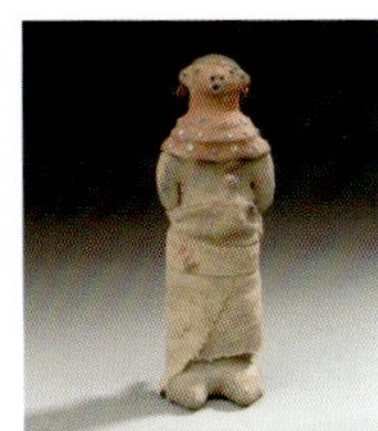
Doll
Clay, cloth, glass beads, metal, pigment
Turkana style
Purchased from Craft Caravan Gallery, New York, in 1984–5
H. 15.5 cm, W. 5.2 cm, D. 6 cm
ROM 2009.126.122

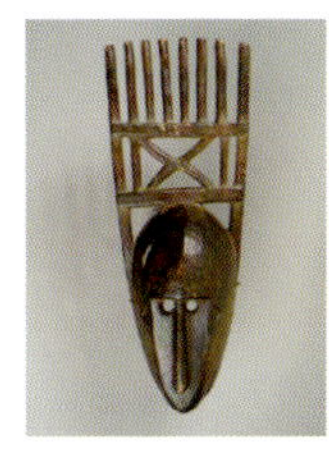
Mask
Wood
Bamana style
Purchased from Craft Caravan Gallery, New York, in 1984–5
H. 53.5 cm, W. 20.5 cm, D. 11.2 cm
ROM 2009.126.143

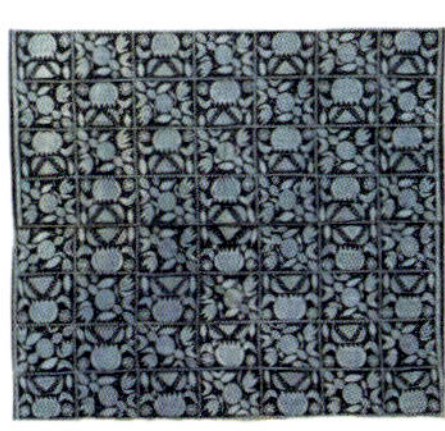
Adire cloth
Cotton
Yoruba style
Purchased from Craft Caravan Gallery, New York, in 1985
L. 196 cm, W. 170 cm
ROM 2009.126.229

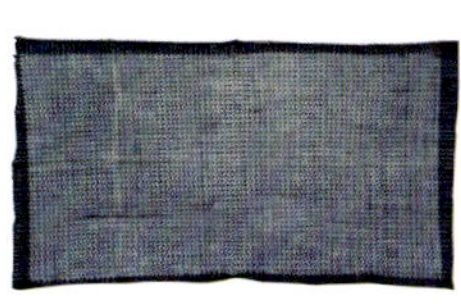
Adire cloth
Cotton
Yoruba style
Purchased from Craft Caravan Gallery, New York, in 1985
L. 151 cm, W. 82.5 cm
ROM 2009.126.230

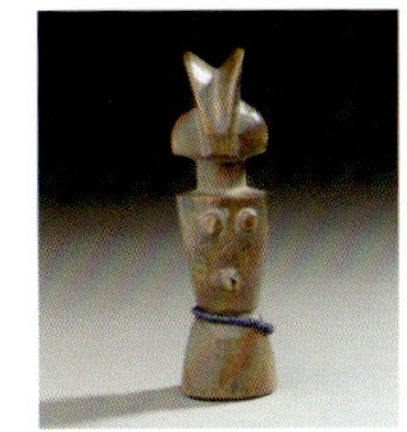
Doll
Wood
Zaramo style
Purchased from Kahan Gallery, New York, in 1993
H. 10.5 cm, W. 3 cm, D. 3.5 cm
ROM 2009.126.123

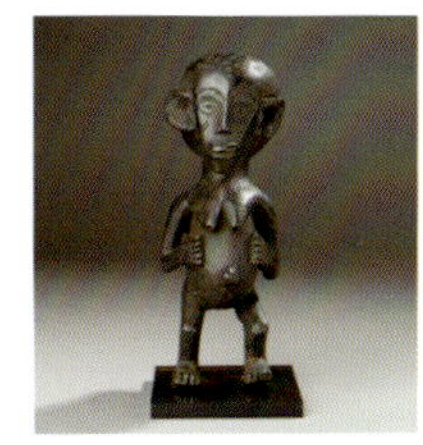
Figure
Wood
Purchased from Kahan Gallery, New York, in the mid-1980s
H. 25.3 cm, W. 9.8 cm, D. 11 cm
ROM 2009.126.267

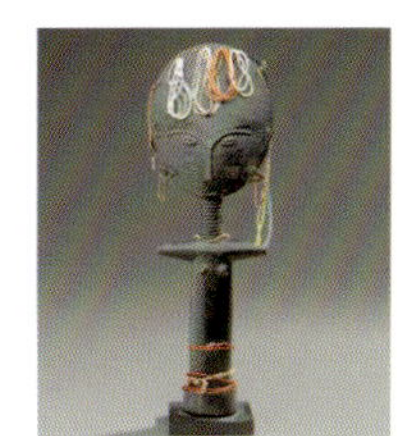
Doll
Wood, fiber, glass beads
Asante style
Purchased from Kahan Gallery, New York, in 1985
H. 25 cm, W. 8.9 cm, D. 5 cm
ROM 2009.126.97

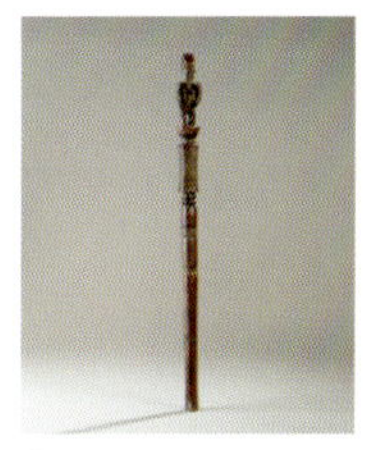
Staff
Wood
Zaramo style
Purchased from Kahan Gallery, New York, in 1993
H. 53 cm, W. 4 cm, D. 2.5 cm
ROM 2009.126.135

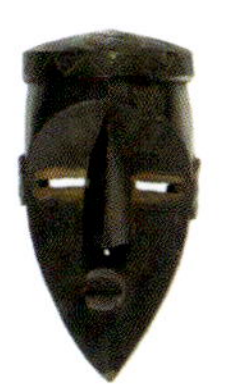
Mask
Wood
Lwalu style
Purchased from Kahan Gallery, New York, in the mid-1980s
H. 31.7 cm, W. 16.9 cm, D. 16.3 cm
ROM 2009.126.216

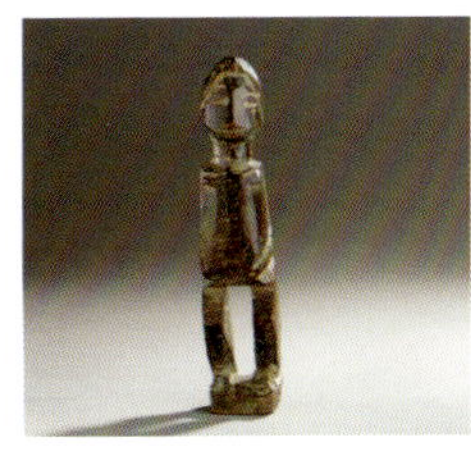
Figure
Wood
Limba style
Purchased from Kahan Gallery, New York, in 1986
H. 21 cm, W. 4.5 cm, D. 4 cm
ROM 2009.126.89

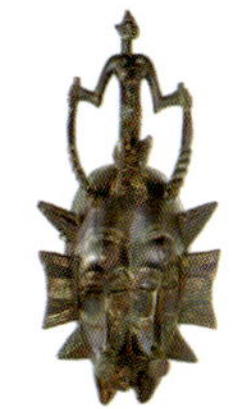
Mask
Wood
Senufo style
Purchased from Tribal Art Gallery, New York, in 1982
H. 40.7 cm, W. 19.6 cm, D. 8.8 cm
ROM 2009.126.187

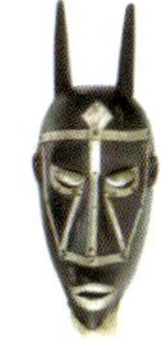
Mask
Wood, metal
Marka or Sorogo style
Purchased from Tribal Art Gallery, New York, in 1987
H. 33.5 cm, W. 13.5 cm, D. 9.3 cm
ROM 2009.126.146

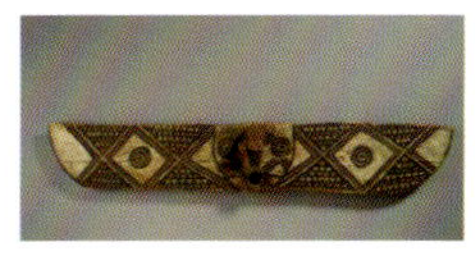
Butterfly mask
Wood, pigment
Bwa style
Purchased from Tribal Art Gallery, New York, in the mid-1980s
H. 23 cm, W. 136 cm, D. 17.3 cm
ROM 2009.126.153

Europe and North America (1959–2004)

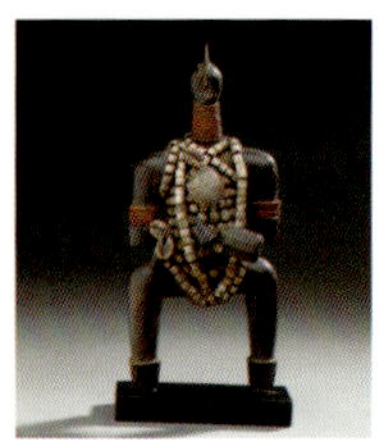
Doll
Wood, leather, shells, glass beads, seeds, bone
Namji style
Purchased from Hamill Gallery, Boston, in 2004
H. 27.1 cm, W. 12.8 cm, D. 10.8 cm
ROM 2009.126.111

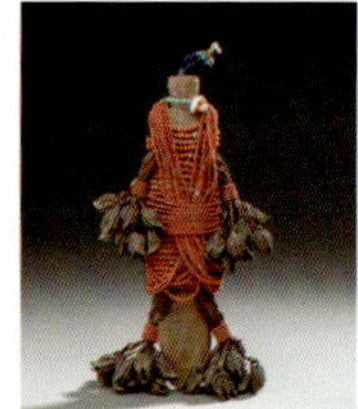
Doll
Wood, leather, shells, glass beads, seeds, bone
Purchased from Hamill Gallery, Boston, in 2004
H. 30.6 cm, W. 17 cm, D. 5.8 cm
ROM 2009.126.124

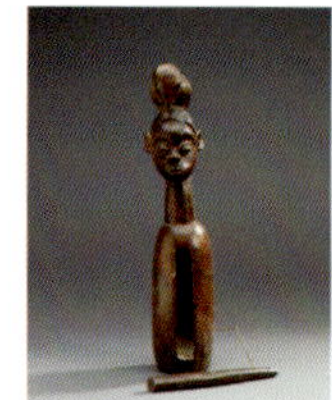
Slit drum
Wood
Yaka style
Purchased from Hamill Gallery, Boston, in 2004
H. 36.1 cm, W. 8 cm, D. 8.5 cm
ROM 2009.126.224

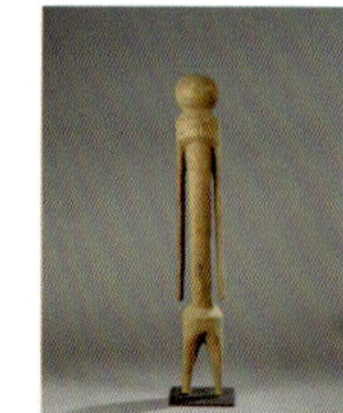
Figure
Wood
Moba style
Purchased from Hamill Gallery, Boston, in 2004
H. 86.5 cm, W. 14.5 cm, D. 14 cm
ROM 2009.126.260

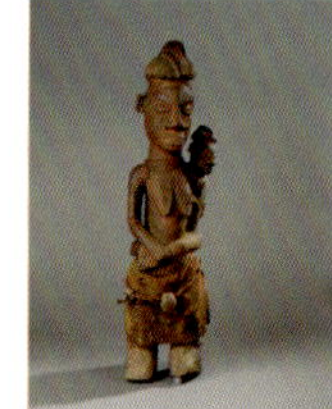
Mother and child figure
Wood, cloth, shells, fiber, pigment
Yaka(?) style
Purchased from Hamill Gallery, Boston, in 2004
H. 80.5 cm, W. 24 cm, D. 23 cm
ROM 2009.126.70

Unrecorded Place and Date of Acquisition

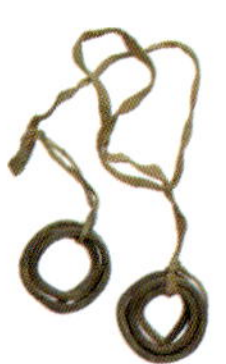
Ear ornament
Brass, leather
Maasai style
L. 57 cm, W. 3.7 cm
ROM 2009.126.255

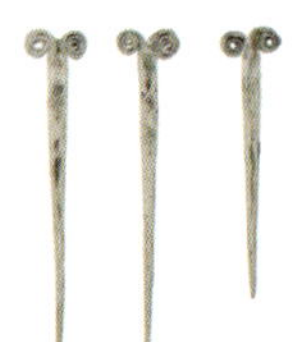
Hairpins
Aluminum
min L. 6 cm, max L. 11.8 cm
ROM 2009.126.320–337

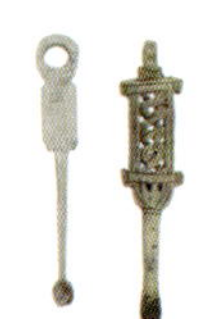
Ear spoon
Aluminum
Ethiopian style
L. 6.5 cm, W. 0.9 cm, D. 0.2 cm
ROM 2009.126.338

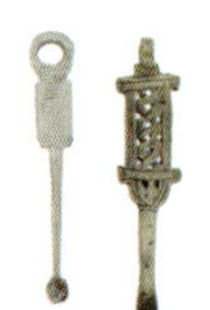
Ear spoon
Aluminum
Ethiopian style
L. 7 cm, W. 1.6 cm, D. 0.2 cm
ROM 2009.126.339

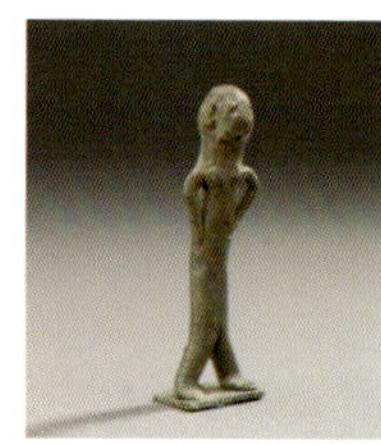
Figurine
Aluminum
Senufo style
H. 6 cm, W. 2 cm, D. 1 cm
ROM 2009.126.344

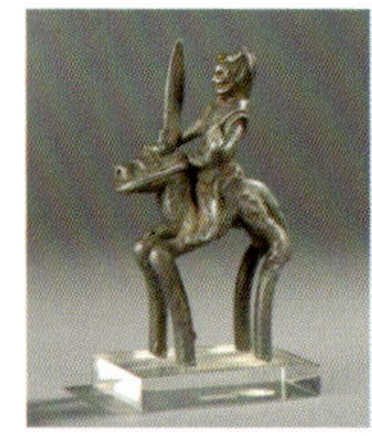
Rider figurine
Aluminum
Senufo(?) style
H. 12 cm, W. 4 cm, D. 8.5 cm
ROM 2009.126.347

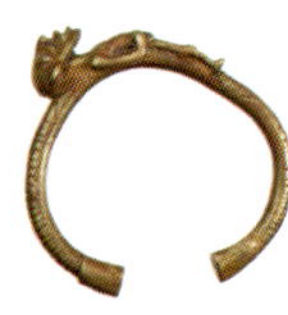
Bracelet
Brass
Senufo style
H. 2 cm, Diam. 8.5 cm
ROM 2009.126.354

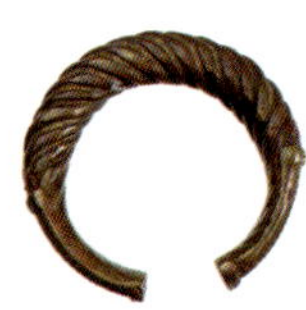
Bracelet
Brass
Akan style
H. 2.3 cm, Diam. 8 cm
ROM 2009.126.356

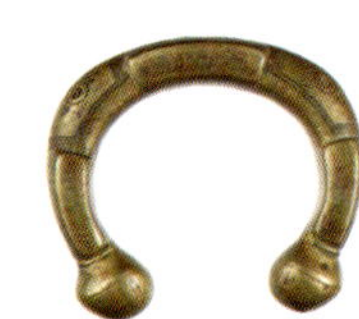
Bracelet
Brass
H. 2.6 cm, W. 10 cm, D. 8.5 cm
ROM 2009.126.363

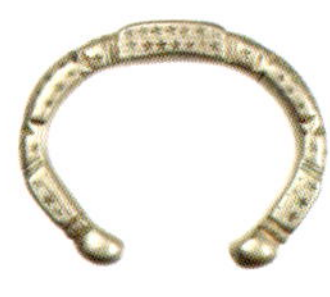
Bracelet
Silver alloy
H. 1.8 cm, W. 9.5 cm, D. 7.7 cm
ROM 2009.126.364

Unrecorded Place and Date of Acquisition

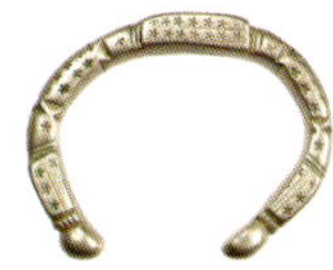

Bracelet
Silver alloy
H. 1.8 cm, W. 9.5 cm, D. 7.7 cm
ROM 2009.126.365

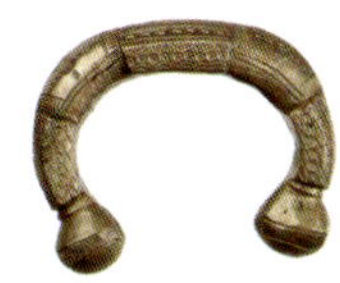

Bracelet
Silver alloy
H. 3 cm, W. 9.3 cm, D. 8 cm
ROM 2009.126.366

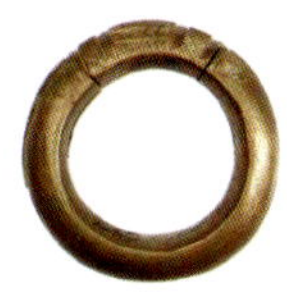

Bracelet
Brass
H. 2.2 cm, Diam. 6.8 cm
ROM 2009.126.367.1–2

List of Plates

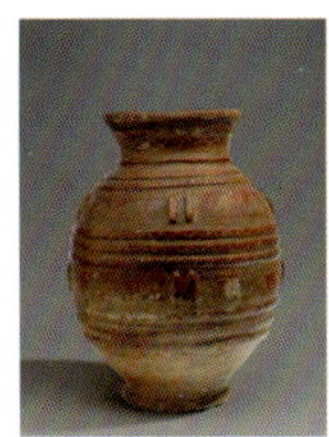

Pot
Unidentified artist or workshop
Bamana style
Terracotta
Purchased from a dealer in Dakar, Senegal, in 1988
H. 56 cm, D. 33 cm
ROM 2009.126.234

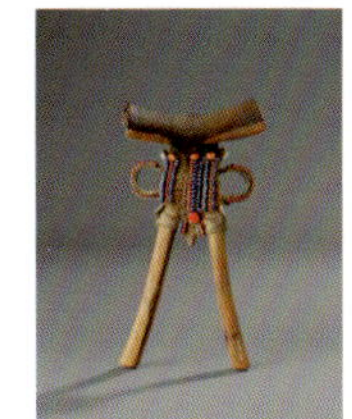

Headrest
Unidentified artist or workshop
Pokot or Turkana style
Wood, leather, glass beads
Purchased from a gallery in Nairobi, Kenya, in 1964
H. 20.3 cm, W. 10.5 cm, D. 5.4 cm
ROM 2009.126.40

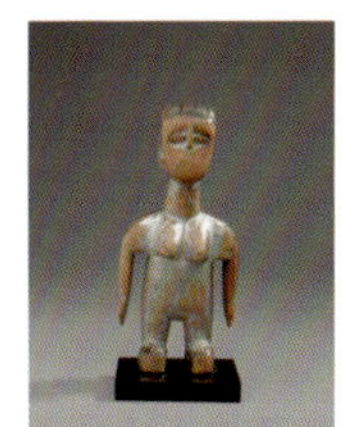

Doll
Unidentified artist or workshop
Ewe style
Wood
Purchased from dealer Arouna in Lomé, Togo, in 1973
H. 16.7 cm, W. 8.7 cm, D. 5 cm
ROM 2009.126.102

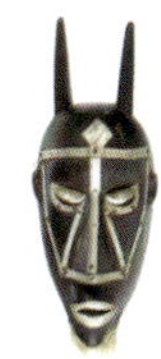

Mask
Unidentified artist or workshop
Marka or Sorogo style
Wood, metal
Purchased from Tribal Art Gallery, New York, in 1987
H. 33.5 cm, W. 13.5 cm, D. 9.3 cm
ROM 2009.126.146

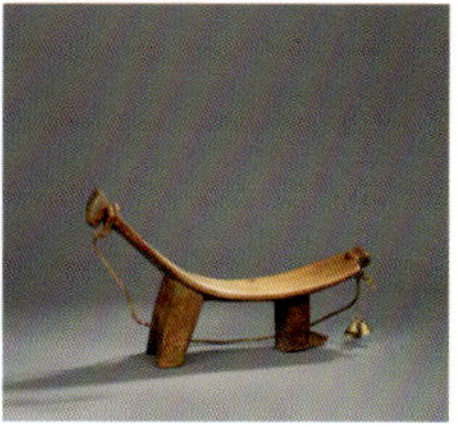

Stool
Lobi style
Unidentified artist or workshop
Wood, fiber, brass, wire
Purchased from a dealer in Ouagadougou in 1981
H. 31 cm, W. 13 cm, D. 52 cm
ROM 2009.126.14

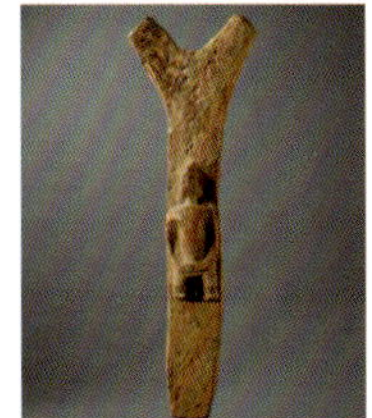

Toguna architectural post
Unidentified artist or workshop
Dogon style
Wood
Purchased from Craft Caravan Gallery, New York, in 1983
H. 182 cm, W. 59 cm, D. 25.5 cm
ROM 2009.126.311

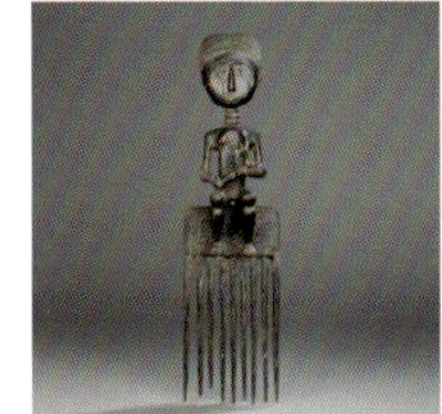

Comb
Unidentified artist or workshop
Asante style
Wood
Purchased from a dealer in Accra in 1973
H. 46 cm, W. 11 cm, D. 7 cm
ROM 2009.126.54

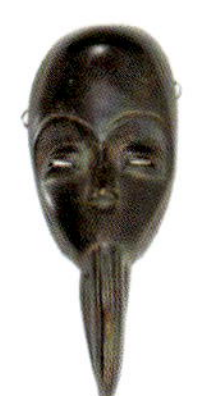

Unidentified artist or workshop
Dan style
Wood
Purchased from a dealer in Abidjan, Côte d'Ivoire, in 1985
H. 37 cm, W. 15.1 cm, D. 11 cm
ROM 2009.126.149

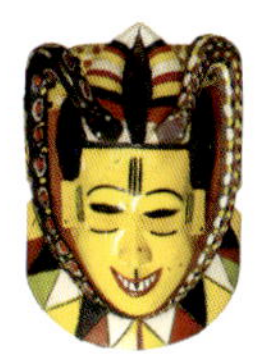

Mask
Unidentified artist or workshop
Guro style
Wood, pigment
Purchased from a dealer in Abidjan in 1987
H. 31.5 cm, W. 22 cm, D. 12.2 cm
ROM 2009.126.178

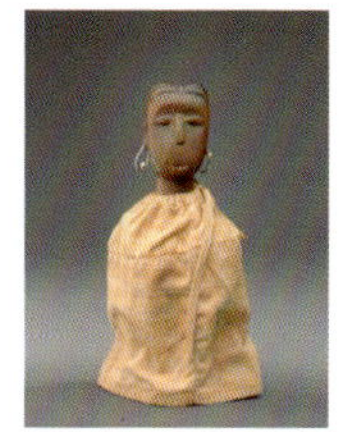

Doll
Ewe style
Unidentified artist or workshop
Wood, cloth, metal
Purchased from dealer Arouna in Lomé, Togo, in 1973
H. 18.5 cm, W. 10 cm, D. 8 cm
ROM 2009.126.104

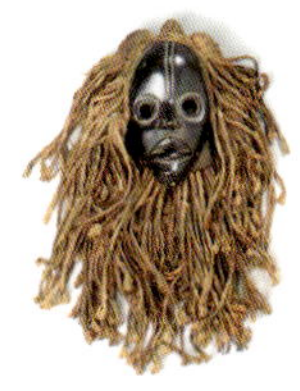

Mask
Unidentified artist or workshop
Dan style
Wood, metal, fiber
Purchased from a dealer in Abidjan, Côte d'Ivoire, in 1985
H. 58 cm, W. 37.4 cm, D. 11 cm
ROM 2009.126.167

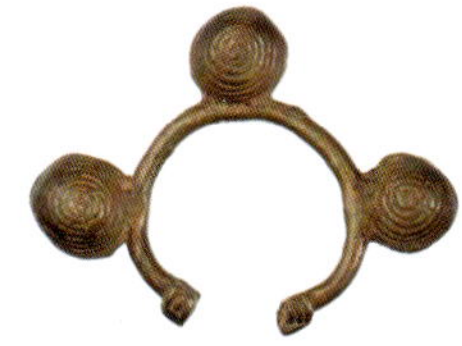

Bracelet with bells
Unidentified artist or workshop
Dan style
Brass
Purchased from a dealer in Abidjan, Côte d'Ivoire, in 1981
H. 2.5 cm, W. 10 cm, D. 7.5 cm
ROM 2009.126.368

LIST OF GALERIE AMRAD AFRICAN ARTS PUBLICATIONS

Non-Fiction and Videos by Esther A. Dagan

The Spirit's Image: The African Masking Tradition—Evolving Continuity by Esther A. Dagan, 1992, 264 pages, 450 b/w photos, 18 colour plates, 203 drawings, 9 diagrams, maps, bibliography. Includes masks from 103 ethnic groups.

African Dolls: For Play and For Magic by Esther A. Dagan, 1990, 143 pages, 180 b/w photos, 2 colour plates, drawings, maps, bibliography.

Emotions in Motion: Theatrical Puppets and Masks from Black Africa by Esther A. Dagan, 1990, 176 pages, 218 b/w photos, 4 colour plates, drawings, maps, bibliography.

Spirits Without Boundaries: 26 Single-Headed Terracotta from Komaland, Ghana by Esther A. Dagan, 1989, 64 pages, 46 b/w photos, 1 colour plate, drawings, maps, bibliography.

Tradition in Translation: Mother and Child in African Sculpture, Past and Present by Esther A. Dagan, 1989, 160 pages, 215 b/w photos, 4 colour plates, drawings, maps, bibliography.

When Art Shares Nature's Gifts: The Calabash in Africa by Esther A. Dagan, 1989, 160 pages, 232 b/w photos, 27 colour plates, drawings, maps, bibliography.

Asante Stools by Esther A. Dagan, 1988, 52 pages, 34 b/w photos, drawings, maps, bibliography.

Dance in Africa by Esther A. Dagan, 1987, VHS Video Cassette, 58 minutes, English narration, includes dances from 13 African countries, Dakar Festival, 1966.

Man and His Vision: The Traditional Wood Sculpture of Burkina Faso by Esther A. Dagan, 1987, 64 pages, 181 b/w photos, maps, bibliography.

Man at Rest: Stools and Seats from 14 African Countries by Esther A. Dagan, 1985, 64 pages, 130 b/w photos, maps, bibliography.

Non-Fiction By Other Authors

The Spirit's Dance in Africa: Evolution, Transformation, and Continuity edited by Esther A. Dagan, 1997, 43 essays by scholars from various fields, 352 pages, 600+ b/w photos and illustrations, 30 colour plates, graphs, tables, glossary, maps, bibliography.

Cheri Samba: The Hybridity of Art by Bogumil Jewsiewicki, 1995, 104 pages, 50 b/w photos, 30 colour plates, bibliography.

Drums: The Heartbeat of Africa edited by Esther A. Dagan, 1993, 36 essays by scholars from various fields, 224 pages, 275 b/w photos, 4 colour plates, 192 drawings, glossary, maps, bibliography.

Fiction by Esther A. Dagan

In Search of Characters by Esther A. Dagan, short stories in a two-act play with film sequences, 2004.

Jerusalem: Snapshots from a Distance by Esther A. Dagan, 8 short stories, 2003.

Mask: 8 Short Stories by Esther A. Dagan, 2002.

CONTRIBUTORS

SILVIA FORNI is Curator of Anthropology in the Department of World Cultures at the Royal Ontario Museum. She is the curator of the African collection and responsible for the permanent and rotating display of African artworks in the Shreyas and Mina Ajmera Gallery of Africa, the Americas and Asia-Pacific. She is also Associate Professor of Anthropology at the University of Toronto. Since 1998, she has been conducting research in Cameroon, and more recently in Senegal and Ghana. She has published essays in several journals, including *African Arts* and *Critical Interventions: Journal of African Art History and Visual Culture* and recently contributed chapters to the edited volumes *African Art and Agency in the Workshop* (2013) and *African Art, Interviews, Narratives: Bodies of Knowledge at Work* (2013). Currently, she is working with Doran Ross on an exhibition and book on Asafo flags from Ghana.

TILL FÖRSTER is an anthropologist and art historian. He holds the chair of social anthropology and is founding director of the Centre for African Studies Basel at the University of Basel, Switzerland. He has specialized in visual culture and political transformations in West and Central Africa and conducted field research for many years, mainly in Côte d'Ivoire and Cameroon. His recent publications focus on questions of governance and social creativity in northern Côte d'Ivoire and on urban visual culture in Cameroon. He has edited *African Art and Agency in the Workshop* (2013) with Sidney Kasfir and *The Politics of Governance* (2014) with Lucy Koechlin.

CATHERINE M. HALE is the Phyllis Wattis Curator of the Arts of Africa and the Americas at Stanford University's Cantor Arts Center. Previously, she was Curator of African and Non-Western Art at the University of Iowa Museum of Art, and has curated exhibitions of African art for the Carleton University Art Gallery and Agnes Etherington Art Centre at Queen's University. One of her most recent projects is the Art & Life in Africa website and related exhibition (2014), which she developed in collaboration with Professor Christopher D. Roy. Hale's research focuses on the arts of the Asante peoples of Ghana, West Africa. She holds a PhD and MA in African Art History from Harvard University.

CHRISTOPHER D. ROY is Elizabeth M. Stanley Faculty Fellow and Professor of African Art History at the University of Iowa. His interest in Africa began in 1966 when he hitchhiked from Paris to Jerusalem and back across North Africa, through Algeria, Tunisia, Libya and Egypt. He enrolled in the Peace Corps in 1970 with his wife Nora, and they served for two years in Ouagadougou. Following the Peace Corps, he enrolled at Indiana University and received his PhD in 1979. In the following years, he made numerous research trips to other parts of Africa, including Nigeria, Ghana and South Africa. From 1994 to 1997, he directed a project to produce a CD-ROM titled "Art and Life in Africa," now available online. From 1999 to the present, he has returned repeatedly to Burkina Faso to record the daily lives and spectacular mask performances of the peoples of that country.

CHRISTOPHER B. STEINER is Lucy C. McDannel '22 Professor of Art History and Anthropology and Director of Museum Studies at Connecticut College. He is the author of the award-winning book *African Art in Transit* (Cambridge, 1994) and co-editor with Ruth B. Phillips of the volume *Unpacking Culture: Art and Commodity in Colonial and Postcolonial Worlds* (University of California Press, 1999).

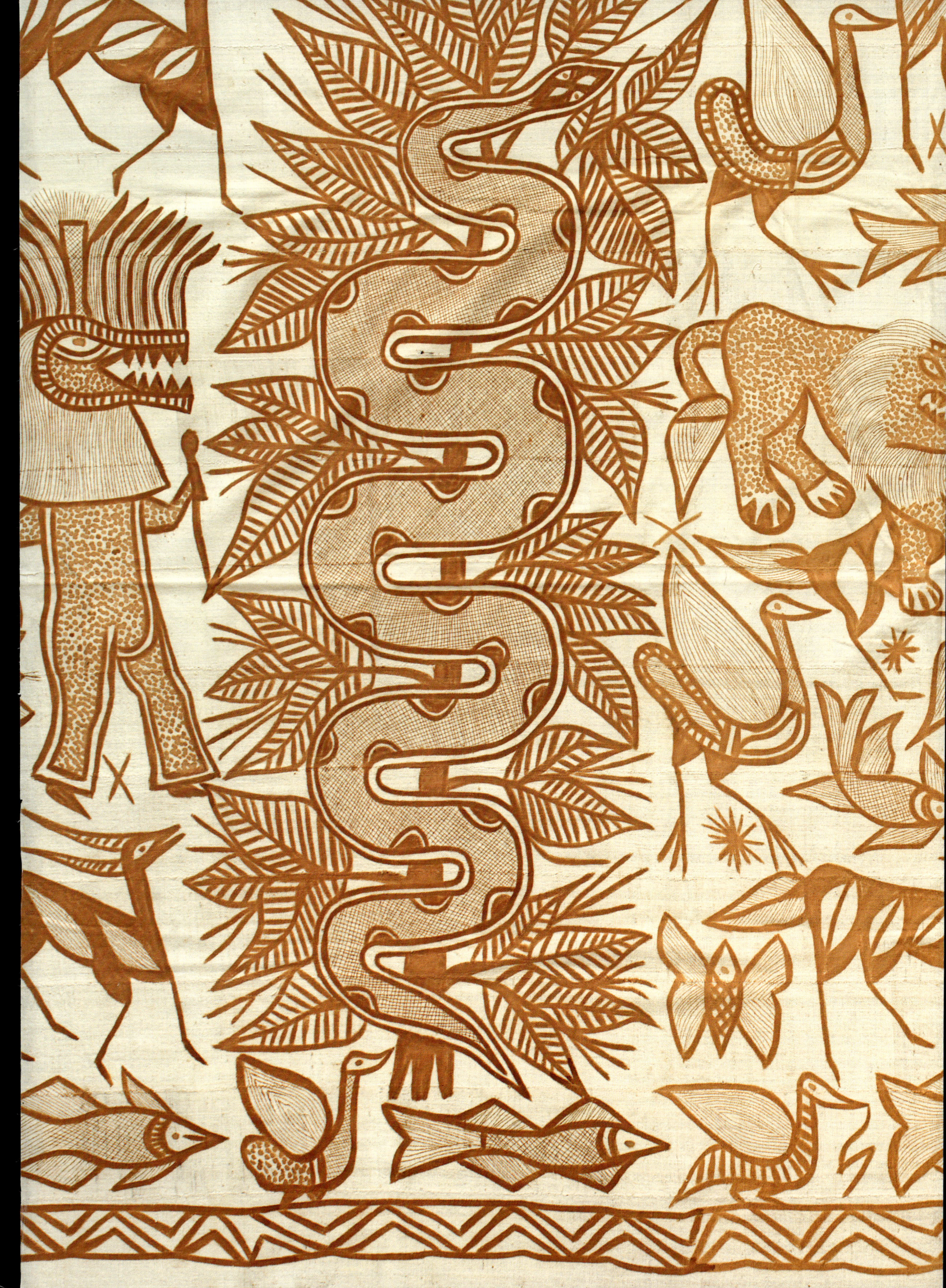

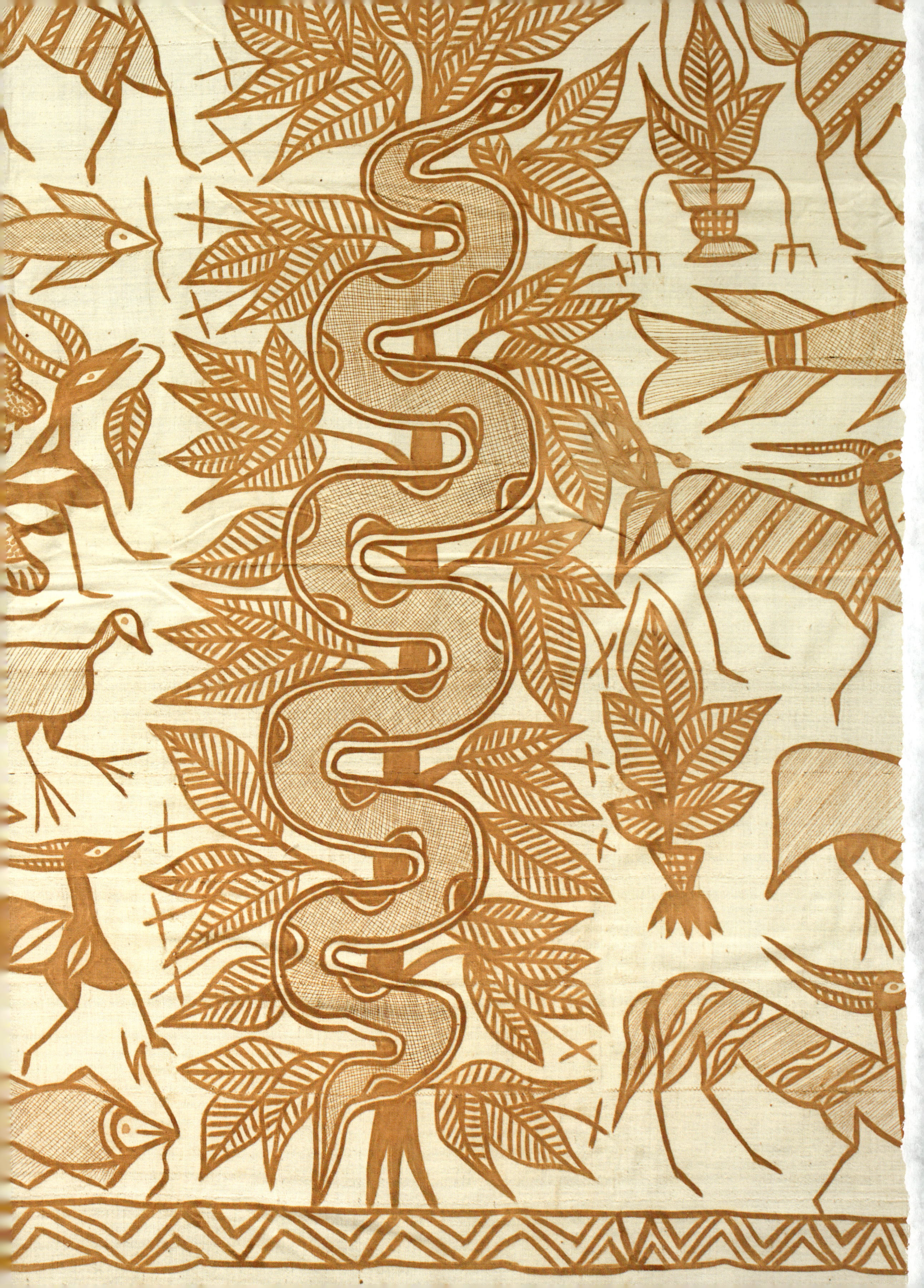